For Reference

Not to be taken from this room

The American
Presidents Ranked
by Performance

The American Presidents Ranked by Performance

by Charles F. Faber *and*
Richard B. Faber

McFarland & Company, Inc., Publishers
Jefferson, North Carolina, and London

Library of Congress Cataloguing-in-Publication Data

Faber, Charles F., 1926–
The American presidents ranked by performance /
by Charles F. Faber and Richard B. Faber
p.   cm.
Includes bibliographical references and index.
ISBN 0-7864-0765-4 (illustrated case binding : 50# alkaline paper) ∞
1. Presidents — Rating of — United States.   2. Presidents —
United States — History.   3. Presidents — United States —
Biography.   4. Political leadership — United States.
5. United States — Politics and government.
I. Faber, Richard B., 1932–   II. Title.
E176.1.F215   2000
973'.099 — dc21   99-87873

British Library Cataloguing-in-Publication data are available

Manufactured in the United States of America

*McFarland & Company, Inc., Publishers
Box 611, Jefferson, North Carolina 28640
www.mcfarlandpub.com*

To the memory of our parents,
Inez McAlister Faber and Richard Andrew Faber

ACKNOWLEDGMENTS

We wish to thank various friends and relatives for their love, understanding, and encouragement. Without their support, this book could never have been written. Especially, we want to thank Pat and Pam for their patience and forbearance during our years of research. We express our appreciation to Pamela Faber and Elizabeth Faber for their research assistance. Patricia Faber and Deborah Webb carefully read the entire manuscript and provided insightful criticism. We thank them for their valuable contributions.

With gratitude, we acknowledge the help of the research librarians of the Des Moines Public Library. We also appreciate the many kindnesses of staff members of the Lexington Public Library, the University of Kentucky Library, and the Sharon (MA) Public Library.

Our lifelong love of learning was instilled in us by our parents. It was enhanced by two of our former professors at Coe College — Howard White and Don Fehrenbacher — who inspired us with their knowledge, enthusiasm, and dedication to the principles of justice and democracy. We also owe more than we can say to the late Roald Campbell of the University of Chicago and Herbert Margulies of the University of Northern Iowa.

CHARLES F. FABER
RICHARD B. FABER

TABLE OF CONTENTS

INTRODUCTION

Who were the greatest American presidents? Which presidents were least successful? These are intriguing questions that have engaged the attention of both the general public and professional historians, whose job it is to chronicle the past and assess the significance of people and events. Ratings of presidents have been published over the last half century in books, professional journals, and the popular press. Clinton Rossiter called presidential rating "a Favorite Indoor Sport of history-minded Americans."[1] Barry Riccio suggested that this favorite indoor sport of historians has perhaps become too much of a pseudo-professional sport brought outdoors. He writes that it may be time to retire it to the parlor.[2] On the other hand Robert Murray and Tim Blessing ask: "If number one can be determined in athletics, in rental car agencies, and in fast-food chains, why not in the presidency?"[3]

Why not indeed? Three approaches to the rating of presidents have been used in the last fifty years. Best known are the polls of scholars and of the general public. There have been books based entirely on the opinion of a single individual. Lastly, there have been studies based on classification schemes which have attempted to change the endeavor from a purely subjective activity to a more scientific effort.

The present book represents a fourth approach. After extensive research, we relied upon our own judgments rather than conducting a poll. The presidents were not only rated, but also ranked in order. In contrast to other studies the criteria for the ratings were stated, and positive and negative indicators for each criterion were also established in advance, so we knew not only the precise criteria on which to base our ratings, but also what evidence to look for to judge the extent to which each criterion was met.

An obvious feature of the present study is that it is a more recent undertaking than the others, and thus it includes more presidents than most of the earlier studies. Also, we have been able to take advantage of more recent biographies of the subjects, several of which included material based on recently released presidential papers that were not available to earlier scholars.

REVIEW OF PREVIOUS STUDIES

Polls

In the last fifty years at least eight polls have been conducted in which historians and or other respondents were asked to rate the presidents.

The first of these polls was conducted in 1948 by Arthur M. Schlesinger, Sr., of Harvard University, one of America's most eminent historians. The results of his poll were published in *Life*[4] and received a great deal of public attention. Schlesinger polled 55 scholars, the majority of whom were historians. Respondents were asked to place each president in one of the following categories: Great, Near Great, Average, Below Average, or Failure. No criteria were specified for the ratings other than the requirement that the test in each case was to be "performance in office, omitting anything done before or after."[5] His survey identified six presidents as Great: Lincoln, Washington, Franklin Roosevelt, Wilson, Jefferson, and Jackson. Theodore Roosevelt, Cleveland, John Adams, and Polk were Near Greats. Grant and Harding were named as Failures, while Tyler, Coolidge, Fillmore, Taylor, Buchanan, and Pierce were listed as Below Average.

Fourteen years later Schlesinger administered

a second poll, this time surveying 75 "experts," including 58 historians. (The remainder were mostly political scientists or journalists.) This time Schlesinger's findings were published in the *New York Times Magazine*.[6] In his two polls Schlesinger used similar procedures. Respondents were again asked to place each president in one of the five categories. Again no specific criteria for the ratings were given. The professor wrote: "Each participant in the poll applied his measuring rod in accordance with the relative importance he attached to the complex factors that helped make or break the particular administration."[7]

Rankings from the two polls were similar. Jackson was demoted from Great to Near Great, while Truman, not included in the first survey, entered the ratings as a Near Great. The same eight names appeared in the Below Average and Failure categories. Again the results were given a great deal of public attention and acceptance.

In 1968 Gary M. Maranell, a sociologist at the University of Kansas, conducted a survey that enlarged and updated the Schlesinger polls.[8] He selected a random sample of 1,095 informants from the membership of the Organization of American Historians and received 571 usable responses. He asked the respondents to rate the presidents on an 11-point scale on each of seven dimensions. Maranell then totaled the points and ranked the presidents in seven different tables. Lincoln was rated first in General Prestige and Accomplishments; Franklin Roosevelt headed the dimensions of Strength of Action, Presidential Activeness, and Respondents' Amount of Information; Wilson was identified as exemplifying the most Idealism, while Kennedy led in Flexibility. Although Maranell did not have a scale for Overall Greatness, he used the General Prestige scale for comparisons with the Schlesinger polls and found only minor differences. Kennedy, who was not included in either of the earlier surveys, emerged as number ten on Maranell's General Prestige dimension.[9]

In 1981 a historian at William Penn College, David L. Porter, asked 41 eminent scholars to rate the presidents. He utilized the same procedures as Schlesinger, but included recent chief executives who had not yet held the office at the time of the earlier surveys. His findings

were very similar to those of Schlesinger's second poll. Theodore Roosevelt and Wilson exchanged positions in the top two groups, and Lyndon Johnson (not rated by Schlesinger) replaced Cleveland among the Near Greats. Five of Schlesinger's Below Average presidents retained that ranking, with Buchanan slipping to Failure. Andrew Johnson fell one notch to Below Average while Grant moved up one category to that estate. Harding remained a failure, joined by the newcomer Nixon as well as the fallen Buchanan. The results of his poll were published in 1987.[10]

In 1982 Steve Neal, a political reporter for the *Chicago Tribune,* surveyed 49 historians or political scientists, each of whom had published a biography or other scholarly work on a president. He asked his respondents to rate the chief executives on a scale of zero to five in five categories (leadership, accomplishments, political skill, appointments and character.) He also asked them to list the ten best and the ten worst presidents in history. The findings were published in the *Tribune*.[11] The rankings based on point totals did not agree completely with the ranks in the lists of ten best and ten worst. Neal's ten best included nine of the eleven Greats and Near Greats identified by Porter's poll. (John Adams and Lyndon Johnson were missing from Neal's list.) The other spot in Neal's ten best was filled by Eisenhower, who had been ranked only Average in the Porter poll.

A far more extensive survey than any of the earlier efforts was undertaken in 1982 by Robert K. Murray, professor of history at Pennsylvania State University, and one of his doctoral students, Tim H. Blessing. They sent out nearly 2,000 questionnaires in an attempt to survey all American historians who held the Ph.D. degree, the rank of assistant professor or higher, and were listed in the American Historical Association's *Guide to Departments of History* for the past two years. They received 846 usable responses. Results were reported in a journal article[12] and elaborated upon in a book.[13]

Murray and Blessing did not designate criteria for their respondents to use, but through means of an exhaustive questionnaire sought to determine *post hoc* the criteria that the respondents had in fact utilized. The Murray-Blessing poll yielded four Greats (Lincoln, Franklin Roosevelt, Washington, and Jefferson) and four Near Greats (Theodore Roosevelt, Wilson, Jackson, and Truman). All of the presidents in the top two categories had been named among the ten best in the *Tribune* poll. At the bottom of the rankings Murray and Blessing listed five Below Average presidents (Taylor, Tyler, Fillmore, Coolidge, and Pierce) and five Failures (Andrew Johnson, Buchanan, Nixon, Grant, and Harding.) Again the resemblance to Neal's findings was striking, with the substitution of Taylor for Carter being the only departure from the *Tribune's* ten worst.

In 1989 William J. Ridings, Jr., and Stuart B. McIver polled 719 individuals, most of whom were historians but also included politicians, journalists, and "celebrities." Participants were asked to rate the presidents in five categories: Leadership Qualities; Accomplishments and Crisis Management; Character and Integrity; Political Skill; and Appointments. They were further requested to provide their own list of the ten best and the ten worst presidents and to provide a letter grade from A to F on each chief executive. Some time later (date not specified) the pollsters conducted an update in which the original respondents were asked to rate Presidents Bush and Clinton, who had not been included in the original poll. About two-thirds of the participants responded. The results of the two polls were in some way combined and presented to the public in a book entitled *Rating the Presidents.*[14] This survey rated all of the presidents, including William Henry Harrison, who served only 30 days in office. The top eight presidents in the Ridings-McIver ratings were: Lincoln, F. Roosevelt, Washington, T. Roosevelt, Wilson, Truman, and Jackson. The bottom eight were Tyler, W. Harrison, Fillmore, Pierce, Grant, A. Johnson, Buchanan, and Harding.

The third Schlesinger Poll was conducted in 1996 by Arthur M. Schlesinger, Jr., nearly 50 years after his father introduced the presidential polling game. Using the same methodology as his father, the younger Schlesinger obtained similar results. Lincoln, Washington, and Franklin Roosevelt were rated Great; Jefferson, Jackson, Polk, Theodore Roosevelt,

Wilson, and Truman were identified as Near Greats. The Failures were Pierce, Buchanan, Andrew Johnson, Grant, Harding, Hoover, and Nixon. Schlesinger's findings were reported in the *New York Times Magazine.*[15]

Interesting and useful though these polls may be, they all suffered from the same major flaw. None of them specified in any meaningful detail the criteria to be used in the ratings. Even the Murray-Blessing study, which criticized the other polls for failing to define the criteria for the ratings, was similarly flawed. Attempting to infer the criteria from examining the relationships between the respondents' answers and certain variables does not seem to us to be an adequate substitute for specifying the criteria in advance.

In none of the polls were the respondents required to rank the presidents in order of greatness. Instead, the usual procedure was to have the respondents group the chief executives in categories to which the researcher gave numerical values. The researcher then calculated a mean score for each president and ranked the chief executives according to this average score. If Lincoln emerged at the top of this ranking, it does not mean that any of the respondents actually said that he was the greatest president. It merely reflects the fact that his mean score was the best when calculated according to the categories in which the raters placed him.

In addition to polls of scholars there are also national public opinion polls. None of these has published a rating of all the presidents. In July 1945 the National Opinion Research Center at the University of Denver asked a nationwide cross section of the general public whom they regarded as two or three of the greatest men who ever lived in this country. The question did not specify that presidents were to be named, but seven of the top twelve mentioned were presidents, past or present, and one (General Eisenhower) was to become president within a decade. The seven chief executives listed, in order, were Franklin Roosevelt, Lincoln, Washington, Wilson, Jefferson, Theodore Roosevelt, and Truman. Non-presidents were Thomas Edison, Henry Ford, Benjamin Franklin, and Generals Eisenhower and MacArthur. As Thomas A. Bailey pointed out, the public is always influenced by presentism.[16] Eight of the twelve top individuals were figures of the twentieth century.

Dr. George H. Gallup, the foremost public opinion pollster of his time, attempted a poll in 1956. The question was: "What *three* United States Presidents do you regard as the *greatest*?" The plan was to canvass 1,800 respondents, but the venture was abandoned after only a partial sample when it became obvious that the average American does not know enough about our past to give a meaningful response.[17] The incomplete results showed Franklin Roosevelt topping the list, followed in order by Lincoln, Washington, Eisenhower, Truman, Wilson, Theodore Roosevelt, Jefferson, Hoover, and Coolidge. Again the phenomenon of presentism is dominant. The five most recent presidents all made the list, even though two of them — Hoover and Coolidge — are not highly regarded by historians. Only three of the top ten were eighteenth or nineteenth century presidents, and these were the great American heroes Washington, Lincoln, and Jefferson.

Ratings by Individuals

Most of the ratings of presidents by individuals were inspired by Schlesinger's first poll. In none of them were all of the presidents ranked. The most common procedure has been for the author to identify from seven to ten of those whom he believed to be among the better presidents (using either poll data or his own stated or unstated criteria) and then explain why his chosen ones were great.

Best known of these efforts is that of the political scientist and historian Clinton Rossiter, in his book *The American Presidency*.[18] Rossiter gave his highest praise to active presidents, especially those who took the initiative in times of crisis. Among those he applauded were the usual honorees: Washington, Jefferson, Jackson, Lincoln, the two Roosevelts, Wilson, and Truman. He also had good things to say about some lesser lights — Cleveland, Hayes, and Andrew Johnson. Rossiter felt that a president could earn the mantle of greatness only by holding office during difficult times. "This standard may work unfairly on Presidents who live under sunny skies," he wrote, "but that is

the way history is written."[19] Great presidents should also enjoy using power. "To be a great President a man must think like a great President," he opined, "he must follow Theodore Roosevelt and choose to be a Jackson-Lincoln."[20]

Morton Bolden edited an anthology of essays, *America's Ten Greatest Presidents*.[21] Bolden chose his ten based on their rankings in the first Schlesinger poll. Each of the ten essays, written by a different scholar, extolled the virtues of the subject. The presidents included were: Washington, John Adams, Jefferson, Jackson, Polk, Lincoln, Cleveland, Wilson, and the two Roosevelts. Although Bolden admitted that rating America's presidents is as difficult as handicapping thoroughbreds, he accepted Schlesinger's Big Ten because the pollster had found a large measure of agreement among the "experts" doing the ratings.

Schlesinger's ratings were also used by the political scientist Herman Finer in his book *The Presidency: Crises and Regeneration*.[22] Activism and power were the watchwords for Finer, who also noted the importance of conviction, courage, cleverness, coherence, constancy, and charm.[23]

Not long after the assassination of President Kennedy, journalist Eric Sokolsky wrote *Our Seven Greatest Presidents*.[24] His hero, Kennedy, made the list of seven, along with Franklin Roosevelt, Truman, Jefferson, Jackson, Polk and Lincoln. Our nation's first president did not make the top seven because Washington was not enough of an activist for the journalist's tastes.

Perhaps the most useful of the books purporting to rate presidents is *Presidential Greatness* by Stanford historian Thomas A. Bailey.[25] After devoting several chapters with titles like "Measuring the Immeasurable," and "The Barriers of Bias" and documenting the shortcomings of the ratings systems, Bailey himself rated all of the presidents from George Washington through Lyndon Johnson. Bailey recognized more explicitly than the other scholars playing the ratings game that if we are going to make ratings with even a rough degree of plausibility, we must first set up measuring rods. He assembled a list of more than one hundred tests which the ideal president ought to pass. He then condensed his list to 43 items, 35 of which applied to all chief executives and 8 additional items that applied chiefly to twentieth-century presidents.[26] Even with the use of these criteria Bailey refused to rank the presidents in order. Instead he used the 43 tests to determine whether he agreed or disagreed with the general appraisal made by the experts in the Schlesinger polls.

"If we must rank Presidents," wrote Bailey, "Washington, in my judgment, deserves the place at the very top."[27] He was not so generous in his ratings of some of our other revered presidents. He downgraded Jefferson and Jackson. Lincoln fared a little better. "We can hardly deny him a place somewhere among the Greats, though he may not have been a Super-Great," was his verdict on Honest Abe.[28] Bailey stated that Theodore Roosevelt and Woodrow Wilson were at best "Near Greats."[29] He said that Franklin Roosevelt can hardly be denied a place in the highest echelon of American presidents.[30] On the last two presidents that he rated — John Kennedy and Lyndon Johnson — Bailey stated that perspective was too short to permit a satisfying evaluation. He clearly admired Kennedy and thought that if he had served a full eight years, he would probably have been ranked by the experts as a Near Great or even a Great.[31] With Johnson there was not only a lack of perspective but also of a complete record, as Bailey's book was written in 1966 while Johnson was still in office. Bailey demonstrates that his caution about lack of perspective and lack of a complete record was well founded with these words:

> Great Presidents generally have had big wars, and with the escalation of bombing and shooting in South Vietnam, Johnson may enjoy this added advantage as he eagerly seeks an honored place beside Lincoln, Wilson, and Franklin Roosevelt. "What Lyndon wants, Lyndon gets," it was said. And if he can avoid a physical breakdown or an economic depression, he may conceivably get there yet. If crisis times make great men, he is well on his way to greatness.[32]

Contrary to Bailey's view, the escalation of the war in Vietnam proved not to be an advantage to Johnson, but rather it was his downfall. Opposition to the war was the principal reason he did not seek re-election only two years after Bailey's book was published.

In 1997 *America's Nine Greatest Presidents* by Frank R. King, an instructor at the Community College of Southern Nevada, was published. As might be expected, King included Washington, Jefferson, Lincoln, and the two Roosevelts among his elite nine. Also included are Monroe, Polk, Truman, and Eisenhower, all of whom make some, but not all, of the other lists. Monroe, especially, is frequently underrated. King's most notable omission is Wilson. King examines the legislative, military, and political accomplishments of each man and analyzes each president's character, values, progressiveness, and political performance.[33]

Classification Schemes

William D. Pederson of Louisiana State University has been perhaps the most avid promoter of the use of classification schemes in the rating of presidents. Pederson and his colleague Ann M. McLaurin publicized the "psychoanalytical" scheme of Duke University's political science professor James David Barber,[34] which they reprinted in their book *The Rating Game in American Politics*.[35] Their hyperbole included the following:

> The James David Barber essay on "Analyzing Presidents" ... is doubtless the most controversial essay in the text, and one of the most debated approaches in political science. Barber claims the ability to predict presidential behavior! Indeed, several years before Nixon's resignation, Barber predicted that Nixon was likely to undo himself in a crisis. Although Barber was not able to foretell Watergate, he did classify Nixon's personality as one of the most dangerous types to have in the White House. The essay reprinted in the text outlines the four-fold typology that Barber uses to separate the mentally healthy from the unhealthy.[36]

Barber posited that two gross dimensions outline the main types of presidential character:

> First, divide the Presidents into the more active and the less active. Then cut across that with a division between those who seemed generally happy and optimistic and those who gave an impression of sadness and irritation. These crude clues tend to symptomize character packages. The "active-positive" types tend to show confidence, flexibility, and a focus on producing results through rational mastery. The

"active-negative" tends to emphasize ambitious striving, aggressiveness, and a focus on the struggle for power against a hostile environment. "Passive-positive" types come through as receptive, compliant, other-directed personas whose superficial hopefulness masks much inner doubt. The "passive-negative" character tends to withdraw from conflict and uncertainty, to think in terms of vague principles of duty and regular procedure.[37]

Incredibly, Barber writes that Eisenhower fits the passive-negative type.[38] Ike's famous infectious grin apparently gave Barber an impression of sadness and irritation. As far as the present writers are concerned, this misjudgment alone makes it difficult to view Barber as an expert judge of character, style, or personality, let alone mental health.

As for Barber's so-called prediction that Nixon would undo himself in a crisis, Barber's exact words are: "The danger is that Nixon will commit himself irrevocably to some disastrous course of action, as, indeed, his predecessor did."[39] This is not a prediction of Watergate, but a warning that Nixon might make a mistake similar to Lyndon Johnson's commitment to the war in Vietnam. Indeed, Barber assigned Nixon and Johnson to the same typology—active-negative.[40]

Pederson adds Jackson, Wilson, Polk, Cleveland, Andrew Johnson, and both Adamses to this type.[41] Were all of these dangerous and mentally unhealthy?

Incidentally, Barber said George Washington fits best the passive-negative type. Pederson said this anomaly is "probably due to modern views of the presidency carried over into another age, as well as Barber's lack of research on early American presidents."[42]

Pederson took the dimensions of flexibility and activeness from Maranell's study and made a four-fold presidential typology of active-flexible, active-inflexible, passive-flexible, and passive-inflexible.[43] There was a high correlation between his adaptation of Maranell's typology and Barber's typology as it applied to twentieth century presidents. This led Pederson to suggest that Barber was actually evaluating presidential flexibility-inflexibility to a greater extent than he realized.[44] Nevertheless, Pederson proceeded to adopt without explanation the Barber nomenclature and referred to presidents as active-positive, active-negative, passive-positive, and passive-negative.

Then Pederson calculated the number of amnesties granted by each president by means of proclamation or executive order. Next he attempted to relate the amnesty record to the personality type. Forty amnesties were counted, of which fifteen were granted by Presidents Lincoln and Johnson immediately following the Civil War.[45] Rather than stating the obvious—that there was a greater need for amnesties following a civil war—Pederson attributed this to their presidential types, even though Lincoln was active-positive and Johnson was active-negative.[46] The other 31 presidents in the study granted a total of 25 amnesties among them, an average of fewer than one each.[47] Even with this small number of cases, Pederson claims that the amnesty record tends to support Barber's typology of presidential character.[48] He made this assertion even while noting that McKinley granted the largest number of individual pardons to deserters up to that time in American history, thus obviating the need to issue any amnesties.[49] Pederson thought McKinley's action supported his hypothesis.[50] Some of his other examples seem equally farfetched to the present writers.

Although we would not say that the Barber and Pederson typologies are thoroughly discredited, we will observe that none of the other principal sources on presidential rating games mentioned them. Obviously, the claim that Barber's typology is one of the most debated approaches in political science is not supported by the literature we reviewed.

THE PRESENT STUDY

In the present study we relied upon our own judgments. We did not conduct a poll. We did not psychoanalyze the presidents or classify them by personality types. We judged them, rather, by their accomplishments. As stated above, we specified the criteria for the rankings in advance, and we also established positive and negative indicators for each criterion in advance, so we knew not only the precise criteria on which to base our ratings, but also what evidence to look for to judge the extent to which each criterion was met. Each president was given a positive, neutral, or negative score on each applicable criterion. We added up the points, and the presidents were ranked accordingly. Thus, we can say that the president who ranked number one met the criteria to a higher degree than the one who was ranked number two, and he in turn outscored number three all the way down to the bottom of the list.

Another obvious advantage to the present study is that it is a more recent undertaking than the polls, and thus we had access to recent scholarship regarding several of the presidents. Our study also includes more chief executives than most of the earlier efforts. For example, the earliest Schlesinger poll included only 29 presidents. The polls conducted in the early 1980s included 36 presidents. Sufficient time has now passed that we are able to add Presidents Reagan, Bush, and Clinton to our study, giving us a total of 39. As in all of the previous studies, except the Ridings-McIver survey, we omitted Presidents William Henry Harrison and James Garfield, neither of whom served long enough to compile a presidential record.

We started our project by constructing the rating system. The rating system calls for the presidents to be rated in five performance areas: Foreign Relations; Domestic Programs; Adminstration and Intergovernmental Relations; Leadership and Decision Making; and Personal Qualities.

These performance areas were arrived at by the present authors through our own analysis of presidential duties. They do not differ widely from the major functions identified by political scientists — symbolic leadership; program design and priority setting; crisis management; legislative and political coalition building; program implementation; and oversight of governmental routines.[51] Nor do they depart significantly from the roles traditionally used by historians to describe the job of the president: head of state; executive administrator; commander-in-chief; primary law enforcer;

domestic-policy initiator; main foreign-policy planner; party leader; and symbolic national spokesman.[52] Each of the functions and roles designated by the political scientists or historians shows up in our criteria either as a performance area or as a sub-area within one of the main areas. Since we were concerned with performance, we did not consider such appearance and background factors as age, physical appearance, health, education, previous experience, and religion. Nor were we concerned with traits, such as flexibility, idealism, decisiveness, courage, activism, or passivism, except insofar as they affected performance. In our review of the literature the closest thing we found to our performance areas and sub-areas was Thomas Bailey's 43 yardsticks for measuring presidential performance.[53]

Within each performance area there are ten sub-areas. For each sub-area a positive indicator and a negative indicator are given. For each positive indicator met a president was awarded a plus one or plus two score, depending upon how strongly he met the criterion. Similarly, chief executives meeting negative criteria were assigned scores of minus one or minus two. Thus, it is theoretically possible for a president to attain a score in each area ranging from minus twenty to plus twenty. With a total of five areas the possible range on a president's total rating is from minus 100 to plus 100. We recognize that in any given sub-area neither the positive nor the negative indicator might apply. In such case the president is given zero points in that sub-area.

With the rating scale in front of us we examined the performance of the presidents. We read two or more scholarly works and consulted numerous additional sources for each chief executive We rated each president on the criteria that we had specified in advance; then we ranked the presidents according to their scores.

CRITERIA AND RATINGS

FOREIGN RELATIONS

The president is in charge of the foreign policy of the United States. His constitutional authority derives from Article 2, Section 2: "The President shall be commander-in-chief of the army and navy of the United States, and of the militia of the several states...he shall have power, by and with the advice and consent of the Senate, to make treaties, provided two-thirds of the senators present concur; and he shall nominate, and with the advice and consent of the Senate, shall appoint ambassadors...and other officers of the United States."

The power to declare war is not a presidential prerogative; it is reserved to Congress. However, thus far in our history Congress has never declared war except on the recommendation of the president and has never refused to declare war when asked to do so by the chief executive. The president's role as commander-in-chief of the armed services gives him the ability to take military action against foreign nations (or domestic uprisings) without the formality of a declaration of war. President Truman's "military action" in Korea is perhaps the most famous example of such an event, but it was by no means the first, nor was it the most deadly undeclared war into which our presidents have led us. Our first undeclared war was against France. In the opinion of Alexander Hamilton, President John Adams had the power to repel attacks, but not to order reprisals without congressional approval. In 1801 Tripoli declared war on the United States. Without asking Congress for a declaration of war President Jefferson ordered the navy to blockade Tripoli's ports and bombard its fortresses. On April 15, 1861, the day after the fall of Fort Sumter, President Lincoln issued a call for troops to "enforce the nation's laws." The South considered this action the equivalent of a declaration of war. The Civil War cost more American lives than any other war in history, declared or undeclared. During the early part of the twentieth century United States presidents almost routinely sent troops into Latin American countries to restore order and protect our interests. The most famous of these excursions was the pursuit of Pancho Villa in Mexico during the Wilson administration. In terms of casualties the most costly undeclared foreign war in which American troops were engaged was the Vietnam conflict during which three different presidents sent troops to fight and die in that Asian land. More recently President Bush fought the undeclared Persian Gulf War and President Clinton has sent American troops into several foreign trouble spots. It cannot be denied that the president's role as commander-in-chief of the armed forces makes his a formidable power in the conduct of foreign relations.

The president's power to make treaties is limited by the necessity to secure approval of two-thirds of the Senate. Throughout our history as a nation this limitation has led to some notable struggles between the chief executive and the Senate, with the most notable being President Wilson's fight to secure ratification of the Treaty of Versailles and U.S. membership in the League of Nations. Sometimes presidents have been able to negotiate executive agreements with other nations in order to avoid the necessity for Senate approval. Presidents have also avoided the necessity for treaty ratification by a two-thirds Senate vote by securing majority passage of joint resolutions in both houses.

That the president's choices for ambassadorships and other diplomatic offices affects our foreign policy is too obvious to require explanation. The secretary of state, appointed by the president and responsible to him, heads the state department and is regarded nominally as the nation's leading spokesperson in foreign affairs. However, the president himself frequently functions as the nation's chief diplomat. Wilson, for example, took personal charge of conducting foreign relations, relegating his secretaries of state to minor roles. Even when a strong secretary, such as Charles Evans Hughes or John Foster Dulles, has taken the spotlight, he has remained the president's subordinate and has seldom acted against the wishes of the chief executive. The summit conference in which the President of the United States meets with the leaders of our most powerful allies or competitors was started by President Roosevelt during World War II and has been used as a vehicle for personal diplomacy by most of the presidents since then. The outcomes of these meetings have been some of the most significant events of our times. The power of the president in foreign relations has grown tremendously since the early days of the Republic when James Madison thought President Washington's neutrality proclamation violated the forms and spirit of the Constitution by exalting executive powers in foreign affairs.

In our Rating Scale we have divided the area of Foreign Relations into ten sub-areas, and specified criteria, denoted as positive or negative indicators, as follows:

1. Performance Area —
Promoting Interests of the United States Through Foreign Relations

1.1. WAR OR THE AVOIDANCE OF WAR

Positive Indicator — The president used diplomacy to prevent the United States from becoming involved in war against our national interests. When the national interest required it, he effectively led the United States in war against an enemy.

Negative Indicator — The president failed to utilize diplomatic means to prevent the United States from being drawn into a war against our national interests. Even though our national interests would have been promoted by taking action against an enemy, he failed to take appropriate steps. He led the United States into war against a perceived enemy when it was against our national interest to be so engaged.

1.2. APPROPRIATE USE OF MILITARY FORCE

Positive Indicator — The president consistently used military force or potential military force to promote our national interests.

Negative Indicator — The president used military force or threat of military force in a way that was detrimental to our national interests; failed to use military force or the build-up of military strength and resolve to protect national interests.

1.3. PEACEKEEPING

Positive indicator — The president used diplomatic means, such as treaties or international agreements, to preserve or bring about peaceful relations between the United States and another nation or used our good offices to settle disputes among foreign nations.

Negative indicator — By failing to act effectively in keeping the peace among nations of the world, the president allowed the national interests of the United States to be injured; brought about temporary peace at the expense of future stability through appeasement, bluffing, bullying, or other inappropriate means.

1.4. INTERNATIONAL RELATIONS

Positive indicator — The president consistently promoted the national interests of the United States by engaging in appropriate relations with other nations; used the granting or withholding of diplomatic recognition of other countries as a tool for promoting our national interests; took action to promote cooperation among nations; led in the establishment of regional alliances to promote security of the area; worked with heads of other governments with whom he had mutual respect.

Negative indicator — The president failed to utilize cooperative relations with other nations when it would have been in the national interest of the United States to have done so; granted or failed to grant diplomatic recognition to other nations when such action or failure to act was contrary to our own best interests; failed to participate in appropriate regional alliances when the opportunity presented itself or used regional alliances in a way that was detrimental to our long-term interests; failed to command the respect or the confidence of other world leaders or did not have a working relationship with them.

1.5. NEIGHBORLINESS

Positive indicator — The president consistently advanced national interests of the United States by taking actions to show we deserve the friendship and support of our neighboring nations in the Western Hemisphere; used diplomatic recognition, economic aid, or other means to encourage development of stable democracies abroad.

Negative indicator — The president harmed the national interests of the United States by inappropriate behavior toward our neighbors in the Western Hemisphere; cooperated with military dictatorships or other repressive regimes to the detriment of other people's hopes for democracy.

1.6. INTERNATIONAL RIVALRY

Positive indicator — The president consistently behaved toward our international rivals in a manner that demonstrated the United States was strong enough and determined enough to protect our national interests against predators.

Negative indicator — The president failed to demonstrate the strength, courage, or will necessary to deter foreign rivals from taking actions harmful to our national interests.

1.7. INTERNATIONAL TENSIONS

Positive indicator — The president helped ease international tensions by demonstrating to foreign rivals that despite our resolve to protect our own national interests, we had no designs against them.

Negative indicator — By threats, jingoism, or saber-rattling the president caused other nations of the world to regard the United States as a danger to their well-being.

1.8. WORLD OPINION

Positive indicator — The president conducted foreign policy in such a way as to enhance favorable public opinion toward the United States throughout the world.

Negative indicator — The president conducted foreign policy in such a way as to alienate public opinion toward the United States throughout the world.

1.9. TARIFF POLICIES

Positive Indicator — The president promoted tariff policies that had long-term beneficial effects.

Negative Indicator — The president promoted tariff policies that in the long run had harmful effects on world economy or on the economic well-being of the United States.

1.10. PROMOTION OF ECONOMIC WELL-BEING ABROAD

Positive Indicator — The president followed practices that led to an increase in world trade in a way that was fair and beneficial to all nations; used economic aid or followed trade policies and other economic practices that increased the standard of living of people in other nations.

Negative Indicator — The president followed practices that decreased world trade or followed practices that led to exploitive or unfair trade arrangements; assisted American companies in the economic exploitation of people in other countries.

Franklin D. Roosevelt emerges as our greatest president in the area of foreign relations with seventeen out of a possible twenty points. Roosevelt, of course, led the nation to victory in World War II. As commander-in-chief, he made superb appointments of George Marshall as chief of staff, Dwight Eisenhower as supreme commander in Europe and Douglas MacArthur as the supreme commander in the Pacific. Roosevelt inspired his fellow Americans to a magnificent all-out effort of production on the home front. His cooperation with Allied leaders, such as Churchill and Stalin, contributed mightily to the Allied victory. The adoption of the Atlantic Charter by Roosevelt and Churchill and the president's "Four Freedoms" speech are examples of FDR's inspirational leadership.

Prior to our entry into the war, Roosevelt had already made his mark in foreign relations. He attempted to use diplomacy to prevent the conflagration. In 1938 he proposed to convene the entire diplomatic corps to the White House so he could urge upon them world peace, the reduction of armaments, and equal access to raw materials. He dropped the plan when Chamberlain rejected it. Roosevelt was appalled by the appeasement at Munich. The lend-lease program with Great Britain was helpful to both countries. It enabled Britain to hold off the Nazis while the United States built up its military preparedness. Delaying our entry into the war until the Japanese attack on Pearl Harbor assured a more enthusiastic, united war effort than had we entered earlier.

But Roosevelt was far more than a great wartime leader. He started the "Good Neighbor" Policy with Latin America and withdrew U.S. troops from some Caribbean republics, repealed the Platt Amendment, settled oil disputes with Mexico, signed reciprocal trade agreements and nonaggression treaties with several Latin American nations, and signed several reciprocal trade agreements with Canada. His administration concluded more than twenty trade treaties, most of which lowered tariffs. These had beneficial long-term benefits to the United States and to other nations as well, although importation of foreign foodstuffs may have temporarily hurt some American farmers. By attending the 1936 Inter-American Conference for the Maintenance of Peace he became our first president to visit South America while in office.

Roosevelt recognized the Soviet Union in 1933, which was in our national interest. His refusal to recognize the Japanese puppet state of Manchukuo was also appropriate. However, his long delay in recognizing the DeGaulle government-in-exile during the war was not helpful. He attempted to use recognition or non-recognition of eastern European governments in 1944 in ways that would be helpful, but this was almost impossible to do under the conditions of Soviet occupation and the perceived need to bring the Soviets into the war against Japan.

Roosevelt wanted to see an end to colonialism abroad and supported independence for India, for Indo-China, and for some of the countries of Africa. Although he cooperated with military dictators in Latin America, he favored self-determination for those countries rather than having them ruled by the United States. He believed that independence is a prerequisite to democracy.

Cooperation with Britain, the Soviet Union, and other nations during the war was vital not only to winning the war but also to the creation of peacekeeping machinery after the war. Roosevelt proposed that the alliance that fought the Axis become an organization for world peace and suggested the name United Nations for it. The groundwork for the San Francisco conference establishing that organization was laid shortly before the president's death.

In summary, Roosevelt was truly a world leader. He conducted international relations in such a way as to promote the self-interest of this country while enhancing world opinion of the United States as a strong, peaceful, fair, and dependable member of the world community.

RANKING OF THE PRESIDENTS IN FOREIGN RELATIONS

President	Ratings on Criteria by Sub-Areas										
	1.1	1.2	1.3	1.4	1.5	1.6	1.7	1.8	1.9	1.10	Total
1. F. Roosevelt	2	2	1	2	2	1	1	2	2	2	17
2. Jackson	2	2	0	2	1	2	2	2	2	2	16
3. Washington	2	1	1	2	0	2	2	2	1	1	14
3. Buchanan	1	1	0	2	1	2	2	2	1	2	14
3. Truman	1	1	1	2	2	2	0	2	0	2	14
6. Madison	1	1	0	2	2	2	1	2	1	1	13
6. Monroe	2	2	2	1	2	2	2	2	-2	0	13
6. Van Buren	1	2	1	1	1	1	2	1	2	1	13
6. Taylor	2	2	0	2	1	2	2	1	1	0	13
6. Wilson	2	1	1	1	0	0	2	2	2	2	13

President		1.1	1.2	1.3	1.4	1.5	1.6	1.7	1.8	1.9	1.10	Total
	Ratings on Criteria by Sub-Areas											
6. Clinton		0	1	2	2	2	1	1	1	1	2	13*
12. J. Adams		2	1	1	1	0	2	1	2	1	1	12
12. Kennedy		1	1	1	2	1	2	0	1	1	2	12
12. Nixon		0	2	1	2	0	2	2	2	0	1	12
15. J. Q. Adams		1	1	0	2	2	2	2	2	−1	0	11
15. Ford		1	1	0	2	2	2	1	1	0	1	11
15. Carter		1	0	2	2	2	1	1	1	0	1	11
18. Lincoln		2	1	0	1	0	2	2	2	0	0	10
18. T. Roosevelt		2	0	2	2	0	2	2	0	0	0	10
20. Jefferson		2	2	0	1	0	2	1	2	−1	0	9
21. Hayes		2	0	0	1	1	1	1	1	0	1	8
21. Cleveland		1	0	0	1	1	2	1	0	1	1	8
21. Taft		0	1	1	1	0	1	1	1	1	1	8
21. Hoover		2	0	1	1	2	−1	1	2	−1	1	8
21. Bush		1	−2	1	2	−1	1	1	1	2	2	8
26. Fillmore		1	1	0	0	1	1	2	1	0	0	7
26. A. Johnson		2	−1	0	1	1	1	1	1	1	0	7
26. Harding		1	0	2	1	2	0	2	1	−2	0	7
29. Tyler		1	0	1	0	−2	1	0	1	2	1	5
29. Arthur		1	2	0	1	1	0	0	0	0	0	5
31. Polk		−1	0	0	1	−2	2	0	0	2	1	3
31. Reagan		0	−2	0	2	−2	1	1	0	2	0	3
33. Coolidge		1	−1	2	1	0	1	1	1	−2	−2	2
34. Pierce		1	1	0	−1	−2	1	−1	−1	1	2	1
34. Eisenhower		2	1	1	0	−2	2	−2	−1	0	0	1
34. L. Johnson		−1	−1	0	1	1	1	0	−1	0	1	1
37. Grant		2	−1	0	−1	−1	1	1	1	−2	−2	−2
38. B. Harrison		0	−2	0	1	0	2	−1	0	−2	−2	−4
39. McKinley		−2	−2	1	2	−2	1	−2	−1	−1	−1	−7

DOMESTIC PROGRAMS

No specific presidential duties in relation to domestic programs are mandated by the Constitution. The document simply says that Congress shall have the power to promote the general welfare of the United States and to make all laws that shall be necessary and proper for executing such power. The duties of the president are to see that such laws are faithfully executed and to recommend such further measures as he judges necessary and expedient.

Gradually there has come about in this country the belief that one of the president's chief responsibilities in the domestic arena is the management of the nation's economy, particularly the federal budget. There is now a general expectation that the president will in normal times attempt to balance the budget and keep the national debt within bounds, but that he will increase spending as necessary to fight a depression or a war. This view was not held by framers of the Constitution, nor by our early presidents. Andrew Jackson was perhaps the first chief executive to assert presidential control over the nation's finances. President Polk institutionalized some of Jackson's changes and started on the road to budgetary control. Further improvements to the budget process were made by Presidents Taft, Wilson, and Harding. President Clinton was the first to have the power of line item veto in congressional appropriations, but this power was declared

*Preliminary rating as of October 27, 1999

unconstitutional. Franklin D. Roosevelt was the first president to put the full force of his office behind an effort to pull the country out of a major economic depression.

Another domestic area in which the president is now expected to have a major impact is that of the rights of groups and individuals. Prior to the adoption of the Fourteenth Amendment, the role of the federal government in this arena was extremely limited. Lack of interest on the part of chief executives and opposition from the courts kept the potential impact of the Fourteenth Amendment dormant for several generations. Then the activism of President Truman, the Warren Court, and Lyndon B. Johnson brought the role of the government in the advancement of citizens' rights to the foreground.

An indication of how the responsibilities of the executive branch have grown over the years may be seen in a listing of the cabinet level departments dealing primarily with domestic affairs: treasury, justice, interior, agriculture, commerce, labor, housing and urban development, transportation, energy, education, health and human services, and veterans affairs. In addition to these departments, there are more than fifty independent agencies. The majority of these have been created in the present century.

As Charles A. McCoy wrote: "The Presidency of the United States is much more than what the Constitution and the laws of the United States proclaim it to be. Rather, it is an institution shaped primarily by the energy and vigor of past occupants." [54] In rating the presidents on domestic programs, we have not given earlier chief executives negative scores for failing to act in sub-areas in which no previous president had acted, as the expectations for their performance were so much less in these categories. The innovative president is rewarded for his innovation, but his predecessors are not penalized. His successors, however, are expected to live up to his standards.

In our Rating Scale, we have divided the area of Domestic Programs into ten sub-areas and specified criteria, denoted as positive or negatives indicators as follows:

2. Performance Area — Improving Life in America Through Domestic Programs

2.1. FISCAL POLICIES

Positive Indicator — The president pursued governmental fiscal policies which had the effect of stimulating the economy in times of economic recession and which restrained inflation in times of economic growth; decreased or increased governmental spending depending upon the national interest; took action to maintain strong economy or to improve a weak one and dealt effectively with economic problems, such as inflation, panics, depressions, or recessions.

Negative Indicator — The president failed to utilize governmental power to promote economic stability; took actions which caused economic downturns, or failed to take remedial actions when downturn occurred; failed to prevent runaway inflation or to bring inherited inflation under control.

2.2. AGRICULTURE, CAPITAL, AND LABOR

Positive Indicator — The president promoted policies facilitating ownership of family farms and agricultural stabilization; led Congress to pass legislation regulating trusts, monopolies, and holding companies, or vigorously enforced existing legislation; led Congress to pass legislation protecting right of labor to organize, bargain collectively, and strike when necessary, or took other action to improve the lot of the working man or woman (or child); sought to maintain a balance of power between capital and labor.

Negative Indicator — The president allowed monopolistic practices to go unchecked; used powers of government to improve status of favored classes over common people, workers, or small farmers; used power of government to weaken organized labor, to break strikes, or to prevent unionization; failed to support child-labor laws, minimum wage, or other actions to improve working conditions.

2.3. DEALING WITH PUBLIC WELFARE

Positive Indicator — The president promoted governmental programs to prevent poverty or to alleviate effects of existing poverty;

used the power of the presidency to promote the welfare of all people through providing social security, guaranteed health care, food for the poor, pure food and drug standards, and protection against crime.

Negative Indicator — The president failed to use power of government to help poor people or promoted policies which increased amount or severity of poverty; used governmental power in ways that were detrimental to the health, safety, or welfare of the people.

2.4. TAX POLICIES

Positive Indicator — The president promoted tax policies which placed burden of taxation on those most able to pay.

Negative Indicator — The president shifted burden of taxation from upper income taxpayers to middle or low income persons.

2.5. INTERNAL IMPROVEMENTS, CONSERVATION, AND ENVIRONMENTAL PROTECTION

Positive Indicator — The president pursued governmental policies which improved transportation and communication, such as rivers, harbors, canals, highways, railroads, mass transit, airports, airline safety, postal service, telephone and telegraph, radio, television, or computer technology; conserved natural resources, promoted flood control, and provided environmental protection.

Negative Indicator — The president failed to utilize governmental power to promote internal improvements; allowed monopolistic control of transportation or communication to be used against the public interest; failed to conserve natural resources or to protect the environment.

2.6. RACIAL JUSTICE

Positive Indicator — The president worked to combat slavery, the slave trade, extension of slavery, segregation, or other racial injustice; used the power of the presidency to support civil rights through desegregation, affirmative action, voting rights, or anti-discrimination programs; used power of presidency to support rights of Native Americans.

Negative Indicator — The president supported slavery, the slave trade, extension of slavery, or racial segregation; opposed desegregation, voting rights, and anti-discrimination programs; treated Native Americans in discriminatory or unfair manner.

2.7. CIVIL LIBERTIES

Positive Indicator — The president supported freedom of speech and press and the right of peaceful dissent; supported freedom of religion and opposed religious bigotry.

Negative Indicator — The president stifled freedom of expression and/or punished dissenters; showed no concern for freedom of religion or practiced discrimination against persons of other religions.

2.8. MINORITIES

Positive Indicator — The president supported non-discriminatory immigration policy and opposed discrimination based on national origin or citizenship status; supported women's suffrage, equality of women before the law; supported equal employment opportunities for all; appointed qualified persons to office regardless of gender, race, religion, national origin, sexual orientation, or disabilities.

Negative Indicator — The president opposed immigration by persons of color or certain national origin; treated unfavored immigrants as second-class persons; opposed women's rights to vote, own property, serve on juries, or otherwise receive equal treatment of the laws; opposed equal employment legislation; appointments to cabinet positions, federal judgeships, etc. limited to members of favored groups.

2. 9. HUMAN DIGNITY

Positive Indicator — The president insisted on humane treatment of all individuals in the United States; took action aimed to help secure human rights abroad; treated all persons with respect, regardless of status; tried to improve the lot of the homeless, to alleviate poverty, or to insure justice for any unfavored group or individual.

Negative Indicator — The president allowed mistreatment of individuals in the United States; ignored human rights abuses by foreign countries; showed disdain or contempt for individuals based on social class, financial status, or membership in an unfavored group, put property rights above human rights.

2.10. EDUCATION, CULTURE, AND RECREATION

Positive Indicator — The president supported policies favorable to public schools and colleges; promoted vocational training and workforce development; supported the arts and humanities, museums, preservation of historic sites, creation of national parks and recreation areas, and the educational use of media such as radio, television, and computer networks.

Negative Indicator — The president opposed federal aid to education, favored policies that would weaken the public schools; opposed federal aid to the arts and humanities; failed to support national parks, historic sites, and recreation areas; failed to support the educational use of media.

Franklin D. Roosevelt heads the list of presidents ranked according to their accomplishments in Domestic Programs with eighteen points out of a possible twenty.

Roosevelt was the first president to attempt on a large scale to alleviate poverty in the United States. He unleashed the full powers of the federal government to combat the depression. When he took office thousands of unemployed workers were standing in bread lines to get food for their families, many farmers and city workers had lost their homes; more were about to lose them because they could not make their mortgage payments; banks were failing by the thousands. Roosevelt immediately declared a bank holiday, while government officials inspected their books. Banks found to be in good condition were allowed to reopen and supplied with money by the treasury. The president called a special session of Congress and proposed bills for congressional approval. Among the many important programs established were the Agricultural Adjustment Act, the Tennessee Valley Authority, the National Industrial Recovery Act, the Civilian Conservation Corps, the Works Progress Administration, Social Security, the Federal Deposit Insurance Corporation, and the Securities and Exchange Commission. Many more New Deal programs were aimed at relieving suffering from the depression and stimulating the economy to bring about recovery. Although full recovery did not come until wartime, all

future presidents must try to emulate Roosevelt's efforts.

Despite campaigning on a platform of reducing expenditures and balancing the budget, Roosevelt quickly found out that federal "pump priming" was the best way to stimulate the economy. When he backed away from spending in 1937, a recession occurred, so he again used fiscal policies to stimulate the economy. During the war he instituted price controls, rent controls, and other fiscal measures to prevent inflation from getting out of hand.

The National Labor Relations Act of 1935, giving labor the right to organize and bargain collectively, was passed without administration support, as Roosevelt thought the National Recovery Administration made it unnecessary. Only after the Senate passed the bill did Roosevelt endorse it. Roosevelt thought that sit-down strikes were illegal, but refused to use federal troops to remove strikers from the General Motors plants. In 1938 Roosevelt became interested in reviving the anti-trust laws and anti-monopolistic regulations that had been dormant for some time. He appointed Thurman Arnold as assistant attorney general in charge of anti-trust activities. Congress authorized a National Economic Committee to investigate monopolies.

The Agricultural Adjustment Act was a comprehensive plan for the rehabilitation of agriculture. It was declared unconstitutional in 1936, and passed again with revisions in 1938 as a soil conservation measure, with acreage allotments, benefit payments, storage loans for surpluses, and marketing quotas. The Frazier-Lemke Moratorium Act of 1935 prohibited creditors from holding foreclosure sales for a period of five years, provided that the farmers involved could make reasonable payments on their mortgaged property. When this law was declared unconstitutional, it was passed again with minor changes and withstood court scrutiny.

The Tennessee Valley Authority was authorized to construct dams for flood control and for the generation and distribution of electricity. It also was authorized to develop new forms of fertilizer and to take such other steps as it saw fit to promote the agricultural and industrial development of the region. Although the rural electrification program was the best known product of TVA, the agency also made great contributions in the areas of erosion control, expansion of commercial navigation, and creation of recreational facilities. It also cooperated with local authorities in providing public health services, experimented with low-cost housing for the benefit of its employees, and made other contributions to the general welfare.

Roosevelt utilized the progressive income tax not only on individuals, but also on corporations. No president has done more to shift the burden of taxation to those most able to pay. Perhaps the most revolutionary of all the New Deal programs was social security, which provides old-age annuities, unemployment insurance, and more adequate care for the poor, the dependent, and the disabled.

He issued an executive order banning discrimination in defense industries and in government because of race, creed, color, or national origin. He created the Fair Employment Practices Commission and appointed qualified persons to office, regardless of gender or religion. He appointed Frances Perkins as secretary of labor, the first female cabinet member in the history of the United States. His Four Freedoms speech was an inspirational statement for civil liberties and human rights. There were two blots on Roosevelt's record,

however. He interred Americans of Japanese ancestry in concentration camps during the war, and he did not try very hard to admit Jewish refugees to the United States. It was not until 1944 that he agreed to take Jews in excess of the quota.

Perhaps more than any previous president, Roosevelt used the power of the presidency to promote the general welfare of all of the people. Abraham Lincoln and his successor, Andrew Johnson, are tied for second in the Domestic Programs area. Harry Truman and Lyndon B. Johnson are tied for fifth, and Woodrow Wilson ranks sixth.

The president with the worst record in Domestic Programs is Ronald Reagan. Reagan cut taxes on wealthy Americans in the hope that their prosperity would trickle down to the lower income groups. The theory did not work, and the gap between rich and poor widened. Budget deficits skyrocketed, burdening future generations with an enormous national debt. Reagan also allowed the nation's infrastructure to deteriorate and opposed measures to protect the environment.

Other chief executives with negative ratings in this area are Franklin Pierce, George Bush, U. S. Grant, James Buchanan, Calvin Coolidge, Richard Nixon, Jerry Ford, Dwight Eisenhower, and Benjamin Harrison.

RANKING OF PRESIDENTS IN AREA OF DOMESTIC PROGRAMS

President	Rating by Sub-Area										
	2.1	2.2	2.3	2.4	2.5	2.6	2.7	2.8	2.9	2.10	Total
1. F. Roosevelt	2	2	2	2	2	1	2	1	2	2	18
2. Lincoln	2	2	2	2	1	1	2	2	2	1	17
2. A. Johnson	2	2	1	2	2	1	2	1	2	2	17
4. Truman	2	1	2	2	1	2	1	2	2	1	16
4. L. Johnson	1	1	2	1	2	2	1	2	2	2	16
6. Wilson	2	2	2	2	1	0	1	2	1	2	15
7. Kennedy	2	1	2	1	1	2	1	1	1	2	14
7. Clinton	2	0	1	1	1	2	1	2	2	2	14*
9. T. Roosevelt	2	2	2	0	2	0	1	0	1	2	12
10. Taft	1	1	1	2	2	0	1	1	1	1	11
10. Carter	−1	0	1	1	2	1	1	2	2	2	11
12. J. Q. Adams	1	0	1	0	1	2	2	0	2	1	10

*Preliminary rating as of October 27, 1999

| President | Ratings on Criteria by Sub-Areas | | | | | | | | | | |
	2.1	2.2	2.3	2.4	2.5	2.6	2.7	2.8	2.9	2.10	Total
12. Jefferson	−1	1	0	1	1	2	2	0	2	2	10
14. Madison	−1	1	1	0	0	2	2	0	2	1	8
14. Hoover	−1	1	−1	2	2	2	1	1	0	1	8
16. Washington	2	0	0	1	1	0	2	0	1	0	7
16. Van Buren	2	2	1	2	0	−1	1	0	0	0	7
16. Taylor	1	0	0	1	1	1	1	1	1	0	7
19. J. Adams	2	0	0	1	0	2	−1	0	1	0	5
19. Monroe	−1	0	0	1	0	1	2	0	2	0	5
19. Jackson	1	2	0	2	1	−2	1	0	0	0	5
19. McKinley	1	−2	1	0	1	1	2	−1	1	1	5
23. Hayes	0	−1	0	0	1	1	0	1	1	1	4
24. Fillmore	2	0	0	1	2	0	0	−2	0	0	3
24. Cleveland	−1	0	−2	1	1	1	2	1	0	0	3
26. Harding	1	0	−1	−2	0	0	2	−1	2	1	2
27. Tyler	−1	1	0	0	1	−1	2	0	−1	0	1
27. Polk	2	0	−1	2	0	−1	0	0	−1	0	1
29. Arthur	−2	0	0	0	0	1	0	−1	0	1	−1
29. B. Harrison	−1	−1	−2	−2	1	0	1	2	0	1	−1
31. Eisenhower	0	−2	−1	−1	1	2	−2	0	0	0	−3
32. Ford	1	−1	−2	−1	−2	0	1	0	0	0	−4
33. Buchanan	−2	0	−2	−1	−1	−1	2	1	−1	0	−5
33. Coolidge	−1	−2	−1	−2	0	0	1	0	0	0	−5
33. Nixon	−1	0	0	0	0	−1	0	0	−2	−1	−5
36. Grant	−2	−2	−1	−2	−1	1	−1	0	1	1	−6
37. Pierce	1	−2	−2	1	0	−2	1	−2	−2	0	−7
37. Bush	−2	−1	−1	2	0	−1	−2	0	−1	−1	−7
39. Reagan	−2	−2	−1	−1	−2	0	1	1	−1	−1	−8

ADMINISTRATION AND INTERGOVERNMENTAL RELATIONS

Without defining the term "executive power," the Constitution states that the executive power shall be vested in a President of the United States. In addition to his duties in foreign relations and as commander-in-chief of the armed forces of the United States, the president may require the opinion, in writing, of the principal officer in each of the executive departments, and he shall have the power to grant reprieves and pardons for offenses against the United States. The Constitution gives the president power of appointment for certain offices. It says that he shall from time to time give to the Congress information on the state of the Union, that he shall recommend to their consideration such measures as he shall judge necessary and expedient, and that he may sign or veto bills passed by Congress. The Constitution further requires the president to take care that the laws be faithfully executed.

The functions of any chief executive include the overseeing of an administrative process, involving such activities as planning, organizing, staffing, directing and coordinating the work of subordinates; communicating; budgeting. In addition, the chief executive of the United States has a role in helping establish the extent of the authority of the executive branch and its relationship to the other branches, to the states, and to the people. Therefore, we have titled this section Administration and Intergovernmental Relations.

What is the extent of the executive power? Many of the earlier presidents were very scrupulous about not overstepping their constitutional limits. For instance, the role of the president in legislation was viewed by some presidents as quite minimal. The term used in the Constitution is "recommend to the consideration of Congress." Strict constructionists tended to believe they had only the power to recommend, not to attempt to influence or persuade Congress to support their proposals. More activist presidents have used many tactics to secure congressional approval, such as imposing party discipline, cajoling, arm-twisting, pleading, threatening, bargaining, calling in their "IOUs," or appealing to the people over the heads of Congress. Despite the fact that the Constitution clearly states that the president may veto a bill if he does not approve of it, some early presidents thought they had no right to veto a bill passed by both houses of Congress unless they believed it to be unconstitutional. Other presidents have used the veto or the threat of a veto as a potent legislative weapon. Does the power to appoint carry with it the power to dismiss? If the appointment must receive approval by the Senate, can the president dismiss an appointee without Senate approval? Andrew Jackson was the first president to answer these questions in the affirmative. Several presidents refused to approve the expenditure of federal funds for badly needed roads, canals, and other internal improvements because they thought such expenditures were unconstitutional. Thomas Jefferson thought the Louisiana Purchase stretched the Constitution to its limit. The question of states' rights was not settled by the Civil War and the Fourteenth Amendment, but has been a problem for some recent presidents as well.

In our Rating Scale, we have divided Area Three into ten sub-areas and specified criteria, denoted as positive or negative indicators, as follows:

3. Performance Area —
Administering the Executive Branch of Government Effectively and Efficiently and Relating Appropriately to Other Branches

3.1. DEVELOPING AN EFFECTIVE PLAN FOR OPERATING THE EXECUTIVE BRANCH

Positive Indicator — The president developed a set of goals and objectives and laid out an organized plan for their accomplishment; engaged in long-term planning and visualized the problems that must be overcome to move the nation forward.

Negative Indicator — The president either made no long-term plans or allowed the distractions of the present to prevent him from focusing on long-term goals; operated the office of the presidency without a set of consistent, well-conceived goals and objectives; reacted to events on a day-to-day basis rather than proactively.

3.2. ORGANIZING THE EXECUTIVE DEPARTMENTS FOR EFFECTIVE ACTION

Positive Indicator — The president organized the executive departments and personnel according to sound administrative principles; established clear organization patterns, communication channels, and procedures for accomplishing national goals and maintaining high standards of performance.

Negative Indicator — The president failed to institute the structure necessary to accomplish the administration's goals; ran the executive branch in a disorganized, haphazard manner.

3.3. STAFFING THE EXECUTIVE BRANCH

Positive Indicator — The president appointed the appropriate number of well-qualified persons to positions for which they were suited in executive branch departments and agencies; appointed strong, capable cabinet officers, who were effective advocates for their departments while cooperating with other department heads on matters of national interest; held employees to high standards of conduct, preventing corruption or scandal from marring his administration.

Negative Indicator — The president allowed bickering among cabinet members to give the appearance of a government in disarray or allowed an assertive cabinet member to appear to be speaking for the government while in fact he is speaking only for himself. Presidential appointees enriched themselves by improper conduct in office or otherwise tarred the administration with corruption and scandal. Appointive offices were under-staffed, overstaffed, or filled by unqualified or otherwise unsuitable personnel.

3.4. DIRECTING THE WORK OF EXECUTIVE BRANCH PERSONNEL

Positive Indicator — The president assigned personnel to appropriate roles, helped them develop clear goals and objectives based on residential priorities, gave them authority to carry out their duties, and held them responsible for results.

Negative Indicator — The president failed to give subordinates clear assignments, delegated excessive or insufficient authority, or failed to hold personnel responsible for producing desired results.

3.5. COMMUNICATING

Positive Indicator — The president developed and maintained an effective system of two-way communication with executive branch employees, the Congress, and the public; kept people informed of what they needed to know, without unnecessary secrecy; reported to the people and to the Congress through speeches, writings, or press conferences on the president's perception of national needs and problems, as well as on plans, priorities, and accomplishments of the administration; worked with the press in a relationship of mutual respect. Although some members of the press naturally opposed some parts of his program, neither the president nor the press pursued a vendetta against the other.

Negative Indicator — The president engaged in one-way communication only; engaged in unnecessary secrecy; failed to keep people informed of matters of national concern; failed to use appropriate channels of reporting, failed to report to significant segments of the nation, failed to include all the types of information that should be reported. The relationship between the press and the president deteriorated to such a point that it interfered with presidential proposals receiving a fair hearing or diminished the office of the president in the eyes of the public at home or abroad.

3.6. CONTROLLING EXPENDITURES

Positive Indicator — The president secured from Congress ample funds to work toward important national priorities, without excessive or wasteful spending; developed or maintained procedures to insure that governmental expenditures fell within reasonable limits, including expansion as required by real national emergency.

Negative Indicator — The president failed to secure adequate funding for national needs; failed to exercise oversight on governmental expenditures; allowed departments to overspend in absence of emergency; increased national debt in time of peace or prosperity.

3.7 EFFECTIVE OPERATIONS

Positive Indicator — Executive branch departments and agencies were well-administered and accomplished important goals and objectives.

Negative Indicator — Some executive departments or agencies were poorly administered, failed to achieve goals and objectives, or followed their own agendas rather than following national priorities.

3.8. WORKING WITH CONGRESS

Positive Indicator — The president secured overwhelming support from members of his own party in the Congress for passage of legislation supportive of presidential goals; secured support from a significant portion of opposition party, thus enabling programs to be passed; maintained a climate of cooperation with opposition to the point that they did not try to sabotage his administration; secured congressional support for a bipartisan foreign policy.

Negative Indicator — Enough members of his own party opposed presidential programs to allow their defeat in Congress. The president was unable to secure enough support from the opposition to pass proposed legislation; allowed his relationship with the opposition to deteriorate to the point that it damaged his presidency; allowed opposition from congressional opponents to prevent the nation from appearing united in support of the administration's foreign policy.

3.9. JUDICIARY

Positive Indicators — The president nominated and secured congressional approval of highly qualified candidates for judicial positions; maintained the independence of the judiciary branch, with mutual respect between the president and the courts.

Negative Indicator — The president nominated inferior candidates for federal judgeships; developed an antagonistic relationship with the judiciary.

3.10. THE PEOPLE VS. THE SPECIAL INTERESTS

Positive Indicator — The president put public interest ahead of self-interest; would "rather be right than president"; acted in the best interests of all the people, rather than responding only to the demands of particular pressure groups; mobilized powerful interest groups (such as labor unions, chambers of commerce, manufacturer's associations, religious organizations, etc.) to exert pressure in a successful effort to secure enactment of his programs. The president was respected by the public and used this respect to further his goals for the nation.

Negative Indicator — The president put getting re-elected, rewarding friends, or satisfying personal goals ahead of doing what was best for the country; gave paramount consideration to the desires of one group — such as business, labor, or agriculture — rather than considering needs of all the people. The president was a tool of the special interests who promoted their own agenda through him, instead of vice versa, or the interests were so antagonized by the president that they defeated his programs. The president was so disrespected by public opinion that it was difficult for him to get his programs enacted, to govern effectively, or to interact effectively with leaders of other nations.

In Area Three George Washington ranks as our greatest president. As the nation's first chief executive under the new Constitution, it became Washington's lot to organize the government, appoint officeholders, establish a working relationship with the Congress and with the judiciary, and to develop the relationship between the new government and the people. In a world ruled by kings and princes, he became one of the first leaders chosen by his fellow citizens to be president of a modern republic. He met this formidable challenge superbly.

As the first president of a new nation, Washington set a precedent for the future with every act. His main goal was the establishment of a strong national government and the preservation of unity. He believed this goal would bring peace and prosperity. He thought his foreign policy of non-involvement in alliances and Hamilton's economic plans would accomplish this goal. Although he postured as a benign administrator who merely carried out the dictates of Congress or the policies collectively agreed upon by his principal counselors, Washington himself was actually the long-term planner for his administration.

There was no administrative structure in place when Washington took office. He had to create the entire apparatus. He was well-equipped for this task. First, he acquired the facts, which he weighed carefully. Once he reached a decision, he carried it out with vigor and tenacity. He organized the executive departments, the federal court system, and the diplomatic corps for effective action.

To fill the newly created positions, Washington appointed well-qualified persons from all sections of the country. Varied political views were represented among his appointees. The two most important posts were assigned to the men who became the leaders of the first two political parties to develop in the new nation. For secretary of treasury he chose the brilliant Alexander Hamilton, who became the leader of the Federalists and was the president's closest advisor on domestic policies. For secretary of state he chose the equally (if not more so) brilliant Thomas Jefferson, who became the leader of the anti–Federalists. For secretary of war he chose his old friend General Henry Knox, whose political savvy and military experience suited him well for the position. These three secretaries headed up departments created by Congress. They, along with the attorney-general, were known unofficially as the president's cabinet. For attorney-general, Washington selected Edmund Randolph, former governor of Virginia and a member of the Constitutional Convention. This was a powerful line-up to get the new administration started on its journey over "untrodden ground."

In organizing the executive branch of the government Washington not only had to create positions, staff them, and develop working relationships among the components, but he also had to find a way to finance the new government. In this task he followed the advice of his secretary of the treasury. Hamilton proposed that the national government should pay the foreign debt, pay the domestic debt at face value, assume the unpaid war debts of the separate states, and issue interest-bearing bonds to secure the funds for these payments. Money would have to be raised to pay the interest on its bonds and the salaries and other expenses of government. Hamilton proposed to obtain the necessary funds from the sale of public lands, collection of customs duties on imports, and the collection of excise taxes on products such as whiskey. Hamilton also proposed creation of a national bank in which money coming into the treasury could be deposited and which could also make investments and issue notes. Some of these matters were quite controversial, but when Washington became convinced they were necessary for the financial stability of the new nation, he supported them and secured congressional approval.

Washington established the power to select and nominate executive officials for the approval of Congress and the power to remove them if they proved unworthy, without the necessity for congressional approval. For a variety of reasons, none of his cabinet members served throughout the president's two terms in office. Hamilton and Jefferson, each the leader of a different faction, did not work well together. At first there were anti–Federalists as well as Federalists in the cabinet, and Washington kept the government unified despite the factionalism. Eventually, all the anti–Federalists were replaced by Federalists. Washington held appointees to a high standard of conduct. James Monroe, envoy to France, accused of misconduct in the press, was recalled. Randolph, after moving from the attorney-generalship to head the state department, was falsely accused of treason, and resigned.

As soon as conflict between the nascent political parties developed, Washington started holding formal cabinet meetings, abandoning his earlier practice of conferring privately with each cabinet officer. Discord was minimized by reaching decisions through consensus.

Washington was elected unanimously before political parties were formed. When factionalism led to the formation of parties, Washington favored the party led by Hamilton. The president secured overwhelming support of the Federalists in Congress. He received enough support and co-operation from the anti–Federalists to pass his domestic programs. His reputation and status enabled him to overcome much of his opposition. Congress was split on foreign policy. The Federalists were pro–British and the Republicans were pro–French. (The opposition party, led by Jefferson, was first called the anti–Federalists. Later Jefferson's supporters were briefly called the Federal-Republicans, then the Democratic-Republicans or simply the Republicans. When Andrew Jackson reorganized the party, it became known as the Democratic party.)

After the midterm elections of 1790 the anti–Federalists, or Republicans, had a majority in the House of Representatives, although the Senate remained under Federalist control by a margin of from three to five votes. Washington was able to persuade enough of the bitterly anti–British opposition party to support the unpopular Jay Treaty for it to receive the two-thirds majority required for Senate ratification. The Jay Treaty was of utmost importance in establishing the security of the young Republic.

Washington left the making of appropriations to Congress because, as he saw it, his task was to make recommendations and then to execute the decisions of Congress. He did exercise the constitutionally mandated oversight over the actions of executive branch offices.

As the first president, it was Washington's job to establish the federal judiciary and to appoint all of the federal judges. He organized the system on a sound and enduring basis and appointed capable, qualified jurists. His choice for the first Chief Justice of the United States was John Jay, a distinguished statesman with the courage to make unpopular decisions. His other court appointees tended to be prominent figures, helping give the court the prestige it needed to function effectively.

Washington was so respected by the people that he seemed invulnerable. He could have been king, or president for life with near-dictatorial power, but he chose the limited powers of the president of a republic. After the formation of political parties, he sided with the minority party, yet maintained public support. Washington always put the public interest first. He always did what he thought was best for the country. Even though his political philosophy caused him to support policies favoring the financial-mercantile interests, he thought he was acting in the best interests of all the people.

RANKING IN ADMINISTRATION AND INTERGOVERNMENTAL RELATIONS

President	Rating by Sub-Area										
	3.1	3.2	3.3	3.4	3.5	3.6	3.7	3.8	3.9	3.10	Total
1. Washington	2	2	2	2	2	1	2	1	2	2	18
2. Wilson	2	2	2	1	1	1	1	−1	2	2	16
3. Jefferson	2	2	2	2	1	1	2	2	0	2	14
4. Truman	0	2	2	2	1	2	2	0	0	2	13
4. Kennedy	0	1	2	2	2	1	1	1	1	2	13
6. Monroe	2	1	1	0	2	1	1	2	0	2	12
6. Lincoln	2	1	1	2	1	0	2	2	−1	2	12
6. Hayes	1	2	2	2	1	0	2	1	1	0	12
6. T. Roosevelt	1	0	2	0	1	0	2	2	2	2	12
6. L. Johnson	2	2	2	1	−1	1	1	2	1	1	12
11. Jackson	2	1	0	2	1	2	2	1	−2	2	11
11. Polk	2	2	2	1	0	2	0	1	0	1	11
11. Eisenhower	0	2	0	1	1	0	2	2	2	1	11
14. Cleveland	1	2	1	2	1	0	1	0	0	2	10
14. F. Roosevelt	1	0	0	0	2	1	2	2	−1	2	9
16. B. Harrison	2	1	1	1	2	−2	2	0	1	0	8
17. J.Q. Adams	0	0	2	1	0	0	1	0	2	1	7
17. Van Buren	0	2	−1	−1	1	2	0	1	2	1	7
17. Taft	2	1	0	−1	−1	1	1	1	2	1	7
17. Clinton	1	0	1	0	1	2	1	−1	1	1	7*
21. Carter	1	1	−1	0	−1	2	1	0	2	1	6
22. J. Adams	1	1	0	−1	−1	1	1	0	2	1	5
22. Madison	1	1	0	−1	2	0	0	−1	1	2	5
22. McKinley	0	0	0	1	2	0	0	1	1	0	5
25. Taylor	0	0	−1	0	−1	0	1	1	1	1	3
25. Bush	−1	1	0	0	1	1	1	0	−1	1	3
27. Fillmore	1	0	0	0	0	0	1	0	0	0	2
28. Buchanan	0	2	1	1	−1	−1	−1	−2	1	1	1
29. Harding	−1	1	−2	0	0	−1	0	1	1	−1	−2
29. Hoover	−1	1	1	0	−2	−1	1	−2	1	0	−2
31. Arthur	0	−1	2	−1	−2	0	0	−1	0	0	−3
31. Coolidge	−1	0	0	−1	−1	1	1	−1	0	−1	−3
33. Pierce	−2	1	1	1	−1	−1	1	−2	0	−2	−4
33. A. Johnson	0	−2	−1	−1	−1	1	−2	0	1	1	−4
35. Ford	1	−1	0	−2	−2	0	−1	−1	0	−1	−7
36. Tyler	−1	1	−1	0	−1	−1	−1	−2	0	−2	−8
36. Reagan	1	0	−2	−2	−2	−2	−2	0	0	1	−8
38. Nixon	−1	1	−2	−2	−2	0	0	−1	−2	−1	−10
39. Grant	−2	−2	−2	−1	−1	0	−1	−2	−1	−1	−13

*Preliminary ratings as of October 27, 1999

LEADERSHIP AND
DECISION MAKING

Nowhere is it written that the president must be a leader, but any effective chief executive must both administer and lead his organization. What is the difference between administration and leadership? Many scholars have addressed this question. While no consensus has emerged, agreement is usually reached on three points. First, the function of both administration and leadership is to elicit human behavior in service of some goal. Second, administration is concerned primarily with management while leadership is more concerned with initiating change. Third, the power of an administrator is based on his formal role within the organization and the authority that is derived from his position, whereas the power of a leader is more personal in nature. The leader relies more on his personal influence and prestige than upon his authority and organizational status. As the nation's chief executive, the president automatically has the authority of an administrator. If he also earns the power of leadership that comes from his personal prestige, he can become much more effective in accomplishing his goals for the nation. The greatest leaders have a vision of a desired future, are able to communicate that vision, and inspire others to work hard to bring it about.

An important part of the job of any executive is making decisions. To be successful an executive must have the courage to make difficult decisions, the prudence to avoid rushing into premature decisions, and the wisdom to select the best alternative course of action based on the available information. Effective decision-making involves analyzing the existing situation, calculating and delineating alternatives, collecting additional information if time permits, predicting possible consequences of each course of action, and choosing the best decision under the circumstances. Political decisions are more difficult than some other kinds of decisions because the human factor plays a greater part. Will the decision be accepted by other parties whose acceptance is essential to its implementation? Is it better to compromise or stick to one's guns? When is half a loaf better

than none? The effective executive constantly reassesses the situation and reconsiders decisions when conditions warrant.

In our Rating Scale, we have divided the area of Leadership and Decision Making into ten sub-areas and established criteria, signified by positive and negative indicators, as follows:

4. Performance Area —
Improving the State of the Nation
Through Effective Leadership and
Appropriate Decision Making

4.1. INSPIRATION

Positive Indicator — Whether by example, exhortation, or charisma the president stimulated or inspired executive branch personnel to a high level of focused, productive effort. He inspired others to view him as an ideal person and to follow him in whatever direction he wanted to lead. The president was able through personal example or through his speeches or writings to inspire the people to an all-out effort to accomplish important national goals.

Negative Indicator — The president allowed executive branch personnel to exhibit uninspired, unfocused, or inappropriate work behavior. His personality was viewed so negatively that people were reluctant to follow him regardless of what he proposed. During his administration a malaise developed. The public was unwilling to exhibit the sacrifice, effort, or unity necessary to promote national well-being.

4.2. PERSUASIVENESS

Positive Indicator — The president was able to persuade others to follow him by convincing them that his was the right course.

Negative Indicator — The president was unable to persuade others to adopt his proposals or to carry out his programs.

4.3. CONFIDENCE BUILDING

Positive Indicator — The president was able to maintain public confidence in the government or to restore it after scandal, depression, or other disaster.

Negative Indicator — The public's confidence in the presidency, in government generally, or in the future of the country was weakened during his incumbency.

4.4. PERFORMANCE STANDARDS

Positive Indicator — The president set high standards of performance for himself and for others. He motivated others toward achieving at a high level.

Negative Indicator — The president allowed members of his administration to engage in inappropriate behavior or failed to hold them responsible for performing their duties at a high level of competence and effectiveness.

4.5. VISION

Positive Indicator — The president had a concept of what the nation and the world *should* be like. He was able to communicate this, unifying the nation and creating a feeling of togetherness and shared national goals among the people.

Negative Indicator — The president had no concept of an ideal society, no dream for the future of his country. His administration was marked by divisiveness, of group against group, of a feeling of no common national purpose.

4.6. CONCEPTUALIZING

Positive Indicator — The president was able to conceive a strategy for getting the country from where it is to where it ought to be.

Negative Indicator — The president was unable to analyze the present situation and develop a strategy for improving the nation's lot.

4.7. WEIGHING ALTERNATIVES

Positive Indicator — Before making a final decision, the president weighed various alternatives and made an informed judgment about the possible consequences of each course of action. In considering alternatives the president listened to subordinates and engaged in fair and honest discussions of the ramifications of the decision. His consideration of alternatives was informed by a wide knowledge and deep understanding of history. The wisdom of his decision making was enhanced by his willingness to learn from past mistakes.

Negative Indicator — Once he decided something should be done, the president jumped in and did it without considering alternate ways of doing it or of considering the views of those who disagreed with him. His decision making was not informed by a knowledge of history or by the lessons learned from his mistakes. The range of alternatives he considered was limited because of his inability or unwillingness to confide in others, to seek their advice, or to engage them in open dialogue.

4.8. INTELLIGENT DECISION-MAKING

Positive Indicator — The president possessed a keen intelligence and utilized it in problem solving and decision making situations.

Negative Indicator — The president used ineffective problem solving and decision making strategies through lack of application of disciplined intelligence.

4.9. COMPROMISE

Positive Indicator — In order to win wider support for a proposal, the president compromised on details but held firm on principle.

Negative Indicator — The president was unwilling to compromise on anything, or refused to stand firm even when a principle was at stake.

4.10. HARD DECISIONS AND EMERGENCIES

Positive Indicator — When faced with a situation where a decision must be made, the president made the decision no matter how tough it was or how severe the consequences if he made the wrong one. The president acted calmly in emergencies, utilizing as careful and prudent a decision-making process as time permitted, but did make timely decisions.

Negative Indicator — The president avoided making hard decisions by postponing action or allowing decisions to be made elsewhere. In emergencies the president acted rashly, rushed to a decision without proper preparation, or was paralyzed into inaction.

In the area of Leadership and Decision-Making three presidents fully satisfied all of the criteria, compiling perfect scores of twenty points each. George Washington, Thomas Jefferson, and Abraham Lincoln were all inspirational leaders, who were able to persuade others to follow their leads. They inspired public confidence. They set high standards for themselves and others. All three had a vision of what the country should become and had the ability to communicate this vision to their fellow citizens. They were adept at conceptualizing strategies. All three were excellent decision makers, skilled at weighing alternatives and reaching intelligent decisions. They knew when to compromise and when to hold firm on principle. These three presidents were courageous, but prudent, decision makers. In no other area did any president attain a perfect score, so it is quite remarkable that these three men all reached the pinnacle of achievement in this one area.

RANKING OF PRESIDENTS IN LEADERSHIP AND DECISION MAKING

President	4.1	4.2	4.3	4.4	4.5	4.6	4.7	4.8	4.9	4.10	Total
1. Washington	2	2	2	2	2	2	2	2	2	2	20
1. Jefferson	2	2	2	2	2	2	2	2	2	2	20
1. Lincoln	2	2	2	2	2	2	2	2	2	2	20
4. Adams	1	2	2	2	2	2	2	2	1	1	17
4. Madison	2	2	2	1	2	1	2	2	2	2	17
4. T. Roosevelt	2	2	2	2	1	0	2	2	2	2	17
7. F. Roosevelt	2	2	2	1	2	2	1	2	0	2	16
8. Polk	0	2	1	2	2	2	2	1	1	2	15
8. L. Johnson	2	1	1	2	2	2	1	1	2	1	15
9. Wilson	1	2	−1	2	2	2	2	2	0	2	14
11. Monroe	2	1	0	2	1	2	2	1	0	2	13
11. Kennedy	2	1	2	2	1	0	1	1	1	2	13
13. Hayes	1	0	1	2	2	1	1	2	0	2	12
13. Truman	0	1	0	2	2	1	2	1	1	2	12
15. Jackson	2	1	2	−1	2	2	0	−1	2	2	11
15. Van Buren	1	2	0	1	0	1	1	1	2	2	11
17. Eisenhower	2	2	1	1	0	−1	1	1	1	2	10
17. Clinton	0	1	0	1	1	1	2	2	0	2	10*
19. Buchanan	1	1	1	1	0	−2	1	2	2	1	8
20. B. Harrison	1	−1	1	2	0	1	0	1	1	1	7
21. Carter	1	1	−1	1	0	0	0	1	1	2	6
22. J. Q. Adams	−1	0	0	0	2	0	2	2	−1	1	5
22. Bush	0	1	0	1	−1	0	1	−1	2	2	5
24. Taylor	0	0	0	0	−1	0	1	1	1	2	4
24. Nixon	0	2	−2	0	2	0	1	1	0	0	4
26. Fillmore	0	0	1	0	0	0	0	0	1	1	3
27. Reagan	1	2	2	−2	0	−1	−2	−1	2	1	2
28. A. Johnson	0	−1	0	−1	1	1	−1	0	1	1	1
29. Cleveland	0	−1	−1	1	−1	−1	0	1	0	2	0
29. McKinley	0	0	2	0	0	0	1	1	−2	−2	0
29. Taft	0	1	1	−1	0	−1	−1	1	−1	1	0
32. Coolidge	0	0	2	0	0	−1	−2	−1	−1	1	−2
32. Ford	−1	0	0	−1	−1	0	−1	0	1	1	−2
34. Tyler	−1	−1	−1	1	−1	1	−1	−1	0	1	−3
35. Harding	0	0	−1	−2	0	−1	0	−2	1	0	−5

Preliminary rating as of October 27, 1999

President	Rating by Sub-Area										
	4.1	4.2	4.3	4.4	4.5	4.6	4.7	4.8	4.9	4.10	Total
36. Arthur	−1	−1	1	−1	−1	−1	0	−1	−1	−1	−7
37. Hoover	−2	−1	−2	1	−2	−1	−1	0	−1	1	−8
38. Pierce	0	−2	−2	0	−1	−2	−2	−2	−1	−1	−11
39. Grant	−2	−1	−2	0	−1	−2	−2	−2	−2	2	−12

PERSONAL QUALITIES

In rating presidents we are concerned primarily with their performance in office. What they did before they became president, what they did after they left the White House, what they did in their personal lives, and the so-called character issues matter to us only as they affect the presidency. A great president should enhance the presidency. In the United States the president is not only the head of government but also head of state. In contrast to nations governed by the parliamentary system, where the prime minister is the head of government and a king, queen, or other dignitary is head of state, the two positions are combined here into one office. Conducting oneself with the dignity that the office requires, instilling pride in one's countrymen, increasing the stature and power of the office, reaching out to the people, and exhibiting high standards of integrity and morality are among the behaviors that enhance the presidency. For want of a better term, we use Personal Qualities to denote those behaviors that elevate or debase the nation's highest office.

As we have done with each of the other Performance Areas, we have divided the area of Personal Qualities into ten sub-areas. Criteria for these sub-areas, expressed as positive or negative indicators, are as follows:

*5. Performance Area —
Enhancing the Presidency Through
Exhibiting Positive Personal Qualities*

5.1. PRESIDENTIAL COMPORTMENT

Positive Indicator — The president conducted himself with the dignity that his office requires.

Negative Indicator — The president demeaned his office by petty, small-minded, mean-spirited, crude, or other inappropriate behavior.

5.2. INSTILLS PRIDE IN COUNTRYMEN

Positive Indicator — The president made people proud to be Americans, made them proud that a man such as he was their president.

Negative Indicator — The president made people ashamed that a person like him was their president, or caused them to feel less pride in themselves and their country.

5.3. INCREASES STATURE OF THE OFFICE

Positive Indicator — The office of the president received more respect both at home and abroad because of the caliber of the person who occupied it.

Negative Indicator — The actions of the incumbent brought the office of the president into disrepute.

5.4. INCREASES THE POWER OF THE PRESIDENCY

Positive Indicator — Through taking bold action into previously uncharted waters or through restoring powers that a previous president had abdicated, the incumbent increased the power of the presidency to act for the good of the nation.

Negative Indicator — The president weakened the presidency by allowing some other agency, such as Congress, to usurp its authority, or by simply not using the power of the presidency to deal with national concerns.

5.5. PUBLIC OPINION AND THE PRESIDENCY

Positive Indicator — The president made the people think that the presidency is the people's office, that the president was "on their side."

Negative Indicator — The president caused the public to feel that the president was uninterested in them, to think that the president feels they are unworthy of his concern, or that the president is their enemy, not their friend.

5.6. PUBLIC ACCESS TO THE PRESIDENCY

Positive Indicator — The president sought input from all segments of the public, and gave thoughtful consideration to input that he received.

Negative Indicator — Access to the president was restricted to a small group of insiders or members of favored classes.

5.7 REACHING OUT TO THE PEOPLE

Positive Indicator — The president used many kinds of formal and informal communications to interact with the people, including among many others: "fireside chats," treating the office as a "bully pulpit," and going over the heads of Congress and other very important persons to appeal directly to the people.

Negative Indicator — The president seemed uninterested in communicating with the people through other than formal channels. He held himself aloof from the people, and they felt this aloofness.

5.8. INTEGRITY AND TRUSTWORTHINESS

Positive Indicator — The president acted consistently on a firm set of moral values and principles. The president could be trusted, his word was as good as his bond, a promise made was a promise that would be kept.

Negative Indicator — The president abandoned his moral principles whenever it was expedient for him to do so. The president could not be trusted to keep his word.

5.9. PERSONAL HONESTY

Positive Indicator — The president acted on the belief that a public office is a public trust and never in any way used his office to benefit himself personally at the expense of the public.

Negative Indicator — The president allowed his personal welfare to influence official decisions.

5.10. PERSONAL MORALITY

Positive Indicator — The president enhanced the prestige of office of the president by the high standard of personal morality he exhibited throughout his life.

Negative Indicator — The president diminished the prestige of the office or his own effectiveness as president by the low standards of morality he exhibited in his personal life.

Abraham Lincoln was the president who exhibited the most positive Personal Qualities, scoring nineteen out of a possible twenty points in this area. Some of his contemporaries would not have rated him so highly, but viewing him through the perspective of history we can see the positive effects he had on the presidency. His homespun mannerisms were ridiculed by his political opponents, but now we honor him for his plain way of speaking and his ability to make a point by telling a humorous story. The president's conduct always honored his country. Lincoln made people proud to be Americans and proud that he was their president. Above all, Lincoln was a patriot, and people responded to his patriotism. He increased the stature of the office through his greatness of spirit, his humility, his humanity, his magnanimity, his patience, his devotion to preserving the Union and especially for his determination to bind up the wounds and bring the nation back together after the war.

By expanding his constitutional war powers, Lincoln increased the power of the presidency to take bold action in emergencies. Sometimes he ruled by decree and proclamation, usurping legislative and judicial powers. His opponents accused him of tyranny, but he was not a tyrant. His temporary usurpation of power was justified by the real emergency of a terrible civil war. He believed that law is the best instrument of justice and that democracy is the best form of government. He was an eloquent spokesman for "government of the people, by the people, and for the people."

Lincoln received visitors in his presidential office certain hours every day, Monday through Friday, even in war time. Anyone could visit, be they powerful leaders or plain people. These visits took up much of the president's precious time, but he needed the input to keep in touch with the feelings of the people. Lincoln became the spokesman for the common man. He reached out to the people in personal meetings with them, in his speeches, and in public letters he wrote. He made it a practice to go over the heads of Congress and appeal directly to the people. Lincoln made the American people think that the president was really working for them and that he was their friend. A master politician and a supreme pragmatist, Lincoln was president of all the people, blending together varied groups and winning support for his administration and the war effort, even when things were going badly on the battlefields. Because of Lincoln, there was an awakening of plain people the world over, looking to America for leadership in their struggle for a better life. To the entire world, Lincoln became a symbol that democracy and liberty could succeed.

Lincoln's integrity and trustworthiness were legendary. He acted consistently on a firm set of moral values and principles. When he compromised, it was for a higher good. Preservation of the Union was to him the highest good, and he subordinated everything else to it. If he could save the Union by freeing all of the slaves, he would free them all. If he could save it by freeing none, he would free none. He viewed the Civil War as a test of whether a democratic government could survive and devoted himself to winning the war to ensure the survival of democracy. He enhanced the prestige of the presidency by holding himself to the highest standard of morality in both his public and personal life. He was personally honest and never used his office to benefit himself personally at the expense of the public. His nickname, "Honest Abe," was well deserved. The presidency was a time of great unhappiness for Lincoln. His beloved son died, his wife suffered emotional problems, and the president himself had long bouts of melancholy. He agonized over the horrors of war, his sympathetic nature making him suffer along with the victims of the conflict. He remained steadfast in his goal to preserve and restore the Union and to offer forgiveness to those who opposed him. With victory in sight at the time of his second inaugural he implored the people to "bind up the nation's wounds; to care for him who shall have borne the battle, and for his widow, and his orphan — to do all which may achieve and cherish a just and lasting peace." Instead of vengeance on the South, he asked for "malice toward none and charity for all." He will forever be an inspiration to free people and to those who long to be free.

RANKING OF PRESIDENTS IN PERSONAL QUALITIES

President					Rating by Sub-Area						
	5.1	5.2	5.3	5.4	5.5	5.6	5.7	5.8	5.9	5.10	Total
1. Lincoln	1	2	2	2	2	2	2	2	2	2	19
2. Washington	2	2	2	2	2	1	2	2	1	2	18
2. Jefferson	2	2	2	2	2	1	1	2	2	2	18
2. T. Roosevelt	1	2	2	2	2	2	2	1	2	2	18
2. Wilson	2	2	2	2	2	0	2	2	2	2	18
6. Monroe	2	2	2	2	2	2	1	2	2	0	17
6. Jackson	1	2	2	2	2	2	2	1	2	1	17
8. Madison	1	2	2	2	2	0	1	2	2	2	16
8. F. Roosevelt	2	2	2	2	2	0	2	1	2	1	16
10. Truman	0	1	0	2	2	2	2	2	2	2	15
11. McKinley	2	2	1	1	2	2	1	1	1	1	14
12. Kennedy	1	2	2	1	2	1	2	0	2	0	13
13. Polk	2	1	1	2	0	0	0	2	2	2	12
13. Hayes	2	0	1	2	0	1	1	2	2	1	12
15. J. Adams	1	1	2	2	0	−1	0	2	2	2	11
15. Van Buren	2	0	1	1	−1	1	2	1	2	2	11
15. A. Johnson	1	1	1	−1	0	2	1	2	2	2	11
15. Cleveland	1	1	1	1	1	0	1	2	2	1	11
15. Eisenhower	2	2	1	0	2	−2	2	1	1	2	11
20. Taylor	1	1	0	0	1	1	1	2	1	2	10
21. J. Q. Adams	2	0	0	0	−1	2	−1	2	2	2	8

President	Rating by Sub-Area										
	5.1	5.2	5.3	5.4	5.5	5.6	5.7	5.8	5.9	5.10	Total
21. Carter	1	−1	0	0	1	0	1	2	2	2	8
23. Tyler	1	−1	0	1	−1	1	0	2	2	2	7
23. Taft	2	0	−1	0	0	0	0	2	2	2	7
23. Reagan	2	2	2	−1	2	−1	1	−2	2	0	7
26. B. Harrison	2	0	1	0	−1	−1	1	0	2	2	6
27. Fillmore	2	1	0	0	0	1	0	1	1	−1	5
27. Bush	1	1	0	0	0	0	−1	1	2	1	5
29. Ford	1	1	1	−1	0	−1	−1	1	1	2	4
29. Buchanan	2	−2	0	−2	−2	1	1	2	2	2	4
31. Coolidge	0	1	0	0	1	−2	−2	1	2	2	3
32. Pierce	−1	−1	0	−1	−1	1	1	1	2	1	2
32. L. Johnson	1	−1	0	2	0	0	0	1	0	−1	2
34. Hoover	1	0	0	0	−1	−2	−2	1	2	2	1
35. Harding	−1	−2	−2	0	0	1	2	1	0	0	−1
36. Clinton	−2	−1	0	−1	2	2	1	−2	0	−2	−3*
37. Arthur	2	−1	−1	−1	−1	0	−2	1	0	−1	−4
38. Grant	0	−2	−2	−1	−1	−1	0	−2	0	0	−9
38. Nixon	−2	−2	−2	0	0	−1	0	−2	0	0	−9

OVERALL ASSESSMENT

All things considered, our greatest president was Abraham Lincoln. The overall assessment of a president is the sum total of his scores in the five Performance Areas. A chief executive satisfying at a high level all of the criteria in any area would receive twenty points. With five areas being scored, the highest possible rating would be 100 points. No one is perfect, not even our greatest president. The Great Emancipator scored seventy-eight points. He ranks first in Personal Qualities with nineteen points and is tied for first in the area of Leadership and Decision Making with a perfect twenty. Lincoln collected seventeen points for Domestic Programs, good for a tie for second in that category. In Administration and Intergovernmental Relations he garnered twelve points and is tied for fifth in the rankings. In Foreign Relations Lincoln scored ten points and ranks in a tie for seventeenth place.

George Washington is second in the overall rankings with 77 points, only one fewer than Lincoln. The Father of His Country ranks first in Administration and Intergovernmental Relations and is tied for first in Leadership and Decision Making. In Personal Qualities he ranks in a tie for second place, while he is tied for third in Foreign Relations. For his Domestic Programs Washington received only seven points, placing him in a tie for fifteenth place. Had Washington scored better in that single category, he might have easily topped the list as our greatest overall president.

Woodrow Wilson and Franklin D. Roosevelt are tied for third. Wilson has a top ten ranking in every category, the only chief executive to achieve that distinction. Roosevelt, who ranks first in both Foreign Relations and Domestic Programs, fared less well in the other areas. Thomas Jefferson achieved a perfect score in Leadership and Decision Making to tie for first in that category, but did not fare well in Foreign Relations or Domestic Programs, and is tied with Harry Truman for fifth place in the overall rankings. Theodore Roosevelt ranks seventh, and John F. Kennedy is eighth. James Monroe and Andrew Jackson are tied for ninth.

U. S. Grant holds the bottom spot in the rankings with a score of minus forty-two. The general received a negative ranking in every single category. He ranks last in Administration and Intergovernmental Relations, last in

*Preliminary ranking as of October 27, 1999

Leadership and Decision Making, and is tied for the bottom spot in Personal Qualities. Franklin Pierce has the next-to-worst overall rating with negative nineteen points. Other presidents who have negative overall assessments are Chester Arthur, Richard Nixon, Calvin Coolidge, Ronald Reagan, and John Tyler. Reagan has the worst record in Domestic Programs. Nixon ranks in a tie for the bottom spot in Personal Qualities. The lowest ranking in Foreign Relations is held by William McKinley, who fared better in other categories,

and has a positive rating overall. Presidential polls usually agree with us in assigning low rankings to Grant, Pierce, Nixon, and Coolidge. Arthur and Tyler receive below average rankings in the polls, but are usually not in the very lowest category. Reagan, of course, is too recent a president to have been included in most polls. Warren Harding, who is frequently at the very bottom of the polls, received negative ratings from us in three of the five categories, but had an overall score of plus one.

OVERALL RANKING OF PRESIDENTS

President	Foreign	Domestic	Admin.	Leadership	Qualities	Overall
1. Lincoln	10	17	12	20	19	78
2. Washington	14	7	18	20	18	77
3. Wilson	13	15	16	14	18	76
3. F. Roosevelt	17	18	9	16	16	76
5. Jefferson	9	9	14	20	18	70
5. Truman	14	16	13	12	15	70
7. T. Roosevelt	10	12	12	17	18	69
8. Kennedy	12	14	13	13	13	65
9. Monroe	13	5	12	13	17	60
9. Jackson	16	5	11	11	17	60
11. Madison	13	8	5	17	16	59
12. J. Adams	12	5	5	17	11	50
13. Van Buren	13	7	7	11	11	49
14. Hayes	8	4	12	12	12	48
15. L. Johnson	1	16	12	15	2	46
16. Polk	3	1	11	15	12	42
16. Carter	11	11	6	6	8	42
18. J. Q. Adams	11	10	7	5	8	41
18. Clinton	13	14	7	10	−3	41*
20. Taylor	13	7	3	4	10	37
21. Taft	8	11	7	0	7	33
22. A. Johnson	7	17	−4	1	11	32
23. Cleveland	8	3	10	0	11	32
24. Eisenhower	1	−3	11	10	11	30
25. Buchanan	14	−5	1	8	3	21
26. Fillmore	7	3	2	3	5	20
27. McKinley	−7	5	5	0	14	17
28. B. Harrison	−4	−3	8	7	6	14
28. Bush	8	−7	3	5	5	14
30. Hoover	8	8	−2	−8	1	7
31. Tyler	4	0	−6	−3	9	4
32. Ford	11	−4	−7	−2	4	2

*Preliminary rating as of October 27, 1999

President	Foreign	Domestic	Admin.	Leadership	Qualities	Overall
33. Harding	7	2	−2	−5	−1	1
34. Coolidge	2	−4	−3	−2	3	−4
34. Reagan	3	−8	−8	2	7	−4
36. Nixon	12	−3	−10	4	−9	−6
37. Arthur	5	−1	−3	−7	−4	−10
38. Pierce	1	−7	−4	−11	2	−19
39. Grant	−2	−6	−13	−12	−9	−42

UNDERRATED AND OVERRATED PRESIDENTS

Of the ten highest ranked presidents according to our criteria, all but two rank in the top ten of every presidential poll reviewed. The two exceptions are James Monroe and John F. Kennedy. Monroe, who is tied for ninth place in our rankings, ranges from twelfth to eighteenth place in the polls. Monroe is the most underrated of all U.S. presidents. His administration was marked by some of the most brilliant diplomacy in American history. He served in a time of peace, prosperity, and domestic tranquillity. His administration was known as the "Era of Good Feelings." Perhaps he would have fared better in the polls had there been more crises for him to face. Kennedy, of course, was not included in the earlier polls. We rank him eighth, whereas the other polls rank him from ninth to fifteenth.

Among the presidents who rank in our second ten, five are generally underrated. In eleventh place in our rankings is James Madison, who ranks from tenth to seventeenth place in the polls. Although half the polls rank Madison within two places of our ranking, he is definitely underrated. Martin Van Buren ranks thirteenth according to our criteria, but is rated from fifteenth to twenty-first in the polls. He was hurt by his reputation as a manipulative politician and by the inevitable comparisons to his charismatic predecessor, Andrew Jackson. Rutherford Hayes ranks fourteenth in our judgment. One poll agrees with this ranking, and one places him even higher — in thirteenth place. However, the other polls all rank him

between twentieth and twenty-fifth. Hayes was never able to overcome the stigma of the "stolen election" of 1876. Jimmy Carter, whom we rank in a tie for sixteenth, is perhaps the most underrated of our second ten. The other polls rank him from nineteenth to twenty-fifth. Carter's relations with the press hurt him, as did his failure to rescue the hostages from Iran. His reputation is in the process of being rehabilitated. We predict that future polls will deal more generously with the Georgian. Zachary Taylor ranks twentieth according to our criteria. The polls place him somewhat lower, ranking him from twenty-fourth to twenty-ninth. Serving less than a full term, Taylor unfortunately died while the debates about the Omnibus Bill were still raging.

The most overrated president is James K. Polk. We rank him in a tie for sixteenth place. The polls rank him from eighth to twelfth. He is honored by poll respondents for expanding the boundaries of the United States by conquest. Having the foremost historian of his era as his press agent perhaps had an effect also. Other presidents ranking significantly higher than they deserve (in our opinion) include Grover Cleveland, Dwight D. Eisenhower, and William McKinley. Although not highly rated in any polls, Herbert Hoover and Chester A. Arthur fare better in the polls than in our rankings.

At the present time Ronald Reagan, George Bush, and Bill Clinton have been ranked in only two polls each. It is too early to say they are underrated or overrated. However, we rank Clinton higher and Reagan and Bush lower than do the existing polls.

GEORGE WASHINGTON
1789–97

	RATING POINTS	RANK
FOREIGN RELATIONS	14	3 tie
DOMESTIC PROGRAMS	7	16 tie
ADMINISTRATION	18	1
LEADERSHIP	20	1 tie
PERSONAL QUALITIES	18	2 tie
OVERALL ASSESSMENT	77	2

BACKGROUND

George Washington was born in Westmoreland County, Virginia, on February 22, 1732, the son of a wealthy planter. As a teenager he worked as a surveyor. At the age of 20, Washington was commissioned as an officer in the Virginia militia. He engaged in several campaigns against the French and Indians. In 1758 he was elected to the House of Burgesses where he served about fifteen years. In 1774 and 1775 he was a delegate to the Continental Congress where he became a prominent member of committees dealing with military matters. In 1775 Congress elected Washington commander-in-chief of colonial troops. Washington's heroism and charismatic leadership during the Revolutionary War made him America's most respected hero. At the end of the war Washington returned to Mount Vernon and the life of a Virginia planter. In 1787 he was elected president of the Constitutional Convention. As presiding officer, Washington took little part in the great debates on the Constitution, but his leadership helped keep the convention together.

NOMINATION AND ELECTION

Strange as it seems in this era of interminable presidential campaigns, our first chief executive was not nominated for and did not run for the presidency. In 1788 there were no contending political parties, no nominating conventions or caucuses, and no presidential campaigning. The electoral college met in New York City on February 4, 1789. Washington was everyone's choice for president, but under the constitutional provisions of that time, electors had to vote for two persons, with the individual receiving most votes becoming the president and the one with the second highest number of votes becoming the vice president. Washington received the unanimous vote of the 69 electors present. John Adams received 34 votes and was elected vice president.

By the time the second presidential election came around, Washington was still the unanimous choice for president, but opposition had arisen to some of his policies, especially to those espoused by his secretary of the treasury, Alexander Hamilton. This opposition was led by Thomas Jefferson and James Madison of Virginia and by Aaron Burr and George Clinton of New York. They made John Adams the object of their attack and tried unsuccessfully to replace him in the vice-presidency. Washington, of course, was re-elected president, receiving all 132 votes.

FOREIGN RELATIONS

Washington was successful in his major goal of keeping his country at peace. When France went to war with Great Britain, Spain, and Holland in 1793, Washington favored strict neutrality. The Proclamation of Neutrality, passed by Congress and signed by Washington, negated the Franco-American Treaty of 1778 and enabled the United States to remain neutral. Washington had avoided involvement in a European war. Fortunately, Washington never had to use military force or the threat of military force against any other nation.

During Washington's administration the national interest was best served by policies of neutrality and the avoidance of alliances. At that time, of course, there were no international organizations for peace, and our neighbors in the Western Hemisphere were still colonies of European powers, so there were no logical alliances to join. As soon as possible Washington established diplomatic relations with Great Britain, France, and Spain.

Problems with all three nations were solved through diplomacy. Edmond Genet, the new French minister to the United States, seemed determined to draw Americans into war on the side of France. Genet tried to outfit warships in American ports and send them into action against the British. Washington asked France to recall Genet because he endangered American neutrality. Genet was removed from office, but allowed to remain in the United States. Neutrality was maintained. Washington also successfully handled other problems with France.

Relations with Britain deteriorated in the early 1790s. British warships accosted American ships carrying food to France and seized their cargoes. They sometimes took sailors from American ships and impressed them into the British Navy. Americans accused the British of stirring up trouble with the Indians on the western frontier and of refusing to abandon forts they had surrendered in 1783. Washington sent John Jay to London in 1794 to negotiate a settlement of these grievances. The treaty called for the British to give up the frontier forts and insured continuing trade between America and Britain, but it contained no promise that Britain would refrain from stopping American ships and impressing seamen. The Senate approved the Jay Treaty by a vote of twenty to ten, despite the bitter opposition of the anti–Federalists.

Difficulties with Spain centered on disputes over the possession of Florida and the mouth of the Mississippi River. On behalf of the United States Thomas Pinckney negotiated the Treaty of San Lorenzo el Real, in which Spain recognized the 31st parallel as the southern boundary of the United States and agreed to let Americans land their goods tax-free at New Orleans. By means of this treaty both the United States and Spain gained free use of the Mississippi River.

Agreement was reached with the Barbary pirates to release American prisoners and to stop harassing American ships. In return Washington agreed to pay $800,000 ransom, plus an annual tribute of $24,000. Although this action freed American prisoners, the payment of a tribute to the pirates set a bad precedent.

Washington favored the establishment of free commerce with the trade centers of Europe. Although the Tariff of 1792 provided some protection for American hemp and iron, it was more of a revenue-raising measure than a protective tariff. Its low rates encouraged world trade, as did Washington's domestic economic policies. Debt retirement enhanced the reputation and credit of the new nation. The National Bank restored confidence in the government. Both the Jay Treaty and the Pinckney Treaty benefitted world trade and promoted peace and prosperity for the United States.

Washington aimed to establish a powerful national government, so strong that America would be considered respectable by European powers. He intended to persuade both Americans and Europeans that we act for ourselves and not for others. He demonstrated by his consistent policies of neutrality and non-aggression that he had no designs against any foreign nation. During the eight years that Washington was in office, the United States became recognized as a viable nation — one that was not going to break up and disappear.

As the first president of the Republic, Washington navigated uncharted waters and successfully pursued foreign policies that helped establish the United States as a strong, peaceful, fair, and dependable member of the world community of nations. The Jay Treaty with Great Britain, the Pinckney Treaty with Spain, and a treaty with the Indians of the Northwest were all concluded in 1795. These treaties were of great importance in establishing the security of the new republic. They enabled Washington to end his administration as the chief executive of a viable nation at peace in a warring world.

DOMESTIC PROGRAMS

One of the major tasks facing the new nation as its first president took office was getting the country's finances in order. Because of inflation, Washington inherited a depreciated currency. Foreign governments questioned the financial viability of the new nation. Washington's secretary of the treasury, Alexander Hamilton, suggested that the foreign and domestic debt should be funded at par and the war debts of the states should be assumed by the new central government. After much debate, Congress voted for funding the debt at par. The assumption of debt plan, however, was defeated in the House of Representatives by two votes, whereupon Hamilton and Jefferson made their famous deal. Jefferson agreed to support assumption in return for Hamilton's support in moving the nation's capital to the South. Next Hamilton proposed creation of a National Bank. This, too, was passed, despite the opposition of Jefferson and his supporters.

The assumption of state debts and the creation of a National Bank restored a sound currency and curtailed inflation while stimulating the economy. Hamilton's policies gave foreign nations confidence in the financial stability of the United States. The stronger central government and Hamilton's economic program brought prosperity to the new nation. However, there were valid objections to the program. Funding the debt at par meant that the owners of government securities received full value for them. In many cases these were bankers, merchants, or speculators who had bought the securities at reduced rates from the original owners, farmers, shopkeepers, or soldiers, who had received them for services or supplies they had provided during the war. The assumption of state debts did not seem fair to those states that had small debts. The debate over the National Bank focused largely on whether the government had constitutional authority to create such an institution.

The Articles of Confederation had not given the central government enough power to deal effectively with the postwar Depression of 1784 and 1785. Under the Constitution, Washington dealt with the inherited problems effectively, and the nation prospered. The National Bank provided a source for the accumulation of capital and a means of providing a greater amount of credit, as well as a source of revenue.

Taxes were extremely low during Washington's administration, with the vast majority of governmental receipts coming from customs. In 1791 the government put a federal tax on whiskey makers. The law permitted government agents to enter homes to collect money from operators of home stills. Protests led Congress to exempt small-scale producers from the tax. Some whiskey makers in Pennsylvania still refused to pay the tax. United States marshals were sent to western Pennsylvania to arrest leaders of the opposition. Several persons were killed or wounded before Washington sent troops to stop the conflict, which became known as the "Whiskey Rebellion." Actually, there was not widespread resistance and the term rebellion is hyperbole. This action by the president strengthened the new national government, as it demonstrated its resolve and ability to enforce the nation's laws.

Washington promoted the general welfare by introducing policies that brought peace and prosperity to the country. Welfare programs as we know them today were not considered the responsibility of the central government. Nor was there governmental involvement in the regulation of business or labor.

George Washington was a slave-owning Southern planter. He believed that blacks were ignorant, lazy, careless, deceitful, and could not be trusted. He authorized his overseers to whip slaves. Their housing was poor and the food inadequate. As president he signed into law the Fugitive Slave Act of 1792. However, he was clearly troubled by the institution of slavery and by his own station as a slave owner. When he left Philadelphia for home in 1797, he left behind some of his house slaves, in effect granting de facto emancipation. He left instructions in his will that his slaves were to be freed upon his widow's death.

In many ways Washington's views toward Native Americans were ahead of his time. He had overcome his youthful prejudices and envisioned the assimilation of Indians into the society of white settlers. He used force against Native Americans in the Northwest. After suffering defeats in 1790, the army decisively defeated the Indians at the Battle of Fallen Timbers in 1794, bringing peace to the area. The "Indian problem" in the Southwest was settled by accommodation.

Washington was a strong supporter of the Constitution and its amendments, including the Bill of Rights, which were added during his administration. Although he did not advocate passage of the First Amendment, he strongly enforced its provisions after it was adopted. He upheld the right of every sect to freedom of worship and equality before the law. He condemned all forms of bigotry, intolerance, discrimination, and persecution due to religion.

In regard to treatment of minorities, human rights, and according dignity to all, our first president did not have an outstanding record. Women's suffrage had been defeated in the Constitutional Convention. The first organized movement for women's rights occurred during Washington's administration, but he took no public position on women's rights. All of his major appointments to federal office were white males, as were all major presidential appointments for the next one hundred years or more. Washington was a member of the aristocracy. His friends and close associates tended to be from the same class. Yet as an officer in

the army, suffering with his troops at Valley Forge and elsewhere, he learned to appreciate the qualities of his countrymen with less-favored backgrounds. He strongly favored a democratic form of government, with equal rights and opportunities for all. His economic policies favored an elite class of businessmen, merchants, and planters, but he sincerely believed that these policies would promote the general welfare of all the people.

ADMINISTRATION AND INTERGOVERNMENTAL RELATIONS

In the area of Administration and Intergovernmental Relations, Washington scored 18 out of a possible 20 points and ranks as our greatest president. For details of his achievements in this area, see the Criteria and Ratings section of this book.

LEADERSHIP AND DECISION MAKING

Washington was a towering figure, viewed by many of his countrymen as an ideal person. The respect he commanded served to hold opposing factions together, united behind the charismatic leader. Through his personal example, Washington was able to inspire the people to work hard to accomplish important national goals. Washington had charisma at a time when the nation needed the inspiration that a strong and persuasive leader could provide. He was successful in persuading others to follow him. His heroic persona captured the popular imagination. His wartime popularity carried over into the presidency.

Washington won public confidence and support, thus unifying the new nation at a critical time in its history. He rebuilt confidence in the national government, following a period of weakness under the Articles of Confederation. Most people were confident that Washington would do what was right for the country, and Washington was devoted to doing what he thought was right. He set high standards for himself. From subordinates he expected a standard of performance similar to his own.

Our first president had a vision for his

country. He envisioned America as a mighty nation. Its empire would consist of hegemony over the North American continent, with trade with Europe. Unity would permit expansion and procure tranquillity, safety, prosperity, and liberty. The America he envisioned would become a fortress.

In planning how to meet his goals for the nation, Washington sought advice from his cabinet and advisors. He usually sided with Hamilton, but did not blindly follow him. Hamilton was the point man in his economic program. Hamilton neither led nor was led by Washington. The two men shared a common outlook. Washington felt that Great Britain held the key to the fulfillment of his dream for America. Ultimately he and Hamilton concluded that ties with Britain were crucial to the realization of their plans for the United States. British trade offered the fuel to drive the American economy, solidify the Union, and bind the mercantile class to the new government.

In making decisions, Washington would gather the facts, weigh alternatives carefully, and blend planning with action to achieve the desired result. Washington was not a scholar. As the first president, he had no predecessors to study. He had no lessons learned from history to guide him. Naturally, he made mistakes. He learned from these mistakes and did not repeat them, even though he was loath to admit making them. If things went wrong, frequently someone else got the blame. But the amazing thing is that with no precedents to guide him he made no disastrous mistakes — no tragic missteps that could so easily have derailed the new nation as it set out on its perilous journey. In his book, *Presidential Greatness,* Thomas A. Bailey writes: "He made no major mistakes — something that cannot be said of any of his successors who served long enough to make a mistake."[55]

Washington's decision-making was characterized by courage, compromise, reassessment, and intelligence. Courage was one of Washington's greatest assets. As president, he signed the Jay Treaty, knowing that much opposition existed. A public outcry resulted, but the president held fast. His military experience enhanced his ability to act in a crisis as president. He remained calm, judicious and never panicked. He could compromise when necessary, but never gave in on principle. "None who knew him," wrote his biographer John E. Ferling, "regarded him as a genius, but some ascribed to him a quality that perhaps was even more desirable. He realized his limitation, they said; he had learned to elicit advice, sifting and sorting and weighing the counsel, with great deliberation, he made up his mind."[56]

PERSONAL QUALITIES

George Washington always conducted himself with dignity and in an appropriate manner. He knew that every part of his conduct could set a precedent for the behavior of future presidents, and he very consciously tried to set the example that he felt was appropriate for the chief executive of a republic. As the first president, he set a standard for the office, which resulted in respect at home and abroad. He set a proper tone for the office. Washington made Americans proud to be Americans and proud of their president.

He was concerned over etiquette. He asked John Adams and Alexander Hamilton for advice on his relationship with the public. He had to decide whether he should meet people freely or see none, whether he should keep open house or have receptions only on national holidays, whether he should accept invitations to private tea parties and how often he should receive visitors. He soon learned that access to the president had to be restricted. President Washington was so overwhelmed by people wanting to see him that he decided to allow one one-hour levee per week open to the public. For additional visits appointments would have to be made. In order to reach out to the people Washington made a trip visiting all 13 states. Given the difficulties of travel in those days, this was quite an impressive feat. Needless to say, he was very well received.

Through such measures as establishing a National Bank, assuming state debts, quelling the Whiskey Rebellion, defeating the Indians at Fallen Timbers, accommodating the Indians of the Southwest, and successfully dealing with foreign nations, Washington enhanced the power of the national government and established the power of the presidency.

Washington knew how to make himself beloved. He developed this facility as a Revolutionary War general. This art was practiced during his presidency as well, greatly to the benefit both of the man and of the office he held.

Washington's integrity was legendary. His character was frequently referred to as noble. He was considered trustworthy. His entire life and career demonstrated his integrity and dependability. Parson Weems's story about his chopping down the cherry tree and telling his father, "I cannot tell a lie," was probably not true, but Washington deserved his high reputation for truthfulness. He tried to refuse a salary for serving as president, as he had for commanding the army during the Revolutionary War, but Congress voted him one anyway. He profited personally from the selection of the Federal District site, but the decision to relocate the nation's capital was not made in order to enrich the president. It was made in order to facilitate the compromise between Hamiltonians and Jeffersonians over the assumption of state debts. Washington lived in elegant style. In 1790 Hamilton's treasury granted him more than he was due, but this was offset by underpayments of the same amount in two other years.

Washington was not the paragon of virtue and morality that the legends and myths about him would have us believe. He was human. He had a temper. Whenever he felt that his integrity was being questioned, his temper was sure to flare. Sometimes he could lose it for less cause, such as being kept waiting a few minutes to see someone he had summoned. However, Washington's character had a bright side that far outweighed any negatives. His virtues of courage, integrity, determination, devotion to duty, and trustworthiness were so strong that he brought tremendous prestige to the office of the president. At the very time our new nation needed a great president in order to survive, Washington insured not only that we survived, but that we thrived.

OVERALL ASSESSMENT

George Washington attained 77 out of a possible 100 points and ranks as our second greatest president. In the area of Adminstration and Intergovernmental Relations he scored highest of all the presidents. In the area of Leadership and Decision-Making he had a perfect score and ranks in a tie for first. He ranks in a second place tie in Personal Qualities and is tied for third in Foreign Relations. Only in the area of Domestic Programs does Washington fail to rank in the top three. The United States was indeed fortunate to have a man such as he for its first president.

JOHN ADAMS

1797–1801

	RATING POINTS	RANK
FOREIGN RELATIONS	12	12 tie
DOMESTIC PROGRAMS	5	9 tie
ADMINISTRATION	5	22 tie
LEADERSHIP	17	4 tie
PERSONAL QUALITIES	11	15 tie
OVERALL ASSESSMENT	50	12

BACKGROUND

John Adams was born on October 30, 1735, in Braintree (now Quincy), Massachusetts. Son of one of the community's civic leaders, Adams entered Harvard at the age of 16 and graduated four years later. After teaching school for three years, he entered the practice of law. In 1770 he was elected to the General Court (legislature) of Massachusetts where he served until 1774. He was a delegate to both Continental Congresses where he became one of the leaders pushing for independence and served on several important committees, including the one that wrote the Declaration of Independence. During most of the next decade, Adams served abroad, as minister to France, to the Netherlands, and to Great Britain.

In 1788 he returned to the United States where he was being mentioned for the vice-presidency. He did not actively seek the office, but he obviously felt he deserved the honor and did nothing to discourage his supporters. In March 1789 Adams received word that he had been elected vice president. He was re-elected four years later. He found service in the vice-presidency considerably less exciting than those heady times a few years earlier when he had been one of the leaders in the struggle for independence.

NOMINATION AND ELECTION

When George Washington gave his Farewell Address, he expected John Adams would succeed him as president. The Federalist members of the House and Senate met in a caucus and, though they made no formal nomination, agreed that they would support Adams. For his running mate they agreed upon Thomas Pinckney. The opponents of the Federalists rallied around Thomas Jefferson as their presidential candidate. Aaron Burr was their choice for vice president. There was no organized campaign. The candidates stayed at home and made no speeches. The battle was fought by their supporters in political rallies and in pamphlets, newspapers, and letters. Character assassination and mudslinging were widely practiced by both sides, but not by the principal candidates.

Adams received a total of 71 votes, one more than a majority. His running mate, Pinckney, received 59 votes. The opposition presidential candidate, Thomas Jefferson, received 68 votes, and thus was elected vice president. Clearly, the method of selecting the president and vice president was flawed, but no changes were made until after the election of 1800.

FOREIGN RELATIONS

By acting decisively John Adams prevented a war with France. This was his most important accomplishment as president. One of Adams's first acts as president was to call a special session of Congress to consider relations with France. He recommended the arming of merchant vessels, the enlargement of the naval force, and the reorganization of the militia. He sent three envoys to Paris where French diplomats offered to negotiate a treaty if the United States would pay a bribe to the French foreign minister. This so-called "X Y Z" affair aroused a patriotic fervor in the United States. As the threat of war loomed, Adams issued an executive order arming the merchant ships and signed an act that established the Navy Department. For two years, from 1798 to 1800, American ships preyed on French commerce. Over 80 French ships were captured in this "undeclared war." Adams made preparations for an army, selecting George Washington as the ranking general. Adams received advice from Europe that France would resume negotiations. On February 19, 1799, Adams forwarded to the Senate the nomination of William Murray to serve as minister plenipotentiary to France. There was opposition, but a commission was appointed as a compromise. Adams simultaneously reopened prospects for diplomatic relations with France, ended all speculation about an alliance with England, and called into question the need for an American army. The mission was successful. In September 1800 Napoleon, who had overthrown the previous French government, signed an agreement ending the crisis.

Through diplomacy Adams set the precedent in the United States for peace and the avoidance of foreign alliances. Avoiding war with France was a wise and statesmanlike course of action. It was the first substantive implementation of the message of Washington's Farewell Address, a precedent for American isolation from European wars that would influence American foreign policy for a century. Although the Adams peace mission was successful, the news did not reach this country in time to help him in the election of 1800.

During Adams's administration, there was no change in the existing tariff laws, which were for revenue only, resulting in a strong, growing economy. In addition to benefitting the United States, the low tariff also increased world trade.

The treaty with France showed Adams's strength and determination to avoid war. By diplomacy conducted during his term, Adams demonstrated that we had no designs on other nations. Adams's foreign policy decisions enhanced the prestige of the United States throughout the world.

DOMESTIC PROGRAMS

As president, Adams maintained a strong and growing economy. No economic panics or depressions occurred during his presidency. Inflation was not a problem. For the most part he maintained the tax and fiscal policies of the Washington administration. In 1798 Congress imposed a very unpopular direct property tax to pay for Adams's policy of building up the army and navy. Several hundred rioters in eastern Pennsylvania protested the tax, released federal prisoners, and "arrested" federal marshals. Their leader, John Fries, was convicted of high treason and sentenced to be hanged. Two years later Adams issued a general amnesty freeing Fries and others. During Adams's administration the federal debt increased by only two million dollars.

Adams believed that slavery was evil. He opposed its extension to any more parts of the country. He showed uncommon foresight in seeing the possibility that a war over slavery could destroy the Union. He made no changes in the Indian policy set by the Northwest Ordinances of 1785 and 1787. His administration took no action when white settlers move into prohibited areas.

Although Adams was one of the leaders of the American Revolution, which brought about the freedom of expression in which he believed, he signed the Alien and Sedition Acts in a time of national danger. Even though these restrictive laws, repugnant to believers in civil liberties, were not strictly enforced, Adams hurt the cause of freedom by signing them into law. The first act changed the period of residence required for full citizenship from five to fourteen years. The second act authorized the deportation of all aliens regarded as dangerous to public safety. It expired in 1800 and was not renewed. The third act authorized the arrest, imprisonment, or banishment of enemy aliens in the time of war. It was never applied. The fourth act provided fines and imprisonment for persons who entered into combinations to oppose execution of national laws, foment insurrection, or to write, publish, or utter false or malicious statements about the president, the legislature, or the government. Under this act ten Republican editors and printers were convicted of sedition.

As a Unitarian, Adams supported freedom of religion and opposed religious bigotry, but his administration did nothing to advance religious freedom.

ADMINISTRATION AND INTERGOVERNMENTAL RELATIONS

For the first time in American history, a change of administrations took place when Adams replaced Washington in the Executive Mansion. As a Federalist and an admirer of Washington, Adams tried to continue the goals and objectives of his predecessor. The long-range planning in which the new president engaged was mainly aimed at maintaining economic growth through peace.

To further Adams's plans to strengthen the navy, Congress created the Department of the Navy in 1798. Otherwise, Adams made no important changes in governmental organization. Any failures in the Adams administration were due not to the organizational structure, but to people in his administration not supporting him.

Adams retained Washington's cabinet and executive branch personnel, including some who were opposed to Adams and were disloyal to him as president. Although his unwillingness to use the spoils system may seem commendable, it actually had unfortunate consequences for the president, his administration, and the country. Due to opposition and disloyalty of some of his personnel, Adams had problems directing the work of the executive branch. His problems were confounded by his failure to have taken over the leadership of the Federalist party while vice president, allowing this to go by default to Alexander Hamilton. Eventually, he fired Secretary of State Thomas Pickering and Secretary of War James McHenry. The firings enabled him to take control of his own administration at the cost of intensified anti-administration feelings among one faction of the Federalists.

Adams did not enjoy good relations with Congress. The Federalists, Adams's own party, split, with one faction following Hamilton in opposition to the president. At first this opposition was covert, but when Adams became aware of it, the contention became open. Adams received some support from the anti-Federalists. He did not let them damage his presidency, even though the opposition took over in the next election. Adams failed to get bipartisan support for his foreign policy. Nevertheless, he was successful in accomplishing his major foreign policy goals.

In his annual message of 1800 Adams recommended a reform of the national judiciary. The reform was pushed diligently by the Federalists in Congress. In 1801 a bill was passed establishing six circuits instead of three. As a result, 23 new federal judgeships were created. At once the president began submitting nominations for the new posts. Some of the judges whom Adams appointed declined the position. The Senate delayed confirmation of others, but completed action just before Adams's term expired. No new nominations were made on the president's last day in office, but the commissions of three judges who had been nominated earlier were signed that evening. Nevertheless, Adams's opponents raised the charge that the president stayed up half the night signing commissions for a host of Federalist judges. Regardless of the dates of their nomination or confirmation, the newly appointed justices were falsely called "Midnight Judges." Actually, Adams was able to nominate and secure Congressional approval of highly qualified candidates for judicial positions, including the much-respected John Marshall as Chief Justice.

Adams favored the financial, manufacturing, and mercantile interests as had Washington before him. Nevertheless, he always tried to put the public interest first, and he truly wanted to be president of all the people. He was hampered by political factionalism and sectionalism. Many of the president's policies succeeded, but he failed politically. Not only was Washington a tough act to follow, but Adams also had to cope with the Hamiltonians in his own party and with the Jeffersonians in the other.

LEADERSHIP AND DECISION-MAKING

John Adams did not have a charismatic personality, but he was well-respected and he inspired people through his personal example and through his writings. He could be very persuasive through the sheer intellectual force of his arguments. Despite the split with Hamilton, which divided his own party, and the opposition of the anti–Federalists, he was able to get many of his programs enacted.

In 1797 the fragile new republic underwent its first change in administration. How would the new president fare? How would he meet the challenges posed by Great Britain and France in the international area? Through his forcefulness and determination, Adams strengthened the office of the president and the position of the United States in the world. Although he faced opposition, he won confidence in the government and in the presidency. Adams was a man of unimpeachable character, and he expected his appointees to meet his own high standards. He fired some subordinates when he discovered their disloyalty. He never allowed the popularity or unpopularity of any course of action to sway him the least bit from doing what he thought was right.

Adams had a dream for the future of the United States. He believed that America could grow into a great nation if we avoided war, re-

mained neutral, and steered clear of alliances. He was interested in seeing the country expand westward. He created a navy that could protect our coasts and shipping. By avoiding war he believed we could concentrate on building a great country through internal growth.

Before making a decision, Adams considered alternatives, and then made a solid decision. Even in the face of opposition, he had the strength and courage to make the necessary decisions, whether they were popular or not. Despite having a fiery temper, he could usually remain calm in emergencies and make a decision based on logic, rather than upon emotion. He learned from the Washington administration, from his study of European history, and from his mistakes. Possessing one of the great minds of his era, he used his intelligence to promote national unity and to preserve the Constitution. As president, Adams continually evaluated and reevaluated his programs and decisions. After he was out of office, he reassessed his administration with the benefit of hindsight, trying to be as fair and objective as humanly possible.

Adams refused to compromise his principles, even when a slight compromise would have smoothed the way to the accomplishment of some objective. He had scorn for politicians who pandered to popular sentiment. He would not commit any act that he regarded as devious, even in order to win an election. His unwillingness to compromise and his unwillingness to engage in the smallest hypocrisy cost him a great deal of political capital. In 1799 he did make a necessary compromise when he agreed to expand the peace mission to France from one man to a committee. This compromise gained wider support and enabled Adams to obtain the desired action, a treaty with France. But this compromise did not involve the sacrifice of his principles, something he would not do under any circumstances.

PERSONAL QUALITIES

Except for the times he lost his temper, Adams conducted himself with the dignity appropriate to the high office of President of the United States. Adams instilled pride in the American people. Because of the caliber of the man he was, the office of the president increased in stature. Due to his leadership, the presidency increased in power. Although Adams was not re-elected in 1800, the people liked him. In his era, presidential elections were not determined by how well the people liked a candidate, but by the proclivities of the electors and by the machinations of the politicians who manipulated them.

Public access to the president was limited during the Adams administration. The Alien and Sedition Acts had a repressive effect on public input. Adams did not seek advice from wide segments of the public, nor did he bother with public explanations of his point of view. In twenty-five years of writings after his presidency was over, Adams explained reasons for his activities as president. Unfortunately, he did not do this while in office.

Adams embraced a version of virtue that went beyond a mere ideological conviction. For Adams, virtue demanded a high level of disinterestedness and a purity of public spirit. To Adams, a promise made was a promise to be kept. He could be trusted completely. Known as "Honest John Adams," he was totally honest, with a standard far higher than that of most contemporary politicians or other citizens, for that matter.

Of all the political leaders in this nation's history, none exceeded Adams as far as personal and public morality are concerned. He was absolutely above reproach.

OVERALL ASSESSMENT

In the various categories John Adams ranged from a low of five points each in Domestic Programs and Administration and Intergovernmental Relations to a high of seventeen points in Leadership and Decision-Making. Overall, he accumulated 50 out of a possible 100 points and ranks twelfth among the 39 presidents rated.

THOMAS JEFFERSON
1801–09

	RATING POINTS	RANK
FOREIGN RELATIONS	9	20
DOMESTIC PROGRAMS	10	12 tie
ADMINISTRATION	14	3
LEADERSHIP	20	1 tie
PERSONAL QUALITIES	18	2 tie
OVERALL ASSESSMENT	70	5 tie

BACKGROUND

Thomas Jefferson was born April 13, 1743, at Shadwell, the family plantation in Albemarle County, Virginia. His father was prominent in civic affairs and his mother was a member of one of Virginia's wealthiest, most influential, and well established families — the Randolphs. After graduating from the College of William and Mary, Jefferson studied law with Judge George Wythe. In 1767 he was admitted to the bar. He designed and supervised the building of his home, Monticello. In 1773 he gave up the practice of law to devote time to public affairs and to supervise the operations of his plantation. He served in the House of Burgesses from 1769 until 1775, when he was chosen as a delegate to the Second Continental Congress. He chaired the committee appointed to write the Declaration of Independence and prepared the draft declaration. In September 1776 Jefferson resigned from Congress and returned to the Virginia House of Delegates.

Jefferson was elected to three terms as gov-ernor of Virginia, but resigned after the 1781 election. In 1783 he was elected to Congress, where he served one year before resigning to join John Adams and Benjamin Franklin in Europe to negotiate treaties of amity and commerce. When Franklin resigned as minister to France, Jefferson replaced him. In 1789 George Washington appointed Jefferson secretary of state. Jefferson's conflicts with Secretary of the Treasury Alexander Hamilton led to the development of America's first political parties. The Federalists adopted Hamilton's principles; Jefferson led the anti–Federalists, or Republicans.

In 1794 Jefferson resigned as secretary of state and returned to Monticello. By 1796 he had become concerned about the centralizing tendencies of the government. He became the Republican candidate for president, running against John Adams. Jefferson received 68 electoral votes to 71 for Adams. According to the Constitution the person receiving the second largest number of votes became vice president. As vice president, Jefferson took no active part in the Adams administration. He presided over the Senate and strengthened his leadership of the Republican party. After the Alien and Sedition Acts were passed in 1798, Jefferson wrote a series of resolutions declaring the acts unconstitutional. The resolutions set forth the compact theory of the Union and were used later by advocates of nullification and secession.

NOMINATION AND ELECTION

Midway through Jefferson's term as vice president he began laying the groundwork for the 1800 presidential race. At that time presidential candidates were not expected to campaign openly for office, but Jefferson promoted his own candidacy behind the scenes by writing letters, supporting Republican newspapers, circulating pamphlets, and urging his friends to write anonymous pieces for the press on his behalf. Republican members of Congress caucused and nominated Aaron Burr for vice president. By consensus Jefferson was already the party's presidential candidate, and the caucus did not bother to nominate him. Soon thereafter the Federalists in Congress met and recommended that John Adams and Charles Cotesworth Pinckney be supported equally as the Federalist candidates. Behind the scenes Hamilton worked secretly to defeat Adams and secure the election of Pinckney. His primary hope rested on the prospect that South Carolina electors might cast their votes for Jefferson and Pinckney in the same way they had voted for Jefferson and Thomas Pinckney in 1796. During the campaign Jefferson defined the issues and developed the Republican platform. He favored states' rights, reducing the national debt, free trade, freedom of speech, and freedom of religion. He opposed a standing army, expansion of the navy, foreign alliances, and the Alien and Sedition acts. Jefferson focused on opposition to Federalist principles and policies, not on personal attacks on Adams. Not all of his supporters followed his example. But some of the most vitriolic attacks on Adams came not from Republicans, but from Hamilton and his fellow Federalists.

South Carolina foiled Hamilton's plans by giving its votes to Jefferson and Burr. It ap-

peared that Jefferson had been elected president. Then the defect in the Constitution, which had become obvious in 1796 but not fixed, again reared its ugly head. Jefferson and Burr had each received 73 votes, Adams had 65, Pinckney 64, and John Jay one vote. Several Republican electors had considered withholding a vote from Burr in order to prevent a tie, but all were convinced that someone else would do so. None did. Jefferson and Burr were tied. The contest was not over.

The election went to the House of Representatives, where each state had one vote, regardless of population. Many Federalist Congressmen decided to vote for Burr in an effort to deny the presidency to Jefferson. Some of these favored Burr; others hoped to prevent the election of either man, in which case Congress would name an acting president until a new election was held. The new Republic faced a constitutional crisis in its first test of transferring control of the presidency from one political party to another. On February 9, 1801, the House agreed to go into continuous session until a president was chosen. If no choice were made by March 4, the country would be without a president until a candidate received the required majority, the vote of nine states. The electoral returns were opened and counted on February 11. As expected, Jefferson and Burr were tied with 73 votes each. The House immediately began balloting. On the first ballot Jefferson received the votes of eight states, Burr received the votes of six states, and the delegations of two states were divided. The results remained the same, ballot after ballot. Finally, on the 36th ballot, taken on February 17, Federalists from the two divided states cast blank ballots, giving Jefferson those two states in addition to the eight he already had. The election was finally over.

Before the election of 1804 was held, the Twelfth Amendment to the Constitution was adopted, providing for separate ballots for president and vice president. On February 25, 1804, the Republican members of Congress convened and nominated Jefferson for a second term. Burr, having fallen out of favor, was replaced by George Clinton as the vice-presidential candidate. The Federalists recommended Charles Cotesworth Pinckney for president and Rufus King for vice president. The Federalists stood no chance, for Jefferson's first term had been a brilliant success. Of the 17 states taking part in the election, Jefferson carried all but two. He received 162 electoral votes to 14 for Pinckney.

FOREIGN RELATIONS

In foreign affairs Thomas Jefferson's success as Minister to France encouraged him to play for big stakes in the international arena. The game was dangerous as France and England were in a struggle for dominance in the western world. There was a risk that our nation could be devoured or reduced to puppet status. Yet there were great opportunities as American commercial prosperity and the acquisition of Louisiana attested. Jefferson obtained what he really wanted, control of the Mississippi River, without going to war for it. The vast Louisiana territory came as an unexpected bonus.

Jefferson's greatest crisis of his first term resulted in the greatest triumph of his presidency. When Jefferson took office, Florida and Louisiana were under Spanish control. Rumors circulated of a secret treaty between Spain and France for the retrocession of Louisiana to France. Jefferson did not want the port of New Orleans to fall into the hands of a strong power like France. In 1802 Spanish officials suspended the right of Americans to deposit goods coming down the Mississippi. The Federalists demanded action, many of them seeking military measures against Spain. War fever swept the land. Jefferson nominated James Monroe as a special emissary to France and Spain to negotiate on the explosive issues. The negotiators hoped to purchase New Orleans and the Floridas. Meanwhile, Spain restored the right of deposit at New Orleans and affirmed that the right was preserved in the treaty of cession to France. When Monroe arrived in Paris, he and Robert R. Livingston, the minister to France, quickly accepted an offer by Napoleon to sell all of Louisiana to the United States. On May 2, 1803, they signed a treaty ceding Louisiana to the United States for $15 million. The Floridas were not included and the boundaries were vague. The United States gained territory doubling the size of the nation and bringing the entire Mississippi and Missouri rivers within its borders. Jefferson was elated. Despite his doubts about the constitutionality of the act, he submitted the treaty to the Senate, which ratified it by a vote of twenty-four to seven.

A lesser crisis occurred in Tripoli. For many years the pirates of the Barbary states had been preying on traffic in the Mediterranean, looting the ships of nations that refused to pay tribute. Most countries, including the United States, paid tribute rather than risking war. Jefferson was opposed in principle but went along with the practice briefly until May 1801 when Tripoli demanded more money. When the president refused, Tripoli declared war on the United States. In 1803 the pirates seized an American ship, the *Philadelphia.* Jefferson acted swiftly and decisively. Without asking Congress for authority to do so, he sent every available ship to the region. American naval forces burned the *Philadelphia* and defeated the pirates. In 1805 Tripoli agreed to end demands for tribute. Jefferson agreed to pay ransom for the release of the crew of the *Philadelphia.* The United States continued to pay tribute to the other Barbary states until 1815. The defeat of Tripoli helped world trade.

Following the *Chesapeake* Affair, in which a British ship attacked an American vessel, Jefferson promoted an embargo against England and France. Napoleon announced the Berlin Decree, forbidding trade in British goods with the European continent, would now apply to the United States. King George III proclaimed the right of impression would be applied to naval vessels and merchant ships of the United States. The embargo stopped legal American trade. Until the embargo was passed, Jefferson's tariff policies had been beneficial. Then America's economy was hurt by the stoppage. This embargo was temporary and was damaging to world trade for only 14 months.

Jefferson showed the world that the United States was growing stronger and would not give in to the European powers. He used bold diplomacy to ward off international rivals and prevent them from any goals of further western conquest. The standing of the United States in world opinion was enhanced as Jefferson successfully played his risky games with the European powers.

DOMESTIC PROGRAMS

During his first term, Jefferson abolished internal taxes, including the federal tax on liquor that had set off the Whiskey Rebellion. By eliminating unnecessary offices and expenses, he was able at the same time to reduce the national debt. The government was supported by taxes on the consumption of foreign goods, paid by those who could afford to buy luxuries. Prosperity was maintained until the Panic of 1807 struck. Like all depressions, this panic had multiple causes, but it was blamed on the Embargo Act of 1807. Jefferson miscalculated the effects of the embargo, which was self-defeating and eroded the economy of the United States, without hurting the European economies. The embargo hurt the commercial interests, but stimulated manufacturing interests of the mid–Atlantic states. Never intended to be permanent, it was repealed in 1809.

Jefferson viewed the United States as an agrarian nation. He favored the manufacturing of articles for our own consumption and the use of commerce for trading surplus agricultural commodities for other needs. In his inaugural address he spoke of encouraging agriculture and of commerce as its handmaiden. Although he himself was a large landowner, he saw the small farmer as the backbone of the nation. Before becoming president he had helped end primogeniture and entail in Virginia. As president, he continued to promote policies facilitating the ownership of small farms. Under Jefferson the balance of power began to shift from men of great fortunes to small farmers, shopkeepers, and artisans. Jefferson believed that government was to serve the ends of the common men as well as to protect property rights. Common men everywhere — the poor, the underprivileged, and the dispossessed — still use the creed of democratic liberalism, of which Jefferson was the most eloquent spokesman, in their struggle to attain a more equitable status in society.

Even though he was a slave owner, Jefferson recognized the evils of the system. He had tried to include in the Declaration of Independence a pledge to end slavery. This was defeated by southern planters and New England politicians whose constituents grew rich from the slave trade, but Jefferson continued to oppose the institution. His Ordinance of 1784 outlawed slavery in all the western territories. When it was superseded by the Ordinances of 1785 and 1787, the prohibition against slavery was continued in the territory north and west of the Ohio River, but slavery was allowed to spread into the lands south of that river. With the expiration of the Constitution's 25-year moratorium on constitutional action on slavery, Jefferson recommended a law effective January 1, 1805, to abolish the slave trade. This passed Congress, and a major step forward was taken. Jefferson did not abolish slavery, but he did stop the legal importation of slaves.

In his second annual message to Congress, Jefferson spoke of good relations with our Indian neighbors. His administration provided tools and implements and sent instructors to teach them agricultural and household arts. He thought the aboriginal inhabitants would need to adapt to the white man's way of living in order to survive. Before the Lewis and Clark expedition, he asked the explorers to treat the natives in the most conciliatory manner; to explain to them our wish to be neighborly, friendly, and useful to them; and to find what items of trade could be interchanged.

For many years both preceding and following his presidency, Jefferson devoted strenuous efforts toward getting his native Virginia to develop a comprehensive system of public education. As president, his efforts were limited by the prevailing view that the federal government had no role in education. One of the purposes of the Lewis and Clark expedition, for which Jefferson secured a small appropriation from a reluctant Congress, was to advance our geographical knowledge.

Jefferson supported freedom of speech and press and the right of peaceful dissent. He said, "I have sworn upon the altar of God eternal hostility against every form of tyranny over the mind of men." He had been a champion of liberty his entire life. However, Jefferson sometimes let his emotions take over. He hated Aaron Burr and branded Burr a traitor before his trial. He put up with General Wilkinson's civil right violations in order to "get" Burr. This transgression aside, Jefferson was one of the most eloquent spokesmen for freedom of expression who ever lived. His administration let the Alien and Sedition Acts lapse and returned money to persons who had been fined under those laws. He influenced Congress to repeal the Naturalization Act, reducing the residency requirement for naturalization once again to five years.

Among all our presidents, none believed more strongly in freedom of religion or opposed bigotry more forcefully than did Jefferson. Before his presidency he had written Virginia's Statute on Religious Liberty. He advocated separation of church and state. He was unfairly attacked for his religious views, being called an atheist, an infidel, and worse. He never answered criticisms of his religion or his private life. For the most part Jefferson kept quiet about his faith but lived by it. He was comforted by his faith when he was attacked for being "irreligious."

An eloquent spokesman for human rights, Jefferson believed in humane treatment of all individuals in the United States, including Indians and slaves. His words in the Declaration of Independence were a high expression of human rights, as were his actions in opposing the slave trade, in opposing the Alien and Sedition Acts, in promoting education, and in supporting freedom of expression and freedom of religion.

Jefferson believed that all persons should be treated with respect and dignity. His views on freedom, education, and democracy were predicated on a belief in the essential dignity of all persons, regardless of their station in life. He believed all persons were created equal, and were equally entitled to life, liberty, and the pursuit of happiness, and he acted vigorously and effectively on this belief.

ADMINISTRATION AND INTERGOVERNMENTAL RELATIONS

Jefferson developed his goals and objectives in the first year of his administration. He used these in planning for his entire tenure in office. He excelled at long-range planning, not only for his administration but for the centuries ahead. He had the ability to overcome problems and move the country forward. Although

he was idealistic, Jefferson was also pragmatic enough to make plans that were achievable.

He organized the executive branch well and did an outstanding job of running it. The executive branch departments and agencies were well-administered and accomplished important goals in harmony with the president's aims. Employees worked together with department heads and the president in teamwork that led to much success.

Jefferson made some great appointments to his cabinet and to other positions. Among the best were James Madison as secretary of state and Albert Gallatin as secretary of the treasury. However, he made some appointments on the basis of friendship. The nominations of two friends, John Page and William Short, did not receive Senate confirmation. However, these mistakes were more than offset by the brilliance of some of the other appointments. The cabinet worked in harmony and successfully. Cabinet members were brought into matters outside their departments and advised on everything.

Jefferson was masterful at directing the executive branch. He often hinted or made suggestions about an idea of his, which was then taken up and developed by subordinates who sometimes did not realize that the accomplishment was not their own idea. Through this method, Jefferson usually got what he wanted.

Jefferson believed in open communications except for some necessary secrecy in the area of foreign affairs. Negotiations leading up to the Louisiana Purchase, for example, were conducted in secret. He reported to the Congress and the nation in annual addresses and in writing. He was a great writer, and wrote all of his speeches himself in longhand.

Jefferson received the needed support from his own party. John Randolph, a floor leader and chairman of the Ways and Means Committee, often opposed Jefferson to no avail. Randolph headed a faction of the Republican Party called the "Quids." Randolph and the Quids were unable to defeat the president's programs, as the president had overwhelming support in the House of Representatives. Despite being a strict constructionist, Jefferson believed he had the power not merely to recommend legislation to Congress, but to influence or persuade Congress to adopt his proposals, using his leadership of the Republican party to that end.

Federalists feared reprisals for their having opposed Jefferson in the elections of 1796 and 1800, but these fears proved unfounded. Jefferson reached out to the Federalists as the minority party to work with the Republicans for the good of the nation. While party differences widened under Adams, the parties came closer together under Jefferson. The president received some support from the opposition. The changeover of administrations was much different than in other revolutionary countries, particularly France. Jefferson had bipartisan support from Congress on some foreign policy issues, but not all. For example, the approval of Monroe as a special emissary to France and Spain was approved by a straight party vote, with all of the Federalists opposed. Only one Federalist voted to approve the treaty relating to the Louisiana Purchase. The Federalists, as well as Jefferson and the Republicans, were concerned with the growing threat of war. The Embargo Act was passed with bipartisan support.

Republicans controlled the executive and legislative branches, but not the judiciary. John Marshall and other Federalist holdovers from the two previous administrations controlled the judicial branch. Repeal of the Judiciary Act was a priority for Jefferson. Adams had used it to pack the bench with Federalists. Jefferson managed the repeal bill through Congress. John Pickering, a federal district court judge suffering from insanity, refused to resign. Jefferson presented a case for impeachment to Congress. The House impeached, the Senate convicted, and Pickering was removed. Supreme Court Justice Samuel Chase made several intemperate charges against Republicans. He was impeached, but the Senate failed to convict. An antagonistic relationship with the judiciary developed.

Jefferson favored the common people. Even though he had some enemies and critics, Jefferson was very popular with the people. Public respect helped him achieve his goals. The public considered him a great man before, during, and after his presidency.

Jefferson was always more concerned with the public interest than with personal gain or fame. He said, "This government is the world's greatest hope." He really believed that, and his actions were guided by the determination to see that hope realized. Jefferson was the president of all the people, the first to be a representative of the common man, the first to recognize the importance of the West, the frontier, and agriculture.

LEADERSHIP AND DECISION MAKING

Jefferson was a leader of great vision. Only he and Aaron Burr among contemporary political leaders saw the great importance of the West. In his first year he set goals for eight years in office. He proposed federal aid to education and a federal role in internal improvements, such as roads. The president had a concept of what the nation and the world should be like. He had been one of the founders of the first modern democracy. He was a reformer and idealistic in his hopes for the country, but he was pragmatic in his assessment of what works in the real world. Jefferson conceived a strategy for getting the country from where it was to where it ought to be.

He led swiftly and boldly when necessary. He inspired most to view him as an ideal person, whose lead they wanted to follow. Jefferson's speeches were scarcely audible, so it became the practice to have them published in the newspaper, before they were spoken. A brilliant writer, he inspired people by his writings to all-out effort to accomplish important goals. As for personal example, he dressed as a common man, dispensed with aristocratic manners and pageantry. He was informal compared to Washington and Adams. He really inspired the ordinary people. The president was very persuasive, and usually huge majorities supported him. Jefferson developed friendships based on trust and respect. Many of the people he relied upon shared the same philosophy, which led to harmony during his administration. He was able to maintain public confidence even when the embargo caused economic hardships. Scurrilous attacks on Jefferson's character did not cause the people to lose confidence in their president.

Jefferson set the highest standards for himself, often working late into the night and then rising early the next morning. He set higher standards for Madison and Gallatin than he did for others with less ability. Jefferson did not need to surround himself with weak people whom he could dominate nor with strong people to take over his work. Madison and Gallatin discussed with the president in private meetings each idea of each plan. They were not "yes men" to the president, but spoke their minds whether agreeing or disagreeing with Jefferson.

He knew when to act boldly and when to let Congress act first. He was a master of timing. When his Republican party took office, he saved democracy by not taking reprisals against the Federalists. Instead he recognized the rights of the minority. By deliberately preferring the use of reason over the use of force, he avoided the mistakes made in the French Revolution.

Jefferson saw and carefully weighed alternatives and made informed decisions. He was pragmatic and willing to compromise in order to win wider support for a proposal. He appeared to be yielding on the surface, but firm underneath. Jefferson continually evaluated programs, such as the unsuccessful embargo until it was repealed.

He was a man of extraordinary courage. He made hard decisions boldly on the war with Tripoli, the Louisiana Purchase, the Lewis and Clark Expedition, and the *Chesapeake* Affair. As president, Jefferson acted calmly and quickly in emergencies, utilizing as careful and prudent decision-making as time permitted, and after due consideration making timely decisions.

PERSONAL QUALITIES

Jefferson conducted himself as a common man instead of as one of the privileged classes. This made an impression not only in this country, but world-wide. His public conduct was above reproach. He refused to talk about his private conduct or to answer charges of scandalous behavior. He did away with much pomp and ceremony that was not really necessary. He treated his subordinates with respect and promoted harmony throughout the government.

Jefferson instilled pride in his country's citizens, making them proud to be Americans and to have such a man as their president. Jefferson and his countrymen really believed in the type of democratic government that was developing in the United States. Jefferson proudly served to help found this government and to improve upon it as president. Jefferson was a man of the highest caliber. Because he served his country so well, the status of the office increased both at home and abroad, but especially at home. Jefferson was a genius and with two more geniuses in the cabinet helping him, his accomplishments and achievements increased the stature of the office.

Jefferson respected the Constitution. He boldly took action in the "grey area," where it was unclear whether or not he had constitutional power to act, most notably in the war with Tripoli and the Louisiana Purchase. The power of the presidency was enhanced, and this power was used for the good of the country. Jefferson's use of the Constitution was not a paradox. He still believed in strict construction. He believed the president should be concerned mainly with foreign affairs and that domestic matters should be left to the states. He offered constitutional amendments to allow his proposed programs on education and internal improvements, but did not attempt to push them through Congress. He was a reformer, but believed that "No more must be attempted than the nation can bear." Jefferson's actions on the war with Tripoli, the Louisiana Purchase, and the Lewis and Clark Expedition all reflected favorably on the president and increased the power of the presidency.

Jefferson did much more than his predecessors to make the presidency a "people's office." His common approach, his simplicity, and his great dedication to his work convinced the majority of the people that the president was "on their side." An avid reader, Jefferson received a great deal of written input from his advisors, newspapers, letters, and pamphlets. This input was carefully considered and used. The president reached out to the people through his actions and writing, but not much through speaking or personal contact. He discontinued the practice of holding levees at the Executive Mansion.

The president was guided by a philosophy of government and a sense of integrity that he shared with his cabinet and the rest of the executive branch appointees. He was a man of principle. Thoroughly trustworthy, Jefferson could always be relied upon. He never gave up on a plan, a principle, or a friend. Jefferson was completely honest. He took no bribes, and no government funds were spent for his personal private use. As the government prospered, his personal finances went badly.

Jefferson was a man of the highest moral character. In his public life there were no scandals. He refused to discuss his private life. A man of the Age of Enlightenment, he devoted his life to applying reason to the betterment of humanity.

OVERALL ASSESSMENT

Thomas Jefferson was one of the greatest Americans who ever lived. In his presidency he did not quite reach the heights that he attained outside that office, but he still scored 70 out of a possible 100 points. He ranks in a tie for fifth among the 39 presidents rated. In the category of Leadership and Decision Making he scored twenty points, one of only three perfect scores attained.

JAMES MADISON

1809–17

	RATING POINTS	RANK
FOREIGN RELATIONS	13	6 tie
DOMESTIC PROGRAMS	8	14 tie
ADMINISTRATION	5	22 tie
LEADERSHIP	17	4 tie
PERSONAL QUALITIES	16	8 tie
OVERALL ASSESSMENT	59	11

BACKGROUND

James Madison was born March 16, 1751, in King George County, Virginia. In 1769 he entered the College of New Jersey (now Princeton University). He completed the regular course at Princeton in two years and returned to Montpelier, his father's plantation. In April 1776 he was elected as a delegate to the Virginia convention and served on the committee to draft a state constitution. In October he was elected to the House of Delegates. From 1777 to 1779 he served on the governor's council of state. In 1779 he became the youngest member elected to the Second Continental Congress, where he served until 1783. From 1784 to 1786 he was again in the House of Delegates. Madison pushed through the assembly a bill for religious liberty that had been introduced originally by Jefferson.

In 1786 he attended the Annapolis convention and was again elected to the Second Continental Congress. With Alexander Hamilton he took the lead in calling for a convention to revise the Articles of Confederation. He played a major role in the debates on the Constitution. He wrote the Virginia Plan, which favored representation based on population. His compromise solved the congressional apportionment problem. He made other suggestions of such import that he earned the name, "Father of the Constitution." In addition to his role in drafting the document, he kept copious notes, which are our best source of information about the proceedings of the convention. Along with Alexander Hamilton and John Jay, he wrote the *Federalist Papers,* which were influential not only in securing ratification of the Constitution but also in our understanding of the American constitutional system. Madison was elected to the Virginia convention on ratification and led the successful fight for acceptance of the Constitution.

From 1789 to 1797 he served in the United States House of Representatives. During his first year in Congress, he proposed twelve amendments to the Constitution and was their leading advocate. Ten of the amendments were ratified and became known as the Bill of Rights. While in the House he declined President Washington's invitation to join a mission to France and to serve as secretary of state. In 1798 he drafted the Virginia Resolutions which maintained that the Alien and Sedition Acts were unconstitutional. In 1799 he was again elected to the Virginia House of Delegates. In 1801 he was appointed secretary of state by President Jefferson and served in this post throughout Jefferson's administrations. The Louisiana Purchase was the most significant event in foreign relations during Madison's tenure. Madison was so influential in foreign affairs that Jefferson's enemies claimed that the president was completely dominated by his secretary of state.

NOMINATION AND ELECTION

In 1808 a caucus of Democratic-Republican congressmen endorsed Madison as the party's presidential candidate. George Clinton was selected as the vice-presidential candidate. The Federalists nominated Charles Cotesworth Pinckney for president and Rufus King for vice president. The Federalists ran their campaign almost entirely on opposition to Jefferson's embargo. They accused Madison of subserviency to Napoleon and a hostility to England that led to the hated embargo. In November Jefferson released to Congress the 1808 diplomatic correspondence of the secretary of state. The charges of truckling to France and warmongering toward England were disproved by the official letters. Madison won the election handily, with 122 electoral votes to 47 for Pinckney and 6 for Clinton.

In 1812 the Democratic-Republican congressional caucus endorsed Madison for a second term. The vote was unanimous because disaffected congressmen, who preferred De Witt Clinton, boycotted the caucus. Clinton disassociated himself from the Democratic-Republican party and became the candidate of anti–Madison forces in both parties. Opposition to the war became the theme of the Clinton campaign. Madison was a bystander in the contest. He made no speeches, wrote no papers, conducted no campaign, and made virtually no comments on the upcoming election.

Madison won re-election with 128 electoral votes to 89 for Clinton.

FOREIGN RELATIONS

Just before Madison took office, the Embargo Act of 1807 was repealed. To replace the embargo, Congress passed the Non-Intercourse Act, which opened trade to all countries except Great Britain and France. In spite of this act British and French warships continued to stop American ships. In 1810 Congress reopened trade with both Britain and France on the provision that if Britain would end its attacks on American ships, the United States would stop trade with France, and vice versa. Napoleon announced that he would revoke the Berlin Decree on the understanding Britain would revoke the Orders in Council. Madison then announced he would stop all trade with Britain unless the Orders in Council were withdrawn within three months. Meanwhile, Napoleon issued new regulations against American shipping, no less severe than those that had been repealed. The British refused to revoke the Orders in Council. The British fleet came to the American coast, fired at American vessels, searched them, and impressed their seamen. With war imminent, responsible statesmen in both countries worked for peace. In an encounter between an American ship and a British man-of-war, the American ship triumphed, leading to a burst of pride in American naval strength. In addition to the naval indignities, the situation on the western frontier led many Americans to favor war. In the Northwest the Indians had been supplied with British war material and were in constant communication with the British. Britain refused to vacate military posts on the Great Lakes. Britain was accused of fomenting the Indian uprising that culminated in the Battle of Tippecanoe. At the time of the attack at Tippecanoe, Tecumseh was in the South, stirring up the Creeks and Cherokees to join his confederacy. A group of congressmen called the War Hawks clamored for war. For years Madison had tried diplomacy as a means of preventing war. He knew the United States was unprepared for war, and that New England merchants feared war would destroy trade. But he knew the nation could tolerate no more insults from Great Britain. Pressed by fiery young congressional leaders such as Henry Clay, he finally recommended war. On June 16, 1812, the Orders in Council were revoked, but it was too late. The House had already voted for war, and two days later (before the news reached the United States) the Senate concurred in the declaration of war. Ironically, the war the president had tried so hard to avoid became known as "Mr. Madison's War." More appropriately, it might have been called "Mr. Clay's War."

Our national interests were promoted by the War of 1812. The war demonstrated that republican institutions have the capacity to sustain a war. The expansion of manufacturing in the war effort led to a stronger national economy. The naval victories indicated America's potential to become a naval power. The victory at New Orleans made a hero of Andrew Jackson and greatly enhanced American self-esteem. The war preserved American territorial integrity. Most importantly, the United States reached full national consciousness. Our independence had been acknowledged previously on paper. Now it was realized in fact.

Although Madison had spent 35 years in government and had excellent qualifications and experience in nearly all governmental areas, he had no experience or special qualifications for commander-in-chief of the armed forces. Nevertheless, he did remarkably well with a small, unprepared army and a much smaller navy in a sharply divided nation. The army started poorly, improved, and finished strongly. His biographer said that the deepest underrating of his work has been as commander-in-chief.[57] He kept a firm hand on the tiller during a war that rent the American people asunder. Historians tend to underestimate the difficulties caused by refusal of New England to participate in the war effort. Madison prevented potential sedition from flaring into civil war.

After the war, an American fleet was sent to the Mediterranean, where the Algerian pirates had renewed their raids on American commerce. Two Algerian frigates were seized. The Dey of Algiers agreed to release all American prisoners and signed a treaty renouncing molestation of American commerce and the exaction of tribute. Similar treaties were signed with Tripoli and Tunisia.

Madison looked forward to a future world federation. He wrote that the federal principle could be modified to indefinite extensions of space. If there are physical obstacles to worldwide extension, Madison wrote, they would be reduced by new inventions and improvements in communications and transportation.

Madison believed in recognizing the independence of all former Spanish colonies in America that had revolted against Spain. In 1808, when Napoleon occupied Spain, a number of Spanish colonies set up autonomous regimes, but did not declare themselves independent. President Jefferson and Secretary of State Madison took the position that the United States had a common interest with those colonies seeking independence and that we should stop European powers from influencing events in the Western Hemisphere. More pressing events stopped Jefferson from doing anything about it. In 1810, as president, Madison sent special agents to South America who were instructed to give unofficial encouragement to the insurgents by affirming the good will of the United States. South American agents were permitted to reside in the United States and purchase supplies and maintain indirect and unofficial contact with the government. The Monroe Doctrine was a logical outgrowth of the policies of Jefferson and Madison.

In 1810 a "West Florida convention army" stormed the Spanish fort at Baton Rouge and declared the territory of West Florida to be a free and independent state. The convention then sent President Madison a declaration asking the United States to take the territory under its protection as an integral part of the United States. In response Madison signed a proclamation directing territorial officials to take possession of the country between the Mississippi and Perdido Rivers on the grounds that the land was part of the Louisiana Purchase. In 1815 the president thwarted an American filibustering force about to sail from New Orleans in an attempt to conquer Texas.

Madison had a much better record in foreign relations than is usually recognized. He wanted peace with honor, but was unable to prevent war due to the intransigence of Britain and the treachery of Napoleon. The War of 1812 and the action against the Dey of Algiers proved that the United States would stand up for its rights. The stature of the United States in world opinion and in our own self-respect was much higher at the end of his administration than at its beginning.

DOMESTIC PROGRAMS

Madison was so preoccupied with foreign affairs that he introduced few domestic programs until 1815. He took office during an economic decline. Due to continuing difficulties with Great Britain and France, Madison was unable to restore American trade to the level needed to help pull the country out of its economic woes.

When war broke out, Congress refused to increase taxes to pay for the costs. The administration had to depend on loans to finance the war. As a result, the national debt grew more during Madison's administration than during any other prior to Buchanan's. Inflation was a natural accompaniment of the deficit. The president was weak in the area of fiscal policies. In 1813 his most trusted advisor, Secretary of the Treasury Albert Gallatin, took a leave from the treasury and went to Europe on a peace mission in response to an offer by Russia to mediate the conflict between Great Britain and the United States. During Gallatin's absence, financial chaos existed until Alexander J. Dallas took over as secretary of the treasury. During the last two years of Madison's second term, prosperity returned.

After the war, Madison was able to give primary attention to domestic affairs. He pointed with satisfaction to the revival of public credit and the great increase in revenues that occurred with peace, but said the absence of a uniform national currency suggested the probable need of a national bank. In adjusting import duties he said part of the purpose should be the introduction and maturing of manufacturing establishments. When the House and Senate squabbled over the nature of the legislation needed to implement provisions of the peace treaty, Madison went ahead on his own and exercised the discretionary power it gave him to reduce import duties. Congress created

a second Bank of the United States, and Madison signed the bank bill.

Congress passed a steady stream of presidential measures. Manufacturers were protected and revenue stabilized by a new tariff. It was a modest tariff and promoted trade, unlike the high protective tariffs that came later to harm world economy by stifling trade. Internal taxes were continued, and the land tax cut in half. Veterans' pensions were authorized.

Well ahead of his time, Madison proposed a Corps of Invalids to be organized to help support the aged and disabled through useful service. Although this proposal was not adopted by Congress, it demonstrated Madison's concern for poverty — a concern very rare among our early presidents. Another proposal that was not adopted by Congress was his plea for a national university to be established within the District of Columbia.

Madison said that the country needed a system of roads and canals that could best be constructed and administered by the national government. Even though he continued signing appropriations for the Cumberland Road, he thought a national system on the scale needed was prohibited by the Constitution, so he proposed an amendment to make it possible. Disregarding the president's constitutional scruples, Congress took preliminary steps for a Delaware-Chesapeake canal, a road from Ohio to Louisiana, and other internal improvements. In his veto message Madison told Congress that he believed federal development of roads and waterways was important to the nation's prosperity, but that he could not approve an unconstitutional act. Congress passed the bill over his veto.

For his time Madison had an advanced view on race relations. Although he was a slave owner, he recognized the evils of slavery. He favored the gradual elimination of slavery, fearing that immediate abolition would bring convulsions to the country more disastrous than the consequences of slavery itself. He believed the condition of slaves was much better than before the Revolutionary War, due to the sensitivity to human suffering growing out of the war. Yet he believed slaves could never be truly happy in a condition of servitude. He intended to free his slaves in his will, but when the time came he did not do so in order not to impoverish his widow.

Madison was a good friend of his "red children." When he praised William Henry Harrison for his bravery at Tippecanoe, he did not know that the general had advanced fifty miles into Indian territory which the president had forbidden him to enter. Madison sent soldiers to drive the white settlers off Indian lands in Mississippi Territory, but it was not done because of a misrepresentation by General Andrew Jackson. Madison sent a directive to Jackson that while Cherokees and Creeks gave permission for a military road to New Orleans, no lands could be obtained from them upon principles inconsistent with their ideas of justice and rights.

One of the greatest advocates of freedom of conscience as an inborn human right, Madison never wavered in his support of freedom of speech, press, assembly, and religion. Even during the War of 1812, when the Federalists opposed the war and some New Englanders talked secession, Madison imposed no sedition laws, and abridged no freedom of speech. He did not muzzle the press or restrict civil liberties in any way even when the British burned the Capitol. His insistence on protecting the right of people to dissent prevented civil strife during his administration. He was urged to stifle personal attacks upon himself, but to his credit he refused. Reacting to a congressional resolution for a day of prayer, Madison invited those piously disposed to give thanks and offer supplications to the "Great Parent and Sovereign of the Universe." This stirred political and religious criticism. Despite advice to the contrary, Madison held firm to his position.

Madison insisted on humane treatment of all individuals, including Indians and slaves. He treated all persons with respect, regardless of race, religion, economic status, or gender. His view that a woman's talents need not be confined to the home were unusual in a man of his times.

ADMINISTRATION AND INTERGOVERNMENTAL RELATIONS

In his inaugural address Madison listed the principles and purposes of his administration.

His first principle was to cherish peace and friendly intercourse with all nations having similar dispositions. He proposed to maintain sincere neutrality toward belligerent nations. He emphasized support for the Constitution and for civil liberties, especially freedom of religion and the press. He intended to promote agriculture, manufacture, and commerce by constitutional means and to support science and education in the same manner. He listed no specific plans to accomplish these purposes. War prevented him from achieving many of his aims.

Madison organized his administration well, but made some mistakes in staffing. In order to mollify the powerful Senator Samuel Smith of Maryland, Madison placed the senator's brother, Robert Smith, in charge of the State Department. The latter was unqualified for the post. As long as Smith was in the post, Madison had to be his own secretary of state, even writing all of the correspondence for that office. Other choices, such as William Eustis for secretary of war and Paul Hamilton for secretary of the navy, were made for reasons of sectional politics. He retained the superbly qualified Albert Gallatin in the treasury post.

The president completely dominated his cabinet. He lacked the ruthlessness needed to force resignations from incompetent department heads, taking their work upon himself. Eventually Smith agreed to resign in exchange for an appointment as minister to Russia. He was replaced by the able James Monroe. Eustis resigned in response to congressional pressure. Madison apparently did not recognize the secretary's inadequacies and would have kept him on. After Madison's first three choices turned down the post, John Armstrong was appointed to head the War Department. Armstrong also proved unsuitable. As commander-in-chief, Madison was handicapped by his lack of military experience and his reluctance to fire incompetent generals and department heads. Madison's performance improved over time. In 1814 he replaced Armstrong with Monroe, who did double duty as head of both the State and War Departments.

During the war there was much necessary secrecy. Otherwise, people were kept informed. Madison had a thin, frail voice and did not communicate well as a public speaker. However, he wrote exceptionally well. Most of his writings have been preserved for posterity. His journal of the Constitutional Convention and his contributions to the *Federalist Papers* were more important than anything he wrote as president.

After seven years of harmony, the Democratic-Republican party had become riddled with factions during Jefferson's last year in office. Although rebellious, the party supported most of Madison's proposals in Congress. The Federalists opposed Madison and the war, and some New Englanders even planned unsuccessfully to secede from the Union. A bipartisan foreign policy during the War of 1812 was denied to the president. Opposition from the Federalists as well as from factions within his own party made for a divided country during wartime. Increasing sectionalism intensified the divisions.

Early in his first term Madison solidified relations with the judiciary. Governor Snyder of Pennsylvania announced that he intended to use the militia to resist a decree of the Supreme Court of the United States transferring Revolutionary War prize money from the State of Pennsylvania to Gideon Olmstead. A confrontation between the Pennsylvania militia and a United States marshal occurred. Madison gave the governor a graceful way to back down and pardoned the militia leaders before they had to spend a day in prison. The principle that states would obey orders of the Supreme Court was upheld. During his two terms Madison had the opportunity to appoint only two Supreme Court justices. One of his appointees, Joseph Story, was one of the most distinguished jurists in the nation's history.

Madison devoted over 35 years of his life to public service, all in the public interest. He warned against the dangers of factionalism and special interests. He was always concerned about the general good of all the people. He had the support of the common man. He was supported by farmers, planters, the West, and the new manufacturing interests, but he was bitterly opposed by some of the older manufacturing and commercial interests of New England. He was respected by the public, as evidenced by his election and re-election. His popularity fell in the early years of the War of 1812 as the war went badly, but soared to new heights following the victory at New Orleans.

LEADERSHIP AND DECISION MAKING

Although lacking in charisma, Madison was a respected leader. As "Father of the Constitution" and Jefferson's secretary of state, he was respected before his administration began, and that respect continued, although it wavered somewhat in the early part of the War of 1812. Through his personal example and his writings he was able to inspire the people to efforts to continue the war to its end. He was able to maintain leadership during the war and restore confidence after the war. He was also inspirational in his writings about government, freedom, and human rights. The president set the highest performance standards for himself. Some of his appointees were high level achievers, but he allowed some members of his administration, such as Armstrong, to engage in inappropriate behavior and to perform unsatisfactorily.

With an eye to the future, Madison was a man of great vision. In his final message he advocated: a decimal system of weights and measures, revision of the criminal code, creation of a department of the interior, federal aid to education, and a system of appellate circuit courts. He spoke of peace and respect abroad. He foresaw constitutional strength and liberty as destined programs. He even looked forward to a world federation. The president was able to conceive a strategy for domestic reform, but was prevented by the war from achieving it.

Madison was quick in thought, cautious in conduct, looking to the consequences of the decision before acting, but firm of decision when the course was set. He was a genius, one of the most intelligent of all our presidents. More importantly, he used this acute intelligence in decision making. Courage and patience were additional strengths. He frequently accepted a compromise in order to win support for a proposal. He had a rather rebellious Congress during most of his tenure, but he usually got what he wanted.

It took great courage for Madison, president

of a new nation with a small army and navy, to lead the country into war with Great Britain, one of the great powers. He showed intelligence and courage in not silencing his critics, but permitting freedom of speech and press amid vicious personal attacks on him and on his programs, particularly during the dark days of the war. The president acted calmly and went to war only when it seemed inevitable.

Madison, one of the most scholarly of all our presidents, carried the history of the world in his mind and called upon it in making decisions. He constantly reassessed the situation and changed course accordingly. For example, soon after war was declared he learned that the British government might have been amenable to further negotiations. Thinking he might have made a mistake, he immediately tried to make peace, but the British refused. During the war he learned from his mistakes and changed strategy and tactics as the situation required.

PERSONAL QUALITIES

The president's conduct was above reproof. He was honest, sincere, and dedicated. He treated everyone with the utmost fairness. Madison continued the informal, common-man approach of Jefferson. He treated his subordinates with respect, at times allowing them to remain in office after they should have been removed.

Because of Madison's great intellect, eloquent writing, and devotion to the principles of liberty, the office of the president gained respect. Although a strict constructionist, Madison believed in implied powers. However, he would not under any circumstances go beyond what he believed was constitutionally permissible. His courage and vision contributed to the power of the presidency.

The majority of the people always thought Madison was on their side. Despite all the claims made by the Federalists and by opposing factions within his own party, there is little doubt that he would have been overwhelmingly elected to a third term had he desired it.

Public access to the president was limited during to the war. During peacetime, Dolley Madison held Wednesday night receptions and was an excellent hostess, one of the most popular first ladies in our history. James Madison reached out more in his writing than through personal contact.

Madison acted consistently on a firm set of moral principles and values. He was completely trustworthy, a man of great personal integrity and patriotism. History records not a single dishonest act that he committed in his entire life. He never took a bribe, nor misused public funds. Although there was a minor scandal in his administration involving exemption from arrest for debts among army recruits, Madison was not personally involved. There were no public or private scandals involving him personally. He was a man of the highest moral character.

OVERALL ASSESSMENT

Like his friend Jefferson, James Madison is one of the greatest Americans who ever lived. Like Jefferson, he, too, made perhaps his greatest contributions outside the presidency. In Madison's case this would be his help in drafting the Constitution, in securing its adoption, in explicating its meaning, and in adding the Bill of Rights to it. All of his life Madison held with undeviating zeal to freedom of conscience and other personal rights and liberties; firm adherence to the republican form of government, based on the will of the people; and passionate devotion to the Union. As president he received 59 out of a possible 100 points and ranks in eleventh place among 39 presidents rated.

JAMES MONROE
1817–25

	RATING POINTS	RANK
FOREIGN RELATIONS	13	6 tie
DOMESTIC PROGRAMS	5	19 tie
ADMINISTRATION	12	6 tie
LEADERSHIP	13	11 tie
PERSONAL QUALITIES	17	6 tie
OVERALL ASSESSMENT	60	9 tie

BACKGROUND

James Monroe, the son of a prosperous planter, was born April 28, 1758, in Westmoreland County, Virginia. At the age of sixteen he entered the College of William and Mary to prepare for a career as a lawyer, but dropped out in 1776 to enter the army. In 1779 he began law studies under Thomas Jefferson. Admitted to the bar in 1786, he spent most of his career in public service. In Virginia he served as a member of the state assembly, governor, and participant in the convention on ratification of the Constitution — which he opposed because it made the national government too strong and lacked a bill of rights. At the national level he served in Congress, in the United States Senate, as a diplomat in Europe under three presidents, and in two cabinet posts under President Madison. Securing the Louisiana Purchase was his greatest diplomatic success.

NOMINATION AND ELECTION

In the 1816 presidential election a Democratic-Republican victory was almost assured. The nation was once again prosperous, and the public was satisfied with the outcome of the War of 1812, firmly believing it to be a great victory. Madison did not seek a third term. It was widely believed that his chosen successor was James Monroe. Opposition to Monroe centered mainly on objections to the continuation of the Virginia Dynasty. The Democratic-Republican congressional caucus selected Monroe over William H. Crawford by a vote of 65 to 54. Badly discredited by their opposition to the war and by the ill-starred Hartford Convention, the Federalists made no nominations but generally supported Rufus King of New York for president. With no political issues at stake and the Federalists unable to pose a serious threat, the election of 1816 was one of the calmest in the nation's history. Monroe carried sixteen states to three for King. The electoral count was 217 for Monroe, 34 for King.

With the Federalists in disarray, no serious candidate emerged to challenge Monroe in 1820. With no opposition, Monroe carried all states and received 231 of the 232 electoral votes. One elector cast his vote for John Quincy Adams, even though Adams was not a candidate.

FOREIGN RELATIONS

Monroe's chief accomplishments were in the field of foreign affairs. Without going to war Monroe acquired Florida; extended our territorial claims to the Pacific; sustained America's rights, dignity, and honor abroad; prevented Russian control of Oregon; caused Spain to abandon its claims north of the 42nd parallel; and announced the Monroe Doctrine. Monroe and his secretary of state, John Quincy Adams, used skillful diplomacy to promote our national interests by peaceful means.

Monroe strengthened our defenses. A show of military force encouraged Spain to cede Florida. Amelia Island, a haven for pirates, was temporarily occupied by General Gaines. After Seminole Indians massacred a party of American soldiers and their families, Monroe sent Andrew Jackson to take command of American troops in the area. Exceeding his authority, Jackson invaded Florida, occupied Pensacola, and hanged two British subjects who had been stirring up the Seminoles. Monroe rebuked Jackson for his actions and restored Pensacola to Spanish rule. The incident proved that Spain was unable to maintain order in Florida and led to Spain's willingness to cede East Florida to the United States for $5 million and to relinquish all claims to West Florida. The United States and Spain agreed on the Sabine River as the western boundary of the Louisiana Purchase. The threat of military action contained in the announcement of the Monroe Doctrine kept European nations from trying to restore Spain's former colonies in Latin America and from further colonization in the Western Hemisphere.

The trading post of Astoria had been established by John Jacob Astor and taken by the British in 1813. In 1818 Britain restored Astoria to the United States, American fishing rights along the Newfoundland and Labrador coasts were recognized, and the boundary between the United States and Canada was established from Lake of the Woods along the 49th parallel to the Rocky Mountains. The Rush-Bagot agreement, signed with Great Britain in 1817, prohibited fortifications on the Great Lakes.

In 1822 the Czar of Russia announced that Russia claimed the Pacific coast from the Bering Strait to the 51st parallel and that no ships from other countries would be allowed to come within 100 miles of this shoreline. After lengthy negotiations, Russia agreed that it would establish no posts south of 54 degrees 40 minutes and gave up its claim to control the seas off the Pacific coast.

During the Napoleonic Wars, many of the Spanish colonies in Latin America had broken away and declared themselves independent countries. In 1822 Monroe sent a special message to Congress proposing recognition of seven independent republics. In 1823 the Quadruple Alliance of Austria, France, Prussia, and Russia proposed that the colonies be ruled as small kingdoms by Bourbon princes. The British foreign minister proposed that the United States and Britain act together against intervention in the New World by the European powers. Secretary of State Adams took a firm stand that the United States should not join with England but should act independently. America's response was in the president's annual message to Congress in December 1823. Adams and Monroe together wrote the portion of the address that later became known as the Monroe Doctrine. It became the cornerstone of American foreign policy for many years.

The Monroe Doctrine advanced the national interests of the United States and showed that we deserved the friendship and support of our Latin American neighbors. To Monroe his doctrine had a moral character; it was not an assertion of imperial mission as later interpreted. Nations of the Quadruple Alliance were annoyed at the pronouncement, which they branded arrogant. Nevertheless, they soon abandoned their plans to intervene in Latin America. Monroe's message demonstrated that we were determined to protect our national interests.

The Monroe Doctrine reduced international tensions by preventing wars between European powers and the new Latin American republics. The diplomatic settlements with Great Britain, Russia, and Spain further reduced international tensions. By announcing his doctrine in his annual address, Monroe focused attention upon his statement as a declaration of American policy and made a greater impact on world opinion than if the principles had emerged through diplomatic notes. His announcement helped the United States achieve a national identity. World opinion of the United States was also enhanced by Secretary Adams's dispatch justifying the acquisition of Florida. It was a declaration that the United States was assuming its rank as an equal among the nations of the world.

The only negative in Monroe's foreign relations was the tariff. Congress had already raised rates with the Tariff of 1816, passed during Madison's administration. Its effects were felt during Monroe's watch. In addition, Congress raised the rates on iron in 1818 and raised rates in general in 1824. In the long run these protective tariffs had a harmful effect on America's trade. Albert Gallatin, minister to France, helped secure a commercial treaty with France. A trade treaty with England failed to receive ratification.

DOMESTIC PROGRAMS

During most of Monroe's administration the country was generally prosperous. He tried to develop programs to help each segment of the economy. However, his programs failed to prevent the Panic of 1819 or to restore prosperity after the depression hit. The president and Congress did very little to combat it. However, William H. Crawford, as secretary of the treasury, did much to alleviate the hardships of persons who had purchased public lands from the government in good times under the terms of 25 percent down and 25 percent in each of the next three years and now found themselves unable to keep up their payments. Under Crawford's plan, the settlers were given a choice of either taking up to eight years to complete their payments or to gain clear title to whatever portion of the land had already been paid for and forfeit the remainder. There were no comprehensive remedies involving

government because the causes of the depression were only dimly understood. The president kept saying it was only temporary and urged frugality, economy, and industry. He tried to insure monetary stability and relaxed mortgage terms on land purchased from the government. The depression lasted three years.

Monroe doubted the constitutionality of the federal government building roads and waterways and urged the adoption of a constitutional amendment authorizing internal improvements. By 1822 the heavily traveled Cumberland Road was in need of repairs. Congress passed a bill appropriating the necessary funds and also authorizing the federal government to build tollhouses and tollgates, to appoint collectors, and to set tolls and penalties for nonpayment. After deliberation, Monroe concluded that while Congress could appropriate funds for repairs, it could not administer tolls and penalties. He explained his objections to Congress and vetoed the bills. Congress upheld this, his only veto. The following year he signed a bill for repairs only. In 1824 he signed the Survey Act, authorizing surveys for roads and canals of national importance.

Monroe reduced by $67 million the national debt incurred in the War of 1812. However, more loans were made during the depression. Deficits were hidden by Secretary of the Treasury Crawford for political reasons. Wartime taxes had been eliminated and Monroe did not restore them. He failed to act to stimulate the economy or to alleviate poverty. Except for approving pensions for Revolutionary War veterans and easing mortgage payments, little was done to promote the general welfare.

Monroe was a slave owner who recognized the evils of slavery but did not know how to end it. In 1819 he endorsed legislation providing for the return to Africa of Negroes illegally seized there. Monroe approved of the formation of the American Colonization Society and supported its establishing a country in Africa, where freed slaves were sent. In gratitude to the president, the first settlement (and later capital of Liberia) was named Monrovia. Monroe failed to achieve Senate ratification of an international slave trade convention with England. Publicly, the president stayed out of the controversy over the admission of Missouri to the Union, believing it was his constitutional duty to remain impartial. Privately, he favored the admission of Missouri as a slave state. When the Missouri Compromise reached his desk, he signed it even though he had doubts about the constitutionality of excluding slavery from the territories.

Monroe believed in a humanitarian Indian policy. The public demanded Indian-owned lands without proper compensation and the forcible removal of Indians to the west. Monroe wanted to "civilize" the Indians and issue individual plots to them, thus ending tribal ownership of Indian lands. Amid the mistreatment of Indians by the territorial governments, Indian agents, and land speculators, Monroe pled for Congress to define the character of Indian rights and to stop breaking treaties.

Our fifth president was a strong champion of freedom of expression and freedom of religion. He had opposed ratification of the Constitution because it failed to guarantee basic rights. After the Bill of Rights was added to that document, he became one of its strongest supporters. Although a slave owner, Monroe believed in human rights and dignity for all. That this seeming contradiction is true is borne out in his efforts to end slave trade and in his humane treatment of Indians.

ADMINISTRATION AND INTERGOVERNMENTAL RELATIONS

Monroe stated his goals and objectives in his inaugural and annual messages. He carefully laid out plans for their accomplishment. The president was a skillful planner. The great accomplishments in foreign affairs came about by planning and hard work by the Monroe administration. He organized the executive branch well. He made some excellent appointments of well-qualified and capable men, most notably John Quincy Adams as secretary of state and John C. Calhoun as secretary of war. He retained Madison's appointees in the treasury and navy departments and as attorney-general. Adams had had seven years of diplomatic experience in St. Petersburg, London, and Ghent. He was a great writer and is considered among our greatest State Department heads. Calhoun

was a superior secretary of war. William H. Crawford, secretary of the treasury, though highly competent, was antagonistic toward Monroe because of their rivalry for the presidential nomination in 1816 and Crawford's ambition to become president in 1824. Adams, Calhoun, and Crawford each had large followings and their popularity helped Monroe get his programs enacted during his first six years in office.

Unfortunately, some of Monroe's appointees were involved in scandals. Theodorick Bland, a judge in Baltimore, and Joseph Skinner, postmaster in Baltimore, were suspected of involvement with pirates. Bland owed his appointment to the intercession of William Winders and William Pinkney, who were active in defending shipowners prosecuted under neutrality laws. There was mismanagement of the second Bank of the United States.

Monroe operated the executive branch on a consensus basis. He called frequent cabinet meetings. Sometimes he had already made up his mind and met only to secure agreement among his department heads. He wanted unanimity in decisions he had made himself. At other times he sincerely wanted the advice of his cabinet, such as on the constitutionality of the Missouri Compromise.

Although Monroe was a poor public speaker, he went on a four-month-long tour of the nation in 1817, traveling as far west as Detroit. His tour helped build unity and a national identity. He was received with such enthusiasm that the trip was a personal triumph for him. His reception in New England, the erstwhile Federalist stronghold, was so enthusiastic that the term "Era of Good Feelings" was applied to his administration. The president kept his employees and the public well informed. He met with every visitor who came to the White House. Monroe enjoyed good relations with the press until the election of 1824 approached. The sensitive president had his feelings hurt by some of the newspaper attacks on him. Monroe reported to the Congress annually through written messages read by the clerk. The texts of the addresses were printed in the press.

Monroe controlled government expenditures, reducing outlays to such an extent that the national debt was greatly reduced. During the depression following the Panic of 1819 he called for further cuts in expenditures. Congress made even greater cuts in some programs than the president had requested.

Monroe was an effective administrator. The State Department, in particular, accomplished important goals during his tenure in office. His administration was marked by some of the most brilliant diplomacy in American history. In the domestic arena, the accomplishments were less spectacular, partly because of the president's sincere belief that he should not exceed his constitutional authority, which Monroe interpreted rather narrowly. Monroe's effectiveness may have been undermined somewhat by his secretary of the treasury, who had his eye on the presidency in 1824.

During the Era of Good Feelings, Monroe had virtually a one-party system, as the Federalists were won over to the Republican party after the election of 1816. The president was unopposed for re-election in 1820. Until 1823 he was highly successful in getting his programs approved by Congress. After 1822 the one-party system did not serve him well. Unlike Jefferson or Madison he could not impose party discipline by saying that opposition to his programs would help the Federalists. Monroe was the head of the nation, but not the leader of a party. Unable to use party unity as a means of realizing presidential policies, he saw the party fragment as various potential presidential candidates put their personal ambitions ahead of the administration's goals.

Monroe's only Supreme Court appointment was Smith Thompson, who was a competent but undistinguished jurist. His most unfortunate appointment was probably that of Theodorick Bland, who had a well-known connection to privateers, to a federal district court in Baltimore. Otherwise, his relationship with the judiciary was satisfactory.

The president tried to please all interest groups and sections to gain universal support. The public respected Monroe, as demonstrated in his tour of the nation. Public enthusiasm and popular demonstrations occurred not because Monroe was a hero, not as a tribute to his personal popularity but as a symbol of national unity. He was the President of the United States, and the country had achieved a national identity. Monroe deserved his status as a symbol of the nation, for he had always put the public interest above his own private interest and tried at all times to be a president of all of the people.

LEADERSHIP AND DECISION MAKING

Most people liked Monroe. He had a rare ability to put men at ease by his courtesy, his lack of condescension, his frankness, his essential goodness, and his kindheartedness. He inspired people by his personal example and by his thoughtful and well-constructed written messages. Although a poor public speaker, he was persuasive in informal conversations and in small groups. He was very open and talked with everyone who came to the White House to see him. Public confidence was built up by Monroe's foreign policy achievements and by his program of nationalism. When the Panic of 1819 struck, confidence waned. He tried to rebuild it by saying the depression was only temporary. He did not know how to remedy the economic ills.

The president set high standards for himself. He was a tireless worker. He motivated others, particularly his strong cabinet. Monroe was not a visionary as Madison and Jefferson were. He was more of a pragmatist. However, his foreign policy achievements were of utmost importance to the future of the nation. He conceptualized a strategy of gaining consensus within his cabinet and then utilizing the strength of his cabinet members to gain enactment of his programs. This strategy was highly successful during the first six years of his administration.

As a rule, Monroe acted slowly. He wanted to be sure that he had weighed carefully all of the alternatives and their possible outcomes before deciding. Monroe was not a scholar. He did not have a swift nor a rich mind, but he used good judgment. A tireless worker, his application and intensive study gave him the knowledge and understanding to use his intelligence wisely. The president reassessed his programs when the need to do so became evident.

In emergencies, Monroe was not afraid to make tough decisions, but he did so calmly with full realization of possible consequences. He acted wisely in an emergency when General Jackson exceeded his authority by invading Florida. Instead of censoring Jackson, a popular hero, and apologizing to Spain, a weakened power, Monroe took advantage of the situation and negotiated the secession of Florida to the United States.

PERSONAL QUALITIES

Last of the leaders from the Revolutionary War era to serve as president, Monroe was a picture of old-fashioned dignity. He was as unfailingly courteous toward his subordinates as he was toward men of power and prestige. As an experienced and skillful former diplomat, he knew how to act as an honorable representative of the nation.

Pride in their nation and their president surged in postwar America. The status of the office increased while Monroe was president, as did the status of the nation. Monroe increased the power of the presidency by actions in foreign relations. However, he deferred to Congress on domestic legislation. He did not use the power of party leadership to influence Congress. He believed he could veto legislation passed by Congress only when it was unconstitutional.

Almost all Americans supported Monroe. The vast majority still believed in him even when the upcoming elections of 1824 brought criticism of the president from politicians and the press. Monroe found public input valuable to him in his work. Although the president did poorly at formal speeches, he wrote well and excelled at many kinds of informal communication. He reached out to the people through personal contacts and written messages.

Monroe acted consistently on a firm set of moral values and principles. He was trustworthy and a man of integrity. Personally honest, he spent over forty years in public service and retired a poor man. He was dedicated to protecting the nation's purse strings. However, he was unable to keep his own property after leaving office. He had to ask Congress to grant him the expense money owed to him by the government.

Shortages in the White House funds were discovered in 1822. Monroe, who made good the funds in question, was requested to appear before a House investigating committee. As a matter of principle and citing the precedent of some of his predecessors, he refused to appear, thus upholding the constitutional separation of powers between the legislative and executive branches.

OVERALL ASSESSMENT

Overall, James Monroe received 60 out of a possible 100 points. He ranks in a tie for ninth place among the 39 presidents rated.

JOHN QUINCY ADAMS

1825–29

	RATING POINTS	RANK
FOREIGN RELATIONS	11	15 tie
DOMESTIC PROGRAMS	10	12 tie
ADMINISTRATION	7	17 tie
LEADERSHIP	5	22 tie
PERSONAL QUALITIES	8	21 tie
OVERALL ASSESSMENT	41	18

BACKGROUND

John Quincy Adams was born July 11, 1767, in Braintree (now Quincy), Massachusetts. His father was one of the leading statesmen of the Revolutionary War era and served as the second president of the United States. A brilliant, precocious child, young Adams at the age of 14 was named secretary to Francis Dana, the first American diplomat in Russia. In 1783 he rejoined his father, a commissioner to the court of France, as his private secretary. In 1785 he returned home and entered the junior class at Harvard, from which he graduated in 1787.

After his graduation from Harvard, Adams studied law. In July 1790 he was admitted to the bar. On May 30, 1794, President Washington appointed him minister to The Netherlands. This appointment was followed by other diplomatic assignments. In 1802 he was elected to the Massachusetts senate and from 1803 to 1808 he served as a United States Senator. In 1809 he was appointed minister to Russia. In 1811 President Madison nominated him for the

Supreme Court, but he declined. In 1814 Madison sent him to negotiate peace terms with England, ending the War of 1812. He served as minister to England from 1815 to 1817. In 1817 President Monroe appointed him secretary of state, a post he filled with distinction throughout Monroe's two terms.

NOMINATION AND ELECTION

Following the election of 1820, organized political parties gave way to the "Era of Good Feelings." The Federalists did not choose to compete again in a national contest. The once-powerful congressional caucus was a thing of the past. Several able candidates, all of whom claimed to be Republicans, were available. It was widely assumed that President Monroe would bestow his blessing on his secretary of state, and John Quincy Adams would become the next president. However, Monroe decided to take no part for or against anyone. Three major candidates emerged to challenge Adams — Secretary of the Treasury William H.

Crawford, Congressman Henry Clay, and General Andrew Jackson.

Clay campaigned for Western expansion, internal improvements at federal expense, a protective tariff, the United States Bank, and recognition of the South American republics. Crawford, endorsed by ex-presidents Jefferson and Madison, campaigned for states' rights, against the tariff, and against internal improvements. Adams and Jackson were both for the tariff and internal improvements.

Adams received 84 electoral votes; Jackson amassed 99 votes, a plurality, but far short of the 131 needed for a majority. Jackson also received a plurality in the popular vote, but little importance was attached to this. Crawford collected 41 electoral votes and Clay received 37.

Under the constitutional provisions of the time, the House of Representatives had to choose a president from among the three candidates receiving the highest number of electoral votes, with the delegation from each state having one vote. As the fourth-place finisher, Clay was no longer in the race, but his support was vital for the winner. Thirteen states voted for Adams. Jackson received the votes of seven states, while Crawford received the votes of only four states.

Rumors circulated that a corrupt bargain had been made between Adams and Clay. Charges of corruption were ridiculous, for John Quincy Adams was one of the most incorruptible men ever to grace American public life. Clay's support for Adams was based on his antipathy for Jackson and his belief that his own chances for the presidency in the future would be enhanced by an 1824 election of Adams.

FOREIGN RELATIONS

Adams served four years as a peacetime president. Although there were some differences and problems with other nations, Adams thought they were not worth going to war over, and war was avoided. A nationalist, Adams built up our armed forces and pursued policies to promote the long term interests of the United States without resorting to the threat of military force. With his years of experience as a diplomat and secretary of state, Adams

worked well with heads of other nations. Keeping the peace was one of his great accomplishments.

Adams was a friend and supporter of the new Latin American nations. As secretary of state, he had contributed to the writing of the Monroe Doctrine. As president, he wrote that in order for the United States to preserve good relations with South America we must observe and preserve a system of kindness, moderation, and forbearance.

In our differences with Great Britain Adams did not give in. Rufus King, as minister to England, could accomplish nothing with George Canning, the British foreign minister. King finally resigned because of ill health. Adams replaced him with Albert Gallatin, an extraordinarily skillful diplomat. Gallatin was supposed to have discretionary authority to act, but on the Oregon question Adams stood firm, insisting on the 49th parallel because he did not want to appear weak to his Jacksonite opponents. The joint occupation agreement was renewed for another ten years. Gallatin signed a treaty with Great Britain that settled the amount of indemnity for the slaves carried away during the War of 1812. Adams was pleased with this development.

Adams's success in foreign affairs eased international tensions and enhanced public opinion toward the United States throughout the world. The world continued to view the United States as a strong and peaceful nation.

The least successful aspect of Adams's foreign relations was his signing of the Tariff of Abominations. Passed by Congress in an effort to embarrass Adams, its rates were inconsistent and absurd. Adams had wanted a high protective tariff, but not the law that was passed. Whether he signed it or vetoed it, he would be subject to ridicule. As he believed that any bill that was passed by both houses and was constitutional should not be vetoed, he reluctantly signed it. Despite the tariff, prosperity continued in the United States. World trade was damaged, however.

DOMESTIC PROGRAMS

The nation was prosperous during Adams's four years, even though his political enemies opposed his every act. Adams believed that government should improve the condition of those who are parties to the social contract and that no government in whatever form can accomplish its objectives unless it improves the condition of those over whom it is established. This view clashed with the views held by advocates of states rights. There was much opposition by those who wanted a strong party government, not a presidential program of good works. Adams tried hard, but because of political opposition was unable to alleviate poverty among those who did not share in the general prosperity. In his third annual message, he spoke of a debt owed to the remaining Revolutionary War veterans and proposed aid, but Congress did not act on this proposal.

Adams believed in the gradual elimination of slavery. As president, he was not an abolitionist, for he wanted to avoid civil war. His greatest work against slavery was performed after his presidency was over when he served in the House of Representatives. He was a champion of liberty and of civil rights, particularly those of freed slaves. He stood for Indian rights against Governor Troup of Georgia and prevented an Indian war. Indian land was preserved when Adams discovered that the Treaty of Indian Springs was fraudulent. Adams issued a warning letter to Troup, and the governor backed down. Later all the Indians in Georgia were driven off their lands and Adams's humane Indian policy ended in futility. But he had preserved their rights for a while. By the arrest of two murderers, war with the Winnebago Indians in Michigan was averted.

Adams believed strongly in freedom of speech and press and the right of peaceful dissent. He earned for himself the nickname "Old Man Eloquent" for his speeches on human rights in the House of Representatives after his presidency. A Unitarian, Adams supported religious freedom. He believed in the humane treatment of all individuals. He fought against slavery. He fought for decent treatment of American Indians. Although he was falsely accused of being a monarchist, an aristocrat, and an elitist, Adams really believed in dignity for all.

ADMINISTRATION AND INTERGOVERNMENTAL RELATIONS

In his first annual message to Congress, Adams laid out his goals and objectives. Not one of his proposals was enacted by a hostile Congress. His plans for what he wanted to do were well drawn, but his strategy for accomplishing them was sadly lacking.

He kept in office all those appointed by the previous administration who wanted to stay. Secretary of the Treasury Crawford resigned, unwilling to serve under the new president with whom he differed politically. Two other members of the Monroe cabinet were elected to national office — Secretary of State Adams as president and Secretary of War Calhoun as vice president. All the others were retained in office. Every employee whose term or commission expired was returned except in the case of misconduct. Many of these people were not loyal to the president, but to Andrew Jackson or others bent on making Adams fail. He appointed Henry Clay as secretary of state, giving additional ammunition to those who had charged a "corrupt bargain." Clay urged him to clear out his enemies and appoint his friends to office, but Adams refused. He would not accept any support based on expected employment or favoritism.

The organization of the executive branch was satisfactory. The appropriate structure was in place. Adams's problem was that some of the employees were disloyal to the president and willing to sabotage his administration in order to help Jackson win the presidency in 1828. Nevertheless, most of the executive branch personnel performed their duties satisfactorily and produced acceptable results. Adams was far more successful with executive branch performance than he was in his dealings with Congress.

Adams was an excellent speaker and a superb writer. He reported through his annual messages to Congress and through his writings. As the election of 1828 approached the relationship with the opposition press deteriorated to one of the lowest levels in American history. Adams was attacked bitterly with falsehoods. The Adamsite press retaliated by unfairly attacking Jackson and his wife. Their scurrilous attacks on Rachel Jackson were said to have contributed to her death.

The president was unable to secure congressional approval for expenditures he wanted to make to fund internal improvements and to improve the condition of the people. Objections were based largely on the view that the constitution limited the powers of the national government to operate in these areas.

When Adams became president, the political party system had gone into a temporary collapse. With the support of no more than one-third of the population, he became a minority president. During his administration two political parties developed — the National Republicans of Adamsites and the Democratic party of Jacksonites. During the first two years the Adamsites won the speakership of the House, but after the mid-term elections of 1826 Adams's party was in the minority in both houses. Adams had the support of his own party adherents, but there were not enough National Republicans to get his programs through. Most of the time the opposition refused to support the president. Foreign policy was the one area in which the president received some bipartisan support, but even so there were delaying tactics, much criticism, and efforts to hurt him politically.

Adams made his judicial appointments as he did all his other appointments — without regard to whom they supported for president in the election of 1824. He maintained the independence of the judicial branch. He appointed Robert Trimble to the Supreme Court. After serving two years on the court, Trimble died suddenly, but he had already shown evidence of judicial brilliance. To replace Trimble, Adams nominated John J. Crittenden, but the president's term expired before the Senate acted on his confirmation and Crittenden remained in politics rather than joining the judiciary.

The president had the support of the northeastern section and of the manufacturing interests, which was not enough to secure enactment of his programs. The public did not respect Adams as president. Before his election he had been respected as a successful diplomat and secretary of state. After his presidency he again won great respect as a congressman. His presidency was the least successful part of his career. Adams always acted in the public interest as he saw it. He would have liked to have been president of all of the people, but he refused to cater to public opinion. Many of the people were under the spell of Andrew Jackson and failed to appreciate Adams's good qualities.

LEADERSHIP AND DECISION MAKING

Adams was too stiff and formal to develop the charisma needed to be an inspirational leader. He was unable to accomplish some of his goals because he was unable to inspire his followers. He was persuasive and an excellent speaker and writer. He was able to convince many people of the rightness of his cause, but was not able to attract a huge or enthusiastic following. His problems with the public were compounded by the belief that Adams had stolen the election from the popular war hero Andrew Jackson.

The president set very high standards for himself. Despite ill health, he worked extremely long days, rising at 5:00 A.M. and working until 5:00 P.M. Aside from his daily walks, he engaged in little recreation as president. He had no social life, did no entertaining. From dark until he retired at 11:00 P.M. he worked alone in his room on the business of his office. He had little time for personal reading or writing. Always he thought about what was best for the country, not what was best for John Quincy Adams. He failed to insist on similarly high standards from his employees. He fired no one except for gross misconduct. Many of his employees were working for his defeat in the next election, but he refused to discipline them.

In his vision for the country Adams was ahead of his time. In his first annual address he proposed a system of internal improvements, a national university, development of geographic and astronomical science, a uniform system of weights and measures, and improvement of the patent system. Due to overwhelming political opposition it was impossible for Adams to bring these dreams to fruition.

Adams made his final decisions carefully, weighing various alternatives, and making informed judgments about the possible consequences of each course of action. He conducted the public's business openly, discussing his decisions not only with his cabinet, but in his annual messages as well. He acted calmly in emergencies, twice preventing Indian wars. He had the courage to make hard decisions. His refusal to veto bills and fire people was based not on lack of courage, but on constitutional scruples. He believed he did not have the right to veto a bill simply because he disagreed with it or to fire a person simply because that individual opposed the president's policies.

The president refused to compromise on his principles even when it was disastrous for him politically to stick to the high road. For example, when his cabinet members warned him that a potential appointee would sabotage his programs, he would make the appointment anyway if he was convinced the individual was qualified. He appointed Henry Clay secretary of state because he believed Clay was the best man for the position, even though he knew the appointment would be used as "evidence" of a corrupt bargain. His stubbornness in such matters undermined his own presidency.

Adams was a scholar. As an avid reader and lover of books, he was rivaled only by Thomas Jefferson among all our presidents. He learned from his study of history and from his lifelong participation in public affairs. He personally knew every one of our first 17 presidents — from George Washington to Andrew Johnson. He was brilliant, fluent in many languages, the only president to have been a published poet, and one of only four presidents to have been admitted as an undergraduate to Phi Beta Kappa. He used his vast knowledge and intelligence to become an outstanding diplomat and secretary of state. After his presidency was over, he showed his genius as a congressman.

He had the ability to learn from his mistakes. Mistakes made during his presidency were useful to him in his career as a congressman and national figure. Neither his intelligence nor his ability to learn from mistakes were enough to cause him to avoid the political mistake of putting principle ahead of expediency at all times. Because of his refusal to do what was expedient, the presidency was the least successful period of his illustrious career.

PERSONAL QUALITIES

Adams conducted himself in such a manner as to reflect well upon the country he represented before the world. He was dignified and treated others in his government and in foreign governments with respect. At the time Adams was president the people were not particularly proud of him. Many resented the fact that he and not the hero Jackson won the election in the House of Representatives in 1824. In the twilight of his career the people regained their respect for and pride in Adams. They were proud of the fearless congressman, fighting for what he believed was right.

As president, Adams did not increase nor decrease the status or power of the presidency. Constitutional scruples prevented him from taking certain actions. Political opposition defeated many of his programs. Among all of our presidents, he lacked by the greatest margin having majority support. Perhaps two-thirds of the people were opposed to him as their choice for president. With his lack of political skills (or stubborn unwillingness to compromise) Adams was unable to secure enactment of his programs. He did not reach out to the people. Had he gone over the heads of congressional opponents and appealed directly to the people, he might have been successful, but it was not in his character to do so.

Adams was a man of integrity. No president exceeded him in acting always on a firm set of moral values and principles. He was completely trustworthy and completely honest. Accusations of corrupt bargains were unfounded, though widely believed. He was a man of highest morality. His political enemies accused him of many unproven immoralities. The worst they could prove against him was that he spent fifty dollars of taxpayer's money to purchase a billiard table for the President's House. Perhaps a more serious charge could be made that he failed to restrain his supporters from making scandalous charges against the character of Rachel Jackson during the 1828 electoral campaign. Adams did not stoop personally to character assassination, but could he not have reined in his supporters?

OVERALL ASSESSMENT

Like several of our other early presidents, John Quincy Adams was a great man whose accomplishments as president were overshadowed by other achievements in his life. With a total of 41 points, he ranks in a tie for eighteenth place among the 39 presidents rated.

ANDREW JACKSON

1829–37

	RATING POINTS	RANK
FOREIGN RELATIONS	16	2
DOMESTIC PROGRAMS	5	19 tie
ADMINISTRATION	11	11 tie
LEADERSHIP	11	15 tie
PERSONAL QUALITIES	17	6 tie
OVERALL ASSESSMENT	60	9 tie

BACKGROUND

Andrew Jackson was born March 15, 1767, in a log cabin near Waxhaw, South Carolina. A bright and precocious child, he lost interest in his studies and never learned proper grammar or spelling. While only thirteen, he volunteered to fight in the Revolutionary War, was captured, and slashed with a saber when he refused to clean a British officer's boots. After studying law for two years, he was admitted to the bar in 1787. He moved to Nashville, Tennessee, where he served as public prosecutor and engaged in private practice. He soon acquired a considerable amount of land. In 1796 he was a delegate to the Tennessee constitutional convention. He was elected as Tennessee's first Congressman, then appointed to the U. S. Senate, from which he resigned after five months. For the next six years he was a justice of the Tennessee Superior Court. He became wealthy from his farms and business interests. As a general in the War of 1812, he won a number of battles, including the greatest land victory of the war at New Orleans. In 1817 he commanded an expedition against the Seminole Indians in Florida. In 1821 he was appointed military governor of Florida, but soon resigned. In 1823 he was appointed Senator from Tennessee. In 1824 he ran unsuccessfully for the presidency. Although Jackson received a plurality, no candidate received a majority. Thus, the election went to the House of Representatives, which chose John Quincy Adams. Jackson's followers charged that the presidency had been stolen by a deal between Adams and Henry Clay. In 1825 Jackson resigned from the Senate to devote his energies to wreaking revenge on Adams and Clay and becoming the next president of the United States.

NOMINATION AND ELECTION

No congressional caucuses were held to nominate candidates for the 1828 presidential election. All nominations were made by state legislatures. Following the election of 1824, the Democratic-Republican party had split into two factions. The faction led by Adams and Clay became known as the National Republicans. Opponents of Adams, led by Jackson and Martin Van Buren, called themselves Democrats. The Tennessee legislature nominated Jackson for president. Sensing that Old Hickory was most likely to win, Van Buren threw his support to the general, as did Vice President Calhoun, and William H. Crawford, whose 1824 campaign for the presidency had been managed by Van Buren.

Adams advocated internal improvements and a protective tariff. Jackson refused to discuss his position on these issues, saying his friends already knew where he stood. Adherents of both candidates generally ignored the issues and focused on personalities. In one of the most vicious campaigns in American history, Adams was unfairly assailed for his use of patronage, for extravagance, and especially for the alleged "corrupt bargain" with Clay. He was also charged with being an aloof aristocrat, out of touch with the people. The president's supporters were even more savage in their attacks upon Jackson's character, calling him a thief, a liar, an adulterer, a gambler, a drunkard, and a murderer. He was castigated as ignorant, cruel, and bloodthirsty. The so-called Coffin Handbill was distributed, charging Jackson with the murder of six militiamen who were executed with Jackson's consent during the War of 1812. Jackson was accused of conspiring with Aaron Burr to commit treason against the United States. Jackson bitterly resented attacks upon the characters of his wife and mother.

One of the enduring myths of American history is that the election of 1828 was a contest between the aristocrats and the common people, with Jackson the people's candidate. Like most myths this one has a grain of truth in it. It is true that many of the small farmers and workingmen supported Old Hickory. It is equally true that his most powerful backers were wealthy, slave-owning, plantation owners and members of the upper class. The election results show that sectional interests were more important than social class distinctions. Adams carried all six New England states; the mid–Atlantic states were divided, and Jackson carried all twelve states of the South and West,

winning the election by 178 electoral votes to 83 for the incumbent president.

In 1832 the Democratic party held its first convention. As Jackson was the unanimous choice for president the only purpose of the convention was to select a vice presidential candidate to replace John C. Calhoun, who had broken with Jackson. Martin Van Buren was nominated for that post on the first ballot. Henry Clay was the candidate of the National Republicans. The campaign of 1832 was quite different from that of 1828. Jackson's veto of the bill to recharter the Bank of the United States dominated all other issues. Jackson was re-elected handily with 219 electoral votes to 49 for Clay and 18 for other candidates.

FOREIGN RELATIONS

Jackson used the threat of military action to promote the interests of the United States, but accomplished his goals without resorting to the use of arms. The greatest foreign relations crisis of Jackson's administration came when Jackson demanded that France pay for damages the French had inflicted on American shipping during the Napoleonic wars. In 1831 France agreed to pay the claims in six annual installments in return for lowered tariffs on French wines shipped to the United States. When the payments were not made on time, Jackson threatened reprisals. The French were outraged by the threats and broke off diplomatic relations with the United States. Jackson built up the nation's naval strength, and military action appeared likely. At this point France agreed to make the payments if Jackson apologized. Great Britain offered mediation, and Jackson accepted, but with the clear understanding that he was to make no apology. After extended negotiations, the case was settled. The payment was made, and France received no apology. The United States gained new respect as a force in international relations.

The British West Indies were opened to American trade for the first time since the Revolutionary War. Claims with the Kingdom of Naples and with Denmark were settled. Colombia ceased its depredations against American ships. A suspended treaty with Mexico was revived. Turkish ports were opened to American shipping. In 1833 a treaty was signed with Siam — the first with an Asian nation. Jackson consistently demonstrated strength, courage, and the will to protect our interests from other countries. Although Jackson's foreign policy was stern and demanding, it was not imperialistic. Other nations realized we were not endangering them. Jackson's success in foreign affairs promoted world peace.

Negotiations for acquisition of Texas had begun during the administration of John Quincy Adams, who offered $1 million for the lands between the Neuces and the Rio Grande. When Jackson became president, he raised the offer to $5 million. Mexico refused, considering the offer degrading. The movement of additional Americans into Texas ended Jackson's hope of purchasing the territory. Within a few years the American settlers revolted and declared Texas an independent republic. Due to our treaty with Mexico, Jackson delayed diplomatic recognition of the Lone Star Republic until his final day in office.

In 1832 Congress passed another high tariff act. An internal crisis developed in the United States when South Carolina declared the tariff null and void. Senator Henry Clay then pushed through a compromise bill that lowered all tariffs for ten years. This action produced long-term beneficial results. Trade agreements that Jackson had reached with other nations, particularly with Britain regarding trade with the British West Indies, benefited all nations and improved international relations.

American prestige reached a new high after Jackson's successful negotiations with France. Public opinion of the United States was enhanced around the world during Jackson's administration.

DOMESTIC POLICIES

In 1832 Jackson vetoed the recharter of the second U. S. Bank because he believed that Congress did not have constitutional authority to create it and that it was an elitist institution that favored eastern manufacturing interests at the expense of the common people. Congress sustained his veto, and the bank was due to expire when its charter ran out in 1836. Jackson sought to hasten its demise by withdrawing

federal funds and depositing them in certain state banks. For this action, the Senate voted to censure Jackson. However, the censure was expunged from the record three years later. State banks extended easy credit and issued paper money freely, leading to increased western land speculation and inflation. Jackson sought to restore economic order by issuing the Specie Circular, which required buyers of public land to pay for it with gold or silver. This order brought inflation and speculation under control, but it also precipitated the Panic of 1837 early in Van Buren's administration. Jackson was the first president to use governmental action in an attempt to improve the economy, and he was temporarily successful. In 1835 the federal government completely paid off its national debt for the first time in history. In 1836 more money flowed into the federal treasury than was spent, and Jackson approved the distribution of the surplus to the states. In the long run, however, Jackson's policies were disastrous.

Jackson spoke against monopoly. One of his objections to the Bank of the United States was that he believed it was a monopoly. He thought its vast powers threatened democratic government. He believed that farmers, laborers, and mechanics should share in the nation's prosperity.

Himself a slave owner, Jackson supported the institution of slavery. He denied civil rights to slaves and to Indians. Jackson felt that Indians were inferior to people of the white race and had no rights to their land if white settlers wanted it. He ordered Indians moved out of the Southeast to lands west of the Mississippi River. The removal of the tribes was a tragedy for Native Americans and a national shame. The Creeks were hauled and driven like cattle under miserable conditions. The Choctaws, thinly clad and barefooted, crossed the Mississippi in zero temperatures. Jackson refused to enforce the Supreme Court decision which ruled against Georgia in favor of the Indians on land claims in that state. By the end of Jackson's administration almost all Indians, except the Seminoles and Cherokees, had been removed from the Southeast. Thousands of Indians, cheated out of their lands, died during the forced migration.

As far as his white fellow citizens were concerned, Jackson worked for the dignity of the common man. He opposed institutions favoring wealth and privilege. He supported freedom of speech, freedom of the press, and the right of peaceful dissent. He supported freedom of religion. In one respect, however, he opposed freedom of the press. In December 1835 he urged Congress to pass a law excluding abolitionist pamphlets from the United States mails. His conception of those worthy of dignity and respect did not include blacks and American Indians.

ADMINISTRATION AND INTERGOVERNMENTAL RELATIONS

In his first annual address Jackson outlined his goals. France must pay American claims for damages during the Napoleonic wars; ports of the British West Indies must be opened to American trade; Texas should be annexed; the national debt should be paid off and the surplus divided among the states for internal improvements; Indians must be moved to the West; an independent Indian state in Georgia must not be established; the president and vice president should be elected directly by popular vote; and the Bank of the United States must be abolished. He planned to appeal to the people to overcome any objections to his goals.

In addition to the department heads serving as his official cabinet, Jackson developed a "kitchen cabinet" of advisors in whom he had confidence. This structure proved useful to the president. In staffing government positions, Old Hickory did not restrict himself to appointing people from an educated, aristocratic, or wealthy elite. He appointed many common people to government posts. Although some of these people were ill-qualified, Jackson made our nation more democratic by opening government service to persons formerly excluded. He retained no department heads from the previous administration, but his spoils system did not lead to an excessively high turnover in lesser positions. During his eight years as president, he replaced about 2,000 of 11,000 federal government employees.

Jackson made some good appointments and

some that were not so good. His cabinet was not particularly distinguished, although some outstanding men served in it at times. No cabinet member served throughout Jackson's two administration. Roger B. Taney served as attorney-general for two years. When Jackson tried to switch him to secretary of the treasurer, the Senate refused to confirm the appointment, the first time in United States history that a cabinet appointee had been denied confirmation. One of Jackson's worst appointments was Samuel Swarthout as collector of customs at the Port of New York. Swarthout stole from the government, setting a pattern of corruption in that post that persisted for decades.

Old Hickory held executive branch personnel responsible for good performance and for loyalty to the president. He quickly fired and replaced personnel, including cabinet members, when he felt changes were needed. When Jackson castigated cabinet members for snubbing Peggy Eaton, the wife of Secretary of State John Eaton, all but one resigned.

Jackson was an outstanding communicator. In addition to his annual addresses, he used informal means of communication. He had an intuitive feel for people. He understood the hopes, dreams, aspirations, and prejudices of the common man and capitalized on this knowledge. He was the first president to appeal directly to the people over the heads of Congress and the courts.

Jackson was an excellent administrator. Prior to his presidency he was used to military command and adjusted easily to civilian administration. He controlled government expenditures so well that he was able to pay off the national debt and distribute a surplus to the states. In order to do this he vetoed some bills that involved spending for privileged groups.

Although Jackson had support of the Democrats in Congress most of the time, he vetoed more bills than any of his predecessors. Unlike previous presidents, he vetoed bills not only for constitutional reasons, but for political, economic, social, or practical reasons. Henry Clay, Jackson's main opponent in Congress, was sometimes successful in sabotaging Jackson's programs and particularly in blocking Senate confirmation of his appointments. Jackson generally had congressional support for his successful, bi-partisan foreign policy.

In regard to the judiciary Jackson did not have a good record. He refused to obey the courts and enforce their decisions, most notably the Supreme Court decision related to Indian lands in Georgia. He maintained that the opinion of the Supreme Court ought not to control other branches of government. After John Marshall died, Jackson appointed Roger B. Taney as chief justice. The Senate, which had denied confirmation of Taney's appointment as secretary of treasury, accepted this nomination. Taney, the first Catholic chief justice, served 28 years in this position until his death in 1864. To this day he remains one of the most controversial federal judges, his name forever linked with the Dred Scott decision. On his last day in office Jackson signed the Judiciary Act of 1837, increasing the number of Supreme Court justices from seven to nine. He appointed five associate justices, the most distinguished of whom was John McLean. One of his appointees, Henry Baldwin, was notorious for erratic behavior. Another nominee, William Smith, declined to serve.

The people championed Old Hickory. His opposition to nullification cost him the support of the South, which had formerly been his stronghold. All other sections of the country and all the interests, except the wealthy elite, supported him. Jackson understood the people better than any previous president. He moved the nation toward greater democracy, furthering the revolution begun by President Jefferson. The common people wholeheartedly respected and supported Jackson. Old Hickory used this support to further his goals for the nation.

LEADERSHIP AND DECISION MAKING

One of the most charismatic of all presidents, Jackson inspired others to follow him. He was a great inspiration to the common people, many of whom regarded him as a great hero who shared their dreams and aspirations. Old Hickory was very persuasive with the masses, if not always with the courts or with Congress. He was able to maintain confidence in the government despite scandals and hard times.

Jackson applied his own high standards to public service. Although most of the people upon whom he was dependent had similar standards, and Jackson motivated them to achieve at a high level, he was often unaware of conditions within departments and was blindly loyal to his friends, especially to those who had fought the British.

The president grew with the office. He saw that economic democracy was essential to security. He visualized a country where farmers and workingmen would share in the fruits of their labor and bastions of privilege based on aristocracy and inherited wealth would fall. He further visualized a nation ever expanding to the westward. Jackson's strategies for moving the country forward were for the most part successful. He became a powerful and exceedingly popular president.

Although he did not go by the book, Jackson was an effective decision maker. He was not a scholar; his learning from history was negligible. Vain and stubborn, he did not learn from his mistakes. Often he developed plans unilaterally, or involved only his kitchen cabinet. He did not weigh alternatives carefully or consider fully the ramifications of his actions. Major decisions were not openly arrived at. The president made all the major decisions himself, and he made them quickly. He seemed to know intuitively what to do. Once a decision was made, he was not likely to reconsider it. In his decision making he was exceptionally courageous and acted with dispatch, even in emergencies. He determined quickly his course of action and carried it out.

The president held firm on principles. When necessary, he could compromise with his political enemies if the national interest required it, such as his acceptance of Henry Clay's compromise tariff. But on matters to which Old Hickory gave the highest priority, such as national security, preservation of the Union, or removal of the Indians, he refused to make compromises, regardless of consequences. Thus, he risked war with France over the shipping claims, broke with Calhoun and lost the support of his Southern backers over the nullification issue, and defied the Supreme

Court on the Georgia land claims. "Our Federal Union! It must be preserved!" he said to the nullifiers. "John Marshall has made his decision; now let him enforce it," he said to the courts. Jackson prevailed in all of these disputes.

PERSONAL QUALITIES

As president, Jackson conducted himself with more restraint and dignity than he had shown at some other times in his life, but he remained true to his real nature. He was considerate of his followers, but lashed out verbally at those who opposed him. His loyalty to Peggy Eaton was shocking to Washington society. The common people approved of Old Hickory and his conduct. They were proud that a man of the people was president.

Jackson increased the stature of the office, earning for it more respect at home and abroad. The conduct of some of his supporters at the time of his inauguration was disgraceful and dishonored the office, but this was a minor incident. In the minds of the people the office of the president was enhanced by Jackson. The people respected Jackson for exercising the power of the presidency in their interest. The spoils systems was popular with many people who had a mind set of "Throw the rascals out."

Old Hickory increased the power of the presidency by his use of the power of appointment and removal of government officials, by increasing the use of the veto power, by attacking the Bank of the United States and the rich and privileged, and by winning the overwhelming support of the people. Although his opponents derided him as "King Andrew," most of the people regarded Jackson's expansion of the powers of the presidency as an advance in democracy. Jackson convinced the people that the presidency is the people's office and that the president was on their side against the privileged few.

More than any previous president, Jackson understood and accepted input from the people. He understood the innermost feelings of people and capitalized on this by appealing directly to them for their support in his battles against Congress and the courts.

Jackson was an honest man and trustworthy. He kept his word, and was exceedingly loyal to friends. His treatment of the Indians was immoral and inconsistent with his other actions. It is the blackest mark upon his presidency. Aside from that very important exception, he acted as a moral, principled man who deserved the praise that his countrymen heaped upon him.

OVERALL ASSESSMENT

Andrew Jackson was a man of many contradictions. Accounts of his presidency usually give more emphasis to his domestic programs than to his international programs, yet his foreign relations were so successful that we rank him second among all the presidents in that area. He was the first president to attempt to use the powers of the federal government to improve the economic condition of ordinary citizens, yet his economic policies brought on the Panic of 1837. He was famed for making the government more democratic, of extending the Jeffersonian revolution, yet he treated Native Americans as though they had no rights whatsoever. He was a capable administrator, but his relations with other branches of government left much to be desired. No other president ever defied the Supreme Court to the extent that Old Hickory did. He had a charismatic personality, yet his leadership style was more authoritarian than participatory. He was a courageous decision maker who sometimes failed to give adequate consideration to the consequences of his decisions. He increased the status and the power of the presidency through his forceful leadership, but sometimes demeaned the office by petty behavior. To a greater extent that any previous president, Jackson tried to use the presidency for the benefit of all white people, regardless of status, but he did not include blacks or Indians among those for whom he showed concern. He was a believer in states' rights, who, when push came to shove, put the welfare of the Union ahead of everything else. With a total of 60 points on a 100-point scale, we rank him in a tie for ninth place among the 39 presidents rated.

MARTIN VAN BUREN

1837–41

	RATING POINTS	RANK
FOREIGN RELATIONS	13	6 tie
DOMESTIC PROGRAMS	7	16 tie
ADMINISTRATION	7	17 tie
LEADERSHIP	11	15 tie
PERSONAL QUALITIES	11	15 tie
OVERALL ASSESSMENT	49	13 tie

BACKGROUND

Martin Van Buren was born December 7, 1782, in Kinderhook, New York. He attended a one-room school in the village. Because of the family's financial situation, there was no hope of his attending college. At the age of 17 he became a law clerk, studied for four years, and was admitted to the bar at 21.

In 1812 he was elected as a state senator. He was re-elected to the state senate in 1816 and soon thereafter was appointed attorney general of New York. In 1820 he outmaneuvered Governor De Witt Clinton and became the dominant leader of his party in New York. For the next several decades he was the Democratic "boss" of upstate New York, just as Thurlow Weed was the boss of upstate New York Whigs. Van Buren was perhaps the first professional politician to serve as President of the United States. Because of his successful political machinations, Van Buren became known as "The Little Magician" and "The Red Fox of Kinderhook."

In 1821 Van Buren was elected to the United States Senate. He was re-elected in 1827, but resigned the following year to become governor of New York. Less than two months later, he resigned from that post to become secretary of state under President Jackson. When Old Hickory and Vice President John Calhoun had a falling out, Van Buren supported the president. Therefore, when Jackson appointed Van Buren as U.S. Minister to Great Britain, Calhoun fought the appointment. By a margin of one vote, the Senate failed to confirm the appointment. Calhoun thought he had destroyed Van Buren's career, but the action backfired. Angered by Calhoun's defiance, Jackson resolved to replace him in the vice-presidency with Van Buren. In 1832 the Little Magician was swept into office as Old Hickory's running mate.

NOMINATION AND ELECTION

President Jackson let it be known that Van Buren was his chosen successor. At the Democratic convention, the Little Magician was nominated unanimously on the first ballot. The hopelessly divided Whigs held no nominating convention in 1836. Their hope was that people in various states would vote for favorite sons rather than Van Buren, thus throwing the election into the House of Representatives, where a Whig might be chosen. The leading Whig candidates were General William Henry Harrison and Senator Daniel Webster. Hugh Lawson White was running as an independent. Calhoun's supporters in the South backed Senator Willie P. Mangum. Judge John McLean was the nominee of the moribund anti–Masons.

There were important issues that might have driven the campaign — distribution of the surplus, disposition of revenue from sale of public lands, internal improvements, chartering of the national bank, slavery and whether Congress had the constitutional right to expunge the records of a previous session. However, the actual campaign hinged mainly on personalities. Van Buren tried to make the election into a referendum on the Jackson administration. His opponents tried to make Van Buren the issue. He was attacked for his dandified dress, his foppish ways, his political style, and his alleged lack of scruples. He was portrayed as a sly and scheming politician.

Van Buren received a bare majority of the popular vote. In the electoral college, he fared better, however, receiving 170 votes to his opponents' combined total of 124.

FOREIGN RELATIONS

Van Buren maintained peace in the face of provocation. The Maine boundary, the *Caroline* Affair, the Mexican claims, and the Texas boundary all presented disputes skillfully handled by the president.

Van Buren used potential military force to keep the peace when two revolutions broke out in Canada. In the first revolution in 1837, Van Buren declared our neutrality. As citizens of northern New York and Vermont were sympathetic to the Canadian rebels, the president sent letters to the governors of these two states demanding strict neutrality. Instructions were sent to federal marshals and district attorneys to take appropriate action against overt acts of American citizens. On January 4, 1838, fight-

ing broke out along the Niagara River. The British had boarded the *Caroline*, a small rebel steamer, on the American side of the river. In an exchange of gunfire, Americans were killed and wounded. After its capture, the *Caroline* was set on fire by the British and sent drifting ablaze over the falls. Van Buren called an emergency cabinet meeting. He called up militia from Navy Island in the Niagara River. At this point Van Buren had the power to call out the militia, to commit United States to strict neutrality, to emphasize the nation's peaceful intent, and to arrest any armed citizens who attempted to cross the border. He felt he needed additional powers. He asked Congress for more latitude in dealing with crises and for an emergency fund. Congress reluctantly gave him authority to extend the length of military service and to call up 50,000 more men, and provided an additional $10 million for war expenditures. The president sent his son John to London to negotiate and General Winfield Scott to the troubled region. The incidents stopped. In the fall of 1838 Maine and New Brunswick became involved in a border dispute. Van Buren called out the militia and asked Congress for funds under the new legislation passed earlier in the year. The president contacted Britain and both sides withdrew.

Van Buren held off annexation of Texas during his term in office. Negotiations led Mexico to resume diplomatic relations with the United States. Through the State Department Van Buren sent a note to Mexico setting forth claims of wrongs done by Mexico to American citizens since Mexico gained its independence. Although the Mexican government accepted responsibility for some of the claims, it kept procrastinating on settling the claims. Not wishing to weaken the shaky Mexican regime, the president did not press for a military solution, but stepped up diplomatic efforts.

The president advanced our national interests through diplomacy with Britain, Mexico, and Texas. He prevented war between the United States and other nations and remained neutral in the Canadian revolutions. He negotiated from a position of strength in our disputes with Britain and Mexico. Despite a clamor from some sections of the country for expansion to the southwest and from another section for northern expansion, Van Buren kept our agreements with Britain and Mexico and indicated no imperialistic designs against them. Tensions on the Canadian border were eased by a show of force and strong negotiation. Van Buren showed our determination to protect our national interests.

The president secured passage of a tariff act by Congress that lowered rates. Although this act reduced government revenues, it had long-term beneficial effects. World trade was encouraged by the tariff reduction and was helpful to all countries, although the economic depression lessened the amount of potential benefits.

Van Buren revitalized the antiquated, neglected army. He built up the navy, replacing tiny, obsolete vessels. During his administration the U.S. Navy discovered the continent of Antarctica. These military and naval developments plus his strong, but non-belligerent foreign policy bolstered public opinion toward the United States in other nations.

DOMESTIC PROGRAMS

Van Buren had been in office only 36 days when the Panic of 1837 started. Since the panic started on Van Buren's watch, he was blamed for it, although the underlying causes predated his administration. Among the causes was speculation in public lands that occurred during Jackson's presidency. Despite Jackson's urging, Congress had refused to limit the sales of public lands to actual settlers. State banks and branches of the Bank of the United States made vast loans to speculators without security in gold or silver. Unable to limit land sales in any other way, Jackson issued his famous Specie Circular, requiring the government to accept only gold or silver in payment for public lands. Banks could no longer make loans without security and the speculation ended. Land sales in the West dropped to a fraction of their former level; building ceased; long lines of rails were left to rust; thousands of laborers were thrown out of work. The cotton market in New Orleans collapsed, and banks failed in New York City. By the end of May 1837 all of the banks had stopped specie payment. By September almost all of the factories in the eastern states

had closed. Over 600 banks failed. For the next four to five years the country suffered through one of the worst depressions in its history.

Van Buren believed that the federal government should not interfere with business and that it had no duty to help those who suffered from the depression. He thought the president's responsibility was limited to keeping the government's finances in order. In a special session of Congress, he secured repeal of the distribution of the surplus and permission for the government to issue treasury notes to meet expenses. He asked Congress for the establishment of an independent treasury where deposits would be safe in the future. He proposed subtreasuries in various parts of the country where government money could be kept. Congress refused to pass the subtreasury bill until 1840. The lowering of tariff rates helped consumers. Twice Van Buren issued treasury notes, stimulating the economy. He declared a moratorium on duty bond payments. Mild though they were, Van Buren's depression measures were considered radical and destructive by business, but he accomplished his primary goal of rescuing the public credit. A recovery brought prosperity temporarily in the winter of 1839-40; then the European depression brought hard times until about 1845.

Van Buren was not the tool of slave-holding planters nor of northern bankers, industrialists, and merchants. His special interest was in the small, independent farmers. One of the first widespread improvements in labor conditions was instituted when Van Buren reduced working hours for government employees to a ten-hour day.

Although Van Buren supported the continuation of slavery in the states where it already existed, he was opposed to its spread. In 1844 he was denied the Democratic nomination for president partly because he opposed annexation of Texas, which would add more slave territory to the United States. In 1848 he was the presidential candidate of the Free Soil party, which opposed the expansion of slavery in the territories. While he was still president, the *Amistad* affair occurred. The captain of a slave ship was killed by Africans, who had been illegally sold into slavery in Cuba and were being transported from one part of the island to another. The Africans told the crew to return them to Africa, but instead they were taken to Long Island, where the ship was seized and the Africans arrested. The secretary of state wanted them convicted of murder and sent to Cuba. However, they were given a trial, adjudged innocent, and allowed to return to Africa.

While Van Buren was president, the Seminole War continued. The army violated a flag of truce to capture the Seminole leader, Osceola, who died in prison. Van Buren continued the removal of the Cherokees. Van Buren did not start the Seminole War nor the removal of the Cherokees; he continued policies that he had inherited from Jackson. Van Buren ordered the removal of the Cherokees to be prompt and humane. His orders were not followed, and soldiers committed atrocities on defenseless Indian farmers.

The president generally supported freedom of speech and press and the right of peaceful dissent. However, he refused to compel the postmasters of the South to deliver abolitionist literature in the mail. Nor did he protest when Congress adopted its "Gag Rule," refusing to receive any further petitions against slavery. Van Buren supported religious freedom and opposed bigotry.

Van Buren continued the spoils system and appointed only white males to office. He favored full civil rights for white immigrants, but condoned slavery and failed to prevent mistreatment of Native Americans. The son of a tavern keeper of modest means, Van Buren rose to the presidency and considered himself a supporter of the common man. Because of his genteel manners and fancy clothes, many of the common people had trouble accepting Van Buren as one of their own.

ADMINISTRATION AND INTERGOVERNMENTAL RELATIONS

Van Buren had been an important part of the Jackson administration. He was a protégé of Old Hickory and owed his election largely to his predecessor's support. He planned a caretaker government. He kept Jackson's cabinet and intended to follow Jackson's policies. In his inaugural address he maintained that the future was bright but not without perils, the greatest of which was the contention that existed over slavery.

In line with his belief that any common man could handle a government position, Jackson had appointed some weak personnel to his administration. Van Buren kept most of these people in office, making few changes in governmental organization or personnel. His most important change in organization was the establishment of an independent treasury and subtreasury system. The Subtreasury Bill was approved by Congress after a long battle. The president fought stubbornly and courageously for this improvement.

One of Jackson's appointees, Samuel Swarthout, collector in New York, was replaced when his term expired in 1838 by Jesse Hoyt. Hoyt discovered a shortage of over two million dollars. An investigation revealed that Swarthout, now out of the country, had been stealing government funds ever since 1829. Federal District Attorney William M. Price not only had helped Swarthout cover up his thefts, but had shared some of the stolen money. Although the dishonest officials had been appointed by Jackson and their thefts discovered by Van Buren's agents, the scandal hurt the Van Buren administration.

Van Buren made changes in his cabinet only when he was forced to by resignation or retirement. He was too slow in removing executive branch personnel who did not produce desired results. Otherwise, executive branch departments and agencies were well administered.

During Van Buren's administration, funds were scarce due to the depression, the Seminole War, the high costs of Indian removal, and the decreased revenue from lower tariff rates. Van Buren opposed using federal funds for internal improvements and economized on spending. He left office with a surplus, instead of the deficit that might have been expected under the circumstances.

Van Buren reported to the people by his inaugural address, by annual addresses, and by the an address to a special session of Congress. The president secured support from most Democrats for his domestic proposals, but incurred bitter opposition from the Whigs. On his foreign policy he secured bi-partisan support, with the divisions being along sectional rather than party lines. Although Congress was slow to act on Van Buren's proposals, most of his programs had been passed by the end of his term.

Always a clever politician, Van Buren made a last minute appointment to the Supreme Court of Peter V. Daniel, who was confirmed by the Senate a few minutes before midnight on March 2, 1841. There was mutual respect between the independent judiciary and the president.

The politician was also a statesman, for Van Buren put the public interest ahead of self-interest. He opposed powerful interests and favored the common people. His defeat in the election of 1840 was largely due to the lasting effects of the depression and the distortions of the campaign.

LEADERSHIP AND DECISION MAKING

Following the charismatic Old Hickory, Van Buren was not able to inspire the people or government personnel the way Jackson did. Nevertheless, important national goals were accomplished in Van Buren's term. Most notable were his foreign policy successes and the creation of the independent treasury.

Known as a master politician, Van Buren could be very persuasive. When necessary he could compromise or make a deal. He set high standards of performance for himself. He worked very hard and put in long hours, sacrificing family life for his career. He was able to motivate some, but not all of his appointees, to similar levels of effort.

Not a scholar nor a visionary, Van Buren was pragmatic rather than idealistic. He had a concept of what the nation should be like, but the divisiveness of sectionalism continued to develop during his administration. The president, who excelled at strategy, was able to accomplish most of his goals. However, he was not able to pull the country out of the economic depression. He was politically courageous in trying to deal with this disaster. His policy was considered radical and destructive by the business community, but he held firm. Well known for his compromises, he refused

to give in on the Subtreasury Bill, and it eventually passed.

Van Buren did not make rapid decisions. He weighed alternatives and made informed judgments about the consequences of his actions. He listened to subordinates and discussed decisions with them. Although he was not college educated and lacked a background in history, he possessed a keen intelligence and used it well. He learned from his mistakes. Van Buren made hard decisions and remained calm in emergencies. For example, he made excellent and timely decisions in the crises along the Canadian border.

Public confidence in the president was weakened by the Panic of 1837. Although this depression was by no reasonable interpretation Van Buren's fault, he received the blame for it from many people. His political opponents capitalized on depression as a means of making the president appeared weak. Van Buren was never able to capture the imagination of the people or stir up the popular enthusiasm that the charismatic Jackson had generated. The Little Magician suffered by comparison with Old Hickory.

PERSONAL QUALITIES

As president, Van Buren conducted himself with dignity. He was always respectful, considerate, and polite to everyone, including his subordinates, foreign diplomats, his opponents, and the common people. The president sought input from all segments of the public. So many people came to see him that some had to be turned away and an appointment made for them.

Although Van Buren followed a powerful president, he, too, took bold action, further increasing presidential power. The stature of the office of the president was increased by Van Buren's foreign policy accomplishments and his successful fight for the Subtreasury Bill. Americans' pride in their country and their president was affected negatively by the economic depression. In addition to the usual contacts, Van Buren made a campaign tour for re-election, speaking directly to the people. He was unable, however, to overcome the effects of the depression and the demagoguery of his opponents. His reputation still suffers from the unfair attacks made upon him in the election of 1840.

Van Buren's repute as a cunning politician obscures the fact that he was a man of high moral principles, who acted consistently in accordance with his beliefs. He was honest and in no way was personally involved in the fraud conducted by some of his subordinates, whom he removed from office as soon as he found out about their abuse of trust. He, himself, could be trusted. He kept his promises. In his entire lifetime he was never involved in scandal or personal immorality. The only legitimate complaint that could be lodged against his character was that he utilized inside information in land speculations while a state senator early in his career. His political opponents overlooked this lapse in moral behavior and concentrated on spurious charges.

OVERALL ASSESSMENT

Van Buren had the misfortune of becoming president only a few weeks before the Panic of 1837 plunged the nation into the deepest depression it had known up to that time. He was unable to bring the country out of the depression during his four-year term of office. Nevertheless, he enjoyed some significant successes, most notably in foreign relations and in his valiant battle for an independent treasury. He scored a total of 49 points on our rating scale and ranks in a tie for thirteenth place among the 39 presidents rated.

WILLIAM HENRY HARRISON
1841

NO RATINGS

Served only one month

BACKGROUND

William Henry Harrison was born February 9, 1773, on the family plantation in Charles City County, Virginia. The Harrisons were a wealthy and prominent family. The future president's father served in the Continental Congress, signed the Declaration of Independence, and was governor of Virginia. Young Harrison's early education was provided by tutors. At the age of 14 he enrolled at Hampden-Sydney College for premedical instruction, then transferred to an academy in Southampton County, and then became an apprentice to a physician. In 1790 he enrolled in medical school at the University of Pennsylvania, but after his father died he abandoned his plans to become a doctor.

In 1791 Harrison joined the army. His most notable engagement was at the Battle of Fallen Timbers. In January 1793 he was appointed governor of the Northwest Territory. In 1799 he was elected as the territory's delegate to the U.S. House of Representatives. From 1800 to 1812 he was governor of Indiana Territory. While still governor, he led a military force against the Indians near Tippecanoe Creek. The battle earned for Harrison the nickname "Old Tippecanoe."

In 1812 Harrison was placed in command of United States forces on the Northwest frontier. He led his troops to a victory over the British and Indians at the Battle of the Thames and became a national hero. The great Indian leader Tecumseh was killed in this battle. Harrison resigned from the army in 1814.

During the next twenty years he served in a variety of political offices — county recorder, county clerk, Ohio state senate, U.S. House of Representatives, U.S. Senate and envoy to Colombia. In 1836 he was one of the Whig candidates for president, losing to Martin Van Buren.

NOMINATION AND ELECTION

For their candidate in the 1840 presidential election, the Whigs were determined to nominate someone who could unite the party. Although Henry Clay was the party's most outstanding figure, he had too many enemies to unite the various factions. Clay's main rivals for the nomination were two military heroes — Generals William Henry Harrison and Winfield Scott. On the first ballot, Clay led with Harrison second and Scott third. For three days the balloting continued with no candidate receiving a majority. Finally, Thurlow Weed persuaded the New York delegation to switch from Scott to Harrison, giving him the nomination.

For vice president the convention selected John Tyler.

The Whigs were too divided to attempt to agree on issues or to adopt a platform. They decided to make the election hinge on personalities. What followed was one of the strangest political campaigns in American history. A newspaper article stated that if Harrison were given a pension and a barrel of hard cider, he would be happy to sit out the rest of his days in a log cabin. The Whigs seized upon the remark and made Harrison the log cabin and hard cider candidate in contrast to Van Buren, whom they depicted as the candidate of palaces and champagne. The wealthy and aristocratic Harrison was presented as a frontiersman and man of the people, while Van Buren, who sprang from humble origins, was vilified as an effeminate, overindulged fop. With the log cabin as their symbol and the slogan "Tippecanoe and Tyler too" the Whigs sang that "Little Van is a Used Up Man." The popular vote was close, with Harrison winning by fewer than 150,000 votes. However, he had an easy victory in the electoral college, 234 to 60.

INAUGURATION AND DEATH

On inauguration day Old Tippecanoe rode to the Capitol on a white charger and delivered his inauguration address on the east portico. Despite the cold and stormy weather, he refused to wear a hat or coat. It took him an hour and 45 minutes to read his speech, the longest inauguration address on record. Harrison caught cold at the ceremonies and lived exactly one month after inauguration day. He died of pleurisy fever (pneumonia) on April 4, 1841.

JOHN TYLER

1841–45

	RATING POINTS	RANK
FOREIGN RELATIONS	5	29 tie
DOMESTIC PROGRAMS	1	27 tie
ADMINISTRATION	−8	36 tie
LEADERSHIP	−3	34
PERSONAL QUALITIES	7	23
OVERALL ASSESSMENT	2	31

BACKGROUND

John Tyler was born March 29, 1790, on the family plantation in Charles City County, Virginia. The Tylers were one of the most prominent families in Virginia, almost as distinguished as their neighbors, the Harrisons. After Tyler graduated from William and Mary, he studied law and was admitted to the bar in 1809. In 1811 he was elected to the Virginia House of Delegates, where he served for five years. In 1813 he became a captain of volunteers, but resigned after a month. In 1817 he was elected to the U.S. House of Representatives, serving two terms. In 1823 he was again elected to the state House of Delegates. Two years later he was elected governor of Virginia. Early in his second term, he resigned to accept a seat in the U.S. Senate, where he served for nearly nine years.

Until he broke with President Jackson over states' rights in 1833, Tyler had been a Democrat. When the Whig party was formed in 1834, Tyler associated himself with the new party,

despite the fact that he still agreed with the Democrats on most issues. In 1836 he resigned from the Senate rather than obey instructions from the Virginia legislature to vote for a resolution expunging censure of President Jackson from the Senate records.

As the Whigs did not have a national nominating convention in 1836, the party fielded three separate vice-presidential candidates. Among them was John Tyler, who received 47 electoral votes, finishing third in the race.

In 1838 he was again elected to the House of Delegates, where he was named Speaker of the House. In the same year he accepted the presidency of the Virginia Colonization Society, whose purpose was to encourage the emigration of free Negroes to Africa.

In 1840 Tyler hoped to return to the Senate, but the Virginia legislature was deadlocked among three aspirants. It was rumored that Whig leaders promised to endorse Tyler for the vice-presidency if Tyler's friends in the legislature agreed to give up their opposition to the senatorial candidacy of William C. Rives. The deadlock in the legislature was not broken in favor of Rives until January 1841, by which time Tyler had already been elected vice president.

NOMINATION AND ELECTION

At the national convention of the Whig party in December 1839, Tyler supported Henry Clay for the presidency. However, when Clay lost the nomination to Harrison, the delegates unanimously decided that the vice-presidential nominee should come from a slaveholding state. Tyler was nominated on the first ballot. For details on the election of 1840, see the section on William Henry Harrison.

Tyler was the first vice president to ascend to the presidency upon the death of the incumbent. There was a dispute as to whether Tyler should become president or acting president. The Constitution states that "in case of the removal of the President from office, or his death, resignation, or inability to discharge the powers and duties of said office, the same shall devolve on the Vice President." The dispute was whether "the same" refers to the powers and duties or to the office. If the powers and duties, but not the office, devolve upon the vice president, he would become an acting president. However, John Tyler claimed the office. When Congress met in joint session of May 31, 1841, a resolution was passed recognizing Tyler as "President of the United States."

FOREIGN RELATIONS

When Tyler took office the Canadian border area had been a tinderbox for years. In November 1841 the president issued a proclamation warning Americans against participating in a planned invasion of Canada. One of the chief accomplishments of the Tyler administration was the signing of the Webster-Ashburton Treaty in 1842. By settling peacefully the border dispute between Canada and the United States, the threat of war with Great Britain was removed. Under terms of the treaty the United States received 7,000 of the 12,000 square miles claimed by both Maine and New Brunswick. Minor adjustments were also made to complete the present Canadian border all the way from the east coast to the Rockies, leaving the Oregon boundary to be settled later. The agreement also established extradition procedures between the United States and Canada for crimes of violence or forgery and called for a cooperative effort to suppress the slave trade. Helping set the climate for approval of the treaty, Secretary of State Daniel Webster won passage of a law granting federal justices the power to free defendants accused of crimes committed on orders from a foreign government.

In 1844 the United States and China concluded the Treaty of Wanghia, promoting peace, amity, and commerce. The United States won access to Chinese ports and gained exemption from the jurisdiction of Chinese law in those ports, thus opening trade with China to American merchants.

These accomplishments helped commerce, decreased world tensions, and enhanced world opinion of the United States. However, their effects were offset in part by Tyler's actions toward Mexico. Tyler had an imperialistic dream of extending our boundaries to Central America, dismembering Mexico along the way and annexing it piece by piece. The only part of this fantasy that he put into practice was the annexation of Texas. Ever since Texas applied for statehood in 1836, annexation of the Lone Star Republic had been a contentious issue. In April 1844 Tyler approved a treaty incorporating Texas into the United States. The Senate refused to ratify the treaty. However, after James K. Polk won the presidency on a pro-annexation platform, Congress passed a joint resolution annexing Texas. Tyler signed the measure. This was the first time in American history that an international agreement was effectuated by a joint congressional resolution instead of by a treaty.

From the Mexican point of view the battlefield treaty of Velasco ending the Texas revolution and recognizing the independence of Texas had been extorted from the captured Santa Anna under duress and was invalid. American annexation would constitute a hostile intervention in Mexican internal affairs. On the other hand, Tyler's position was that the annexation was really a reclaiming of territory that had originally been included in the Louisiana Purchase. This claim is of dubious validity, for those boundaries were indistinct. Tyler further maintained that since Mexico had been unable to subdue Texas militarily, the Lone Star Republic was a free agent to contract international obligations as she saw fit. This proposition perhaps had some validity.

In some instances Tyler used potential military force to accomplish American objectives peacefully. As part of the annexation of Texas, he placed the fleet off the coast of Texas in case Mexico should attack. He urged strengthening of the army and navy and increased the number of naval warships. He brought an end to the war against the Seminoles in Florida. He sent a special message to Congress recognizing the independence of the Sandwich (Hawaiian) Islands. He felt that the Monroe Doctrine should be applied to them. Wishing to settle a dispute with Great Britain, Tyler was willing to accept the 49th parallel as the northern boundary of Oregon. He wanted military posts to be established along the Oregon Trail, but Congress did not act on these suggestions.

Tyler favored a tariff for revenue only. In 1841 it became necessary to increase government revenues. Although Tyler was committed to maintaining the Compromise Tariff of 1833, he signed a tariff extension, which imposed a tax on some items on the free list and raised the tariff on other items taxed at less than the maximum permitted by the 1833 act. In 1842 Congress passed two bills raising the tariff above these rates. Tyler vetoed both bills. Congress then passed another tariff bill, which Tyler found less objectionable and signed, raising rates to the 1832 levels. Although this tariff provided some protection to manufacturers, its main purpose was to raise essential revenue for the government. Tyler favored free trade that would lead to an increase in world commerce, but was forced by practical necessity to impose tariffs. The Senate rejected a treaty that the United States had worked out with the German Customs Union which provided for a mutual reduction in tariffs on certain items traded between the Germans and Americans. Because of opposition from Congress, the treaty with China remained Tyler's only significant contribution to world trade.

DOMESTIC PROGRAMS

Upon ascending to the presidency, Tyler inherited a government facing economic problems. The nation had not recovered from the depression following the Panic of 1837. Estimated revenues for the current year would be less than the necessary expenditures. Tyler proposed to increase revenues by imposing duties on imports and to create a suitable fiscal agent for the collection and disbursement of public revenues. He left it up to Congress to devise plans for creating the fiscal agent, which would replace the Subtreasury system. It is unlikely that Congress would have paid much attention had the president proposed a specific, detailed plan. At first Tyler was unable to improve the nation's economy, and his enemies in Congress deliberately made the problems worse. However, prosperity gradually returned, although neither the president nor Congress are entitled to much credit for the improvement.

Congress passed a bill, signed by the president, repealing the Independent Treasury Act. Tyler proposed a plan for a new national bank, which would avoid the constitutional objections raised by states' rights advocates, by providing that no branch would be located in any state without its consent. Congress rejected this plan and passed a bill with a weak consent provision and other measures that the president found objectionable. Tyler vetoed it, but delayed his veto message until Congress passed a bankruptcy bill, which he favored. Congress again passed a similar bill. For the second time Tyler vetoed the establishment of a national bank.

In his first annual message the president proposed an Exchequer plan. It was tabled by Congress in 1842 and voted down in 1843. Public moneys continued to be deposited in selected state banks and the so-called financial crisis continued. Actually, the budget deficit during Tyler's administration was far less than it had been under Van Buren's and only a small fraction of what it would be under Polk.

Tyler signed a bill providing for the distribution among the states of the proceeds from the sale of federal lands. Although the federal government could have used the funds to meet its projected deficit and he had previously opposed the distribution on constitutional grounds, Tyler approved distribution solely as a relief measure for the states. The bill also granted pre-emption rights to settlers who had occupied and improved and erected a dwelling upon public lands. The holder of such a claim could buy the land up to a maximum of 160 acres for $1.25 an acre. This act was a great benefit to farmers in the Midwest.

Because of his belief in states' rights, Tyler opposed paying for internal improvements out of federal funds. He vetoed a rivers and harbors bill in 1844. However, he approved of appropriating funds to construct a telegraph line from Washington to Baltimore. Although his views on states' rights prevented him from advocating a role for the federal government in education, Tyler did what he could to promote literary and scientific activity. He established a Bureau of Medicine and Surgery in the Navy.

Tyler supported freedom of speech and press and freedom of religion. He opposed the Know-Nothings and others who injected religion into politics. Although Tyler considered himself a true follower of Jefferson, he favored the wealthy class. In the matter of slavery, he put property rights above human rights. Tyler thought the federal government should encourage Native Americans to adopt the trappings of civilization. By the standards of his time, his Indian policy was one of justice and fairness.

ADMINISTRATION AND INTERGOVERNMENTAL RELATIONS

Tyler was thrust suddenly and unexpectedly into the presidency when Harrison died. He took office without a set of goals and objectives. In the foreign policy arena he developed the goals of settling the boundary dispute with Canada and expanding southward and westward into Mexican territory. He had great success on the Canadian border, annexed Texas, but failed to acquire California or other Mexican territory.

Although retaining Harrison's cabinet seemed a prudent thing to do, it turned out to be a mistake. In his brief tenure Harrison had made decisions based on a majority vote of his cabinet. Tyler immediately told the cabinet

that he would discontinue that practice and that he, as president, would make all decisions. In the cabinet were members from different political factions, each jealous of the others. After Tyler's second bank veto, the entire cabinet, except Daniel Webster, resigned in protest. In 1843 Webster resigned in opposition to Tyler's Texas policy, but remained on friendly terms with the president.

Tyler had made some mistakes and had some bad luck with his cabinet appointments. Four of his nominees for cabinet posts were rejected by the Senate. Abel P. Upshur, who succeeded Webster as secretary of state, and Secretary of the Navy Thomas W. Gilmer were killed in an explosion aboard the USS *Princeton* during a presidential inspection of the ship. Attorney General Hugh S. Legare died in office. In addition to the five cabinet members who resigned in protest of Tyler's veto of the national bank bill, two resigned because they disagreed with the annexation of Texas, and Tyler encouraged the resignation of another because he was dissatisfied with his performance. Tyler had a greater turnover of cabinet members than any other one-term president in the nation's history. In the executive departments he was surrounded by political enemies until he purged some of them and appointed replacements who shared his views.

After he had been in office for two years, Tyler reorganized the executive departments according to sound administrative principles. He then assigned personnel to appropriate roles, gave them authority to do their jobs, and held them responsible for performance. The executive departments were now well administered, but few new domestic programs were started and accomplishments in the domestic arena were unimpressive.

At first Tyler could not get needed funds from Congress and the treasury was bare. As the economy improved and revenues were increased, the budget was balanced and the public debt was reduced. Efficient fiscal administration permitted Tyler to reduce federal expenditures without eliminating services.

After Tyler's veto of the second bank bill, the Whig members of Congress adopted a resolution repudiating the president and declaring the alliance between the Whigs and Tyler was at an end. The Whig press thereupon attacked the president viciously. Amid talk of impeachment and assassination, the Whig press and pamphleteers continued their attacks and pursued a vendetta against Tyler, driving him back to the southern Democrats.

Relations between Congress and the president deteriorated badly. He lost the support of his own party in Congress, which rejected many of Tyler's proposals. In turn, he vetoed nine bills passed by Congress, more than any previous president except Andrew Jackson. On Tyler's last day in office Congress, for the first time in history, overrode a presidential veto.

After the president's veto of a tariff bill late in 1842, an effort was made to have him impeached. John Minor Botts, a Whig representative from Virginia, drew up a list of charges against the president and offered a resolution calling for the appointment of a committee of congressmen to investigate the charge. The resolution was defeated by a vote of 127 to 83.

The judicial branch maintained independence in the battles between the other two branches. Tyler appointed five Supreme Court justices, but only one actually served on the court. The others either withdrew or failed to receive confirmation by the Senate.

Tyler communicated through his annual addresses and White House visits. He frequently gave large parties at night, but was unable to reach out to the people. He was uncomfortable around common people. Tyler believed in land ownership as a prerequisite to voting, slavery, states' rights, nullification, secession, and strict construction of the Constitution. These ideas were not popular with the people. His opposition to the national bank and the protective tariff were also unpopular. He lacked Jackson's ability to paint the bank as a villain. The president refused to bend his principles to accommodate public opinion or interest groups. He became so unpopular that he could not get his programs enacted and found it difficult to govern effectively.

LEADERSHIP AND DECISION MAKING

Tyler lacked charisma and was unable to inspire others to follow his lead. Although he had some success in foreign affairs, he was not able to secure passage of most of his domestic agenda and was unable to rally the people to his side. His vision of America was not accepted by most of the people. Tyler was unable to win the confidence of the American public.

Tyler's administration was marked by divisiveness. Much of this was the fault of Tyler's enemies in Congress, but the president's unwillingness to compromise contributed to his problems. Sometimes it is praiseworthy to hold firm on principle, but when the president holds principles that are not shared by the Congress or the people, governing is difficult. Had Tyler been willing to compromise on the second bank bill, his whole administration might have been more successful.

Tyler was a bold and courageous decision maker, but not always an intelligent one. He was not an intellectual, nor did he always use common sense. He acted calmly in emergencies. His greatest weakness as a decision maker was his failure to take into account the political ramifications of his actions.

Not only did Tyler have difficulty in influencing Congress and in leading the American people, but he also had problems within the administrative branch. After the mass cabinet resignations and his purge of 1843, Tyler set standards and motivated executive branch personnel to more dedicated performance of their duties.

PERSONAL QUALITIES

A charming southern gentleman, Tyler comported himself with the dignity appropriate to his position. By his insistence that he was the president, not merely an acting president, he strengthened the office. Because of his accomplishments in foreign relations, Tyler was respected more abroad than he was at home. The American people were not proud of their president. Perhaps vicious attacks by an unfriendly press contributed to this lack of pride by the people, but the greatest cause was that the public did not share the president's beliefs. People were not proud of being governed by an aristocrat with whom they had little in common. Most people felt Tyler was not on their side.

Access to the president was almost unlimited. He received input from anyone during daytime office visits or parties at night. The problem was that he did not give serious consideration to the input he received. Tyler interacted with the people at the White House and communicated by addresses to Congress. Still the people felt he was aloof and out of touch.

Tyler was a highly moral and principled man, even though his political principles were out of favor with the American people. He could be trusted and kept his promises. Completely honest, Tyler never used his office in any way to benefit himself financially. Having spent much of his own money entertaining at the White House, he left office nearly bankrupt. Scurrilous attacks on him notwithstanding, he was of sound moral character. No private or public scandal marred his record.

OVERALL ASSESSMENT

Tyler had some notable successes in Foreign Relations and demonstrated some admirable qualities. However, his deficiencies in other areas pulled his overall rating down to a total of only four points on the rating scale, ranking him in 31st place among the 39 presidents rated.

JAMES KNOX POLK

1845–49

	RATING POINTS	RANK
FOREIGN RELATIONS	3	31 tie
DOMESTIC PROGRAMS	1	27 tie
ADMINISTRATION	11	11 tie
LEADERSHIP	15	8 tie
PERSONAL QUALITIES	12	13 tie
OVERALL ASSESSMENT	42	16 tie

BACKGROUND

James Knox Polk was born November 4, 1795, on his parents' farm in Mecklenburg County, North Carolina. When the boy was 11, the family moved to Tennessee. After attending local academies, he entered the University of North Carolina. Although not brilliant, he applied himself with such diligence that he graduated with first honors in both mathematics and the classics. After graduation, Polk studied law under Congressman Felix Grundy and was admitted to the bar in 1820. In 1823 he was elected to the state legislature. In 1825 he was elected to the United States House of Representatives, where he served for 14 years, with two terms as Speaker. His support of President Jackson earned him the nickname "Young Hickory." In 1839 he was elected governor of Tennessee. In 1840 he was nominated for vice president by the Tennessee legislature, but received only one electoral vote. He was defeated for re-election in 1841 and lost another gubernatorial bid in 1843.

NOMINATION AND ELECTION

When the Democratic convention met in 1844, Polk hoped to become his party's nominee for vice president. Former President Martin Van Buren was the favorite for the presidential nod going into the convention. On the first ballot Van Buren received more than a simple majority of the votes, but not enough to win the nomination under the two-thirds rule. After seven ballots, it became apparent that neither Van Buren nor Lewis Cass, his principal rival, could reach the requisite number of votes, so the convention adjourned for the night. During the night considerable politicking occurred. The next morning, on the eighth ballot, Polk received votes for the first time. During the ninth ballot, the New York delegation produced a letter from Van Buren authorizing the withdrawal of his candidacy if that would bring about harmony in the party. The New York delegation switched to Polk and the stampede started. State after state jumped on the Polk bandwagon. By the end of balloting, the vote was unanimous. For the first time in the United States a major party had selected a real darkhorse as its presidential candidate.

The Whig candidate, Henry Clay. was far better known and more popular than Polk. In this election the personal popularity of the candidates proved to be less important than their stands on the issues. The Whigs tried to make a protective tariff and Clay's "American System" the major issues. Polk ran against the United States Bank and for the annexation of Texas and the acquisition of Oregon. Linking Texas and Oregon together was good strategy. Acquiring Texas appealed to slaveholding Southerners, while securing Oregon appealed to Northerners wanting more free territory. The Democrats adopted as their campaign slogan, "Fifty-four forty or fight," referring to the disputed northern boundary of the Oregon country. Clay was ambivalent on the Texas question, but Polk made annexation one of his principal planks. Polk campaigned for the "Reannexation of Texas and the Reoccupation of Oregon" claiming that both of those extensive territories had already been a part of the United States.

In a close election no candidate received a majority of the popular vote. Polk outpolled Clay by about 38,000 votes. In the all-important electoral college, Polk won 170 to 105.

FOREIGN RELATIONS

No one did more than Polk to promote the idea of manifest destiny — that our nation was destined to rule the whole continent from the Hudson Bay to the Isthmus of Panama. Apparently, Polk put a higher priority on taking Mexican territory than he did on gaining other land, for he went to war over this and compromised or yielded on his other ambitions.

The annexation of Texas was approved by a joint resolution of Congress and signed by President Tyler, three days before Polk took office. Mexico, which refused to recognize the independence of Texas, formally protested the annexation and broke off diplomatic relations with the United States. Polk ordered General Zachary Taylor to occupy a point on or near the Rio Grande and to limit action to the defense of Texas unless war was declared by Mexico.

When Polk received word that Mexico was ready to resume diplomatic relations, he appointed John Slidell as envoy. Slidell was authorized to purchase California and New Mexico if Mexico would agree on a permanent boundary line of the Rio Grande from its mouth to the thirty-second parallel and west to the Pacific. In the face of hostile public opinion, Mexican President Herrera refused to see Slidell.

On January 13, 1845, the secretary of war, acting under instructions from Polk, ordered General Taylor to positions on the left bank of the Rio Grande, thus invading Mexican territory. The first skirmish occurred on April 25. On May 11 Polk submitted his war message to Congress. On various occasions Mexico had intimated that she might acquiesce to the annexation of Texas. Polk's critics charged that the president's action in ordering American troops into Mexican territory was intended to provoke a Mexican attack and precipitate a war. The war enabled the United States to gain New Mexico and California, which could not have been obtained at that time by peaceful means. The Texas dispute could perhaps have been settled peacefully, but Polk wanted more than Texas and was willing to go to war to get it.

The Mexican War remains controversial to this day. As a result of the war, Mexico gave up its claims to Texas and ceded to the United States more than 500,000 additional square miles. Mexico was reduced to about half of its former size and lost some of its most productive land. Some Mexicans still resent this land seizure.

Polk handled the dispute with Britain over the Oregon boundary quite differently. As early as August 1845, he offered to accept the forty-ninth parallel as the boundary line. At that time the British refused. When they asked him to renew the offer in December, Polk refused. On May 21, 1846, he notified Britain that the joint occupation of Oregon was to be terminated within one year, as provided in existing treaties. On June 10 he laid the British proposal before the Senate, and the treaty was ratified on June 15. Thus, Polk settled peacefully by compromise the long-standing dispute over the northwest boundary. He did not have the same desire for war with Great Britain as he had for war with Mexico.

In his dealings with other nations, Polk utilized diplomacy rather than military action. Twice he tried to purchase Cuba, but when Spain refused to sell, he ordered General Butler to prevent our troops from engaging in any filibustering expedition to the island. He declined an offer by Sweden to sell the island of Saint Bartholomew to the United States. When the government of Yucatan offered to yield its sovereignty to any nation able to help it prevent the Indians from exterminating the white population, Polk was ready to annex that country. However, the Yucatan government reached an accord with the Indians before any move toward annexation occurred. Difficulties with Brazil and Buenos Aires were settled peacefully. Polk established diplomatic relations with the new nations of Ecuador and Bolivia. He concluded an important treaty with New Granada, guaranteeing the United States the right of transit across the Isthmus of Panama. Finally, he concluded a postal convention with Great Britain, giving American vessels equal footing with British ships in transporting intercontinental mail.

Polk reinterpreted the Monroe Doctrine to forbid any European interference in North America. Although existing rights of all European nations were to be respected, no transfer of dominion over North American territory could be made from one European nation to another. He also included Hawaii within the scope of North America. This restatement has been called the Polk Doctrine.

Among Polk's achievements was a reduction in the tariff rates. The protective tariff of 1842 was replaced by one for revenue only. Despite the lower rates, it produced greater revenue as trade increased. The new tariff was beneficial to the United States and to other nations. Polk was able to get the measure passed despite strong opposition in Congress and elsewhere.

Polk's accomplishments in foreign affairs were indeed impressive. Unfortunately, his record is marred by the Mexican war. Although we went to war against Mexico, other nations had no reason to fear we would attack them. Polk enhanced the strength of the United States, but not its reputation for being fair or peaceful.

DOMESTIC PROGRAMS

The cornerstone of Polk's domestic program was the restoration of the independent treasury system. Polk levied no federal taxes. Revenue to operate the government came from the tariff, which probably impacted most on those most able to pay. Even though rates were lowered by the Walker Tariff of 1846, revenue increased because the amount of imports climbed. Polk ordered imports stored in warehouses until the duties were collected.

Polk's policies of low taxes and revenue-producing tariff proved economically beneficial even to the manufacturing interests that had wanted protection. His term was marked by relative prosperity, and his fiscal policies were conducive to stability. He ordered department heads to scrutinize expenditures carefully to avoid waste. Although the idea of a comprehensive national budget had not yet been developed, Polk established an office similar to that of director of the budget to help control government expenditures. He operated the government with such frugality that he did not have to raise taxes to pursue the Mexican war. The war did, however, deter him from his plans to reduce the national debt. Instead, the debt increased by some $55 million, the most in any administration since that of James Madison, another wartime president. Even during the war, however, inflation was not a problem due to Polk's policies.

Because of constitutional scruples, Polk opposed spending federal funds for internal improvements, opposed distribution of the surplus to the states, and failed to use governmental power to help poor people, even opposing relief for the poor in the nation's capital, which was governed by Congress. He vetoed rivers and harbors bills because he regarded them as "pork-barrel" projects, as well as constitutionally suspect. His policies were sound, but he could have helped the country by spending the surplus in constructive ways.

Although he was a slaveowner and supported slavery, Polk thought preservation of the Union was more important than extending or restricting slavery. He strongly opposed the Wilmot Proviso. He thought abolitionists were dangerous because they promoted disunion.

He not only owned slaves, but also supported or engaged in the buying and selling of slaves, and did not even investigate when some of his slaves accused an overseer of cruelty.

Polk encouraged his friends to acquire control of a leading Washington newspaper that supported the Democrats in order to insure that it would give him editorial support. At the time this was accepted as an appropriate thing to do, as the administration was "entitled" to have a newspaper friendly to it in the nation's capital. He made no attempt to stifle the freedom of the opposition press.

Polk was a strong supporter of freedom of religion and spoke out against religious bigotry. Yet his record in regard to the Mormons was far from exemplary. He took no action to protect them from mobs in Nauvoo. During the Mexican war he said Mormons should be treated like any other American citizens. They were invited to enlist in the army, but their enlistment was delayed until they reached California. He did not want them armed until California was secure. He made them pay their own way across the continent.

Even though the 1848 meeting at Senaca Falls led by Elizabeth Cady Stanton and Lucretia Mott excited much public discussion and has been called the first women's suffrage convention, Polk took little notice of it. Although he did not show disdain nor contempt for low-status individuals, he did nothing to improve their lot in life. He ignored the hardships of children working in factories and the poverty of immigrants. The Irish who fled the potato famine and the refugees of Central European wars received no help from the President of the United States.

ADMINISTRATION AND INTERGOVERNMENTAL RELATIONS

At the outset of his administration, Polk announced his four major goals — reduction of the tariff, establishment of an independent treasury, settlement of the Oregon question and acquisition of California. He made plans for the accomplishment of these goals. He anticipated roadblocks in his way and skillfully avoided them when possible. In spite of vigorous opposition the goals were all achieved. The settlement of the Oregon dispute required a compromise, and it took a war to persuade Mexico to relinquish California. Nevertheless, Polk was able to claim successful accomplishment of all of his goals.

Polk organized the executive departments well and set clear expectations for his key appointees. He instructed the department heads to hold their subordinates accountable, to devote full time to their duties, and to resign if they became candidates for president or vice president. To his cabinet he appointed only well-qualified, white males. Although he was influenced by political considerations, such as geographical balance, he appointed no incompetents. His cabinet included James Buchanan as secretary of state and George Bancroft as secretary of the navy. He held his appointees to a high ethical standard and to high performance standards. On the other hand, he required them to pledge to support his plans as a condition of employment. The pledge was kept with varying degrees of fidelity. Polk tended to micro-manage the work of his administration.

On his last day in office, Polk signed the bill creating the Department of the Interior. He did not favor the bill, believing it would weaken the power of the states and increase the jurisdiction of the national government. Having no constitutional objections to the bill, he signed it reluctantly.

The president reported to Congress and the public through speeches and in writing. He used his pet newspaper as the administration's mouthpiece. Naturally, he was opposed by the Whig press. He did not engage in press conferences or give-and-take discussions.

Polk required department heads to check expenditures by subordinates. He was extremely protective of government funds. He probably had better control of government expenditures than any previous president. On the whole, government operations were rather effective. John Slidell's diplomatic mission to Mexico was badly mismanaged, but this was an exception. As secretary of state, Buchanan often opposed the president in private and in cabinet meetings, and on a few occasions refused to follow the president's directives, but he never tried to sabotage programs even when he disagreed with them.

Despite factionalism within the Democratic party, Polk secured enough legislative support to accomplish all of his major goals. Polk was unable to secure much support from the Whigs. After they gained control of Congress in the midterm elections of 1846, the Whigs were able to thwart Polk's programs, but by then he had achieved a lower tariff, an independent treasury, and settlement of the Oregon boundary. The Mexican war was already in full swing, and the Whigs were unable to stop it. He secured enough support from the Whigs to gain Senate ratification of the Treaty of Guadalupe Hidalgo, including the acquisition of California, thus enabling Polk to claim accomplishment of all four of his major goals.

Polk did not have a high regard for the judiciary. His appointments to federal judgeships were competent, but not outstanding. During his administration he appointed two Supreme Court justices.

Public opinion was helpful to Polk in getting his programs accomplished, but this was because much of the public agreed with the programs, rather than personally supporting the president. Polk put the public interest, as he saw it, first. When he accepted the presidential nomination, he pledged himself to be a one-term president in order to avoid the danger that desire for re-election might influence his actions. He acted in the best interest of all the people, as he perceived those interests from his limited perspective. He was beholden to no special interest group. However, because of his lack of interaction with the common people and his view that the Constitution severely limited governmental power, he took no direct action to improve the lives of people.

LEADERSHIP AND
DECISION MAKING

Lacking charisma, Polk was not an inspirational leader. Because of his command of the facts and logical argument, he was very persuasive. Public confidence in government was somewhat restored after a sharp decline in the previous eight years. Polk set high standards for himself and others and saw to it that these standards were met as well as possible.

In his vision for America, Polk saw a united, prosperous country, stretching from coast to coast. This was a vision shared by many Americans at the time, although people disagreed on how to achieve unity in a nation divided by slavery. Many people thought that westward expansion should not come at the expense of war, but Polk managed to make it appear that the Mexicans started the war.

Polk was especially good at developing strategies for accomplishing his goals. He weighed alternatives and carefully considered possible consequences of each course of action before making a decision. He was not a scholar, but he knew the principal facts of history and was guided by them. Polk was loath to admit mistakes, but did so occasionally. He rarely made the same mistake twice. When circumstances changed, Polk was able to reverse his stand on issues. For example, earlier he had supported Jackson's state bank policy, but as president he strongly advocated depositing funds in an independent treasury. He led and won a tough fight to accomplish this.

Polk was usually able to compromise on details while holding firm to principles. The terms on the annexation of Texas and the treaty of Guadalupe Hidalgo are examples of this. However, his refusal to compromise on sending Slidell to Mexico as a commissioner rather than as a minister led to the failure of the mission. A compromise might have led to an agreement whereby the war with Mexico could have been avoided. There appears to have been no principled reason for not making this compromise.

During emergencies Polk remained calm and cool, striving always to make decisions on the basis of reason rather than on emotion. Polk had the courage to make hard decisions when necessary, but seldom made them needlessly. When he became convinced that war with Mexico was necessary in order to achieve his objectives, he ordered actions that caused the Mexicans to fire the first shots, thus assuring that Congress would respond affirmatively to his call for a declaration of war.

PERSONAL QUALITIES

As president, Polk conducted himself with dignity and did not engage in behavior that could demean the office. Many Americans took pride in the accomplishments of our troops in Mexico. A stronger president than his immediate predecessors, Polk restored the status of the presidency to nearly what it had been under Andrew Jackson. He greatly increased the power of the presidency in the conduct of foreign affairs. Because of constitutional scruples, however, he did not deal with some domestic problems.

Polk did not make the people think that the presidency was the people's office. He lacked Jackson's common touch. Although the people did not think of the president as one of them, they did not regard him as an enemy. Polk did not seek input from the public. Access was restricted to a small group of insiders, except for office seekers. Polk did not reach out to the people by formal or informal means, but neither did he show disdain or contempt for their views. He was just aloof by nature.

Although Polk could be devious in his political scheming, his personal integrity was above reproach. He always kept his word and was completely trustworthy. He was scrupu-lously honest. He refused to accept gifts to himself or his wife. He never used his office for personal financial gain. Polk exhibited a high standard of personal morality throughout his life. His administration restored the prestige of the presidency, which had lately slipped considerably.

OVERALL ASSESSMENT

On our 100-point rating scale, Polk scored 42 points, ranking in a tie for sixteenth place. In most surveys Polk fares a little better than he does in our rankings. Many historians give him more credit than we do for his role in expanding the boundaries of the United States. While not denying the significance of his accomplishments, we believe his actions leading us into war with Mexico were unjustified. We would further point out that historians' ratings of Polk have been influenced by the writings of George Bancroft, the most eminent American historian of the nineteenth century. Bancroft had been one of the main advocates of Polk's nomination for the presidency, was a trusted member of Polk's cabinet, and was one of Polk's principal advisors. Quite naturally, Bancroft's histories presented a favorable view of Polk's presidency.

ZACHARY TAYLOR
1849–50

	RATING POINTS	RANK
FOREIGN RELATIONS	13	6 tie
DOMESTIC PROGRAMS	7	16 tie
ADMINISTRATION	3	25 tie
LEADERSHIP	4	24 tie
PERSONAL QUALITIES	10	20
OVERALL ASSESSMENT	37	20

BACKGROUND

Zachary Taylor was born in Orange County, Virginia, on November 24, 1784. When he was eight months old, he moved with his parents to Louisville, Kentucky. With little formal education and no military experience, he was commissioned a first lieutenant in the United States army in 1808. He rose steadily through the ranks, reaching the rank of major general in 1846. He participated in military campaigns in the War of 1812, the Black Hawk War, the Second Seminole War, and in the War with Mexico. He was a successful soldier, winning numerous important victories. He disdained fancy uniforms, preferring nondescript civilian clothing. His untidy appearance gave rise to his nickname: "Old Rough and Ready." He was extremely popular with his troops due to his unpretentious ways. During the Mexican War, Taylor became a national hero. While still in the army, Taylor acquired cotton plantations in Louisiana and Mississippi.

NOMINATION AND ELECTION

In 1846 politicians began looking at Taylor as a potential presidential candidate. At first, the general discouraged all efforts to promote his candidacy. By the spring of 1848 Taylor was certain that no Democrat could ease the sectional strife that was dividing the country, and no Whig statesman could win. Therefore, he felt duty-bound to run. He still refused to campaign for the nomination, but his supporters were active on his behalf. By the time the Whig convention met, Taylor had become the most likely nominee. He led on the first ballot and won the nomination on the fourth.

At the Democratic convention the party split over the issue of slavery. The Barnburners, a faction of New Yorkers holding strong anti-slavery views, walked out in a dispute over the number of votes allocated to their delegates. The convention nominated General Lewis Cass and endorsed a platform stating that Congress had no power to interfere with slavery. Minor parties also made nominations. Ex-President

Martin Van Buren became the Liberty Party candidate.

From the beginning to the end of the race Taylor performed his peacetime army duties and tended to his cotton plantation. He went on no campaign tours and delivered no political speeches. His supporters campaigned spiritedly, however, as did those of Cass and Van Buren. Despite the general's reticence, this was no lackluster campaign. There were plenty of bonfires and rousing songs and more than enough vituperation. The election was extremely close. Taylor and Cass each carried fifteen states. The third man in the race held the balance of power. Not counting New York state, Taylor and Cass each received 127 electoral votes. But in New York Van Buren polled over 120,000 votes. Had these votes gone to Cass, he would have been elected. But the split between the two New York factions allowed Taylor to carry the state and win the presidency 163 electoral votes to 127. The popular vote gave Taylor a plurality, but not a majority.

FOREIGN RELATIONS

During his short time in office, Taylor dealt very well with a series of crises in foreign relations. His most notable success was the Clayton-Bulwer treaty, which prevented a possible war with Great Britain over Nicaragua. He also stopped American agitation to annex Canada, and enforced the Neutrality Act of 1818 against Germany. He took strong actions against French and Portuguese diplomats who were violating American law, but settled the matters peacefully. Taylor resisted calling the militia into service against the Seminoles. His refusal to allow punishment of the whole tribe because of the murder of one white man averted another Seminole War. He also prevented an Indian War from breaking out on the Rio Grande. He used the threat of military force in order to advance American interests while keeping the peace. He threatened Spain with war if they ceded Cuba to Great Britain, and ordered troops to use force if necessary to prevent the invasion of Cuba by American expansionists. He threatened to take military action against Texas if the Texans used force in the boundary dispute with New Mexico.

Taylor consistently promoted the interests of the United States in his relations with other nations. He strongly defended U.S. interests against threats from other nations and at the same time put the brakes on American expansionists who wanted to take over Canada, Mexico, Central America, and Cuba. Despite the fact that he gained his greatest fame as a general in the War with Mexico, he treated that country and its people with respect and in return gained their friendship.

Although he took a firm stand against threats to this country, Taylor's foreign policy decreased international tensions. His actions concerning Canada, Nicaragua, and Cuba smoothed troubled waters. When Hungary, under the leadership of Kossuth, was struggling to win independence from Austria, Taylor would not allow Americans to give aid to the revolutionists while Austria was still the legitimate governing power. He announced that if Kossuth were successful, we would recognize his government. In the meantime, we would not interfere in the internal matters of another nation.

No major impact on world trade was made by the Taylor administration, other than the generally beneficial effect of lowered international tensions. Although the Whigs had traditionally been a high tariff party, rates were not raised significantly during Taylor's term. Coal and iron interests pressed Taylor to raise rates. The secretary of state and the secretary of the treasury both supported these interests. Taylor, however, refused to call a special session on tariffs.

DOMESTIC PROGRAMS

Taylor was fortunate to have been elected president in a time of prosperity. Taxes were low and Taylor saw no need to raise them. He was able to reduce the national debt, which had been incurred to pay for the Mexican War. In common with other Whigs of his era, Taylor favored the federal government investing in internal improvements, such as building canals, roads, and railroads. He was one of the first to propose a transcontinental railroad, but nothing was done about this during his lifetime.

Taylor was a slave owner who purchased more slaves to work on his plantations. He treated his slaves very well, but still kept them in slavery. He strongly opposed extension of slavery into new territories, but supported it where it already existed. He was a supporter of civil liberties. He supported the rights of immigrants, and opposed the Know-Nothings, who wanted to restrict immigration and deny political office to immigrants. He treated Indians far better than did most American presidents. Taylor insisted on the humane treatment of all individuals in the United States. To a greater degree than most of his contemporaries, Taylor treated all persons with respect, regardless of status. One of the things that made him a national hero in the first place was his showing ordinary soldiers as much respect as he showed generals.

ADMINISTRATION AND INTERGOVERNMENTAL RELATIONS

As president, Taylor ranked his goals and objectives in priority order, with preservation of the Union as his number one goal. All his plans were designed to achieve this end. He did not have comprehensive, detailed plans, but he had his priorities straight.

Taylor made no substantial changes in the organization of the executive branch. He proposed the creation of a Bureau of Agriculture within the Department of the Interior, but this recommendation was not adopted by Congress. Some of Taylor's department heads were good people, but overall his was not a distinguished cabinet. Federal offices were staffed with a desire to reward supporters, punish enemies, and attain geographical balance. Nepotism flourished. Taylor was more of a spoilsman than Jackson, who is credited with introducing the spoils system. The overall quality of his appointees was about the same as that of his immediate predecessors. Three of his cabinet members were engaged in an activity that brought some disrepute to the cabinet — the Galphin affair. Their involvement was entirely legal but of questionable ethics and allowed one of them to make a huge profit financially from settlement of a claim against the United States. The payment of the Galphin claim was a one-time event. No harm to the nation's finances occurred by keeping the incumbents in office. However, the affair damaged the president's political standing. He would have been better served by calling for their immediate resignations. Taylor did not do a particularly good job of directing the activities of his assistants, perhaps placing more faith in them than was warranted.

Although he governed frugally and was able to reduce the public debt, Taylor should not received too much credit for this. Congress controlled the purse strings and used its power of appropriations as a weapon in some of its battles with the president. Taylor was the first president to be elected with his party a minority in both houses of Congress. To make matters worse, his party was split along sectional lines on the important issues related to slavery.

During his brief time in office, Taylor appointed one justice to the Supreme Court — a capable, if undistinguished man, who resigned after writing a strong dissent in the Dred Scott decision. Taylor wanted the courts to settle the boundary dispute between Texas and New Mexico, saying this was a judicial matter with which neither the president nor the Congress should interfere.

A poor public speaker and an ineffective writer, Taylor sometimes had difficulty communicating with the public. His letters and speeches were written by others, but he always studied them carefully before signing them to be certain they reflected his views. As was the custom of the day, he hosted levees at the Executive Mansion where he could receive input from the public. He allowed his friends to establish a newspaper in Washington that was authorized to speak for the president.

Taylor wanted to be president of all the people. His sincere wish was to be a non-partisan, non-sectional president. His non-partisan approach to issues was not a pretense, but an honest reflection of his deep concern for the whole country. He was highly respected by the people, mainly because of his war record rather than his political record.

LEADERSHIP AND DECISION-MAKING

As a general, Taylor had been an inspirational leader. As president, however, he was less successful. He was not an inspiring speaker, nor did he have a charismatic personality. Although Taylor could be persuasive at times, he was unable to get a hostile Congress to follow his lead on many matters. He set high standards for himself, but he did not always succeed in motivating others to achieve at a high level. The public's confidence in government did not change much during Taylor's administration.

Taylor had a vision of what the nation and the world should be like, but he was not able to communicate this well enough to unify the nation and create a shared sense of national goals. The overwhelming national concern of the day was what to do about the extension of slavery into new states and territories. Taylor analyzed the situation and developed a strategy called the "President's Plan." This called for the admission of California and New Mexico to the Union when those territories had adopted constitutions guaranteeing a republican form of government and had applied for admission. The boundary between Texas and New Mexico would then become a matter for judicial determination, as a dispute between two states. The question of slavery would be determined by the wording of each proposed state constitution.

Taylor was unable to persuade others, particularly congressional leaders, to put aside their factionalism and unite behind the President's Plan. Some of the opposition undoubtedly arose from sectional biases, but some of it came from those whose desire to preserve the Union was as sincere and fervent as the president's, but who honestly believed that his plan was not the answer the country needed.

Taylor was intelligent and used his intelligence in problem-solving and decision-making situations. He weighed alternatives and made appropriate decisions based on his estimate of the probable consequences of various lines of action. He listened to advice, but made up his own mind. He did not have a particularly wide knowledge and understanding of history, but was not as ill-informed as some of his critics have charged. Taylor was willing to compromise on many matters in order to win support for a proposal, but held firm on any principle that he regarded as important. Some parts of the Omnibus Bill proposed by Congressional leaders in 1850 violated principles that the president held dear, and he would not compromise. There was little likelihood that the Omnibus would have passed, but Taylor made it clear that he would veto it if it did pass. After Taylor's death, the Omnibus was split into the several separate bills that became known as the Compromise of 1850, passed the Congress, and were signed by Fillmore.

Taylor had the courage to make a hard decision and stick to it, and was willing to accept the consequences of his action, even if it led to war. Fortunately, war never resulted from any of his presidential decisions. In emergencies he remained calm, utilizing as careful a decision-making process as time permitted. Had he lived and Congress had passed the Compromise of 1850, he surely would have vetoed parts of it. We do not know what the results of such a veto would have been. If the South had accepted his veto and not seceded, the Civil War might have been averted. But had any states left the Union, the war might have started ten years sooner, for Taylor would have used the military to enforce the federal laws and put down any revolt.

PERSONAL QUALITIES

The president comported himself with the dignity that his office required, judged by the standards of the times. (Today we might not think it dignified for a president to chew tobacco and spit in a box by his desk, but it was acceptable behavior in his time.) He never demeaned the office by small-minded or mean-spirited actions. The people were proud that a war hero such as "Old Rough and Ready" was their president. His actions in the area of foreign relations enhanced that pride, but his domestic policies received severe criticism from his political enemies. Taylor's 16 months in the White House did little to affect the stature of the office or the power of the presidency.

Except for those who believed in the extension of slavery, the people thought President Taylor was on their side. He gave great access, receiving input from all segments of society. He reached out to the people through personal appearances, even gravely risking his health on a trip to the Northeast. He was a poor public speaker and was unable to use his office as a bully pulpit, but he made the people feel he was interested in them.

Taylor acted consistently on a firm set of moral principles and values. He had great integrity. The president was honest in his personal life and in his official life. He never used his office to benefit himself financially, although he did use his position to appoint friends and relatives to governmental offices. Taylor enhanced the prestige of the presidency through the high standard of personal morality he exhibited throughout his life, both in public and in private.

FINAL DAYS

On the Fourth of July 1850, a very hot day, Taylor stood several hours in the sun at the laying of the cornerstone of the Washington Monument. When he returned to the President's House, hungry and thirsty, he is said to have eaten bowls of cherries and drunk cold milk. Whether from the heat or the food and drink, the president became ill and developed severe cramps. His doctor diagnosed the problem as cholera morbus, a gastronomic upset. Despite being treated with calomel and opium, the president continued to grow weaker from the effects of vomiting and diarrhea. On July 9 he died.

At the time of the president's unfortunate death, the nation was facing the unsolved problem of what to do about slavery. Soon after Taylor's demise the crisis was eased when Millard Fillmore signed the bills making up the Compromise of 1850. The problem was not solved; its resolution was merely delayed. In a little more than ten years the Union broke up and it became the lot of Abraham Lincoln to struggle to restore the Union and to try another solution to the problem of slavery in the United States.

OVERALL ASSESSMENT

Overall, Zachary Taylor received 37 out of a possible 100 rating scale points. He ranks twentieth among the 39 presidents rated. His greatest achievements were in the area of Foreign Relations, where he ranked in a tie for sixth among all the presidents. His weakest performance was in the area of Administration and Intergovernmental Relations, showing that a lifetime of military leadership does not necessarily prepare one to administer well the nation's highest civilian office. Where Taylor would have ranked had his administration not been cut short by his untimely death will never be known. We do know that he achieved enough in his 16 months in office to deserve a higher ranking than presidential polls usually give him.

MILLARD FILLMORE

1850–53

	RATING POINTS	RANK
FOREIGN RELATIONS	7	26 tie
DOMESTIC PROGRAMS	3	24 tie
ADMINISTRATION	2	27
LEADERSHIP	3	26
PERSONAL QUALITIES	5	27 tie
OVERALL ASSESSMENT	20	26

BACKGROUND

Millard Fillmore was born in a log cabin on his parents' farm in Cayuga County, New York, on January 7, 1800. He attended school for only brief periods. At the age of 14, he was apprenticed to a cloth-dresser. In 1819 he bought his freedom from a second apprenticeship for $30. He studied law, worked as a law clerk, and taught elementary school. In 1823 he was admitted to the bar and opened his own law office in East Aurora, New York. In 1828 he was a delegate to the Antimasonic convention. With the help of Thurlow Weed, he was elected to three terms in the New York state assembly. In 1832 he was elected to the U.S. House of Representatives as an Anti-Mason. In 1834 he resigned from that party and spent the next two years consolidating Whig power in western New York. In 1836 he was elected to Congress and served three terms, rising to chair the influential Ways and Means Committee. In 1844, with Weed's backing, Fillmore decided he wanted to run for vice president. However, Weed's choice

for governor of New York became incapacitated and Weed decided he preferred Fillmore in Albany rather than in Washington. Weed passed the word to his friends to deny Fillmore the vice-presidential nomination. Fillmore considered this as a betrayal by Weed, but he was powerless to prevent it. Reluctantly, Fillmore became the Whig nominee for governor of New York, but lost. In 1847 Fillmore was elected to the comptrollership of New York state, the most powerful office in the state as far as financial matters were concerned.

NOMINATION AND ELECTION

In contrast to recent conventions wherein the presidential nominee selects his running mate, Zachary Taylor made no public statement about his preference for vice president. As a matter of fact, the general remained in Louisiana and did not learn of his own nomination until well after the selection of his running mate had been made. Taylor's managers, however, had indicated their support for

Abbott Lawrence, an anti-slavery textile man-ufacturer from Massachusetts. Going into the convention, Lawrence was a heavy favorite. This situation changed quickly as soon as Taylor was nominated, however. A Massachusetts delegate, objecting to a proposal that Taylor's nomination be made unanimous, offered a res-olution to the effect that the Whig party would pledge itself to abide by the nomination of Tay-lor if he would agree to the principle of no ex-tension of slavery over territory now free, and to the protection of American industry. These comments probably doomed Lawrence's can-didacy. Fillmore's chances were given a con-siderable boost when a Clay supporter made an emotional appeal to the party to unite behind the New Yorker.

Fourteen names were placed in nomination. The first ballot was close, with Fillmore re-ceiving 115 votes to 109 for Lawrence. On the second ballot most of the favorite sons were eliminated. Fillmore was then nominated eas-ily, with almost twice as many votes as Lawrence.

In the presidential campaign that followed, Taylor stayed home in Louisiana. Fillmore re-futed charges by Southerners that he was an abolitionist. He never mentioned slavery in the territories or the federal government's respon-sibility for it there. He turned down a proffered alliance with the Native Americans (Know-Nothings). He bid for the Irish vote by ex-tending his sympathy for Ireland's plight in the potato famine and for its subjugation to Eng-land. Fillmore also campaigned for Taylor in New York, and had a part in quelling anti–Tay-lor sentiment that threatened to split the party at a meeting called by Thurlow Weed in Al-bany in August. Weed's real intentions in call-ing the meeting are not clear, but it ended with the party leaders united in promoting the Tay-lor candidacy.

Taylor died in office, and Fillmore became president on July 10, 1850.

FOREIGN RELATIONS

Fillmore's foreign policy was to promote, by honorable means only, every legitimate inter-est of Americans. He avoided a possible war with Spain by refusing to exact vengeance against that country for the execution of Amer-icans who had illegally invaded Cuba. Troubles in Nicaragua flared up again when an Ameri-can vessel failed to pay port dues at San Juan. An English brig-of-war gave chase and fired a round at the American ship, forcing the captain to heave to and pay the fee. Fillmore promptly ordered an armed vessel to the scene. The cri-sis was short-lived. Negotiations among the United States, Great Britain, Costa Rica, and Nicaragua solved the problem temporarily. Then Nicaraguan revolutionists took over and would have nothing to do with the treaty.

When Austria protested that the United States had sided with the revolutionist Kossuth, Fillmore approved Secretary of State Daniel Webster's note saying that if Austria attempted to retaliate, the United States was "quite will-ing to take their chances and abide their des-tiny." The American minister to Turkey inter-ceded and won freedom for Kossuth, who had fled to that country.

The United States had been the first to ac-knowledge Hawaii's national existence. Several times prior to Fillmore's administration the State Department had served notice on foreign powers to respect Hawaii's independence. For example, in 1843 a British naval officer had seized the islands, and the United States an-nounced that we might feel justified in using force if necessary to prevent the islands from falling into the hands of a European power. In 1849 Napoleon III seized Honolulu. In response to American protests, the French withdrew. The problem arose again during the Fillmore administration. In 1851 France presented the Hawaiian king with a list of demands that would reduce the islands to a French protec-torate. Webster informed Napoleon that Ha-waii must remain independent in spirit as well as in law. The French withdrew their demands.

For the most part Fillmore's foreign rela-tions record was free of bluff, bombast, and aggression. He supported the sending of bat-tleships to Japan as a show of strength in the opening of that nation's ports, a process that started in the Taylor administration and was achieved in the Pierce administration. Fill-more refused to threaten to use force against Mexico to protect the Tehuantepec railroad project, and Judah Benjamin lost his $100,000 investment there. Rather than challenge Peruvian claims to the Lobos islands, he had the treasury pay the fees that Peru charged Boston merchants for taking guano from the islands.

Fillmore tried to increase world trade, particularly with China and Japan. His efforts to build a canal across Nicaragua were aimed at facilitating commerce. He assisted his merchant friends in the economic exploitation of third world countries, but stopped short of using troops to help with a railroad in Mexico. (Somewhat at odds with his attempts to help world trade was his view on tariffs.) He favored a high protective tariff, and as chairman of the Ways and Means Committee had pushed a higher tariff through during Tyler's administration, but he did not raise it significantly while president.

Fillmore consistently tried to ease international tensions by demonstrating that we had the resolve to protect our national interests, but that we had no designs against other nations. Especially notable in this regard was his reassurance to Spain that we would not try to "liberate" Cuba. His warning to France in regard to Hawaii was an example of our resolve. Although not exactly in the field of foreign relations, his strengthening of the defenses at Fort Sumter when South Carolina threatened secession was another example of his willingness to take strong action to protect our national interests. He was a good neighbor to the other countries in the Western Hemisphere as demonstrated by his actions with regard to the Mexican railroad, the Nicaragua canal, and the Peruvian guano. Fillmore's conduct of foreign policy enhanced public opinion of the United States throughout much of the world.

DOMESTIC PROGRAMS

Due to increased industrialization, the development of railroads, and the settlement of new agricultural areas in the Midwest, the United States enjoyed a period of prosperity under Fillmore. Although the president's economic policies favored the business and commercial interests, the wages of labor kept pace with inflation and agriculture also prospered during his administration. Fillmore was clearly on the side of capital, but he was not anti-

union, and the labor unions grew in strength during his administration. He thought one of the main functions of government was to help business. He advocated granting federal lands to subsidize railroad building and thought both the states and federal governments should help build and improve canals, rivers, and harbors for the benefit of the commercial classes.

Fillmore did not use the governmental powers to promote the general welfare, except insofar as the public was helped by internal improvements. Although the improvements were for the benefit of business, there were some "trickle-down" effects. The president kept taxes low and continued reducing the national debt.

Fillmore believed that slavery was wrong and that at some time in the distant future it might disappear, at which time the freed slaves should be sent back to Africa. Meanwhile, slavery was permitted by the Constitution, and the duty of the president was to uphold the Constitution. Strongly anti-abolitionist, he signed a more stringent Fugitive Slave Law and favored its vigorous enforcement. He supported the Compromise of 1850.

In common with many whites of his era, Fillmore regarded blacks as inferior. Although he favored allowing immigration to continue, he was for restricting the rights of immigrants to vote and would limit government office-holding to natural born citizens. Both before and after his presidency he was an important leader of intolerant political parties — the Anti-Masons and the Know-Nothings — but his actions as president were not notably bigoted. He supported freedom of speech and the press and strongly favored separation of church and state, opposing government support of Catholic schools.

Fillmore clearly preferred the company of wealthy business and professional people, but never showed disdain or contempt for the less fortunate. In his strict enforcement of the Fugitive Slave Act he put property rights above human rights. He would not have phrased it that way; his view was that everybody must obey any law that is constitutional.

ADMINISTRATION AND INTERGOVERNMENTAL RELATIONS

Fillmore had two major goals — to save the Union from dissolution and to achieve the economic programs of the original Whigs. His short-term plans were aimed at the accomplishment of these two goals. Circumstances prevented him from doing much long-range planning.

Fillmore's organization of the executive branch was in no way remarkable. He followed the usual practices of believers in the spoils system, but did take ability into consideration along with political concerns. His best-known appointee was Daniel Webster as secretary of state, but the great orator was in poor health much of the time and the president directed foreign relations himself. All in all Fillmore's administrative style was typical for a president of his era.

In his relations with Congress Fillmore was persuasive on the matter of the Texas boundary. Otherwise, Congress seemed dominant. The Compromise of 1850 was a congressional achievement, rather than an administration initiative. Fillmore's main contribution to the Compromise was agreeing to sign it.

Fillmore used federal court appointments as a means of rewarding political friends or punishing political enemies. He never even gave lip service to the view that an independent judiciary should remain free from political patronage. His one appointee to the Supreme Court was undistinguished.

As president, Fillmore gave paramount consideration to the interests of one group — the commercial class. This was not because he caved in to their pressure, but because he truly believed that government should help business, that what was good for business was good for the country. He tried very hard not to favor one section of the country over another because he wanted desperately to hold the nation together. During his administration he was more popular with the people than his present reputation would lead one to believe. He enjoyed meeting people, especially wealthy people, merchants, and so-called leading citizens.

How effective was Fillmore's administration? He was successful in the short run at least. Prosperity increased during his administration. The nation remained at peace. The Compromise of 1850 staved off the threat of immediate southern secession. Whether the Compromise merely postponed the inevitable or whether it might have prevented the Civil War from ever happening will never be known. A few years later the Kansas-Nebraska Act was passed and the die was cast. But for a while the Compromise was a success. Fillmore's biographer, Robert J. Rayback, wrote: "As if by magic, the clouds of disunion, which still hovered threateningly over the nation, disappeared....In ten short weeks, Fillmore's administration had solved the problem of territorial government that had plagued Congress ever since American and Mexican troops first clashed four years ago."[58] Of course, the problem of slavery in the territories was not really solved, but the union did not fall apart during Fillmore's watch.

LEADERSHIP AND DECISION MAKING

Although Fillmore said he had no ambition to be president, clearly he aspired to political leadership most of his adult life. He was not a charismatic leader. He was frequently in a leadership position because of his ambition, his hard work, his study of the issues, and his ability to survive in political warfare. He did not often get others to follow him because he persuaded them of the rightness of his cause; he more often used political intrigue or manipulation.

Fillmore's vision was of a nation of peace and prosperity, untorn by sectional strife. He achieved peace and prosperity, and temporarily reduced sectional strife. He was not forward-looking enough to be called visionary. He was an intelligent man, but he was not particularly adept at conceptualizing the grand strategy for accomplishing his goals. Fillmore did not set high performance standards for himself and his subordinates. Because Fillmore presided over a period of prosperity and lessened tensions, the level of confidence the people had in him and in their government was high at that time. Because his achievements in the domestic arena were so transient in nature,

Fillmore's reputation has suffered greatly at the hands of modern interpreters of the period.

Because of the unavailability of quality schooling in his youth, Fillmore was not well-educated in a formal sense. He read widely and attempted to make informed decisions. He usually considered alternatives and listened to the advice of his political cohorts before making a decision. He apparently did not learn easily from past mistakes, as Thurlow Weed outfoxed him on numerous occasions before he caught on.

In order to achieve his ends, Fillmore was willing to compromise. On important principles he would usually stick to his guns rather than give in. He did not view the Compromise of 1850 as a violation of his principles in any way. Normally, Fillmore had no trouble making hard decisions and sticking to them. One exception to this rule came when he postponed announcing his decision to not run for re-election in 1852. The delay left him in the race, but his known reluctance to run enabled his political opponents to gain a lead that he could not overcome in the nominating convention. He usually remained cool in emergencies. His ability not to be flustered by political intrigue improved with practice.

PERSONAL QUALITIES

Fillmore conducted himself with dignity. He was unfailingly courteous and affable. He was handsome and looked every inch the president. During his time in office, Americans were proud of their country, and many of them were proud of their president. The fact that Fillmore has been ridiculed by some modern writers does not detract from his acceptance by his contemporaries. Fillmore neither added to nor subtracted from the stature of the office. As a Whig, he did not believe in increasing the power of the presidency.

Sectional divisions and political factional-

ism were the main determinants of public opinion about Fillmore during his lifetime. The president sought advice from many segments of the population (including the common people) and took this advice into consideration in formulating his plans. He had a great deal of contact with people, but he never went over the heads of Congress to appeal directly to the people to support his programs. He believed in deferring to Congress.

Fillmore acted consistently on his values of saving the Union and promoting commerce. He sometimes changed his mind about which particular policies would best meet those goals, but he never wavered on the goals themselves. His relationship with other politicians was marked by inconsistency, however. His political friends and enemies sometimes switched identities.

Fillmore was personally honest in that he never stole from the public purse. He saw nothing wrong in using political influence to help his adopted city of Buffalo prosper. In his view that was how the game of politics was played. He got moderately rich during a career in politics through accepting favors from friends and supporters. These favors were in no way bribes. There was no impropriety involved. The favors did not influence his policies or programs.

Fillmore was a politician through and through. This meant cooperation with Thurlow Weed when he thought it was to his advantage. It meant taking control of the Anti-Mason party to gain a foothold in politics in the early days and accepting the nomination of the Know-Nothings in his later years. Otherwise, his moral conduct was acceptable.

OVERALL ASSESSMENT

Millard Fillmore received 19 out of a possible 100 points on the rating scales and ranks 26th among the 39 presidents rated.

FRANKLIN PIERCE

1853–57

	RATING POINTS	RANK
FOREIGN RELATIONS	1	34 tie
DOMESTIC PROGRAMS	–7	37 tie
ADMINISTRATION	–4	33 tie
LEADERSHIP	–11	38
PERSONAL QUALITIES	2	32 tie
OVERALL ASSESSMENT	–19	38

BACKGROUND

Franklin Pierce was born in Hillsboro, New Hampshire, on November 23, 1804. He attended Phillips Exeter Academy and Bowdoin College, from which he graduated in 1824, ranking third in his class. After studying law under New Hampshire Governor Levi Woodbury, he opened his own law office in Concord and soon embarked upon a political career. Elected to the state legislature, he boarded with his father, by now the governor. Re-elected, he became speaker of the house at the age of 26. In 1833 he was elected to the U.S. House of Representatives where he served two terms before becoming a U.S. Senator. Near the end of his Senate term, he resigned and returned to Concord, where he practiced law for the next five years and honed his political skills within the state Democratic party organization.

In 1846 President Polk invited Pierce to become attorney general, but he declined. In 1847 he was appointed a colonel in the army and was soon promoted to brigadier general. He served under General Winfield Scott on the expedition to Mexico City. During a battle he wrenched a leg that he had injured when thrown from his horse the previous day. Pierce fainted from the pain and lay helpless until the end of the battle. For this, political enemies later falsely accused him of cowardice.

After the war Pierce returned to the practice of law in New Hampshire. Prominent in the state Democratic party, Pierce was chosen to chair a convention called to revise the state constitution. By 1852 he was the leading Democrat in his state, but not yet a major player on the national stage. Nevertheless, the New Hampshire delegation to the Democratic national convention decided to nominate him for the presidency in the event the convention deadlocked. Pierce agreed that his friends could support him, but only on the condition that a real deadlock ensued and some other state entered his name into the balloting.

NOMINATION AND ELECTION

When the Democratic convention met, Pierce was the darkest of dark horses. The four strongest candidates were Stephen A. Douglas, Lewis Cass, James Buchanan, and William L. Marcy. The Democrats were divided on questions relating to the expansion of slavery and the enforcement of the Fugitive Slave Law. The leading candidates fought each other bitterly, and partisan feeling ran high. The two-thirds rule was adopted, making it even more difficult for any candidate to secure enough votes to win the nomination. For three days the delegates voted, but the convention remained deadlocked. On the 35th ballot, a delegate from Virginia placed Pierce's name before the convention, but he received only a few votes. On the 49th ballot James C. Dobbin supported Pierce with an outburst of oratory, and the stampede was underway. When the news reached Pierce, he could hardly believe it.

The Whigs had as much difficulty as the Democrats in choosing a candidate, nominating Winfield Scott on the 53rd ballot. There were minor parties in the fray as well, but the campaign was essentially a two-man race. Pierce supported the Compromise of 1850 and the strict enforcement of the Fugitive Slave Act. Scott's views were obscure. The race featured mudslinging against both major candidates. Pierce was charged with being a coward, a drunkard, and anti–Catholic. Scott was ridiculed for his nickname, "Old Fuss and Feathers," and for some awkward phrases he had once used. He also was accused unjustly of being hostile to foreign-born Americans. Scott made a campaign tour through several states, making a number of speeches in each state. Pierce stayed home and did not campaign.

In the election, Pierce won an overwhelming victory, carrying all but four of the 31 states, giving him 254 electoral votes to Scott's 42.

Two months before his inauguration, 11-year-old Bennie, Pierce's last surviving son, was mangled in a railroad wreck. Both parents saw the child die; neither parent recovered from the loss. Pierce sought refuge in the bottle, with unhappy results.

Pierce's presidency was so unsuccessful that he did not seek a second term.

FOREIGN RELATIONS

In his inaugural address, Pierce said: "My administration will not be controlled by any timid forebodings of evil from expansion." His actions as president show clearly that national expansion was one of his goals. In 1853 he advocated the annexation of Hawaii. His plan fell through, partly because of the death of King Kamehameha. Unsuccessful in attempts to purchase Cuba, three of Pierce's diplomats issued the infamous Ostend Manifesto, declaring that if Spain freed its slaves but would not sell Cuba, the United States would be justified in taking the island by force. Although the American people had supported Pierce's expansionist policies, they turned against him when they learned of the Manifesto. Cuba remained a Spanish possession.

Pierce's foreign policy goal of obtaining new territory for the United States through aggressive imperialism led to disputes with other countries and threats of war. However, Pierce preferred negotiation to war, and although he led us to the brink he never pushed us over the edge. When a southern route through Mexican territory seemed to be the best location for the construction of an American railroad to the Pacific, the Pierce administration peacefully acquired the land in a transaction known as the Gadsden Purchase. When a dispute arose about the boundary between Chihuahua and New Mexico, we again were on the verge of war. In 1854 Chihuahua, under the direction of Mexican President Santa Anna, took armed possession of the disputed territory. For a time war between the United States and Mexico seemed inevitable, but the problem was settled by negotiations. The United States paid Mexico $10 million to relinquish its claims to the region.

Treaties involving governments in Nicaragua and Santo Domingo were worked out, but never ratified. In Nicaragua Pierce recognized the filibustering regime of the American adventurer, William Walker. This recognition was encompassed in the Dallas-Clarendon agreement, but the U.S. Senate added so many amendments that the British turned it down. A treaty acquiring Samana Bay from the Dominican Republic also failed of ratification. British and French representatives protested the Samana cession and that item was stricken. The Dominicans added a provision prohibiting racial distinctions among Dominican citizens when traveling in the United States. The administration withdrew the treaty without submitting it to the Senate.

Pierce's conduct of foreign policy had mixed results on our relations with other nations. Although potential military force and the threat of force did not help Pierce acquire much new territory, it did make other countries aware of the growing power of the United States. The United States assumed a more powerful role in international affairs, demonstrating to rivals our strength. On the other hand, his aggressive, imperialistic foreign policy frightened neighbors and created hostility toward the United States. It certainly alienated public opinion toward this country throughout much of the Western Hemisphere. By threats and annexation attempts the United States became regarded as a danger to the well-being of other nations. However, Pierce's jingoism was more rhetoric than action.

Pierce favored increased trade and a lower tariff. He was successful in obtaining a modest tariff reduction. A reciprocal trade agreement was reached with Britain, which greatly reduced trade barriers between the United States and Canada. With a few restrictions, it also opened the fishing waters of each country to the fishermen of the other.

Trade with Japan was opened by the Perry mission, with beneficial results to all nations. At Pierce's insistence, a trade treaty with Japan was ratified by the Senate in 1854. The Danish tolls problem was brought to a head and was settled in the Buchanan administration. American trade was increased world wide to everyone's benefit.

DOMESTIC PROGRAMS

Pierce was fortunate to become president during a time of prosperity. He took no action on the domestic economy, and the nation's prosperity continued. Taxes were low and the Pierce administration reduced the tariff. Pierce did not have to deal with inflation or deflation. Spending was reduced in every department except the War Department, which was increased to build up the armed forces in support of Pierce's expansionist foreign policy. The decrease in spending for domestic programs was not necessarily in the national interest, as no new programs were started during the entire administration, although some were needed.

Even in prosperous times, there was poverty in the land. The president strongly opposed any governmental help for the poor. He vetoed the Dorothea Dix Bill to provide institutional care for the indigent mentally ill. The Pierce administration opposed the right of labor to organize. The secretary of war, Jefferson Davis, threatened to fire bricklayers who were working on the capitol annex if they persisted in trying to organize. The bricklayers failed in their attempt to achieve a closed shop. In struggles between capital and labor Pierce was definitely on the side of capital.

Pierce supported the Constitution and supported the freedoms guaranteed therein, as understood by the strict construction of the times. Before becoming president he had tried to eliminate an anti–Catholic measure from the constitution of New Hampshire. However, he seemed to have no respect for non-whites. He was pro-slavery and put property rights of slaveholders above human rights. He disrespected whites who disagreed with his views on slavery, holding them responsible for sectional ill-feelings. His treatment of Native Americans was harsh and inhumane.

Continuous warfare with the Indians took place throughout Pierce's term. During his administration 52 Indian treaties were "negotiated" (at gunpoint), taking 174 million acres away from the tribes in return for $11 million — considerably less than ten cents per acre. Previous administrations had forced the Indians west of the Mississippi, and now the western lands were wanted for white settlers. The Pierce administration decided that the Indians would be put involuntarily on reservations in two areas — one in what is now Oklahoma and the other one in the Dakotas — and the rest of the land would be opened for white settlement. The secretary of the interior, Robert McClelland, reported that there were 300,000 aborigines and they were costing the government annually more than $2.6 million — nearly nine dollars per Indian. Annuities were still being paid in cash, which McClelland thought inappropriate as it paralyzed efforts for permanent improvement. He thought the best way to care for the "redskins" was to colonize them or place them on reservations, isolating the various tribes within set limits, taking care of them under agents, teaching them to work, and giving them Christian instruction. Native rights and interests were never considered and their traditional way of life was destroyed.

Controversy over slavery was the bane of all presidents who served during the 1850s. None of them was able to solve the problem. Pierce's presidential campaign had centered on his support for the Compromise of 1850, including strict enforcement of the Fugitive Slave Act. He wanted slavery permitted in the territories and wished to acquire new land south of the United States in Mexico or Cuba in order to expand slavery. Pierce thought that all sectional problems were due to the agitation of abolitionists and other Northerners who wanted to interfere with slavery. Sectional feelings worsened during his administration due to disastrous Kansas-Nebraska Act, which Pierce supported. Armed clashes occurred in "Bleeding Kansas." Sectional antagonism reached new heights. The Whig party, already weakened by sectionalism, disintegrated, hastening the birth of the new Republican party. During the Pierce administration sectionalism accelerated from a serious problem to a crisis.

ADMINISTRATION AND INTERGOVERNMENTAL RELATIONS

Pierce's goals were the preservation of the Union, expansion of our population into the unorganized territory of the West, acquisition of new land in Latin America and Hawaii, and the perpetuation and extension of slavery. He failed to foresee problems with his nationalistic and racist policies. Other goals and objectives covered in his annual messages originated with his department heads.

The departments were well run and organized according to sound administrative principles. All members of the administration took their jobs seriously and worked hard. Although Pierce asserted himself on some occasions, the government was mostly run by department heads. Due to the president's weakness, his strong, capable cabinet officers took more initiative, becoming stronger and making most of the decisions for their respective departments themselves. Three particularly strong department heads — Secretary of State William Marcy, Secretary of War Jefferson Davis, and Attorney General Caleb Cushing — dominated cabinet meetings. Each cabinet member made or attempted to make reforms in his department that laid the basis for modern, workable bureaucracy. Except for a hint of collusion between Davis and railroad interests, there was no scandal. For the first time a cabinet remained intact throughout an entire presidential term.

Cabinet members were successful in getting some reforms implemented. Marcy revamped the organization of the diplomatic corps. The secretary of the treasury insisted on strict accountability of government workers and reduced the national debt. The secretary of the navy ordered more ships to be built in navy yards, established new procedures to retire incapacitated naval officers, instituted a new system of rewards and punishment for naval personnel, and refused to reinstitute flogging. He revived the apprenticeship program and raised the pay of seamen. Cushing proposed expansion and reform of the judiciary, but Congress rejected his proposals

Pierce was a poor communicator. He was cordial, appeared presidential, and made friends easily in one-on-one conversation. Congressmen listened to him, but did things their own way. Most of the public and the press lost respect for the president and opposed his programs. Enough members of his own party opposed presidential programs to allow their defeat in Congress, and he was unable to secure enough support from the opposition to pass proposed legislation. Relations with Congress deteriorated to the point that Pierce's presidency was damaged. His party lost its majorities in both houses in the mid-term elections of 1854. The most significant legislation passed during his term was the Kansas-Nebraska Act, introduced by Senator Douglas and regarded as a victory for the administration. This act reopened the question of slavery in the territories and may have made the Civil War inevitable. At the very least, the act was against the national interest in that it polarized the North and South and turned Kansas into a bloody battleground. Pierce exercised nine vetoes; five of them were overriden. The president was so weak that Congressional leaders took over and tried to steer the ship of state.

Pierce was widely perceived as acting only in the interests of the pro-slavery South and the imperialists. Other powerful interest groups were antagonized, particularly those in the Northern states. The public lost respect for the president, making it difficult for him to govern effectively.

LEADERSHIP AND DECISION MAKING

Although Pierce had a magnetic personality, he did not inspire or stimulate executive branch personnel to high levels of performance. Most of them were serious public servants and worked hard despite the lack of presidential leadership. Pierce was frequently unable to persuade others to adopt his proposals or carry out his programs with enthusiasm.

Pierce was not a visionary. He did not communicate his concept of what the nation and the world should be like. He could not create a sense of togetherness, of shared national goals. Instead, his programs caused deviseness and factionalism. Sectionalism festered to such an extent that both the president's own party and the opposition party split into factions. New political movements and new parties that opposed the president and his views came about and grew stronger.

With the help of cabinet members and Congress Pierce could remain calm in emergencies and make hard decisions. But he preferred to compromise. He failed to stand firm in the face of opposition. He not only compromised too much, but often took ambiguous positions on both sides of issues. He wanted to please everybody, and often two persons on different sides would both think they had the president's support. This led to distrust and disrespect for him. The people's confidence in the presidency weakened during Pierce's administration.

The ordinary demands of the office of president were often beyond Pierce's ability. Instead of growing with the job, he was overwhelmed by it. He was unable to analyze situations or to develop appropriate strategies for dealing with problems. Often he was unable to understand the ramification of his decisions. He failed to learn from his mistakes.

PERSONAL QUALITIES

Amiable, gregarious, and so very handsome, Franklin Pierce appeared to be the very model of a nineteenth century president. But appearances can be deceiving. He did not have the "right stuff" to be the nation's chief executive. Too eager to please, too willing to compromise, he failed to exercise presidential leadership.

Pierce was honest and never used his office to benefit himself personally at the expense of the public. In one sense he was trustworthy. He never deliberately went back on his word, but because of his propensity for agreeing with almost everything said to him in private conversation some people thought he broke promises. Pierce acted consistently on his values and principles, but according to his values slavery, racism, and jingoism were acceptable. He was never involved in a scandal in or out of office, other than occasionally appearing under the influence of alcohol. Pierce enjoyed drinking, but he could not hold his liquor. From time to time he would go on the wagon and stop drinking entirely for years at a time. Invariably, he would resume and suffer from it.

The president was available to the public. People who met him on a one-on-one basis or who drank with him in a small group usually liked him. As his wife secluded herself after the death of their last son, they did not entertain in the Executive Mansion. Pierce was often seen at night walking alone in Washington or riding horseback. He would sometimes talk with strangers who intercepted him. Some of the input he received from the public may have been considered by the president in his policy making. Pierce communicated formally to the public in his inaugural address and in four annual addresses. He announced his goals and objectives, including proposals given to him by his department heads. He always went over each speech in advance with his cabinet.

The people were not proud of their president. Some did not respect him because he drank too much. Others objected to his policies, which increased sectionalism. Under Pierce, people became more loyal to their section or faction than to America. Because of the caliber of the person who occupied it, the office of the president received less respect at home and in the Western Hemisphere. In Europe and some parts of Asia, the opposite occurred. America's increased presence on the international scene led to greater respect for the United States and its president.

By abdicating some of his powers to the cabinet and to Congress, Pierce diminished the stature of the presidency. The majority of the American people came to believe that Pierce was opposed to their best interests. Of course, the majority lived in the Northern states. Many of them felt that Pierce was a Northern man with Southern sympathies. He was called a "doughface." Later, Northerners who sided with the South would be called "copperheads." Both terms were contemptuous and hostile epithets.

OVERALL ASSESSMENT

With negative 19 points overall, Pierce ranks as next to last among the 39 presidents rated.

JAMES BUCHANAN
1857–61

	RATING POINTS	RANK
FOREIGN RELATIONS	14	3 tie
DOMESTIC PROGRAMS	–5	33 tie
ADMINISTRATION	1	28
LEADERSHIP	8	19
PERSONAL QUALITIES	4	29 tie
OVERALL ASSESSMENT	22	25

BACKGROUND

James Buchanan was born on April 23, 1791, in a log cabin near Mercersburg, Pennsylvania. After graduating from Dickinson College, he studied law in Lancaster, Pennsylvania, and opened a law office there. During the War of 1812, he enlisted in the army as a private. From 1814 to 1816 he served in the Pennsylvania legislature. In 1816 he returned to the practice of law in Lancaster. In 1820 he entered politics on the national scene, serving in the House of Representatives, the Senate, as minister to Russia and to Great Britain, and as secretary of state.

NOMINATION AND ELECTION

In 1856 four prominent Democrats vied for the party's presidential nomination: President Pierce, Stephen Douglas, Lewis Cass, and Buchanan. Sectional divisions had become pronounced since the Kansas-Nebraska Act had passed in 1854. Douglas had introduced, and

Pierce had signed the act. Both were acceptable to the South and also to the West, for they upheld popular sovereignty, but they faced strong opposition from the Northern, antislavery wing of the party. Cass was unacceptable to the South. This left Buchanan, who had been out of the country as minister to Britain when the Kansas-Nebraska Act was passed and had not taken a position on the act since his return. At the Democratic convention, Buchanan was the favorite. He led from the beginning, but it took seventeen ballots for him to secure the two-thirds majority needed to win the nomination.

By now the Whig party had disintegrated, with its antislavery wing joining the new Republican party. The Republican candidate was John C. Fremont. The Know-Nothing party and the remaining Whigs both supported ex-president Millard Fillmore in his comeback attempt. The Democrats made preservation of the Union their major issue and tried to avoid the slavery question. The Republicans fought slavery with the slogan, "Free soil, free speech, and Fremont." The Know-Nothings attacked both sides.

The voters were excited about only one issue — slavery. Buchanan swept the South and carried five states outside Dixie to garner 174 electoral votes to 114 for Fremont and 8 for Fillmore. Despite his easy win in the electoral college, Buchanan did not receive a majority of the popular vote, but had a plurality with a little over 45 percent.

FOREIGN RELATIONS

In foreign affairs Buchanan developed firm polices that enhanced American prestige abroad. He opened the door to diplomatic relations with the nations of Asia, extending commercial opportunities. He exchanged ministers with Persia and initiated an exchange of ministers with Japan. He obtained trade privileges with China. By treaty, he developed trade on three continents. A treaty was made with France acknowledging the rights of French-born naturalized citizens in the United States. The low tariff of 1857 had been passed the day before Buchanan took office. Although an advocate of free trade, he asked for higher rates for needed revenue. It did not pass. His slogan was "Free seas and free trade."

The president's experience as a diplomat helped him establish better relations with Great Britain. By an arrangement between the governments of the United States and Great Britain, the cruisers of each were empowered to board vessels of either nation suspected of engaging in the African slave trade. In 1858 British cruisers in the Gulf of Mexico became quite active and boarded about 30 American vessels in the course of only a few weeks. Buchanan protested and the British government halted the practice. The problem of British possessions in Central America was solved when Britain signed treaties with Nicaragua and Honduras that were satisfactory to the United States. The right of transit in Central America was established. Congress, however, rejected Buchanan's proposal to build canals and roads across Nicaragua or Panama.

An incident in the Pacific Northwest for a time exacerbated feelings between Britain and the United States. The San Juan Islands in Puget Sound were disputed between the two nations. The height of hostility and absurdity was reached when a pig belonging to an Englishman raided the garden of an American, who shot the pig. The so-called "Pig War" ensued. Troops of both nations rushed in. War was threatened, but both nations agreed to arbitration. The islands were awarded to the United States.

The show of military force secured for the United States the right of transit in South America. An American steamer was dispatched under a naval commander to survey various rivers in South America to determine their navigability. Paraguay's President Lopez took exception to American ships steaming up the Parana River. A Paraguayan soldier fired at the ship and killed the helmsman. Buchanan sent a naval contingent to South America. Backed by this force, an American commissioner was able to secure redress.

Buchanan expanded the Monroe Doctrine by asserting that it was the responsibility of the United States to keep order in the Caribbean and Central America. Such disorder existed in the area that European nations threatened to use force to protect their citizens there. Buchanan urged Congress to take action to keep order. Otherwise, he said Europeans would intervene in defiance of the Monroe Doctrine. The European nations did not follow through on their threats. The president eased international tensions by demonstrating to foreign rivals that the United States was determined to protect our interests in the Western Hemisphere. Buchanan worked well with other heads of state with whom he had mutual respect. His aggressive and adventuresome foreign policy, particularly his goals of free seas and free trade, enhanced the United States in world opinion.

DOMESTIC PROGRAMS

Buchanan's administration was damaged by the Panic of 1857. The president did not deal effectively with this depression. Secretary of the Treasury Howell Cobb immediately concentrated government gold in New York City and won thanks from that city's merchants. However, the other departments curtailed public works, which brought much criticism from laborers and others for humanitarian reasons. Customs and land sales dropped. In his annual message of 1857, Buchanan announced reform, not relief. He said the government sympathized, but it could do nothing to relieve the suffering of individuals. The government would continue to pay its obligations in gold and silver, and it would continue public works in progress, but it would start no new projects. The president asked Congress to pass new bankruptcy, banking, and credit laws to prevent future periodic depressions. As for the innocent victims, said Buchanan, rugged individualism would triumph over adversity. The buoyancy of youth and the energy of the people would enable them to recover. Recovery eventually occurred, but not before thousands had suffered the misery of broken lives, starvation, and despair.

Buchanan's so-called reforms actually hurt rather than helped the economy. He promoted policies that were detrimental to the health, safety, and welfare of the people. Although the administration did not have enough money, he refused to raise taxes or seek any additional sources of revenue, other than his ill-fated proposal to raise tariffs. His refusal to help the poor in the Panic of 1857 seems unduly harsh to twentieth century Americans, but it was standard practice in the 1800s.

Buchanan supported freedom of speech and the press and the right of peaceful dissent. He supported freedom of religion and opposed bigotry. He opposed political parties that were prejudiced against non–Protestants, foreigners, and immigrants. He appreciated and respected white people for their personal qualities, regardless of their station in life. However, he condoned slavery and allowed mistreatment of slaves and Native Americans.

Buchanan's record of religious tolerance was challenged by an event that came to be known as the "Utah War" or the "Mormon War." In 1857 a dispute developed between federal judges and local officials. The Mormons refused to give up polygamy, and the land office declined to grant them a title to their lands. Buchanan sent fifteen hundred troops to Utah to enforce federal laws and appointed a non–Mormon to replace Brigham Young as governor. Young received his replacement with

courtesy, but said he would lead his people to Mexico rather than submit to military rule. A violent confrontation was avoided; Buchanan recalled the American troops and restored Young to his governorship.

The most serious problem facing Buchanan was the conflict over slavery. Two days after the president's inaugural address the Dred Scott decision was announced, denying citizenship to any person who had been a slave or was the descendant of a slave. Furthermore, the court declared the Missouri Compromise and all other acts of Congress restricting slavery were unconstitutional, and said that neither Congress nor state legislatures had any authority to restrict the spread of slavery. Buchanan welcomed this decision, saying that it left the question of slavery up to popular sovereignty, where it belonged.

Popular sovereignty was tested and found wanting in Kansas. In 1857 the proslavery group drew up the Lecompton constitution, which would have permitted slavery in that state, and submitted it to the voters for approval. The antislavery settlers refused to vote, and the proslavery forces won the election. Buchanan recommended that Congress accept this constitution. Senator Douglas, the original author of popular sovereignty, opposed it. Largely because of his influence, Congress rejected the proposed constitution. Angered by Buchanan's support of the Lecompton constitution, Northern voters turned strongly against the president. Opposition candidates won control of both houses in the mid-term elections of 1858.

In 1859 sectional tensions were further intensified when John Brown attacked the arsenal at Harpers Ferry, apparently intending to secure arms with which to lead a slave revolt. His subsequent hanging inspired abolitionists to renewed efforts to fight slavery. Ill feeling between North and South escalated.

Buchanan faced the greatest responsibilities of his presidency during his lame duck period. After Lincoln's election, South Carolina seceded from the Union. Six other Southern states soon followed, establishing the Confederate States of America. Buchanan declared that there was no right of secession, but that the Constitution provided no legal way to prevent it. He recommended constitutional revision in a way satisfactory to both North and South as the only way to prevent war. He felt that by remaining calm he could retain the loyalty of the eight slave states that had not yet seceded. Further, he hoped that if left alone the seven Confederate states would soon disagree among themselves and move toward reunion.

When South Carolina demanded that Union troops garrisoned at Fort Sumter be withdrawn, Buchanan refused. He sent the steamer *Star of the West* to reinforce the fort. South Carolina batteries opened fire on the vessel, forcing it to turn back. Buchanan refused to regard this as an act of war. He wished to keep the peace long enough that the new president would have a chance to find a solution. He continued to support the Crittenden Compromise and the call for peace congresses. He was successful in avoiding war through the completion of his term.

ADMINISTRATION AND INTERGOVERNMENTAL RELATIONS

As president, Buchanan developed a set of goals and objectives. In planning for their accomplishment, he depended too much on a hostile Congress. He engaged in long-term planning, but sometimes failed to visualize the problems to be overcome. The slavery issue distracted from everything else.

Buchanan organized the executive departments according to sound administrative principles. He established clear organizational patterns, communication channels, and procedures for accomplishing national goals and maintaining high standards of performance. Buchanan appointed some well-qualified persons to positions for which they were suited. He also made a few bad appointments. Among the strong, capable cabinet members were Secretary of the Treasury Howell Cobb and Attorney General Jeremiah Black. As a former secretary of state and an experienced diplomat, Buchanan ran the State Department himself, performing those duties with the assistance of John Appleton. The official head of the State Department was Lewis Cass, a former general and presidential candidate. A failed hero, re-

garded by some as lazy and senile, Cass was a mere figurehead in the role. However, he held views similar to those of Buchanan and provided some important support to the president in difficult cabinet meetings. As tensions between the sections intensified, cabinet members from the North and South bickered. After the secession of South Carolina, all the Southern members resigned and were replaced by men whose views were similar to the president's. During the last few months, the cabinet was unified.

There were communication problems throughout the Buchanan administration. As president, he reported to the people and Congress by annual addresses, but few people paid much attention to what he said. In Congress and in the press Buchanan was attacked by Republicans and by Democrats, by Northerners and by Southerners. The press continued printing false accusations against Buchanan for five years after he left office. He was blamed for causing the Civil War, which he tried so hard to prevent. In 1868 he wrote an autobiography in which he defended his administration. However, he is still underrated by many historians, at least partly because of his bad press.

Buchanan nominated and secured congressional approval of highly qualified candidates for judicial positions. He maintained the independence of the judiciary with mutual respect, even though much of the public lost confidence in the Supreme Court after the Dred Scott decision. All of the federal judges in South Carolina resigned when that state seceded from the Union.

In his inaugural address, Buchanan announced that he would serve only one term. This announcement plus the growing sectional differences weakened the Buchanan presidency. Douglas took over the leadership of the Democratic party and viciously attacked the president in order to promote his own bid for the presidency in 1860. In the mid-term election of 1858, Buchanan's supporters suffered heavy losses, and the Democrats lost control of the House of Representatives. Opposition from the Republicans and from within his own party made it difficult for the president to obtain congressional approval of his programs. Some of his foreign policies were successful due to bipartisan support, but others failed due to congressional opposition.

Buchanan put public interest ahead of self-interest. He faced opposition from sectional interest groups. The growing antagonism between North and South doomed many of his programs.

LEADERSHIP AND DECISION MAKING

Although not generally credited with great vision, Buchanan had a concept of what the nation and the world should be like. However, he was unable to conceive a strategy for achieving his goals. He left too much to Congress, which failed to take necessary action. Buchanan was unable to unify the nation against rising sectionalism and extremism.

Due to extremism on the slavery issue, Buchanan was unable to persuade Congress to follow him. He was a Unionist and supported national rather than sectional views, whereas Congress was dominated by sectionalism. He used all of his powers of persuasion to avoid the Civil War until after his term ended.

The president's ability to maintain public confidence was challenged by the Panic of 1857, by Bleeding Kansas, by the Dred Scott decision, by the Lincoln-Douglas debates (which further enflamed public opinion), by John Brown's raid at Harpers Ferry and by the secession of South Carolina. Through all these events, Buchanan kept the peace.

Buchanan led his executive departments to productive efforts, except for dealing with the Panic of 1857, until things fell apart after Lincoln's election in November 1860. By his personal example, Buchanan inspired his personnel. He worked hard and was devoted to duty. With the exception of Cass, Buchanan set high standards for his appointees as he did for himself.

Before making a final decision Buchanan usually weighed various alternatives and made an informed judgment about the consequences of each action. He seldom acted too hastily, but perhaps did so in the Mormon affair. Buchanan had a knowledge and understanding of history. He learned from his own mistakes. His natural intelligence was abetted by wisdom acquired from many years of experience in government.

Buchanan was willing to compromise. He was successful in obtaining passage of the English Bill, a compromise that ended bloodshed in Kansas. He favored the Crittenden Compromise as an attempt to solve the slavery problem. Buchanan urged Congress to propose constitutional amendments or to call a constitutional convention to avoid civil war. He endorsed the recommendations of the Virginia Convention.

Despite what some critics have said, Buchanan could make hard decisions. He was calm in emergencies and always in control of himself. The charge that he vacillated during his lame-duck stage is grossly unfair. During that period he worked ceaselessly in an effort to keep the peace.

PERSONAL QUALITIES

Buchanan conducted himself with the dignity that his office required. Because of his strong foreign policy, he increased the respect accorded to the presidency by people abroad. However, because of his inability to prevent sectional antagonism from increasing, he and his office received less respect at home. Buchanan failed to convince people that he had their best interests in mind; many people misunderstood him and resented his domestic policies. The presidency was a thankless job for Buchanan.

As a strict constructionist, Buchanan supported the separation of powers between the branches of government. As he interpreted the Constitution, Congress rather than the president should take the lead in domestic matters. According to his view, Congress should propose and enact the laws; it was the duty of the president to execute them. In his annual address, he placed squarely on the shoulders of Congress the responsibility of solving the nation's problems, thus weakening the power of the presidency. Nevertheless, he did take firm action in several instances, especially in the realm of foreign affairs.

Buchanan received input from all segments of the public. A bachelor, he took daily evening strolls about Washington and frequently talked with people he met. Each week he gave a small dinner for 15 people and a state dinner for 30 guests. He spoke to the people in his inaugural address, in his annual address, and in a special speech after South Carolina's secession.

As president, Buchanan acted on a firm set of moral values and principles. He could be trusted, his word was good, and he kept his promises. He was wedded to the Constitution. As the Constitution condoned slavery, so did he. He believed that a constitutional republic was man's greatest creative invention in government. He believed that man's actions should be controlled by his intellect, not by emotions. He acted on the belief that a public office is a public trust and never in any way used his office to benefit himself financially at the expense of the public. He was investigated by a committee of a hostile Congress, which could find no violations of law or propriety.

Throughout his life Buchanan exhibited a high standard of personal morality. He had mental toughness and moral stamina, He was devoted to duty, tenacious of principle, and was always in control of himself. Buchanan was a man of unimpeachable honesty, of highest patriotism, and considerable ability.

OVERALL ASSESSMENT

In less troubled times his moral character, the breadth of his legal knowledge, and his vast experience would have given Buchanan a chance to be an excellent president. However, the times in which he served were too much for him. He achieved considerable success in foreign relations, but was unable to solve the problems caused by slavery. To his credit, it must be said that no state seceded until after Lincoln was elected and the Civil War did not start while Buchanan was in office. He received 22 rating points and ranks 25th among the presidents.

ABRAHAM LINCOLN
1861–65

	RATING POINTS	RANK
FOREIGN RELATIONS	10	18 tie
DOMESTIC PROGRAMS	17	2 tie
ADMINISTRATION	12	6 tie
LEADERSHIP	20	1 tie
PERSONAL QUALITIES	19	1
OVERALL ASSESSMENT	78	1

BACKGROUND

Abraham Lincoln was born February 12, 1809, in a log cabin near Hodgenville, Kentucky. The Lincolns moved to Indiana in 1816 and to Illinois in 1830. At the age of 22, Abe set out on his own in New Salem. Mostly self-educated, Lincoln attended school no more than a year in his entire youth, but he developed a love of books.

In 1831 Lincoln became a clerk in a store in New Salem. After serving briefly in the Black Hawk War, he became partners in a general store in New Salem, but business deteriorated and the partnership was soon dissolved. For the next three years he served as New Salem postmaster. In 1834 Lincoln was elected to the first of his four terms in the state legislature. About this time he began the study of law. In 1837 he moved to Springfield, becoming a partner in a law office.

In 1846 Lincoln was elected to Congress. Because of his opposition to the Mexican war, he was not nominated for a second term. He re-turned to the practice of law in Springfield and declined appointments as secretary and as governor of the Oregon Territory. In 1854 he became the leader in Illinois of the opposition to the Kansas-Nebraska Act, sponsored by Democratic Senator Stephen A. Douglas. Lincoln was elected to a fifth term in the Illinois state legislature, but resigned shortly thereafter to seek unsuccessfully a seat in the U.S. Senate.

In 1856 Lincoln joined the new Republican party. At the party's first national convention, Lincoln's name was put in nomination as Illinois's favorite son candidate for vice president. He received 110 votes on the first ballot. His supporters switched to William L. Dayton on the next ballot. Lincoln campaigned hard for the unsuccessful Fremont-Dayton ticket, making more than fifty speeches throughout Illinois.

In 1858 the Illinois Republican convention nominated Lincoln to run for the U.S. Senate against Douglas, the Democratic incumbent. Lincoln gained national attention with his acceptance speech in which he said: "A house divided against itself cannot stand. I believe this government cannot endure permanently half slave and half free." The famous Lincoln-Douglas debates followed. Although the Illinois legislature elected Douglas, the debates pushed Lincoln into the forefront of national politics as one of the leading spokesmen for the Republican party.

NOMINATION AND ELECTION

People began talking about Lincoln as a potential presidential candidate, and he was endorsed as a favorite son by the Illinois state Republican convention. When the national convention met in Chicago, William H. Seward was the front-runner. The galleries were packed with Lincoln supporters and Lincoln's managers worked feverishly behind the scenes to line up uncommitted delegates and to secure promises from supporters of other favorite sons to switch to Lincoln on the second or third ballot. As expected, Seward led on the first ballot and Lincoln was second. On the second ballot Seward still led, but Lincoln was close behind. On the third ballot Lincoln surged into the lead and states rushed to join the bandwagon, making his nomination unanimous. Hannibal Hamlin was chosen as the vice-presidential candidate.

The Democratic convention was unable to select a candidate as most of the Southern delegates walked out in protest to the platform endorsing popular sovereignty. The Democrats tried again, and again many Southern delegates walked out, making it impossible for any candidate to receive the two-thirds majority required by party rules. A motion was passed making two-thirds of those present and voting sufficient for nomination. Douglas then won the nomination. The Southern delegates met separately and nominated John C. Breckenridge for the presidency, giving the Democrats two sets of candidates. Meanwhile, remnants of the old Whigs and Know-Nothings formed the Constitutional Union party and nominated John Bell for the presidency.

With the Democratic party split, Lincoln felt confident of victory. He stayed home in Springfield, received hundreds of visitors, and refused to discuss the issues. Douglas campaigned vigorously for popular sovereignty and

warned that a Lincoln victory would mean secession of the South. Breckenridge was the proslavery candidate, supporting the Dred Scott decision. The Bell Ringers, supporting Bell, pledged themselves to preserving the Union and constitutional government.

Lincoln received a plurality of the popular vote, but was far short of a majority. Douglas was second, Breckenridge third, and Bell fourth. Lincoln received 180 electoral votes, not one of them from the South. Breckenridge carried eleven of the fifteen slave states for 72 electoral votes. Bell won three states with 39 electoral votes. Douglas, despite coming in second in the popular vote, carried only one state and received 12 electoral votes.

In 1864 with the Civil War going badly for the North, Lincoln's chances of re-election did not appear bright. A group of Radical Republicans held an Independent Republican national convention and nominated John C. Fremont for the presidency on a platform of more aggressive conduct of the war and continuation of the one-term tradition for presidents which had existed for the last three decades. Fremont later withdrew to support Lincoln. Despite bitter opposition to Lincoln by some Republicans, he easily won his party's nomination for a second term at the regular Republican convention, receiving the votes of all states but one. In order to broaden its appeal, this convention styled itself the National Union convention. Andrew Johnson, a Tennessee Democrat who remained loyal to the Union, was selected as the vice-presidential candidate.

Convinced that the North could not win the war, the Democrats adopted a peace platform. They nominated General George B. McClellan, who accepted the nomination but rejected the platform. Within a few days, the fortunes of war changed dramatically. General Sherman took Atlanta, Admiral Farragut was victorious at Mobile, and General Sheridan drove the Confederates from the Shenandoah Valley. These developments knocked the props out from under the Democratic campaign.

Lincoln won easily. The soldier vote was counted separately, with Lincoln winning it by a huge margin. Lincoln carried 22 states with 212 electoral votes. McClellan received only 21 votes from three states.

FOREIGN RELATIONS

Lincoln avoided war with England and France over the *Trent* affair by releasing James Mason and John Slidell, diplomats of the Confederate States of America, who had been seized and removed from a neutral ship by a United States sloop of war. Another British ship, the *Peterhoff*, while bound for Mexico was seized by the United States for supposedly carrying contraband. Again the president averted war with England by releasing the ship and crew. In both episodes the force used had neither been authorized nor known in advance by Lincoln. These actions were violations of international law, and the president took the necessary action to correct the wrongs. Military force used in our Civil War promoted our long-term interests abroad by showing our strength and resolve and by demonstrating that democracy and freedom can survive.

During Lincoln's administration there were no foreign wars involving the United States. The president was not involved in international peacekeeping. Lincoln could have prevented the Civil War only by accepting the dissolution of the Union, which he was unwilling to do. He insisted on sending provisions to Fort Sumter, where the first shot were fired by the South.

Lincoln recommended diplomatic recognition of Haiti and Liberia, nations governed by black people, promoting future emancipation in the United States and encouraging democracy abroad. However, he also recognized the Maximilian government in Mexico. Archduke Ferdinand Maximilian accepted the throne of Mexico as a puppet of Napoleon III of France. Lincoln permitted this violation of the Monroe Doctrine because we were involved in the Civil War. Under the circumstances, he was powerless to prevent it.

On the seas the president acted consistently to deter our international rivals. The blockade of the Confederate States showed our strength. Although it harmed world trade and the economies of Britain and France by causing a shortage of cotton for their industries, it was necessary and justified by the higher priority of the war. Although Lincoln had campaigned for a high tariff, the war took his attention away from such issues as the tariff or the promotion of economic welfare abroad. Tariff rates were increased during his administration, but more as a revenue-raising measure than for protection.

Lincoln eased tensions with Great Britain by sending private citizens to England to win people over to the Union side. In addition, he used the White House as a pulpit to speak out to the common people of England. His actions after the *Trent* and *Peterhoff* affairs also eased international tensions. World opinion shifted in our favor. After military successes and the Emancipation Proclamation, Lincoln's administration enhanced world opinion of the United States.

DOMESTIC PROGRAMS

In order to pay for the war the government raised taxes, sold bonds, and printed paper money. On the tax front, it increased tariffs, levied sales taxes, and taxed incomes above a certain level. For the first time since 1817 taxes were levied on domestic producers and consumers. The Internal Revenue Act of 1861 levied an income tax for the first time in the nation's history. Although the income tax was declared unconstitutional, it set a precedent for the nation's twentieth century tax structure.

The National Banking Act established for the first time a national currency and permitted a network of national banks. In order for a bank to be chartered, it was required to purchase United States bonds and deposit them in Washington. Then the bank would be allowed to issue notes up to ninety percent of the value of the bonds. This procedure raised funds for the government's war effort, provided the public with safe currency, and allowed the bankers to make a profit.

Before the taxes were collected and the bonds were sold, the government had to have ready money. Its only source was to print paper money called greenbacks, which were not based on gold or silver in the treasury. This led to inflation and caused problems in the future, but it was essential at the time. Altogether about $450 million dollars were issued in greenbacks, while taxes brought in about $667 million and over $2 billion were raised through the sale of bonds.

The war acted as a stimulus to industry in the North. Currency reform relieved the economic problems of the West. Lincoln believed that laborers and farmers should benefit from improvements in the economy. The department of agriculture and land-grant colleges were created. The Homestead Act promoted ownership of family farms, helping in the settlement of the Great Plains. Lincoln believed slavery should be kept out of the territories so the poor, the unemployed, immigrants, and others wanting to better themselves would have more opportunities. Strongly pro-labor in his views, Lincoln supported the right to strike. He favored broad immigration.

Prior to his presidency, Lincoln had favored federal support for improvements of roads, canals, and rivers. During his administration the war took a higher priority, and internal improvements unrelated to the war effort were put on hold.

Lincoln helped end slavery by issuing the Emancipation Proclamation and by proposing the Thirteenth Amendment to the Constitution. He approved congressional bills for the desegregation of the horse-drawn streetcars in Washington and for the acceptance of African-American witnesses in federal courts. He accepted a black ambassador from Haiti. In his last public address, Lincoln urged immediate suffrage for educated African-Americans and for African-American soldiers. This was a small first step leading toward universal suffrage for all Americans. It represented a significant change in Lincoln, who had earlier opposed social and political equality for Negroes. He established the Freedman's Bureau to promote the welfare of ex-slaves. He put down a Sioux uprising in Minnesota. Of 303 Indians sentenced to die for their part in the action, Lincoln commuted the sentences of all but 39, one of whom he pardoned.

Using his war powers, the president by decree authorized the suspension of habeas corpus and declared martial law temporarily during the war. Freedom of speech was preserved, and no espionage or sedition law was passed. There was no real censorship. In the crisis of a civil war, the Constitution was stretched but not subverted. Lincoln supported freedom of religion. He refused to arrest those clergymen who preached against the war in their churches.

Lincoln's war powers were softened by his humane sympathy, his humor, his lawyer-like caution, his fairness toward his opponents, and his overall character. He grieved for the war dead on both sides. Lincoln granted many pardons and commutations for people who received the death penalty, especially for young soldiers convicted of sleeping on guard duty or of desertion. He felt there was too much killing in the war and that soldiers should not be executed.

ADMINISTRATION AND INTERGOVERNMENTAL RELATIONS

Lincoln's main goal was to save the Union by winning the war. A second objective, that of solving the problem of slavery, was subverted to the main goal. The planning of action on slavery depended upon the probable effects on the military and political situations.

At the start of the war, the executive departments, including the military, were not well organized. Sound organization came later. Lincoln called for volunteers for the military a number of times. Eventually, conscription was used to acquire sufficient troops to win the war. At the beginning of the war, the commanding generals were unsuitable. After Lincoln put General Grant in command, the Union went on to victory. As the war progressed toward its end, Lincoln became an outstanding leader in both civil and military matters, a fact that was not recognized until near the end of his presidency. Lincoln's own assertion that he did not control events, but events controlled him is unduly modest. His leadership produced great events.

As cabinet members Lincoln appointed leaders of each faction of the Republican party, men from each section of the country, and Democrats as well. Despite friction and animosity among its members, he skillfully kept this cabinet working. During his first term he sometimes acted without consulting his cabinet. For his second term he selected people who were not national leaders themselves, hoping he could work better with them.

Aside from necessary wartime secrecy, Lincoln maintained effective two-way communication with employees, the army and the navy, and the public. Facing a real national emergency, Lincoln acquired the funds necessary to increase expenditures as needed. A great administrator, Lincoln accomplished his goals.

In Congress, the president's own party was made up of conservative Republicans, Radical Republicans, former Democrats, and former Whigs. A master politician, Lincoln usually maintained the support of this party and all the factions in it, although the Radical Republicans attempted to depose him in the summer of 1864. The Democratic party split into those who supported Lincoln and the war and those who opposed both. Lincoln secured enough bipartisan support to achieve most of his war policies, as well as his foreign policies and domestic programs.

Lincoln ignored a ruling by Chief Justice Roger B. Taney about suspending the writ of habeas corpus. As a wartime president he usurped both judicial and legislative functions during the national emergency. After Taney's death, Lincoln appointed Salmon P. Chase as Chief Justice. During his presidency, Lincoln also appointed four associate justices to the Supreme Court, including both conservatives and liberals.

LEADERSHIP

Lincoln was one of the greatest leaders in American history. Through his personal example, his speeches, and his writings Lincoln inspired the people to an all-out effort to win the war. He was charismatic as an ugly, awkward, plain-spoken story teller and frontiersman. The people viewed him with respect and were willing to follow him. Not since Andrew Jackson had a president had this relationship with the common people. Lincoln was able to persuade others to follow him by convincing them that his views on the Union and on slavery were right. During a hard war, he maintained public confidence. He was re-elected to a second term by a large margin. The president set high standards for himself and others. He removed generals from their commands for

poor performance and kept searching until he found the right military commanders.

One step ahead of the great body of political opinion, Lincoln always led the way. As president, a hard-headed realist and great pragmatist, he had a concept of what the nation and the world should be like. Thinking ahead, he moved the country one step at a time from where it was toward what it ought to be. Each step paved the way for the next one.

Before making a decision Lincoln weighed alternatives and considered consequences. He believed that for great causes, great risks should be taken. Lincoln had the ability for intense application and clear insight, which he applied successfully to military affairs as well as to politics. He possessed a quick mind, which showed in his wit and humor. The Emancipation Proclamation was a product not only of courage and daring but also of considerable ingenuity.

In order to achieve his overriding objective of saving the Union, Lincoln for a long time was willing to accept any honorable compromise. However, he rejected the Crittenden Compromise. He felt that the nation had been troubled too long on the question of slavery and that the time had come to take a stand for what is right. No compromise could be a cure. After Fort Sumter there were no acceptable alternatives to war. During the war, Lincoln faced many tough decisions. Although he agonized over them throughout many a sleepless night, he made them promptly and fairly.

PERSONAL QUALITIES

In the area of Personal Qualities, Lincoln was our highest ranking chief executive with a mark of nineteen points. For a review of this area, see the Criteria and Ratings section of this book.

FINAL DAYS

On the evening of April 14, 1865, five days after Lee surrendered to Grant at Appomattox Court House, Lincoln attended a performance of a play at Ford's Theatre in Washington. A Southern sympathizer named John Wilkes Booth entered the rear of the president's box and shot him in the back of the head. Lincoln was carried, unconscious, across the street to a boarding house. He died the next day.

After the crime, Booth leaped down upon the stage. His spurs caught on an American flag and he tripped, breaking his leg. He limped across the stage and out the back to a waiting horse. He fled, but was pursued by federal troops and trapped in a Virginia barn, which was set afire. Booth was shot, either by himself or one of the soldiers, and died on April 26. Four others were convicted and hanged for conspiracy in the assassination.

The slaying of Lincoln at the victorious end of the Civil War made him a martyr. His fame, nation-wide and world-wide, has lasted more than 130 years after his death and shows no signs of diminishing. He is remembered for preserving the Union, saving our democracy, and helping to end slavery. Most of all he is remembered for his humanity, his charity, and his inspiring words in the Gettysburg Address and his Second Inaugural Address. He is held in affectionate esteem along with George Washington as our greatest national heroes. Both are likely to live forever in the hearts of Americans and lovers of freedom everywhere.

OVERALL ASSESSMENT

Overall, Lincoln ranks as our greatest president. He scored 78 points on the 100-point scale. For a review of his accomplishments, see various parts of the Criteria and Ratings section.

ANDREW JOHNSON
1865–69

	RATING POINTS	RANK
FOREIGN RELATIONS	7	26 tie
DOMESTIC PROGRAMS	17	2 tie
ADMINISTRATION	–4	33 tie
LEADERSHIP	1	28
PERSONAL QUALITIES	11	15 tie
OVERALL ASSESSMENT	32	22 tie

BACKGROUND

Andrew Johnson was born in a log cottage in Raleigh, North Carolina, on December 29, 1808. His father died when Andrew was three. As his mother could not afford to send him to school, he never attended school a single day in his life. At the age of thirteen Andrew was apprenticed to a tailor. At work his foreman read to him and taught him the alphabet. He taught himself to read. In 1826 the family moved to Tennessee, and Andrew opened a tailor shop in Greeneville.

At the age of 19, Johnson was elected to the village council. After two years as alderman, he served as mayor for three years. A defender of the rights of the laboring man, Johnson served three terms in the Tennessee state legislature, ten years in the U.S. House of Representatives, one term as governor of Tennessee, and one term in the U.S. Senate. At the Democratic national convention in 1860, Johnson was Tennessee's favorite son candidate. However, he withdrew in favor of John C. Breckenridge.

After Lincoln's election, Johnson opposed secession and remained loyal to the Union. He remained in the Senate even after his state joined the Confederacy, the only Southern senator to do so. In 1862 President Lincoln appointed Johnson military governor of Tennessee.

NOMINATION AND ELECTION

In 1864 the Republican party was renamed the National Union party in a gesture of solidarity. Lincoln wished to replace his vice president, the radical Republican Hannibal Hamlin, with a war Democrat of vote-getting appeal. General Benjamin Butler was Lincoln's first choice, but Butler declined. Johnson was Lincoln's second choice. For details about the election of 1864, see the section on Abraham Lincoln.

Upon the death of Lincoln, Johnson became president. The assassination plot had included a plan to kill Johnson also, but the assigned assassin backed out and the vice president lived to succeed the fallen leader.

At the Democratic national convention in 1868 Johnson received the second highest number of votes on the first ballot, trailing George H. Pendleton. On the 22nd ballot the convention surprisingly nominated Horatio Seymour, who was not a candidate and did not want the nomination, which he accepted reluctantly.

FOREIGN RELATIONS

Foreign relations and domestic politics frequently intermix. Seldom was this truism more apparent than during the administration of Andrew Johnson. When Johnson became president, the Civil War was almost over. He soon ended it. In areas where the war had continued, surrenders were accepted and the fighting stopped. The peacekeeping about which the president was concerned most was within our own borders and did not involve other nations. Although riots occurred, civil war did not break out again.

Congress continued military rule of the South longer than was necessary, to the detriment of our national interests. Johnson removed the blockade, reopened Southern ports, and ended restrictions on trade by presidential proclamation. He attempted to lower tariffs, but Congress raised them over his opposition. He intended to return to the Southern states their civil government and their representation in Congress. These plans were thwarted by Radical Republicans, who controlled Congress.

In a ticklish international situation exacerbated by domestic politics, Johnson refused to send a warship to the island of Alta Velo off Santo Domingo. The island contained valuable guano deposits which had been exploited by Americans until stopped by Santo Domingo authorities. Managers of the president's impeachment trial attempted unsuccessfully to blackmail the president into armed intervention. Another potential problem arose when Irish Americans invaded Canada during the Fenian movement for the liberation of Ireland. They were driven back by the Canadians and sent home by federal authorities, avoiding any more warfare.

As soon as the Civil War ended, Johnson reasserted the Monroe Doctrine by sending troops to the Rio Grande. In 1866 the United States gave formal recognition to Mexican President Juarez. The French were expelled by U.S. diplomatic pressure in 1867. Maximilian was captured and executed, ending the last attempt by a European power to put a ruler on a throne in the Western Hemisphere.

Great Britain and the United States had differences over British neutrality during the war and the *Alabama* claims, which led to a treaty that the Senate refused to ratify. A resolution was offered to recognize for Abyssinia the same rights in their war with Great Britain that the British had recognized to the Confederacy.

The greatest foreign policy achievement of the Johnson administration was the purchase of Alaska. The ratification of the treaty by the Senate was accomplished through the efforts of Secretary of State Seward. Seward also negotiated a treaty with Denmark for the purchase of St. Thomas and St. John, but the treaty was smothered in the Senate committee on foreign relations.

Johnson told Congress it would soon become necessary for the United States to lend effective aid to the solution of political and social problems in Cuba. He recommended a reciprocity treaty with Hawaii as a guaranty of good will and forbearance, leading to voluntary admission to the Union. He vigorously asserted the Monroe Doctrine in the West Indies.

The French expulsion from Mexico showed our strength and determination. Johnson's foreign policy demonstrated to rivals that while we would protect our interests, we had no designs against them. Johnson was more popular abroad than at home because of the way he conducted foreign policy. His firm, but fair and peaceful, approach to international problems earned him respect abroad.

DOMESTIC PROGRAMS

Upon assumption of the presidency, Johnson spoke of the theme that dominated his career — devotion to the advancement and welfare of the people. He was concerned with the welfare of all the people, including the former slaves. He had promoted the passage of a homestead act in every term he served in Congress. Johnson supported family farms and opposed the aristocratic southern planters. He particularly wanted free land for the improvement and advancement of the poor whites of the South.

In order to keep inflation under control, Johnson gradually called in paper money. He encouraged economy in government spending, reducing the size of the army and navy in order to achieve savings. His tax policies placed the burden of taxation on those most able to pay. He recommended tax and tariff policies that would not bear unfairly on the poor, but would levy on accumulated wealth. He was able to get his tax program enacted because Congress concentrated its attention on defeating his tariff proposals.

Johnson opposed spending federal funds for internal improvements and thought improvements should be up to the states. As governor he had proposed state aid to education, but as president he did not favor federal aid to the public schools because of his states' rights views. In 1867 he appointed as the first U.S. Commissioner of Education Henry Barnard, one of the nation's greatest educational leaders of the nineteenth century.

In 1866 an Indian uprising occurred as railroad construction started on Sioux lands. Fierce hostility arose. The Sioux put under close siege the military posts which were intended to protect the route and annihilated a detachment of troops at Fort Philip Kearny. The conflagration spread terror among scattered ranches and mail stations of a wide region. All railroad construction in Nebraska had to be protected by the military. A peace commission was established and made peace with the Sioux by abandoning the army posts in their territories and changing the route of the railroad. Johnson deserves credit for his fair treatment of Native American concerns.

Johnson was a former slave owner and a Southerner, but slavery ended with the end of the war and the ratification of the Thirteenth Amendment. In his first State of the Union message, the president said that Negro suffrage should be left to the states, former slaves should be protected in all their liberties, in the right to work, to own property, and to receive just pay for their work. He opposed compulsory colonization but favored assisting those who wanted to emigrate. The two races, he

said, should make an effort to live side by side in a state of mutual benefit and good will.

Johnson supported freedom of speech and the press and the right of peaceful dissent. He supported freedom of religion and opposed bigotry. He vigorously opposed the Know Nothing movement and its prejudices against Catholics and foreigners. Johnson opposed injustices of the reconstruction era, the denial of habeas corpus and trial by jury. He opposed abuses under military rule. Most historians believe his vetoes of the Freedman's Bureau Bill and the Civil Rights Bills were based not on an anti–Negro bias but on a desire for reconciliation with the South.

ADMINISTRATION AND INTERGOVERNMENTAL RELATIONS

Johnson developed a set of goals and objectives during his first year in office. His main goals were to preserve the Union and the Constitution. He wanted to establish the nation intact as it was before the war, except for slavery. He wished to open a path to peace and unity. Because of congressional opposition, Johnson was unable to overcome the problems involved in moving the nation forward.

The Radical Republicans in the executive departments disrupted communication channels and the chain of command. Johnson failed to hold personnel responsible for producing results, and the legislative branch sabotaged the performance of the executive branch. Sometimes Johnson was unable to receive sufficient funds from Congress to carry out his programs.

Against the advice of many of his friends, Johnson kept Lincoln's cabinet. From the start there was friction in the cabinet. Secretary of War Edwin A. Stanton was the president's bane. Emotionally unstable, Stanton spied on the White House and other administration offices. When Johnson lifted martial law, Stanton countermanded the order. Before the New Orleans riots the governor of Louisiana wired Johnson for orders; Stanton pigeonholed the wire and did not show it to the president. Two hundred people were killed. When Johnson saw the wire, he blamed Stanton for the riots and those deaths. When the death penalties for the Lincoln assassination were carried out, Stanton tore out a page containing the clemency recommendation of the court on Mrs. Surratt's sentence. After her death, Stanton replaced the torn-out page. When Johnson discovered this, he asked for Stanton's resignation. Stanton refused to resign. The president suspended Stanton and General Grant was named secretary ad interim. The Senate ordered Stanton reinstated under the Tenure of Office Act. Grant broke his promise to Johnson and turned the office back to Stanton. Stanton continued issuing orders without the president's knowledge. Faced with an untenable situation, Johnson fired Stanton in violation of the Tenure of Office Act. This led to impeachment proceedings against Johnson by Congress for high crimes and misdemeanors. After the acquittal, Stanton, who had not yet vacated his office, resigned.

Johnson had communication problems with executive branch employees, the Congress, and the public. His inclination to speak extemporaneously got him into trouble time after time. His advisors urged him to speak only from a prepared, written speech. However, Johnson disregarded this advice. If he had an audience of two or more persons he would give a stump speech.

The president usually kept decisions to himself until he announced them. He did not confide much in anyone. In 1866 Johnson made a campaign trip around the country, breaking the precedent at that time. He made many errors and lost half his newspaper support. Distortions and lies about the president were published. Much later, during the impeachment trial, the president was able to communicate effectively his side of the case.

Following the war, there was a general breakdown in public morality and corruption was widespread. Commissioner of Internal Revenue E. A. Rollins was involved with the Whiskey Ring. Johnson asked for Rollins's resignation and got it. Rollins was indicted, but acquitted as the Whiskey Ring controlled the judge and jury.

Johnson had been elected on the Union ticket with Republican Lincoln. The Republicans were the majority party in both Houses of Congress. Thaddeus Stevens told Johnson during his first year to change his Reconstruction policy. Stevens claimed that only Congress could dictate the terms of Southern Reconstruction. The president replied that he acted under his powers as commander-in-chief and in credence to the constitutional requirement to guarantee to every state a republican form of government. Johnson then lost the support of Republicans in Congress. A power struggle developed between the presidency, which had grown much stronger during the war, and the legislative branch. The Radical Republicans wanted to continue military rule not only to punish the South but also to prevent the return of the Southern states with representation in Congress. Johnson would not compromise his principles and insisted on continuing Lincoln's mild reconstruction policies. The Radicals attempted to seize control by impeachment. Johnson was acquitted by one vote with seven Republicans voting for him along with all the Democrats on three of the eleven articles of impeachment. The Republicans then gave up, ending the trial. Johnson had defended the Constitution and the presidency, although he had been stripped of his powers by acts of Congress.

Johnson maintained independence of the judiciary branch with mutual respect between the president and the courts. Congress failed in its attempts to abolish the Supreme Court. Congress, by keeping military rule in the South over the opposition of the president, avoided habeas corpus and trial by jury long into peace time. Johnson made only one nomination to the Supreme Court, and this candidate failed to win confirmation by the Senate.

Johnson considered himself the president of the South as well as the North. He was a president of all the people. He supported the common man against special interests. He was always for the public interest ahead of self-interest. In his first proclamation of amnesty for Southerners he withheld pardons from fourteen classes of rebels, including high ranking military and naval officers, officers educated at West Point and Annapolis, and rebels who owned property valued at $20,000 or more. This was aimed at the aristocrats whom Johnson blamed for starting the war. The excluded persons could apply individually to the president for pardons. He felt that the common people of the South had been led into a war they really did not want by the aristocracy.

LEADERSHIP AND DECISION MAKING

Not a strong leader, Johnson lacked charisma and failed to inspire people through his speeches or writings. He allowed executive branch personnel — Grant and Stanton, for example — to exhibit inappropriate work behavior. Sometimes he could not persuade others to follow him, but in his impeachment trial seven of his political enemies were persuaded to vote for him. Johnson stated his principles and never wavered. An honest, dedicated and moral person, Johnson strengthened the presidency and our form of constitutional government by refusing to cave in to congressional pressure.

Johnson was not a visionary, nor a scholar. As president he had a concept of what the nation and the world should be like. He had only a few important principles: the welfare and improvement of the common people; the Constitution, with its checks and balances; and restoration rather than reconstruction of the South. The president held to his beliefs, never wavering, unwilling to compromise. He refused to be bribed or blackmailed. Johnson was unable to devise a strategy to implement his programs successfully.

The public's confidence in the presidency and in Congress was weakened by the deadlock between Johnson and the Radicals. However, after his acquittal in the impeachment trial, the stature of the presidency and confidence in the Constitution were restored. The president set high standards of performance for himself, but not for others; he allowed some members of his administration to engage in inappropriate behavior. He should have purged his administration of his enemies long before the Tenure of Office Act was passed.

Before making a final decision, Johnson weighed alternatives and took his time. Johnson made hard decisions. Even during his impeachment he remained calm and behaved appropriately. His weakness was his inability to take people into his confidence. His most important decisions were made alone without cabinet help. Self-educated and well-read, Johnson possessed keen intelligence and applied it to matters of state. In his interpersonal relations, however, he sometimes failed to use his good judgment. His intemperate outbursts gave ammunition that his opponents used against him.

PERSONAL QUALITIES

Johnson conducted himself with dignity except during some of his stump speeches. He was twice accused of giving speeches while drunk — at his inauguration as vice president and on Washington's birthday in 1866. He may have had too much to drink prior to his inaugural speech. If so, this was the only time. He was ill and drank some whiskey to brace himself for the inauguration. Johnson was always dignified while performing his duties.

The common people in both the North and the South usually supported Johnson and were proud of him as president. However, the opposition press printed distortions and lies about him and the unscrupulous Radicals in Congress verbally attacked him constantly. With all this propaganda and with public morality at a low point with widespread corruption, people felt less pride in themselves and their country. Most citizens and newspapers applauded Johnson's impeachment acquittal.

His successful defense of the presidency from the attempted takeover of the government by Congress increased the stature of the office. The defense team of lawyers outmatched, outmaneuvered, and outdebated the managers of impeachment. Johnson, through newspaper interviews, was able to make his side of the case available to the public. The office of the president received more respect at home and especially abroad.

By assuming enormous war powers, Lincoln had usurped from the other two branches. It was Johnson's intent to return war powers to Congress, the Courts, and especially to the states. He attempted to replace military rule with civil government and restore the seceded states to the Union. He felt that the Southern states had never left the Union during the Civil War and were still entitled to statehood. Congress usurped the president's powers — stripped him of all the power they could. Johnson fought Congress to defend the office from destruction, but the presidency was weakened temporarily.

Johnson tried to be the people's president, and the common people thought he was on their side. However, he was not popular enough with the leaders of either party to be renominated for president in 1868. Johnson believed the president should be accessible to any citizen, high or low, great or humble, with or without reason. Every day at certain hours his office was open to all who wanted to see him. Many of his visitors were former rebels seeking pardons. Johnson visited with each for a while and approved stacks of pardons for ordinary Southerners.

Johnson was one of the first presidents to go over the heads of Congress to appeal directly to the people. During the impeachment trial the senate gagged defense witnesses, and Johnson participated in newspaper interviews in order to present his side of the case. He spoke from the steps of the Capitol, criticizing the Joint Committee on Reconstruction. Accompanied by members of his cabinet and by General Grant and Admiral Farragut, he made a political tour of the country, speaking in several cities.

During his entire life, Johnson exhibited a high standard of personal and public morality. He was completely honest and never used his office for personal gain at the expense of the public. He acted consistently on a firm set of moral values and principles.

OVERALL ASSESSMENT

Of a possible 100 points, Johnson scored 32 on our rating system. He is tied for 22nd place among the 39 presidents rated. Johnson found himself in the difficult position of a Democrat, elected by Republicans, as Tyler had been a Democrat elected by Whigs some years earlier. Both men had troubles with Congress, with Johnson's problems being more serious. The power struggle between the president and Radicals in Congress dominated his administration.

ULYSSES SIMPSON GRANT

1869–77

	RATING POINTS	RANK
FOREIGN RELATIONS	–2	37
DOMESTIC PROGRAMS	–6	36
ADMINISTRATION	–13	39
LEADERSHIP	–12	39
PERSONAL QUALITIES	–9	38 tie
OVERALL ASSESSMENT	–42	39

BACKGROUND

Hiram Ulysses Grant was born April 27, 1822, in a two-room cabin at Point Pleasant, Ohio. In 1839 he received an appointment to the United States Military Academy, where his name was mistakenly listed as Ulysses Simpson Grant. The young man never corrected the error. In 1843 he graduated 21st in a class of 39. In 1845 he accompanied General Zachary Taylor to Texas and later participated in the invasion of Mexico. He was transferred to General Winfield Scott's army and went on the march to Mexico City. Under both generals he served with diligence and bravery, twice being cited for gallantry under fire.

After the Mexican War, Grant was stationed at various places, including an assignment on the West Coast. Unhappy and lonely, separated from his family, Grant became intemperate in his drinking. He received a reprimand and resigned from the army in 1854 to rejoin his wife and children. During the next six years, Grant failed at farming, selling real estate, and clerk-ing in a customs house. Disappointed and in financial straits, he obtained a job as a clerk in a Galena, Illinois, leather goods store owned by his two brothers.

When the Civil War broke out, Grant was appointed colonel, and was soon promoted to brigadier general and then to major general. Victories at Fort Henry, Fort Donelson, Shiloh, Vicksburg, and Chattanooga made him President Lincoln's favorite general. In the spring of 1864 Lincoln promoted him to lieutenant general and placed him in command of all Union armies. Under Grant's command, the tide of the war turned and the North went on to victory. He accepted General Lee's surrender at Appomattox Court House on April 9, 1865. After the war, Grant returned to Galena. In 1866 he was honored by Congress as general of the army, the first time this title had been awarded. In 1867-68 he served briefly as acting secretary of war.

NOMINATION AND ELECTION

Grant's lack of political experience did not deter the Republicans, who wanted a candidate who could win the presidency in 1868. As a popular war hero, Grant was a great favorite with the public. He had become estranged from President Johnson, calling for his impeachment, and favoring the Radicals' plan for reconstruction. During 1868 the popular clamor for him grew, and months before the Republican convention met it was obvious that he would be selected. No other candidate's name was presented, and Grant won the nomination by acclamation. Schuyler Colfax was selected as his running mate. Grant accepted the nomination with a short and simple speech. He endorsed the party platform, promised to administer the laws according to the popular will, and ended the address by saying, "Let us have peace," which then became the campaign slogan for the Republicans.

The Democrats nominated Horatio Seymour. Neither Grant nor Seymour participated in the campaign. After a slow start, enthusiasts for the two candidates campaigned with more than the usual mud slinging and name calling. Grant was called a butcher, a liar, a drunkard, a weather cock, and a puppet who lacked real ability or real character. On the other side Seymour was charged with having been disloyal during the war; it was said that his election would damage the nation.

Grant won in a landslide. He carried 26 states with 214 electoral votes to 8 states and 80 votes for Seymour.

In 1872 Grant was again nominated unanimously on the first ballot. Henry Wilson was named as his running mate. Liberal Republicans, opposed to Grant, held a separate convention and nominated Horace Greeley for president and B. Gratz Brown for vice president. The Democrats selected the Liberal Republican ticket as their nominees. At least seven other parties fielded candidates.

The election of 1872 featured negative campaigning. Greeley was ridiculed for such things as his appearance, career, vegetarianism, temperance, and spiritualism. Grant was attacked for corruption, nepotism, favoritism, and neglect of office. Grant's organization amassed a huge campaign chest, by the standards of the time. Funds were collected from Indian traders, contractors, the "Whiskey Ring," and holders of government offices.

Grant did not campaign. At first Greeley did not, either. In September he gave some speeches. Democratic politicians in Indiana asked him to stop speaking, as in their opinion he was doing more harm than good. He returned home.

This time Grant won by a larger margin than in 1868. Grant carried 33 states with 286 electoral votes. Greeley carried only six Southern or Border states. Three weeks after the election he died, heartbroken. The electoral votes from the states carried by Greeley were divided among four persons. Three votes for Greeley were not counted, as he was dead before the votes were cast.

FOREIGN RELATIONS

Most of Grant's foreign policy was delegated to a very capable secretary of state, Hamilton Fish. Successes were mainly due to Fish's action, and failures were usually caused by Grant's acting alone.

Perhaps Grant's greatest achievement as president was the Treaty of Washington with Great Britain, which settled the *Alabama* claims. The two nations agreed to submit the claims to international arbitration. The arbitration panel met in Geneva and awarded the United States $15.5 million. During his two terms, Grant avoided involvement in war. The United States stayed out of the Cuban Revolution. Grant prepared a proclamation according diplomatic recognition to the Cuban rebels. He signed it and sent it to Fish for countersigning and publishing. Knowing that the rebels had no organized government nor effective army, Fish suppressed the document.

Grant informed Germany that the United States would not tolerate intervention in the Venezuelan Revolution and offered Venezuela assistance to prevent the Dutch from using force against that South American nation. Grant's addition to the Monroe Doctrine was: "No territory on this continent shall be regarded as subject to transfer to a European power." The British and Spanish felt we had no designs against them and recognized Grant as a man of peace. By the end of his two terms, world public opinion held Grant in higher regard than did the domestic public.

Under Grant the army was used in domestic affairs — in the occupation of the defeated Confederacy to keep Republican state governments in power and in the West against Indians. The navy suffered from the low state of politics and business during the Grant years.

Grant tried and failed to annex Santo Domingo. A treaty was signed but not ratified by the Senate. Later, annexation by joint resolution failed. Senator Charles Sumner led the opposition to Santo Domingo annexation and exposed gigantic frauds in the annexation scheme. The people of Santo Domingo feared a takeover by the United States would be a detriment to their interests.

Throughout his two terms Grant favored a high protective tariff for the benefit of big business. On this issue Grant received the support of the Republican Congress. The Democrats, who took control of Congress in the 1874 midterm election, were unsuccessful in getting the tariff reduced. Grant's tariff policies hurt world trade and harmed people in other countries. On the other hand, Grant did sign a reciprocity treaty with Hawaii and opened Samoa to American shipping.

DOMESTIC PROGRAMS

Grant's fiscal policies during the Panic of 1873 were counterproductive. In his annual address that year, Grant urged economy in government spending. He stopped appropriations on public buildings not yet started. Public works were to be postponed until the country could afford them. The president wanted a return to specie payment, but not until a favorable balance of trade was reached. Grant proposed elasticity of currency. Next he wanted to prevent speculation.

Inflationists gained control of Congress over hard money advocates. Congress passed a bill that would increase currency, but Grant vetoed it. Grant halted internal improvements. Even during the depression, Grant had no poverty programs except those to help ex-slaves and Indians. He was more interested in aid to business than in helping the poor. He rewarded those who supported his policies. He promoted repressive tax policies, favoring tax breaks for the wealthy and opposing a tax on high incomes.

Grant used the powers of government to favor big business over common people, farmers, and workers. High freight and passenger rates were charged by the railroads, born in fraud and corruption. Farmers united through granges of the Patrons of Husbandry to oppose the railroads. Congress brought pressure on state legislatures to regulate railroad rates. Next Congress opposed the manufacturers and jobbers who sold farm machinery at inflated prices. In these endeavors Congress received no help from the president. In making a bid for the foreign vote, Grant sent a lengthy message to Congress against exploitation of newly arrived immigrants, but nothing was done to improve sanitary conditions of ships or to protect immigrants from being swindled.

Grant supported the right of ex-slaves to vote and hold office. Congress appropriated $2 million for Native Americans, but left no instructions as to how the funds were to be spent. At the suggestion of Secretary of the Interior Jacob Donelson Cox, Grant appointed a board of philanthropists to advise on Indian policy. Grant's program demonstrated his sincere desire to solve the Indians' economic difficulties, even though only six months previously he had wanted to transfer the Indian Bureau to the War Department. The scandals of the era included the corruption of some Indian agents, and Indian wars continued on the frontier. Nevertheless, some historians maintain that Grant had a benevolent attitude toward Native Americans.

However, the army showed no benevolence toward the Indians. After gold was discovered in the Black Hills in 1874, miners poured into the area, disregarding a treaty and violating the Indians' rights. Skirmishes broke out, and the army tried to round up the Sioux and place them on reservations. Under Crazy Horse and Sitting Bull the Indians resisted, leading to the battles of Rosebud and Little Big Horn.

The president proposed a constitutional amendment requiring each state to establish and maintain free public schools for all children, irrespective of sex, color, birthplace, or residence. The amendment would forbid the teaching of religious tenets in the schools, and no funds could be allocated for schools of religious denominations. This progressive and far-sighted proposal was ignored by Congress. One important advance in the fields of education, recreation, and conservation occurred during the Grant administration when Congress created Yellowstone National Park.

ADMINISTRATION AND INTERGOVERNMENTAL RELATIONS

Grant did not develop a set of goals and objectives and plan for their accomplishment. He was not able to engage in long term planning or to visualize problems to be overcome. In his inaugural address he spoke in generalities. He said he would not enforce policies against the will of the people. He spoke of the greatest good to the greatest number. Grant asserted independence from politicians and others because he did not seek the presidency and was elected by all the people. He spoke of executing laws and lowering the national debt. In his first annual message he recommended laws to return to coin payments, redemption of greenbacks, and refunding the debt. He read a section on foreign affairs written by the secretary of state and a report written by the secretary of the treasury.

The president permitted each department head to run his department, with very little oversight from the top. Grant withdrew into his shell and failed to give executive department personnel any definite directions. Two capable cabinet members — Hamilton Fish and George S. Boutwell — ran their departments well and overshadowed the president. Others were less capable, and Grant failed to hold them responsible for producing results.

Grant was accused of nepotism and favoritism in making appointments. Many of his appointees were unqualified and unsuited for their positions. Corruption and scandal tarred the Grant administration. There was an unusually high rate of turnover in the Grant cabinet. Twenty-five different individuals occupied the seven cabinet positions during his administration.

Grant wanted to cut spending. The Treasury Department reduced the national debt, which was regarded as a positive accomplishment. However, more spending was needed in order to pump up the economy following the Panic of 1873 and Grant was still cutting.

Although he wrote his own speeches, Grant did much less writing that did his enemies. He gave two inaugural addresses and annual addresses, but spoke in generalities and platitudes. Lack of adequate reporting to the people, Congress, and the press hurt his presidency.

The president lacked support from his own divided party in Congress and from the opposing Democrats. Grant vetoed 92 bills, far more than any previous president, more than all his predecessors combined. However, only four bills were passed over his veto. He did not have bipartisan foreign policy support. Grant was widely criticized for his judicial appointments. His most controversial appointee to the Supreme Court, Edwin M. Stanton, died only four days after having been appointed and never served on the court. On the other hand, Grant appointed as chief justice a competent jurist, Morrison R. Waite, who served in the position for 14 years.

Grant was so intent on rewarding friends and relatives and giving favors to businessmen that he failed sometimes to do what was best for the country. Because of the scandals and corruption associated with his administration, the president became so disrespected by public opinion that it was difficult for him to govern during his last two years in office.

LEADERSHIP AND DECISION MAKING

Grant had a colorless personality, devoid of dramatic characteristics, of dynamic force. He lacked ambition and was unimaginative, failing to inspire executive branch personnel to productive effort or to inspire the people to accomplish anything. Grant was not persuasive. The president, without ability to rally the people, was inarticulate when bold statements of purpose were needed. He was unable to restore confidence during the depression and after the scandals were revealed. Grant was not a visionary. He tried to achieve practical solutions to problems as they occurred. He was not the policy maker for his party and his administration was marked by divisiveness. During his administration the Republicans were split into three factions — the Radicals, the regulars, and the liberals, or reformers.

During his first term the president allowed members of his administration to engage in inappropriate behavior and failed to hold them responsible for competent work performance. Grant ousted 192 employees prior to the 1872 election due to corruption or inefficiency based on departmental investigations. These investigations were ordered by Grant to weaken the Liberal Republican movement. Regardless of his motivation, Grant deserves credit for the housecleaning that resulted. He really wanted honesty and efficiency in government. However, in his second term the same problem cropped up again. Due to laxity or naiveté he continued to make inappropriate appointments and to supervise inadequately. His second administration was riddled with corruption.

The president was unprepared by experience and was lacking in ability to analyze situations and develop strategy for civilian governance. Grant had become a war hero due to his military qualities and hammering techniques. His decisiveness and obstinacy brought him success in war. As president these qualities worked against him. He was unwilling to compromise. He made decisions quickly without considering alternatives. His decision making was not informed by a knowledge of history or by lessons learned from his mistakes. He made his decisions alone, keeping silent until he had made them, and not seeking advice from competent and unbiased counselors. Grant's military education and experience did not equip him with enough political problem-solving skills to be a successful president. Grant made hard decisions. He handled emergencies well, remaining calm. In this way his army experience was helpful. Overall though, his military leadership did not translate into political skill or effective civilian governance.

PERSONAL QUALITIES

On Grant's inauguration day he refused to ride to the ceremonies with the outgoing president, Andrew Johnson, because of personal animosity between them. Otherwise, Grant conducted himself appropriately as far as manners are concerned. He disdained ceremony, but was polite and respectful to visitors. Rumors of his alleged drunkenness while president were unfounded.

Grant's chief weakness as president was his deplorable judgment of character. Many of his associates were unscrupulous men intent on enriching themselves, and a number of them were unethical and dishonest. The president was manipulated by grafters. He was incredibly naive. Personally honest, he did not realize the evil done by his close associates. Grant's second term was labeled the "nadir of national disgrace." After a depression and scandals, people were ashamed of him. The office of the president lost prestige due to Grant's actions. The presidency was weakened during Grant's administration, not only because of the scandals but also because of Grant's failure to provide leadership. To the detriment of the nation, much of his power was usurped by Radicals in Congress.

Public opinion of Grant plummeted during his second term. This was due not only to the events of his administration, but also partly because of his personality. Although the White House was open socially for two hours every other Thursday night. Grant had a submerged personality and shrank from contacts. The president received input in silence. Often the person speaking to him mistook his silence for approval. Most input was not even considered by the president. As far as formal communications go, Grant spoke at two inaugurals and sent annual addresses to Congress.

Critics charged that the president could not be trusted to keep his word. As examples they cited his turning the office of secretary of war over to Stanton and his failure to follow through on a campaign promise regarding civil service reform. He was also accused of abandoning his moral principles in situations involving his friends. Whenever one of his close associates was caught in wrongdoing, the president was often the first to shield the scoundrel. Grant never took bribes, but he accepted expensive gifts from people when he should not have done so for the sake of appearances. He allowed friendship to influence decisions. However, he stopped James Fisk, Jr., and Jay Gould from cornering the gold market, even though they had been among the principal fund-raisers for his presidential campaign.

Grant was not proven personally guilty of any of the scandals of his administration. His private secretary, Orville Babcock, and two cabinet members, W. W. Belknap and W. A. Richardson, were caught and had to resign.

Many other of his appointees in sub-cabinet level positions were involved, as were many leading businessmen and some members of Congress. The president was a victim, more than an instigator, of the dishonesty and unethical behavior with which his administration is tarred.

OVERALL ASSESSMENT

Grant was our least successful president, receiving negative scores in every area. His total score was minus 42 points, ranking him in last place by a large margin.

RUTHERFORD B. HAYES

1877–81

	RATING POINTS	RANK
FOREIGN RELATIONS	8	21 tie
DOMESTIC PROGRAMS	4	23
ADMINISTRATION	12	5 tie
LEADERSHIP	12	13 tie
PERSONAL QUALITIES	12	13 tie
OVERALL ASSESSMENT	48	14

BACKGROUND

Rutherford Birchard Hayes was born in Delaware, Ohio, on October 4, 1822. His father died before the future president was born. The boy was raised by his mother and her younger brother. Hayes was educated in private schools in Ohio and Connecticut. He graduated from Kenyon College at the head of his class and attended law school at Harvard University. Following his graduation from Harvard, Hayes began practicing law in Fremont, Ohio, moving to Cincinnati in 1849. In 1855 he was a delegate to the Republican state convention. In 1858 he was elected city solicitor of Cincinnati.

When the Civil War started, Hayes became a major in the Ohio volunteers. He was severely wounded in combat at South Mountain, after which he was promoted to colonel. Later he served in the Shenandoah Valley campaign. In 1863 he was promoted to brigadier general and in 1864 to major general of volunteers. While still in uniform, he received the Republican

nomination for Congress. He refused to return to Cincinnati to campaign. Nevertheless, he was handily elected. He did not resign from the army until after the end of the war. He took his seat in Congress and was re-elected in 1866.

In 1867, running on a platform of universal manhood suffrage, Hayes was elected governor of Ohio. He gave the state economical and honest government. He encouraged merit appointments, reduced the state debt, and promoted education, prison reform, and better treatment of the mentally ill. He served two terms. In 1872 he was a delegate to the Republican national convention, where he supported the renomination of President Grant. He was the Republican candidate for Congress in 1872, but lost in the general election. In 1875 he was again elected governor of Ohio.

NOMINATION AND ELECTION

Hayes's victory in the 1875 Ohio gubernatorial race brought him to the attention of national party leaders, who frequently mentioned him as a possible presidential nominee in 1876. When the Republican national convention met, however, Hayes was not the favorite. That role went to James G. Blaine, the former Speaker of the House of Representatives. The administration forces supported Roscoe Conkling, the New York political boss, while the reformers backed Benjamin H. Bristow, the secretary of the treasury and the prosecutor of the Whiskey Ring.

Robert G. Ingersoll nominated Blaine with an electrifying speech that threatened to stampede the convention into a first ballot selection of the Plumed Knight. But the lighting equipment to the hall gave out — the main gas line had been cut. The convention had to adjourn. When voting began the next morning, Blaine led on the early ballots, but was unable to command a majority. On the seventh ballot, Hayes received 384 votes, only 5 more than were needed, to 351 for Blaine. Representative William A. Wheeler of New York was chosen as the vice-presidential candidate.

The Democrats nominated Governor Samuel J. Tilden of New York for president and Thomas A. Hendricks as his running mate. Tilden, prosecutor of the Tweed Ring, had earned a reputation as a great reformer, and the Democrats made reform the main theme of the campaign. The nation had not yet recovered from the Panic of 1873, so the Democrats blamed the depression on the Republicans, but they dwelt chiefly on the scandals and waste in the Grant administration.

Both candidates favored hard money, civil service reform, and withdrawal of the last Federal troops from the South. The Republicans waved the bloody shirt, denouncing the Democrats for their stand during the Civil War. They emphasized Hayes's war record, which they contrasted to Tilden's civilian status during the conflict. The Republican press assailed Tilden's character unmercifully.

For the first time in the history of presidential elections, professional publicity men played a large part in the Democratic campaign. There was a literary bureau, a speakers' bureau, and a bureau of correspondence under the personal supervision of Tilden. Sensing they had a chance to win, the Democrats campaigned hard. On the other hand, Hayes remained silent on the issues of the campaign in order to keep the support of all factions of his party.

On election night Tilden was the apparent winner. Hayes went to bed believing that he had lost the election. However, four journalists sitting up in the offices of the *New York Times*, watching the returns in the early morning hours, realized the election hinged on three Southern states. Managing editor John C. Reid contacted the chairman of the Republican congressional committee, Zachariah Chandler. The two men evolved a plan to dispute enough electoral votes to let Hayes win. The canvassing boards in Florida, South Carolina, and Louisiana were controlled by Republicans. If Hayes could claim all nineteen votes from those three states, he would have a one-vote majority in the electoral college. Amid charges of bribery, falsifying returns, and other frauds the returning boards were persuaded to certify Republican victories in all three states.

When the electoral college met, not only the Republican electors from the three disputed states appeared, but the Democratic electors were there also. Another dispute arose in Oregon. The Democratic governor declared one of the Republican electors ineligible and replaced him with a Democrat. This left Hayes with 165 undisputed electoral votes to 184 for Tilden. With 185 votes required for election, Hayes needed all 20. Which returns were to be considered valid? This decision was up to Congress, where the Senate had a Republican majority and the House a Democratic one. Unable to agree on how to handle the deadlock between the two houses, Congress appointed a special commission to make the decision. On the second of March, only two days before Inauguration Day, the commission delivered its verdict. By a straight party vote of eight to seven, all Hayes electors were accepted, all Tilden electors rejected.

The Democrats were outraged at this development. For a time it appeared that the country might be plunged into another civil war, but Tilden refused to press the issue. It has been said that the Democrats accepted the decision only after they had been promised that Federal troops would be withdrawn from the last two carpetbag states. Hayes denied that he had any part in this bargain. Nevertheless, soon after his inauguration he gave the order to withdraw the troops, thus ending the era of Radical reconstruction.

The final official results show Hayes with 185 electoral votes from 21 states and Tilden with 184 votes from 17 states. In the popular vote Hayes received one-quarter of a million fewer votes than Tilden. Other candidates have received a plurality and lost, but Tilden remains the only presidential candidate to have received a majority of the popular vote and lost.

FOREIGN RELATIONS

Hayes was a man of peace during an age of war. The French attempt to build a canal across Central America was considered by Hayes to be a violation of the Monroe Doctrine. Hayes insisted that if a canal were to be built it must be under American control. War with France was avoided when the French project failed due to yellow fever and mismanagement. Hayes sent troops across the Mexican border to prevent raids by revolutionaries. The raids stopped when the United States recognized the government of Porfirio Diaz. Hayes used the military effectively to promote peace. He did, however, allow the navy to deteriorate badly. Hayes did not intervene in the Russo-Turkish War or the War of the Pacific between Chile and Bolivia.

The interests of the United States were promoted by Hayes's action in Mexico and his firmness on the Central American canal. Secretary of State William M. Evarts was keenly sensitive to all European motions in the direction of Latin America and protested loudly against alleged British encroachment in Guatemala. Hayes had no designs against foreign nations. Blaine's accusation that Hayes wanted to annex Mexico was false. During the Hayes administration there were no changes in the tariff. Secretary Evarts spoke aggressively, seeking foreign markets for surplus manufacturing goods, and pleased American businessmen by revitalizing the consular corps and initiating monthly consular reports that described overseas economies, customs, and governments. World opinion of the United States was enhanced by the actions of the Hayes administration.

DOMESTIC PROGRAMS

Hayes was a man of peace at home as well as abroad. He ended the military occupation of the South by his recall of troops in 1877. During the late 1870s, cattlemen and other groups fought for control of Lincoln County, New Mexico. Hayes ordered the combatants to stop fighting and appointed General Lew Wallace territorial governor. Wallace declared martial law and used troops to end the bloodshed, bringing the Lincoln County War to an end. The Hayes administration also ended, temporarily, a number of Indian wars. The Nez Percé War ended with the surrender of Chief Joseph only 40 miles short of an escape to Canada after a remarkable retreat of more than 1,000 miles.

Although modern historians are sympathetic to the Nez Percé, Hayes actually had a better record in dealing with Native Americans than most presidents in the decades of the 1860s to 1890s. Secretary of the Interior Carl Schurz encouraged more favorable treatment of the Indians and initiated a number of reforms. In the previous administration the Indian Commissioner had awarded contracts and purchased supplies with a disregard for business principles and common honesty. Manipulation and fraud were everywhere. Indian agents put their unqualified relatives on the payroll. During the Grant administration, Indians starved while contractors and agents divided profits. Schurz fired the Indian Commissioner, the chief clerk, and the worst of his subordinates. By completely reorganizing the Indian Bureau, Schurz restored honesty to the Indian service. Hayes's Indian policy included fair compensation for lands taken from the tribes, ownership of land by individual Indians, and industrial and general education, leading to eventual citizenship. By proclamation he ordered the removal of squatters from Indian Territory.

Hayes was a sound money man. He opposed Greenback and silver advocates. The Bland-Allison Act, requiring the federal government to purchase $2–$4 million dollars of silver monthly for coinage, was passed over his veto. It was intended to inflate the currency and thus help farmers and debtors. Prosperity returned late in the Hayes administration, ending the Panic of 1873. His fiscal policies could not be credited with the return of prosperity, which came in spite of them. In 1879 Hayes resumed payment of specie for greenbacks. This policy helped restore business confidence and is sometimes credited with helping business improve.

Hayes favored business interests over farmers and laborers. During a national strike of railroad workers, he issued proclamations against domestic violence and ordered federal troops to four states to suppress the strikes. During the Hayes administration, the economy of the United States completed the change from an agrarian society to an industrial one. The president seemed oblivious to the development of trusts and monopolies. Hayes failed to use the power of government to help the poor.

In some ways the Hayes administration was forward-looking. Secretary Schurz was the first strong conservationist to serve in a presidential cabinet. He tried to protect western timberlands from lumbermen who were destroying resources. Hayes asked Congress to appropriate funds to supplement state education budgets to promote public education. He called for a building for the Library of Congress and for the completion of the Washington monument.

Hayes supported freedom of speech and press and the right of peaceful dissent, but used the military against strikers. He supported freedom of religion and opposed religious bigotry, but he opposed the right of the Mormons to practice polygamy. Hayes was not prejudiced against any nationality. In 1878 the first Chinese embassy officials were received by the president. In 1879 he vetoed a Chinese Exclusion Act on the grounds that it violated a treaty between the United States and China. Secretary Evarts negotiated a new pact, the Treaty of 1880, restricting, but not banning altogether, future Chinese immigration.

Hayes did not disfavor any racial or ethnic group. He was in favor of the Fifteenth Amendment. However, Hayes withdrew the army of occupation and turned the former Rebel states over to local control. By not enforcing the Fifteenth Amendment, local officials returned the South to white supremacy. The rule by the freed slaves, led by

scalawags and carpetbaggers, was ended. Soon the ex-slaves were to lose virtually all of their civil rights, as the South adopted a policy of government by the whites and for the whites. This did not happen during the Hayes administration, though. He refused to sign bills withdrawing the federal marshals from the polls at Southern elections.

ADMINISTRATION AND INTERGOVERNMENTAL RELATIONS

The president's goals were to reform the governmental departments, to restore the Union, to end sectional hostilities, to set up a sound currency, to end the depression, to implement civil service reforms, and to eliminate corruption in government. Hayes successfully visualized how to accomplish most of his goals.

Hayes organized the executive departments and personnel according to sound administrative principles. Executive branch departments and agencies were well-administered by Hayes through capable and loyal department heads. Hayes instituted policies of reform, attacking graft that was firmly entrenched in America in 1877. He announced that efficient service should be the test for office holding. Job applicants were referred to department heads who were made responsible for the selection of their subordinates. This was a major reform in the history of the presidency. Earlier presidents had wasted an inordinate amount of time interviewing office seekers.

The president selected a strong, capable cabinet with the exception of Richard W. Thompson as secretary of the navy, who was fired for accepting a bribe. Hayes had three excellent cabinet members who performed outstanding work — Secretary of State W. M. Evarts, Secretary of the Treasury John Sherman, and Secretary of the Interior Carl Schurz. The New York Custom House had long been a scandal and a disgrace. Hayes appointed the Jay Commission to investigate, and it was discovered that 200 petty politicians, ward heelers to the Stalwart leader, Senator Roscoe Conkling, were paid by the Custom House without performing any work. Hayes ordered the useless men discharged and discontinued the system of rewarding ward heelers with jobs. He fired the three top officials at the Custom House, including the collector, Chester A. Arthur.

An honest person, Hayes eliminated the worst corruption in the executive branch. He assigned personnel to appropriate roles and did a good job of directing their work. He issued an executive order prohibiting electioneering by government officers and disallowing assessments for political purposes on government employees. To help prevent future corruption, he supported a proposed civil service system. However, the Congress refused to act on the proposal.

Hayes had not run for president as a reform candidate or communicated his liberal views to Stalwart leaders who helped win the election of 1876. After the New York Custom House firings, Conkling split with Hayes, dividing the Republican Party. The Stalwarts were completely surprised by Hayes, as were the people. Hayes communicated by inaugural address and annual addresses to Congress and the public. In the White House, Hayes received guests each night after dinner and until bedtime. He communicated his desire for honesty in government and peace in the land.

Sometimes Hayes had trouble getting ample funds from Congress. Appropriation bills often had amendments tacked on them that required vetoes. Hayes was a frugal president and prevented excessive or wasteful spending. The Stalwart faction of the Republican party was unable to control Hayes. They were unable to rule as an oligarchy because the Democrats, the opposition party, came to Hayes's support often enough to prevent it

Hayes appointed two justices of the Supreme Court — William B. Woods and John Marshall Harlan. Harlan was a liberal dissenter in some landmark cases — one in which the federal income tax was declared unconstitutional and in several civil rights cases. His tenure of 33 years on the court is one of the longest on record. He is regarded as among the outstanding jurists in the history of the court. In 1879 Hayes signed an act permitting qualified women members of the bar to practice before the Supreme Court.

One of the more important court decisions of the Hayes era was made by the U.S. District Court of Nebraska, which ruled that an Indian was a person within the meaning of the laws of the United States. This case arose after the government had transferred the Ponca Indians from Nebraska to Oklahoma in violation of a treaty. Suffering from disease and starvation, a band of Poncas under Chief Standing Bear tried to return to Nebraska and were arrested. Judge Dundy released Standing Bear and 25 followers. Hayes realized a mistake was made by violating the treaty and by arresting Standing Bear. He appointed a commission to deal with the matter.

Hayes put public interest ahead of self-interest. As to special interests, he favored business over labor and agriculture. The disputed election of 1876 cost Hayes much public respect. In the opinion of many people, the Republicans had stolen the election from the rightful winner, Tilden. Hayes insisted he had acted honorably in the matter. He was very proud of the statement from his inaugural address: "He serves his party best who serves his country best."

LEADERSHIP AND
DECISION MAKING

The president inspired and stimulated executive branch personnel to high levels of effort by his policies, his reforms, and his personal example. He failed to inspire the people due to his lack of charisma, drab appearance and personality, and poor public speaking capability. Hayes was persuasive enough to accomplish a great deal, but not enough to be renominated. He had said he would not be a candidate for reelection but he probably would have run again if there had been sufficient public demand. The president restored public confidence in the government after scandal and depression.

Hayes set high standards of performance for himself and others. Not since before Andrew Jackson had a president had a policy of basing job tenure on efficient service. He ran the government like a business, rather than as a patronage dispensing operation.

Hayes was a visionary and a reformer. He had a concept of what the nation should be like and did something about it. He fired corrupt government officials. He worked for civil service reform. Through Schurz he brought about reforms in the Indian service. He ended military rule in the South. He stood up to congressional usurpers and restored presidential power. He developed a strategy for getting the country from where it was to where it ought to be.

Cabinet meetings were pleasant, earnest, and efficient. The president listened to subordinates and weighed alternatives. There was not much arguing among Hayes's advisors. The president made business-like decisions. Hayes possessed and used a keen intelligence in solving problems. He did not compromise much. Hayes made some hard decisions when necessary. He vetoed 13 bills passed by Congress, only one of which was overridden. He acted calmly in emergencies.

PERSONAL QUALITIES

Hayes always conducted himself with dignity and never behaved inappropriately while president. He received respect both at home and abroad because of the caliber of person he was. Hayes made people proud of him by his reforms and accomplishments.

By winning back the power of the presidency from the congressional oligarchy, Hayes helped preserve our form of government. If his administration had been dominated by Congress, as had the two previous administrations, our national government could have been in effect converted to a parliamentary system, with the president being reduced to a mere figurehead.

By the end of his administration, people were beginning to think that the president was on their side. Hayes sought input from all segments of the public. He received guests at the White House and made a trip South, reaching out to those people now back in the Union. In 1880 he attended a reunion of his Civil War regiment in San Francisco, becoming the first president to visit the west coast while in office.

Hayes acted consistently on a firm set of moral values and principles. He could be trusted. His word was good; he kept his promises. Personally honest, Hayes never used his office in any way to his own benefit. Hayes exhibited a high standard of personal morality throughout his life. He was never involved in any public or private scandal, except the disputed election.

OVERALL ASSESSMENT

Hayes earned 48 points out of a possible 100, ranking him in a tie for fourteenth place among all presidents rated. He was a better president than is generally recognized. The fact that he served only one term probably hurt his ranking in the polls. Undoubtedly, he was downgraded by some poll participants for having assumed the presidency after an election they think Tilden should have won.

JAMES A. GARFIELD

1881

BACKGROUND

James Abram Garfield was born November 19, 1831, in a crude, one-room log cabin in Cuyahoga County, Ohio. His father died when the boy was 18 months old, and his mother supported the family by working the 30-acre farm. In his early teens, James began to do odd jobs during his vacations from the village school. During 1848-49 he attended Geauga Academy, working his way through school by doing carpentry work and teaching elementary school. From 1851 to 1854 he attended the Hiram Eclectic Institute, earning his way by working as a janitor and teacher. In 1854 he entered Williams College as a junior. He graduated with honors in 1856.

Garfield returned to Ohio as a professor at Hiram College. A year later, he became president of the college. During the Civil War, Garfield was commissioned as a lieutenant colonel in the Ohio volunteers. Upon winning a battle at Middle Creek, Kentucky, he was promoted to brigadier general, the youngest in the Union army. He won promotion to major general after distinguishing himself in the Battle of Chickamauga. While still in the army, he was elected to Congress in 1862. He resigned from the army and was re-elected to the House eight times. He served as chairman of the Appropri-

ations Committee and as a member of several other important committees. He supported the Reconstruction measures of the Radical Republicans and voted for the impeachment of President Andrew Johnson. He served on the commission that settled the disputed Hayes-Tilden election of 1876.

During the Hayes administration, Garfield became Republican floor leader in the House of Representatives. He mediated between the Stalwarts led by Roscoe Conkling and the Half-Breeds led by James G. Blaine. In 1880 he was elected to the U.S. Senate by the Ohio legislature, but before he could take his seat other events intervened.

NOMINATION AND ELECTION

Garfield was the leader of the Ohio delegation to the Republican national convention in 1880, which turned into a confrontation between the Stalwarts and the Half-Breeds. The Stalwarts wanted a third term for U.S. Grant. Conkling and his lieutenant, Chester Arthur, predicted Grant's nomination on the first ballot. Most other observers considered Blaine the front-runner.

On the first ballot Grant led Blaine by 20 votes. Twenty-seven more ballots were taken that day with little fluctuation in the totals. As a non-candidate, Garfield received no votes on the first ballot and only one vote on other early ballots. His boom started on the 34th ballot. On the 35th ballot he received 50 votes. State after state lined up behind the senator-elect from Ohio. Blaine's managers asked Conkling to switch from Grant to Blaine to stem the tide. Conkling angrily refused. The Stalwarts held fast, but Garfield was nominated on the 36th ballot. Conkling moved to make the nomination unanimous. In return, Conkling was given the right to name Garfield's running mate, and Arthur was nominated.

The Democrats nominated General Winfield Scott Hancock for president. The parties were about evenly divided in strength. It was difficult to identify a consistent Democratic or Republican position on any issue. The Republican party was badly divided. Stalwarts and Half-Breeds eyed each other with suspicion and jealousy. Garfield was the ideal candidate to heal party divisions. He lacked political convictions and tried to appeal to all factions. He was a party regular, a pragmatist, and had no enemies.

The campaign was a rather dull affair. The Democratic candidate, General Hancock, had an impeccable record, but was not particularly knowledgeable about political issues. Both major parties boasted of their candidates' war records, heroism, honesty, and integrity. Some excitement was injected into the campaign in late October when a New York weekly printed a forged letter allegedly signed by Garfield in which he advocated the importation of cheap Chinese labor. Although the letter was denounced as a fraud, the Democrats continued distributing thousands of copies. It almost cost Garfield the election.

In the popular vote Garfield edged Hancock by fewer than 10,000 votes. Each man carried 19 states. However, Garfield won the more populous states and received 214 electoral votes to 155 for his opponent.

ASSASSINATION AND AFTERMATH

On July 2, 1881, President Garfield entered a railroad station in Washington, intending to catch a train to New York. A small, shabbily dressed man suddenly appeared, drew a pistol, and shot the president in the back. As Garfield fell to the floor, a policeman seized the gunman, who said, "I did it and will go to jail for it. I am a Stalwart, and Arthur will be President."

The president received two gunshot wounds. One grazed his right arm, doing no serious damage. The other entered the lower back, deflected off a rib, and lodged near the pancreas. He was taken to the White House, where the doctors repeatedly probed the wound with bare fingers and unsterilized instruments in an effort to find the bullet. Three separate operations were performed to drain abscesses and remove bone fragments. Garfield contracted blood poisoning and by September 17 had developed broncho-pneumonia. He died two days later.

The assassin, Charles J. Guiteau, had supported Garfield in the election of 1880 and had sought a diplomatic post in Paris as a reward, but had been rebuffed. Although he claimed to be a Stalwart and a friend of Arthur, he had never been accepted by the Stalwarts as anything more than a hanger-on and was not regarded by Arthur as a friend. He pleaded not guilty by reason of insanity, but despite abundant evidence that he was mentally unbalanced, was found guilty. He was hanged on June 30, 1882.

CHESTER ALAN ARTHUR
1881–85

	RATING POINTS	RANK
FOREIGN RELATIONS	5	29 tie
DOMESTIC PROGRAMS	−1	29
ADMINISTRATION	−3	31 tie
LEADERSHIP	−7	36
PERSONAL QUALITIES	−4	37
OVERALL ASSESSMENT	−10	37

BACKGROUND

Chester Alan Arthur was born October 5, 1829, in a parsonage near North Fairfield, Vermont. He graduated from Union College in 1848, earning a Phi Beta Kappa key. Arthur taught school, studied law, and clerked in a law firm in New York City until he was admitted to the bar and became a partner in the firm. He entered politics and soon earned favor with the Whig boss of New York, Thurlow Weed, who recommended him for a position as engineer-in-chief on the governor's staff with the rank of brigadier general. During the Civil War, he was placed in charge of the Quartermaster General's office in New York City.

When Weed began collecting assessments from government employees, Arthur and his friend Thomas Murphy became collectors for the party. In 1869 Murphy made an arrangement with William Tweed to create the office of counsel to the New York City Tax Commission. The Democratic boss appointed the Republican Arthur to the high paying post. Tax levies were manipulated shamelessly by the Tweed Ring. What Arthur did for Tweed has never been learned, but Arthur became a wealthy man. In 1870 he resigned from the post and soon became one of Roscoe Conkling's lieutenants.

Conkling took control of the state Republican party when he won a Senate battle to confirm Murphy, who had been appointed by President Grant to be collector of the port of New York, one of the nation's greatest patronage plums. Murphy looted the custom house to line his own pockets so brazenly that he was forced out, but was allowed to name his own successor. He chose his close friend, Chet Arthur. As collector, Arthur took orders from Conkling. Despite the new Civil Service regulations, he found jobs for his friends, relatives, and persons favored by Conkling. One of Conkling's most effective spoilsmen, he gradually took charge of the day-to-day operations of the machine. Although assessments were illegal, Arthur secured vast sums through "voluntary contributions" for Grant's re-election campaign in 1872.

During the Hayes presidential campaign in 1876, Arthur's enforcement of voluntary contributions from customhouse employees was severe and ruthless. Despite Hayes's benefits from Arthur's actions, the new president called for civil service reform and started an investigation of the customhouses. Gross inefficiency and corruption were found. Theodore Roosevelt was chosen to fill Arthur's chair, but Arthur refused to resign, and the Conkling machine blocked Roosevelt's confirmation, allowing Arthur to retain the post. After Congress adjourned, Hayes suspended Arthur and appointed Edwin A. Merrit in his stead.

Arthur returned to the practice of law. In 1879 he became president of the Republican Central Committee in New York City and soon also became chairman of the state committee. He was serving in those capacities when the Republican convention met to nominate candidates for the 1880 election.

NOMINATION AND ELECTION

For details of the presidential nomination and election of 1880, see the entry on James A. Garfield.

Arthur was thrilled with the honor of being vice president, but he was little interested in the formal duties of the post, such as presiding over the Senate. What he wanted to do was parcel out government jobs to his and Conkling's friends. He was in New York trying to help Conkling win re-election to the Senate when Garfield was shot. As Garfield's condition deteriorated, Arthur was sounded out on the possibility of his assuming reins of the executive branch during the president's disability. He declined. On September 19, 1881, Garfield died. The next day Arthur took the oath of office.

Arthur wanted to be re-elected and worked toward that end, though not with his accustomed skill and vigor. He was suffering from Bright's disease, a then-fatal kidney ailment. Had the president retained his full political skills, he might have been able to combine forces with another candidate and prevent James G. Blaine from securing the 1884 presidential nomination. With no groundswell of popular support for his re-election, securing the nomination depended on the manipula-

tions of professional politicians, where he had generally fared so well. But not this time. On the fifth ballot Blaine was nominated.

FOREIGN RELATIONS

During the first few months of the Arthur administration, foreign relations were dominated by Secretary of State James G. Blaine, a holdover from the Garfield administration. Blaine resigned in December 1881 and was replaced by Frederick T. Frelinghuysen. At first Arthur approved Blaine's plan to call a Pan-American peace conference. After Frelinghuysen replaced Blaine and discovered some dubious activities by his predecessor, Arthur decided to submit the question of a peace conference to Congress, which took no action, so Arthur canceled the conference. Whether or not the proposed peace conference would have been helpful will never be known. By referring the matter to Congress, Arthur abdicated presidential responsibility for it.

Blaine protested a proposal for European arbitration of a boundary dispute between Colombia and Costa Rica. Blaine insisted that the United States was capable of leading Latin American nations to settle disputes among themselves. European powers seemed eager to intervene in such conflicts, in the hope of expanding their political and economic authority in the area. The United States sought to stop them by taking action to preserve peace and stability. Blaine pushed for the creation of a Central American union. He favored a canal across Nicaragua, under the control of the United States, and thought that a strong, unified government in Central America would increase its chances. Blaine intervened in a dispute between Guatemala and Mexico. When Mexico rejected mediation and sent troops to the area, Blaine warned Mexico that aggression against Guatemala would be deemed an unfriendly act by the United States. He instructed our minister in Mexico to use the influence of the United States to settle the dispute. Diplomatic relations with Mexico deteriorated, the dispute with Guatemala was not settled, and the war continued. Suspicions of American intentions in the struggle had become general.

When Frelinghuysen replaced Blaine, the

United States adopted a less aggressive policy toward our neighbors. Like Blaine, the new secretary wanted a canal across Nicaragua under U.S. control. He sent a letter to London urging total abrogation of the Clayton-Bulwar Treaty. Although Britain refused, Frelinghuysen negotiated a treaty with Nicaragua for joint control of a proposed canal. The Senate amended this treaty, requiring further negotiations. Before the process could be completed, Arthur's term expired. The Frelinghuysen treaty was then withdrawn by President Cleveland. The hopes for a Central American union were abandoned when Guatemala demanded our help against Mexico as a price for joining the union. Arthur refused to intervene in that war and also in a war between Peru and Chile.

The U.S. navy and merchant marine had deteriorated after the Civil War. Arthur called reconstruction of the navy of utmost importance to the national welfare. In 1883 Congress passed a bill authorizing four new ships, far fewer than were needed. Each of Arthur's annual messages to Congress contained strong appeals for funds to build ships. Early in 1885 Congress appropriated funds for four additional ships. Secretary of the Navy William Chandler ordered the establishment of the Naval War College and the Office of Naval Intelligence. He condemned patronage among navy yard personnel, and he made other reforms.

Election returns in November 1882 were seen as a mandate to cut tariffs. Eager to take credit for tariff revision and to prevent the newly elected Democratic majority in Congress from making deeper cuts, the Republicans tackled tariff revision. Arthur called for substantial reductions in tariff. However, Congress passed a bill calling for only minor reductions, and Arthur signed the measure without comment. A commercial treaty with Mexico, a treaty with Spain including a significant reduction in duties by both countries, and reciprocity treaties with the Dominican Republic and Hawaii were all worked out by the administration, but defeated in Congress.

DOMESTIC PROGRAMS

During the Arthur administration the country slowly drifted into an economic depression. There was no adequate diagnosis of the problem and no reliable prescription for its solution. Arthur proposed early retirement of silver certificates and abandoning the compulsory coinage of a fixed amount of specie.

Arthur urged revision of the homestead laws to protect ranchers from homesteaders. He opposed the fencing of public lands. A National Bureau of Labor and a Bureau of Animal Industry were established. The president favored the interests of business over those of laborers and big landowners over small farmers. Arthur vetoed a bill enacting safety and health standards for steamships bringing large numbers of immigrants to the United States. His objection was not to the purpose of the bill but to mistakes in its wording. After Congress revised the bill, he signed it. His conservative views on the role of government prevention him from taking other actions to promote the general welfare.

Arthur proposed the repeal of all internal revenue taxes, except on tobacco and liquor. Congress took no action. Even though there was a surplus, Congress refused to lower taxes. Neither Congress nor Arthur wanted to spend the surplus funds on internal improvements or welfare measures, believing these were not appropriate functions of the national government. Later the economic downturn helped reduce the surplus.

Arthur created a territorial government for Alaska. He vetoed a pork-barrel rivers and harbors bill, but Congress overrode the veto. His secretary of the interior called for the repeal of timber culture and preemption laws. Arthur was interested in preserving forests on the public domain and called unsuccessfully for legislation.

Arthur was unable to accept full Negro equality, but he showed sympathy toward blacks. He appointed several Negroes to government positions and called for federal aid to Negro education. He proposed legislation to prevent intrusion on land set aside for Indians. He outlined measures to help Indians become full citizens and gradually become absorbed into the mass of our citizens. Arthur's administration reflected the public opinion of his day, which was assimilating the Indians, making them into civilized farmers, abandoning Indian culture, and giving up tribal lands. He stressed the need for more Indian schools. He repeatedly called for a law permitting individual land ownership by Indians. Arthur sought to extend state and territorial laws to Indian reservations, so Indians could receive protection of law and maintain in court their rights of person and property. He attempted to protect Indian land from encroachment. He resisted pressure to open up the Indian Territory and protected Zuni land, but mistakenly opened Crow Creek Reservation in Dakota Territory.

In 1879 Hayes had vetoed a bill severely restricting Chinese immigration. It further denied citizenship to Chinese and required every Chinese already in this country to register at the United States Customhouse if he left and wished to return. Arthur vetoed it and Congress was unable to override the veto. After the bill was rewritten with a ten-year rather than twenty-year exclusion, Arthur signed it. Arthur asked Congress to suppress polygamy in the western territories. Otherwise, he had no particular record on civil liberties. He did little for the common people. He urged caution in granting pension claims of Union veterans and proposed an increase in the pension staff to increase its efficiency. He secured the construction of a building for the Library of Congress.

ADMINISTRATION AND INTERGOVERNMENTAL RELATIONS

Arthur had a set of goals and objectives, but he did not appear to have any viable plans to get his programs enacted. He did little in the way of establishing organizational patterns or communication channels. He did not establish procedures for maintaining high standards of performance.

To allay suspicion, Arthur wanted to retain Garfield's cabinet for a time. When the secretary of the treasury resigned, he nominated a Conkling supporter, Charles J. Folger, giving the Stalwarts control of the Treasury. When the attorney general resigned, Arthur nominated Benjamin Harris Brewster for the post. Although Brewster was associated with the Stalwart machine, he was well-qualified and an ad-

vocate of civil service reform. When Blaine resigned as secretary of state, Conkling expected to be appointed in his place, but Arthur knew public opinion would not tolerate the appointment. Instead he named Frelinghuysen, a well-known but respectable Stalwart from New Jersey. As other members of the Garfield cabinet resigned, Arthur replaced them with Stalwarts who had not been tarnished by scandal. From Garfield's cabinet only Secretary of War Robert Lincoln stayed on throughout the Arthur years.

Arthur stated that appointment should be made on fitness for office, tenure in office should be stable, and promotion as far as practicable filled by worthy and efficient employees. But he did not support the use of competitive examinations for appointments or promotions. On appointments Arthur usually heeded the advice of Republican Senators and Representatives from the areas where the appointments were to be made. He granted interviews to office seekers only three days a week, during stated hours. He said he would appoint no one not qualified and would remove no one except for cause and after the offender in question was told of the charges and given time to reply. He did not entirely live up to his promise, but his record as president was far better than could have been predicted from his past performance.

On the matter of political assessments the president declared that no one who declined to contribute would be subject to discharge, but that voluntary contributions were acceptable. At first Congress showed little interest in civil service reform. However, the midterm elections of 1882 convinced a majority of Congressmen from both parties, as well as the president, that there was a real political gain in supporting civil service reform. Arthur dropped his opposition to competitive exams. The Pendleton bill passed by huge margins and was signed by the president. It applied only to federal departments in Washington and to custom houses and post offices with more than fifty employees. Arthur's selections for the Civil Service Commission were acceptable to reformers. Arthur surprised his critics by administering the Pendleton Act effectively and efficiently.

Arthur did not like the work of being president. As collector he had delegated most of his duties to subordinates. As president he could not delegate as much, but he still delegated more than he should have. He failed to hold some of his subordinates to a high standard of performance. Arthur had a poor relationship with the press. He disliked talking to reporters. Without success, he asked them not to quote anything he said. Arthur felt it undignified to share his thoughts through any channel other than formal messages.

Because of the large surplus which he inherited, Arthur had ample funds in the Treasury, but he failed to get Congress to appropriate funds for many of his programs. In other cases the president failed to ask for appropriations because of his view of the limited role the government was supposed to play under the Constitution. Arthur was not successful in his dealings with Congress. Many of the president's proposals were ignored. Tariff revision was postponed, then so weakened as to be insignificant. No decision on presidential succession was made. Needed legislation regarding bankruptcy and relief for the Supreme Court failed to win consideration. In the Forty-Eighth Congress Democrats had a large majority in the House. Sometimes, though, Arthur had as much support from the Democrats as he did from the divided Republican party.

Some executive departments were well administered, with the Navy Department being an outstanding example. The Interior Department also made a good record. The State Department under Blaine pursued the secretary's agenda rather than the president's. The government failed to secure convictions in the star-route cases. When a vacancy occurred in the Supreme Court, Arthur nominated Conkling, but Conkling rejected the nomination. Two appointments were made to the High Court — Horace Gray and Samuel Blatchford — both competent, if undistinguished, jurists.

Arthur had an aristocratic disdain for the public. In return the public showed little respect for him. Arthur had a reputation of always acting in his own self-interest and in the interests of his Stalwart friends.

LEADERSHIP AND DECISION MAKING

Arthur was not an inspirational leader. His reputation as a venal member of the Conkling machine worked against him, as did his poor relations with the press. The fact that he put in short hours at work as president did not encourage government employees to a high level of effort. Although he did not engage in or permit inappropriate behavior, Arthur did not devote a lot of energy or forcefulness to the presidency. The star-route frauds involved among others the secretary of the Republican national committee, Senator Stephen Dorsey, a friend of the president. Even though government attorneys presented massive evidence, the defendants were acquitted. Although the president did nothing improper, critics blamed the administration for failing to get a conviction. Arthur's personal image was damaged unfairly by the trial.

Arthur was seldom able to persuade others to follow him by convincing them that his was the right course. Often the Congress rejected or ignored his proposals. Arthur was unable to communicate a vision of the ideal society. If he had a dream for the future of his country, he did not share it with the people. He had no ideological agenda. Conceptualization was not the president's strong point. He did not develop and communicate a strategy for moving the country forward. The country drifted through the Arthur years without a strong sense of direction from the president.

Very little information is available about the president's decision-making style. He had all of his papers burned before his death, and there are no reliable accounts by his associates. He probably made decisions on his own without consulting many people. There are no accounts of cabinet level discussions of issues.

Arthur was intelligent enough, but there is no evidence of careful application of disciplined intelligence to solving problems or making decisions. He did learn from his own mistakes and grew in stature during his presidency. He was overwilling to compromise. As a man of no ideological convictions and few principles, the idea of holding firm on principle seldom occurred to him. He did refuse to appoint Conkling to the position of secretary of state, but later nominated him for the Supreme Court. Arthur remained calm in emergencies. He postponed decisions whenever possible, and frequently abdicated his decision making authority to department heads or Congress.

PERSONAL QUALITIES

The people were not proud that a man such as Arthur was their president, even though he reformed himself in the executive office. He was unable to overcome memories of his background as a spoilsman. Because he had been a leader in the corrupt Stalwart faction in New York, working for the infamous Roscoe Conkling, and abusing his position at the custom house for the benefit of the Stalwarts, Arthur entered the presidency with an unsavory reputation. As president, however, he engaged in no corruption. Even so, his past somewhat tarnished the office of the president.

Arthur believed in the Whig theory of the presidency. He thought the chief executive was responsible only for the execution, not for the initiation of legislation. He allowed Congress, especially the Senate, to become the dominant branch of government. He thought it was enough that he should be a dignified representative of the American people and provide them with an honest and reasonably efficient administration.

Arthur did not make the people think that the presidency is the people's office, that he was on their side. He did make some proposals that he felt would help the situation of blacks and Native Americans, but never convinced the majority of the people that he cared about them. He should have communicated more regularly and openly with the public. Thrice a week he greeted the general public for an hour. After lunch he saw callers by appointment. There is no evidence that he gave any consideration to input from the public. Arthur would never have considered going over the heads of Congress to the people. He held himself aloof from the masses.

Although he never believed that a public office is a public trust, Arthur never used the presidency to enrich himself at the expense of the public. He had already done that in New York. Although Arthur exhibited a satisfactory level of morality as president, the prestige of the presidency was diminished somewhat by the low standards he had exhibited earlier.

OVERALL ASSESSMENT

Although Arthur did not turn out to be as bad a president as reformers feared, his performance left much to be desired. On our rating scale he received minus ten points and ranks 37th among the 39 presidents rated.

GROVER CLEVELAND

1884–89; 1893–97

	RATING POINTS	RANK
FOREIGN RELATIONS	8	21 tie
DOMESTIC PROGRAMS	3	24 tie
ADMINISTRATION	10	14
LEADERSHIP	0	29 tie
PERSONAL QUALITIES	11	15 tie
OVERALL ASSESSMENT	32	22 tie

BACKGROUND

Stephen Grover Cleveland was born on March 18, 1837, in a Presbyterian manse in Caldwell, New Jersey. While still a boy, he dropped his first name. At the age of 14 he quit school to work as a clerk in a general store. For a while he taught at the Institution for the Blind in New York City. He yearned to attend college, but was unable to afford it. An uncle arranged for him to study law in the offices of Buffalo attorneys. In 1859 he was admitted to the bar. As his help was needed to support his widowed mother and younger siblings, Cleveland paid a substitute to take his place in the army during the Civil War. In addition to practicing law, he served as ward supervisor, assistant district attorney, sheriff of Erie County, and mayor of Buffalo. Cleveland's honest, efficient administration of the city government led to his election as governor of New York in 1883. He continued his program of reform at the state level, standing up to Tammany Hall and insisting that state jobs be awarded on merit, not as patronage plums. He vetoed padded appropriation bills, promoted and signed a civil service bill, and appointed distinguished reformers to the civil service commission.

NOMINATION AND ELECTION

Cleveland's reforms quickly made him a contender for the presidency. The public was disgusted with corruption in government that had been widespread since the Civil War. Cleveland was honest, capable, and electable. His campaign slogan was, "Public office is a public trust." When the 1884 Democratic national convention met, Cleveland was the front-runner. Despite bitter opposition from the Tammany Hall machine, he won the nomination on the second ballot. For his running mate the convention selected Thomas A. Hendricks. The Republicans nominated James G. Blaine, who had long been one of that party's leading figures. However, Blaine was unacceptable to the reform element within the party. The reformers, referred to as Mugwumps, supported Cleveland.

The Democratic platform called for tariff revision, while the Republicans supported a high, protective tariff. Other than that, the parties differed little on the issues. The campaign featured attacks on the personal morality of both candidates. The Democrats said Blaine was tainted with scandal relating to his business deals with a railroad, but nothing was proven. A Republican newspaper printed an accusation that Cleveland had had an affair with a young widow in Buffalo, who had borne him an illegitimate child. Cleveland admitted that he had had illicit relations with the woman. Although he was uncertain of the child's paternity, he had accepted responsibility for it and had paid child support. The scandal nearly cost Cleveland the election, but his defenders pointed out that Cleveland had been a model of integrity in his public life.

As the campaign was ending, it appeared that the contest would be close. The outcome of the election hinged on New York. Unfortunately for Blaine, he attended a meeting in New York at which one of the participants, Dr. Samuel Blanchard, referred to the Democratic party as one "whose antecedents have been Rum, Romanism, and Rebellion." Blaine did not immediately repudiate the words, leading to charges that he was anti–Catholic. He lost New York State, with its large Catholic vote, by a narrow margin. Blanchard's statement may have cost Blaine the presidency. Cleveland outpolled Blaine to win a plurality, but not a majority, of the popular votes. Cleveland carried 20 states for a total of 219 electoral votes. Blaine won 182 electoral votes from 18 states. With 36 electoral votes from New York, Blaine would have won.

In 1888 the Democratic national convention nominated Cleveland by acclamation for a second term. Allen G. Thuman was nominated for vice president. The Republicans nominated Benjamin Harrison. During the campaign, Cleveland continued to talk about lower tariffs and the gold standard. The Republican platform insisted on a protective tariff. Harrison remained at home and said very little. In contrast to the election four years before, personal invective played very little part in the campaign. Cleveland may have been hurt by the statement by the British minister, Sir Lionel Sackville-West, that he hoped Cleveland would win because a Democratic administration would be more conciliatory and friendly to the mother country than a Republican would. The minister's comment undoubtedly cost Cleveland support among Irish-Americans, as well as from other voters who saw no advantage to being conciliatory toward England. Again Cleveland won a plurality of the popular vote. In the electoral college, however, he came up short, with 168 electoral votes to 235 for Harrison.

In 1892, the Republicans nominated President Harrison for a second term. Whitelaw Reid was the vice-presidential nominee. Despite opposition from Tammany Hall, Cleveland won the Democratic nomination on the first ballot. Adlai E. Stevenson was selected as his running mate. The campaign of 1892 was quiet, with neither Cleveland nor Harrison campaigning actively. The main difference between the two major parties was their position on tariff. Some excitement was injected into the scene by the emergence of the People's party, which presented a radical, progressive platform. The new party nominated James B. Weaver for president. For the third consecutive election, Cleveland captured a plurality of the popular vote. In the electoral college Cleveland won easily with 277 electoral votes to 145 for Harrison and 22 for Weaver.

FOREIGN RELATIONS

In both of his administrations Cleveland avoided war. Diplomacy was used in several trouble spots. The potential use of military force protected our interests in others. Cleveland avoided war with Spain over the Cuban revolution. He refused to recognize the insurrectionists as belligerents, made every effort to prevent filibustering expeditions from leaving the United States for Cuba, and urged upon the Spanish government the necessity of granting autonomy to Cuba as a means of ending the fighting. Cleveland continued to withhold diplomatic recognition from the Cuban rebels.

The president and his secretary of state, Richard Olney, went too far in threatening the use of force in a boundary dispute between Venezuela and British Guiana. Fortunately, war was avoided by British diplomacy. Cleveland used the potential of military force in separate events in Hawaii, the North Atlantic, the Bering Sea, Samoan islands, Panama province of Colombia, and Brazil. Some of these actions promoted our national interests; some were detrimental.

Cleveland opposed recognition of the provisional government in Hawaii. During the Harrison administration Queen Liliuokalani had been forced off the throne by actions of American planters in Hawaii with the help of marines from an American warship ostensibly sent there to protect American lives. The United States had negotiated a treaty of annexation, but it still had not been ratified when Harrison left office. Convinced that our actions in Hawaii had been dishonorable, Cleveland withdrew the treaty. He wanted to restore the Queen to her rightful throne.

Cleveland was a strong advocate and enforcer of the Monroe Doctrine. Latin American nations knew that they could count on help from the United States in disputes with European nations. The president demonstrated by his actions that the United States would protect our national interests. The anti-imperialism of Cleveland and his dedication to arbitration demonstrated that we had no designs against other nations. In 1888 Cleveland called for a Pan-American conference, but by the time the delegates arrived in the spring of 1889 Harrison was president.

During his first term Cleveland came out for a low tariff, while his opponents favored a high, protective tariff. The election of 1888 was fought on the tariff issue, with Cleveland losing. After he returned to office by winning the election of 1892, fought on the same issue, the House passed an acceptable tariff bill. The Senate amended the bill 634 times, with nearly all of the changes being favors to special interests. In conference the Senate version was accepted, and it passed both Houses. The president let the bill become law without his signature.

Cleveland withdrew reciprocal trade treaties made by the Arthur administration with the Dominican Republic and with the Spanish Antilles. Reciprocity with Mexico was allowed to lapse. Proposed reciprocal agreements with Colombia and El Salvador fashioned by the Arthur administration were abandoned. Cleveland opposed reciprocity because he suspected the Republicans were trying to set up economic protectorates. Cleveland wanted a general tariff reduction to promote world trade and economic well-being in a way that was fair and beneficial to all nations. However, the Senate wrecked the tariff act and trade did not increase.

DOMESTIC PROGRAMS

The Panic of 1893 had already started before Cleveland's second inauguration. He faced a terrible depression, the worst in American history up to that time. Banks and businesses failed, unemployment increased, prices fell, and farms were lost. The depression worsened and people actually starved. Cleveland's practices failed to bring recovery. Cleveland had two main governmental fiscal policies: staying on the gold standard with a "sound money" policy and lowering tariff rates to expand trade and increase markets. Had it been adopted, his tariff policy could have been helpful. The hard money policy was counterproductive. It helped creditors and hurt farmers, laborers and others who could not pay their debts, thus worsening the depression.

Cleveland recognized that big business needed to be restrained before it became too powerful. He placed the first federal controls on business in 1887 with the Interstate Commerce Act. The Department of Labor was created during his administration. Cleveland recovered more than 80 million acres of public lands from railroads and cattle ranchers. He prevented companies from cutting down publicly owned forests and drove trespassers off the public domain and from Indian lands. Cleveland was not a friend of organized labor. During the Pullman strike, strikebreakers were hired, installed as federal officials, and given the jobs of the strikers. Newspapers falsely reported revolution and anarchy. Attorney General Olney wanted to suppress the strike. Cleveland was reluctant to send troops, so Olney had federal judges issue restraining orders. The army was called out and violence erupted in Chicago.

Cleveland then sided with the railroads and assumed power as commander-in-chief. Soldiers, enlisted by the Department of Justice as deputies, were paid by the General Managers Association, but were certified as federal representatives. Later an official, fully-documented investigation rebuked Cleveland and Olney for failing to protect the rights of labor.

Olney did not prosecute trusts vigorously and was pleased when the government lost cases involving big business. Cleveland believed in trust busting, but at the state level and not at the federal level as advocated by Theodore Roosevelt. The Wilson Tariff Bill contained an income tax — the fairest of all taxes, placing the burden of taxation on those most able to pay. However, the Supreme Court ruled the income tax unconstitutional.

In retaliation for raids by Apaches who had left the reservation, the government embarked upon a campaign to wipe out the non-reservation Apaches. Soldiers were ordered to kill every Indian man capable of bearing arms and to capture the women and children and return them to the reservation. With this one significant exception, Cleveland supported the rights of Native Americans. Among his first acts as president were the issuing of proclamations warning against attempts to settle on Oklahoma lands, closing reservations on the east bank of the Missouri River in Dakota Territory to settlement, and ordering cattlemen to vacate Indian lands on the Cheyenne and Arapaho reservations. He favored legislation for the education and civilization of Indians with a view to their eventual citizenship. Cleveland displayed a paternalistic attitude toward black Americans, Native Americans, and Chinese immigrants. He appointed a few African-Americans to office. He felt education was the key to success for them. For his time, Cleveland was a reformer in the area of Indian policy. He signed the Dawes Act, which he sincerely thought would improve the lot of Native Americans. Unfortunately, the act in the long run had a harmful effect on the welfare of those he was trying to help. The president opposed the Force Bill, aimed at protecting the suffrage of Southern blacks. He thought it would be a dangerous expansion of the power of the central government.

Cleveland supported freedom of speech and press and the right of peaceful dissent. He supported freedom of religion and opposed religious bigotry. Cleveland complained about newspapers, whose sensationalism and outright falsehoods outraged him. Many newspapers of the time advocated intervention in the Cuban insurrection. Spanish atrocities were described, with no mention of those committed by the rebels.

At times Cleveland showed a bias against Chinese immigrants, which stemmed from his belief that desirable immigrants were those who would accept American values and meld into American society. Cleveland opposed nativist movements that would keep out immigrants from southern and eastern Europe. He welcomed them so long as they intended to stay permanently and to accept American ways.

As he opposed using federal money for internal improvements, Cleveland vetoed a rivers and harbors bill. He was unable to overcome the despair that followed the Panic of 1893. During his first administration, he had vetoed a Texas Feed Bill, saying the government should not support people and that farm subsidies were impermissible. Now, as the depression deepened, he still refused to help poor people, believing it was not the government's role to do so.

Cleveland conserved natural resources and protected the environment by protecting the public domain and Indian lands. He supported education, including policies favorable to public schools. He encouraged the establishment of trade schools for southern African-Americans and schools to assimilate Native Americans into American life. By the time of his second inauguration in 1893, Cleveland was interested only in the economy, ignoring developments in education and recreation.

ADMINISTRATION AND INTERGOVERNMENTAL RELATIONS

As his major goals Cleveland favored lowering the tariff, maintaining the gold standard, and running an honest government. A competent, conscientious executive, Cleveland organized the executive departments like a business. He refused to remove federal employees from their positions on the basis of their political affiliation.

In his first administration he had a good cabinet. During his second administration he was unable to get the people he wanted and did not have an outstanding cabinet. One controversial member, Richard Olney, was able and aggressive, but irascible and opinionated. Olney may have influenced the president to make his two worst mistakes, suppressing the Pullman strike and threatening war against Great Britain over the Venezuelan boundary dispute. Cleveland assigned personnel appropriately and gave them the authority to carry out their duties, but in a way that coincided with the president's wishes. Corruption was wiped out in the Departments of Interior, Navy, and Treasury.

Cleveland maintained effective communications with his executive branch employees. He could be blunt and stubborn sometimes. His strained relationship with the press prevented the president and his proposals from getting a fair hearing.

In order to keep the gold standard and sound money, Cleveland had the government issue bonds. Funds needed by the government to improve the economy and help bring about recovery were not requested from Congress. Cleveland vetoed numerous pension "steals" and brought economy to government expenditures. The president was not the leader of his party, nor was he the leader of Congress. His party split over the gold versus silver currency issue. Cleveland could not depend upon Congress for a bi-partisan foreign policy. Success in having his pension vetoes sustained and in obtaining repeal of the Tenure of Office Act made the president bolder in confronting the Senate and the battle was on, with Cleveland winning about as often as he lost.

While Cleveland was president, the Supreme Court reached some unpopular decisions. The income tax was invalidated, an injunction issued during the Pullman strike was upheld, and attempts to check monopolies were made almost impossible. All of these were later reversed: the income tax by constitutional amendment, the trust opinion by reversal by the court itself, and the use of injunctions in

labor disputes by legislation. Cleveland was unfairly blamed for unpopular Supreme Court decisions. The majority of the justices deciding these cases were appointed by other presidents. During his first term Cleveland appointed Chief Justice Melville Fuller and Lucius Quintus Cincinnatus Lamar. During his second he appointed Edward White and Rufus Peckham. White was a dissenter in the income tax case and voted to uphold some anti-trust legislation. He later became the first associate justice to be named chief justice.

Cleveland really believed that public office is a public trust. His campaign slogan was not a ploy to get elected, but a sincere statement of his commitments. He chose to act always for the general good. He made decisions and policies based on what he thought was right. He was not influenced by special interests, nor did he use interest groups to exert pressure to get his programs enacted. The public respected him.

LEADERSHIP AND DECISION MAKING

By example the president inspired executive branch personnel to high levels of achievement. He was unable to influence Congress as he did his own personnel, even though he did set a personal example by his exceptionally hard work. He was a poor speaker and writer, which diminished his ability to impel others to emulate his example. He was not a persuasive party leader who could formulate programs and plans and persuade his party to adopt them willingly. Self-righteousness and narrow thinking may have hindered Cleveland. Due to the worsening depression during his second term, the president could not maintain public confidence in the government. He was unable to conceive a strategy for improving the economy.

Although he was an intelligent and hardworking man, Cleveland was not well-educated nor well prepared for the presidency. In problem solving and decision making situations he used his keen intelligence and firm morality. Cleveland was not a visionary nor a scholar and lacked a knowledge of history. He learned from his mistakes and worked well with his cabinet members, who supported his decisions.

Cleveland clung stubbornly to his beliefs. He might have been more successful had he been willing to compromise a little more. On matters that did not involve an important principle, he did compromise. Cleveland faced emergencies calmly and courageously.

PERSONAL QUALITIES

Cleveland conducted himself with dignity. He was a heavy man — over 250 pounds — but he was neat and well-groomed. As a young man he had frequented Buffalo saloons and beer gardens, but he ceased this practice when he married. Lacking social graces, he had a quality of plainness about him that made him seem human. He was no stuffed shirt. After the scandals of previous administrations, Americans were proud of Cleveland's integrity. Some of his foreign affairs decisions instilled additional pride in his countrymen. Because Cleveland was such an honest and conscientious person, the office of the presidency was increased in stature. However, his failure to deal effectively with the depression cost him some respect.

In his first inaugural address Cleveland said that he meant to be a president who kept to his own duties. After two years in office he realized that the president not only executes laws but must help make them. Recognizing this fact, Cleveland began to battle with Congress over power. The executive branch won its independence, and the power of the presidency increased. Cleveland maintained that only he and the vice president were elected by all the people and that as a president he represented their interests. He was shocked to learn that many Congressmen were beholden to certain individuals or businesses. Until the depression occurred, the people thought the president was on their side. As the depression deepened, farmers, laborers, debtors, and the poor began to feel that Cleveland was not interested in them.

The president received a lot of input from the public, but he may not have considered it seriously. Job seekers were bothersome, consuming time that he could have spent more productively. Going over the heads of Congress, Cleveland appealed directly to the people through speeches, circulars, and a few friendly newspapers. He was not particularly successful in taking his case to the people, but he tried.

Cleveland considered the moral basis of every policy decision he made He was trustworthy. His word was good and he kept his promises. His integrity was exemplary. He never used his office to benefit himself at the expense of the public. As he believed that honesty and efficiency were the appropriate standards for government employment, he worked extraordinarily hard as president. His sense of duty and responsibility was a hallmark of his presidency. He enhanced the prestige of the office of president by the high standard of morality he exhibited throughout his political career.

OVERALL ASSESSMENT

Grover Cleveland was an honest man and a reformer. A stubborn fighter, he refused to compromise his principles for political expediency. He received a total of 32 points and ranks in a tie for 22nd place among the 39 presidents rated.

BENJAMIN HARRISON
1889–93

	RATING POINTS	RANK
FOREIGN RELATIONS	–4	38
DOMESTIC PROGRAMS	–3	30 tie
ADMINISTRATION	8	16
LEADERSHIP	7	20
PERSONAL QUALITIES	6	26
OVERALL ASSESSMENT	14	28 tie

BACKGROUND

Benjamin Harrison was born at North Bend, Ohio, on August 20, 1833. His father was a Congressman, his grandfather was the ninth president of the United States, and his great-grandfather was a signer of the Declaration of Independence. Benjamin graduated from Miami University near the top of his class in 1852 and read law in the offices of a Cincinnati legal firm. After being admitted to the bar, Harrison practiced first in Cincinnati, then in Indianapolis. In 1857 he was elected city attorney. Next he became secretary of the Republican central committee. In 1860 he was elected reporter of decisions for the Indiana Supreme Court. In 1862 Harrison took command of an Indiana infantry regiment as a colonel. After two years of duty in the West, Harrison's unit was attached to General Sherman's army and participated in the Atlanta campaign of 1864. At the end of the war he was commissioned as a brigadier general and cited for gallantry.

After the war, Harrison resumed his law practice and his duties as reporter of the state supreme court. He became one of the leading lawyers in Indiana, earning an excellent income. In 1876 he won the Republican gubernatorial nomination, but lost the general election. The hard-fought race and close election brought Harrison national attention. President Hayes appointed him to the Mississippi River Commission. In 1878 he was elected chairman of the Republican state convention. As chairman of the Indiana delegation to the national convention in 1880, he helped secure the presidential nomination for dark horse James A. Garfield. In 1881 Harrison was offered a cabinet post by President Garfield, but turned it down, preferring a seat in the United States Senate. In 1887 he lost his bid for re-election to the Senate by two votes

NOMINATION AND ELECTION

When the Republican national convention met in 1888, the party's dominant figure was in Europe. James G. Blaine had announced that he was not a candidate, but many people believed he would accept the nomination if it were given to him. In Blaine's absence, the front-runners were John Sherman and Walter Q. Gresham, but neither man was able to come close to the number of votes needed for nomination. After the third ballot, most party leaders wanted to avoid a deadlock by settling on William B. Allison. Chauncey Depew, spokesman for the eastern money interests, was unwilling to accept Allison and suggested Harrison as a compromise selection. From Great Britain, Blaine wired in secret code, advising the convention to nominate Harrison for president and Levi P. Morton for vice president. On the eighth ballot Harrison secured the nomination. Morton was given the vice presidential nod. At the Democratic convention President Grover Cleveland was renominated unanimously. For an account of the election of 1888, see the entry on Cleveland.

When the Republicans met in 1892, the party was still reeling from their losses in the midterm elections of 1890. Some party leaders were ready to dump the president in favor of James G. Blaine, but the Plumed Knight refused to allow his name to be placed in nomination. Harrison was renominated on the first ballot. The Democrats nominated ex-president Grover Cleveland and the radical new People's party named James B. Weaver. For an account of the election of 1892, see the entry on Cleveland.

FOREIGN RELATIONS

In his inaugural address Harrison spoke of the blessings of territorial expansion — increases in population and corporate wealth. Harrison said America's contribution toward world peace would be non-interference in the affairs of foreign governments and arbitration of international quarrels. The vigorous foreign policy of President Harrison and Secretary of State James G. Blaine involved the United States in problems that were settled by diplomacy or left unsettled for future administrations. The principal problems concerned our involvement in Samoa, the Bering Sea, and Hawaii. In Samoa, war with Germany was avoided by the use of diplomacy. A tripartite protectorate was set up with Germany, Britain,

and the United States. Congress authorized the president to declare American dominion over the waters of the Bering Sea. Britain objected to this act, and the matter was referred to an international tribunal. In Hawaii, American planters with the help of marines and sailors from an American warship removed Queen Liliuokalani from the throne early in 1893. The new Hawaiian government asked the United States to make Hawaii a territory. Harrison rushed a treaty of annexation to the Senate. Before the Senate could act, Cleveland returned to the presidency and withdrew the treaty. Separate incidents involving Italy and Chile were ended short of war by apologies and indemnities.

During Harrison's administration a Pan-American conference was held and an international monetary conference was organized. Harrison's inter–American policy was based on improved trade, diplomacy and mutual defense. He wanted to expand foreign markets for the United States. The president talked of a customs union, inter–American steamship lines, trademark and copyright laws, and arbitration treaties. He entertained high hopes for the Pan-American Conference, which created the Pan-American Union.

Harrison built a modern, stronger navy and called for a new merchant marine. He said the flag would follow American citizens in all countries. He insisted on respect for the U.S. uniform and nearly went to war with Chile over it. Although war did not occur, Harrison's policies increased international tensions. American actions in Hawaii, Samoa, the Bering Sea and the incidents involving Italy and Chile may have alienated world opinion toward the United States. On the other hand, the Pan-American Congress may have enhanced opinion of us throughout the world.

Harrison promoted protective tariff policies. The McKinley tariff of 1890 led to higher consumer prices, increasing the cost of living and causing hardships for persons of limited means. Reciprocity provisions of the act were controversial. Democrats claimed that reciprocity was a guise to help American businessmen. Clearly, reciprocity was not fair and beneficial to all nations. The long-term effects of the high protective tariff were harmful to the world economy.

DOMESTIC PROGRAMS

In an era when the use of gold or silver was a leading political controversy, Harrison favored bimetalism. The Sherman Silver Purchase Act was passed, increasing the amount of silver the treasury was required to purchase each month, with the payment to be made in treasury notes, thus increasing the supply of paper money. This helped farmers, laborers, debtors, and the West. However, as most people redeemed their notes in gold, the fear of a drain on the treasury's gold reserves helped cause the Panic of 1893. Another contributor to the depression was the McKinley Tariff Act, which hurt the economy. The president refused Wall Street's demand for a bond issue. The International Monetary Conference ended in failure. The worst effects of the depression were not felt until the second Cleveland administration, but its beginnings occurred in Harrison's term.

The Sherman Anti-trust Act was the first legislation passed regulating big business. Although it turned out to be ineffective, Harrison sincerely believed it would help restrain the trusts. Passed with bipartisan support in Congress, it was not rigorously enforced, and the trusts soon found loopholes. Harrison used the power of government to weaken organized labor and break strikes. At the Homestead Works of the Carnegie Steel Company twenty men were killed in a battle between workers and armed Pinkerton men, resulting in a military guard to protect replacement workers. Thirty miners were killed in the Couer d'Alene area, where striking miners had been locked out. Harrison sent troops to suppress the disturbance. In Tennessee miners battled convict labor and in New York arson, train-wrecking and murder took place during a switchmen's strike.

Farmers received low prices for their produce, but paid high prices for supplies. Indebtedness often contributed to their distress. Reading signs of discontent in the Midwest in the election year of 1890, Harrison made a tour of the region. The McKinley Tariff hit the poor hardest. It soon became apparent that the new tariff would increase the cost of living, and the Democrats charged the administration with causing prices to go so high that farmers and workers would be unable to afford the necessities of life. Harrison did not believe that government programs to alleviate poverty were constitutional.

The president was accused of inconsistency on internal improvements. He vetoed small public works bills while signing a rivers and harbors bill. Appropriations for rivers and harbors were pork-barrel bills, with powerful congressional sponsors, so it is difficult for presidents to prevent their passage. Harrison helped obtain passage of a one million dollar improvement of the Mississippi River channel.

Harrison worked hard to obtain passage of the Force Bill, which would have insured that African-American citizens could vote freely and that their vote would be counted. The bill passed the House, but stalled in the Senate. Small wars between Native Americans and white settlers continued. The Battle of Wounded Knee took place in 1890, and Harrison's policies must bear part of the blame for it. He opened eleven million acres of Sioux land to general settlement. The Navajo reservations were inadequate, leading to incidents when Native Americans spilled over into white man's territory. Harrison did nothing to improve conditions for the Native Americans and permitted their lands to be taken from them. He opened Indian land in Oklahoma to settlement, leading to the Oklahoma Land Rush. In 1892 he opened additional Indian lands in Oklahoma, North Dakota, and Montana to white settlement. Thomas Morgan, Indian commissioner, and Daniel Dorchester, commissioner of Indian education, were strongly opposed by Catholic leaders out of fear they might close Indian schools operated by Catholics. Both men were accused of anti–Catholic bias. Harrison supported freedom of speech and the press and the right of peaceful dissent. He issued an amnesty to Mormons who agreed to future obedience of the anti-polygamy laws.

Harrison appointed some African-American postmasters in large southern cities. He wanted to place more blacks in other federal jobs and received needed support from First Assistant Postmaster General James A. Clarkson, who employed several thousand African-Americans in rural post offices and more as letter carriers and railway mail clerks. He influenced the president to overturn the Treasury Department's unwritten rule barring appointments of blacks to offices in that department. Harrison appointed Norris Wright Cuney collector of the port of Galveston, breaking the Treasury's color line. Frederick Douglass was named U.S. resident minister and consul general to Haiti. During an era of political patronage, Harrison supported civil service reform. Yet his critics charged that he was the king of spoilsman. Within a year 31,000 out of 55,000 postmasters were replaced. Civil service reformers who had supported Harrison in 1888 turned to Cleveland in 1892.

In his inaugural address Harrison pledged social justice for all men. He took action to secure human rights for Americans abroad. In labor disputes and strikes, however, he put property rights above human rights. He showed little concern for the human rights of Native Americans. Harrison was quite generous to veterans. He signed an act granting pensions to Union veterans of ninety days or more service who were disabled and unable to earn a living, whether or not their disability was service related. During his administration the number of pensioners more than tripled.

Harrison attributed American growth to education and religion and appealed for more progress. He asked for universal education. In the 1888 election campaign some Republicans had favored federal aid to education, but it was not enacted by Congress. Harrison doubted the constitutionality of federal action and thought progress should be made at the state and local level. While he spoke to Congress in favor of improvements in education, he made no specific proposals. Perhaps Harrison's greatest contribution in the domestic arena was the preservation of natural recreational areas. He signed an act establishing Sequoia and Yosemite national parks. By presidential proclamation he created many forest reserves, including one adjoining Yellowstone National Park.

ADMINISTRATION AND INTERGOVERNMENTAL RELATIONS

In his inaugural address and in his first address to Congress, Harrison announced his goals: further American growth, a protective tariff, uniform and equal administration of laws, enforcement of the Monroe Doctrine, a modern navy and efficient merchant marine, more convenient coaling stations, better dock and harbor positions, non-interference in the affairs of foreign governments, arbitration of international quarrels, early statehood for territories, a free ballot, veterans' pensions, and enforcement of civil service laws. He called for legislation to protect silver from excessive coinage, to deal with the race question, and to protect the safety of railway workers. Harrison's long-term planning involved getting the support of the legislative branch.

Harrison turned the Native Americans' problems completely over to the secretary of the interior. Harrison himself handled problems dealing with African-American civil rights, veterans' pensions, trusts and monopolies, silver coinage, and the tariff. Blaine was ill much of the time, so Harrison acted as his own secretary of state. He did not fully utilize his employees and did too much himself, not delegating enough authority.

Harrison made some excellent appointments, choosing men on their qualifications and not by patronage, angering political bosses. The president selected a strong, capable cabinet. Benjamin Franklin Tracy as secretary of the navy, helped with what was perhaps the greatest accomplishment of the Harrison administration, the inauguration of a new and modern navy. A vigorous reformer, Theodore Roosevelt was appointed as a Civil Service Commissioner. Roosevelt was honest, conscientious and successful in civil service law investigation and enforcement. In the Bureau of Pensions, the commissioner, James R. Tanner, was forced to resign due to lavish and illegal handouts. In Milwaukee Postmaster George H. Paul was forced to resign due to cheating that occurred on civil service exams. The secretary of the interior, John W. Noble, was largely responsible for the General Land Revision Act of 1891, making it possible to set aside timberlands by presidential proclamation. The secretary of the treasury, the secretary of war, and postmaster general were appointed because of their friendship with Harrison or as rewards for their political support, but these appointments are hardly enough to justify the charges of nepotism and favoritism that were levied against Harrison by his opponents.

An effective orator and stump speaker, Harrison maintained effective two-way communication with the executive branch employees, the Congress, and the public. As president, he made several trips, speaking at many stops to and from his destinations. Harrison had a good relationship with the press. Some politicians criticized the president for appointing too many editors to public office.

Spending during the Harrison administration was extravagant, particularly on veterans' pensions and on internal improvements. The Republican-controlled Fifty-first Congress was labeled the billion dollar congress, for spending nearly that amount between 1889 and 1891. For this extravagance, Congress was criticized by Democrats. Ironically, after the midterm elections of 1890, the Democratic-controlled Fifty-second Congress became the first to vote expenditures in excess of one billion dollars.

When Harrison assumed office, his party controlled both houses of Congress, but the leaders of both houses were unsympathetic to the president. Patronage squabbles and civil service law enforcement cost Harrison support in his own party. The Republicans split on the silver and tariff issues. Democrats were united in opposition to the high tariff. The Populists drew support away from the Republican party. Even with much opposition, most of Harrison's proposed legislation passed. In foreign policy the Democrats and anti-imperialists opposed the annexation of Hawaii. After the Democratic landslide in the elections of 1890, little in the way of legislation was accomplished. All attention in the remaining two years of Harrison's administration focused on foreign policy.

The Circuit Court of Appeals was created by the Harrison administration. A major reform, it freed the United States Supreme Court justices from the duty of service wherever called. Harrison based his nomination of judges on ability, not patronage. Harrison appointed four associate justices of the Supreme Court: David J. Brewer, Henry B. Brown, George Shiras, and Howell E. Jackson. Answering criticism from Republican leaders, Harrison said he never believed in a partisan judiciary. His attorney general was highly regarded for his resistance to partisan pressures in the selection of candidates for the federal judiciary.

LEADERSHIP AND DECISION MAKING

Harrison inspired executive branch personnel by his honesty, his intelligence and knowledge about the workings of various departments. Through speeches and by example he tried to lead the public, but he had only inconsistent success. Lacking both charisma and the common touch, he could not sway the masses. He was persuasive enough with other politicians to get some of his goals accomplished, but he was not so persuasive with the voters. He won the presidency with fewer popular votes than Cleveland received as the losing candidate. Harrison campaigned for the Republican party which suffered big losses in the 1890 Congressional elections. In 1892 he was defeated in his re-election bid. By his personal integrity, the president maintained public confidence in the government after scandals. Harrison set high standards of performance for himself and for others. He replaced inefficient or corrupt officials.

Harrison had a concept of what the nation and the world should be like. He communicated this, but was unable to unify the nation. The people were divided: North and South, West and East, Capital and Labor, Gold and Silver, and Agriculture versus Business. The Republican party split over the tariff and free silver. A third party demanded reforms in business, labor, currency, and agriculture. Because of these divisions, Harrison was only partially successful in getting his programs enacted.

In most cases the president made informed decisions, weighed alternatives, and made informed judgments. Often, however, he acted alone, failing to seek advice from other knowledgeable persons and failing to test his ideas against the judgments of others. His decision about annexing Hawaii at the end of his term was made in haste. Harrison was an intelligent man, but not skillful in interpersonal relations. In order to win wider support for his proposals, the president at times compromised with the Republicans in the House and Senate. The president made hard decisions and acted calmly in emergencies.

PERSONAL QUALITIES

Although he seemed cold and austere, Harrison was polite and dignified. For a time the office of the president received more respect because of Harrison's honesty and his courage in standing up to the political bosses. In the struggle for power between the president and the legislative branch that had been taking place since the Civil War, Harrison may have made some slight gains. It has been unfairly charged that he docilely signed the bills which the Republican Congress laid on his table. Actually, he vetoed 44 bills, many of them passed by the Republican-controlled Fifty-first Congress; only one of his vetoes was overridden.

At first some people were proud of their president, who governed independently from party bosses and political machines, used civil service, and accomplished reforms. However, rising discontent hurt American pride. Laborers complained that cut-throat Pinkerton men were allowed to swarm over the country at will to murder workmen. In addition to laborers, many farmers, miners, anti-imperialists, Southerners, Westerners, and others were extremely displeased with Harrison.

A fine speaker, Harrison made a number of public addresses and tours. He gave an inaugural address and four annual addresses to Congress. Harrison did not seek input from the public. Farmers and laborers felt the president was uninterested in them. Office seekers and visitors bothered him. He ran the administration himself with support from key people, whom he trusted. He disliked small talk and could not tolerate inefficiency or incompetency in subordinates.

The president was a man of integrity and trustworthiness. His actions were not always above reproach, but they were generally well-intentioned. His attempted annexation of Hawaii and his handling of labor disputes seem immoral to us, but they were logical consequences of his sincere belief in the superiority of the American businessman. Harrison was honest in an era of crooked politicians. He honored the office of the president by the high standard of personal morality he exhibited throughout his life. A praying churchman, he was never involved in scandal in his personal life.

OVERALL ASSESSMENT

Overall, Harrison earned a total of 14 points and ranks in a tie for the 28th position among the 39 presidents rated.

WILLIAM McKINLEY

1897–1901

	RATING POINTS	RANK
FOREIGN RELATIONS	–7	39
DOMESTIC PROGRAMS	5	19 tie
ADMINISTRATION	5	22 tie
LEADERSHIP	0	29 tie
PERSONAL QUALITIES	14	11
OVERALL ASSESSMENT	17	27

BACKGROUND

William McKinley was born on January 29, 1843, in Niles, Ohio. He entered Allegheny College, but dropped out because of illness. He worked as a post office clerk and as a school teacher. During the Civil War, McKinley enlisted in the Ohio Volunteers. As a mess sergeant at Antietam, his bravery under fire earned him a battlefield commission as second lieutenant. By the end of the war he had been promoted to brevet major. After the war McKinley attended law school in Albany, New York. Admitted to the bar in 1867, he practiced law in Canton, Ohio, and became active in Republican party affairs. In 1869 he was elected prosecuting attorney of Stark County. In 1876 McKinley was elected to Congress where he served six terms. He authored the McKinley Tariff of 1890. In 1891 he was elected to the first of two terms as governor of Ohio. As governor, he called out the national guard to put down labor disturbances, imposed an excise tax on corporations, secured safety legislation for transportation workers, and restricted the antiunion activities of employers.

NOMINATION AND ELECTION

In 1892 McKinley was one of the leading challengers to the renomination of President Harrison. By 1896 he was the front-runner for the Republican nomination. Mark Hanna financed a campaign trip for McKinley prior to the convention and directed his quest for the nomination, which he won easily on the first ballot. Garret A. Hobart was nominated for vice president. William Jennings Bryan won the Democratic nomination. McKinley planned to campaign on the tariff. However, Bryan made the free coinage of silver the main issue. McKinley dropped his advocacy of silver and came out for the gold standard and sound money. Bryan traveled around the country, making more than 600 speeches. In contrast, McKinley stayed home and spoke from the front porch of his house to delegations that came to see him. Bryan denounced Wall Street bankers as bloated plutocrats responsible for the nation's economic ills. Republicans denounced Bryan as a dangerous radical who would destroy business. It was an epic struggle of the agrarian South and West against the industrial East, of debtors against creditors, of the poor against the wealthy. Minor parties entered the fray. The Populists endorsed Bryan for the presidency. Democrats loyal to the gold standard formed the National Democratic party and nominated John M. Palmer for the presidency. Four additional parties named candidates. McKinley was elected with a bare majority of the popular vote. However, he garnered 271 electoral votes to Bryan's 176.

In 1900 President McKinley was nominated for a second term on the first ballot. As Vice President Hobart had died in office, the Republicans had to choose a new running mate for the president. Despite Hanna's misgivings, the Republican bosses of New York and Pennsylvania persuaded the convention to accept Theodore Roosevelt as the vice presidential nominee. The Democrats again nominated Bryan on the first ballot. Several minor parties offered candidates of their own or endorsed Bryan. The main issue in 1900 was imperialism. The Democrats charged that McKinley had deserted America's time-honored anti-empire policy and had subjugated millions of defenseless people in the lands taken from Spain during the recent war. On the other hand, Republicans claimed that the McKinley administration had liberated ten million people from the yoke of Spanish imperialism. The outcome of the election was never in doubt. Americans preferred to view themselves as liberators, not as oppressors. McKinley increased his electoral vote over his 1896 total, receiving 292 electoral votes to Bryan's 155.

FOREIGN RELATIONS

The Spanish-American War could have been avoided. A Cuban revolution had started in 1895, and Cleveland adopted a policy of neutrality. McKinley also took a neutral position in 1897. However, there was much support for the Cuban rebels in America and in American public opinion. War fever was fanned by Senate jingoes and the Yellow Press. Unlike Cleveland,

McKinley responded to pressure and intervened in Cuban affairs. In 1898, after the destruction of the battleship *Maine* in Havana harbor, McKinley sent an ultimatum to Spain. After some delay, Spain agreed to nearly all demands and ceased hostilities. Nevertheless, McKinley sent his already-written war message to Congress and added the Spanish reply. Congress declared war.

McKinley annexed Hawaii by Joint Resolution after a treaty failed in the Senate. Spain ceded Puerto Rico, Guam, and the Philippine Islands to the United States and evacuated Cuba. The Filipinos had set up their own independent government, so they did not recognize the legitimacy of United States rule. McKinley put down their independence movement by military force. This unjust imperialistic aggression harmed the national interests of the United States.

In other parts of the world, our record was better. The United States remained neutral in the Boer War. McKinley attempted to keep peace by announcing the open door in China. He sent troops as a part of an international force to rescue the legations during the Boxer rebellion. McKinley appointed a commission to work for an international silver convention. The president sent a delegation to the Hague Convention in 1899, which had been called by the Czar of Russia in an attempt to establish machinery for international arbitration. This conference decreased international tensions and contained a germ for future developments.

In McKinley's first term, the Dingley Tariff was passed, creating the highest rates ever and providing reciprocity. McKinley made John A. Kasson head of a special reciprocity division of the State Department. Kasson began negotiating agreements with foreign powers. These agreements were submitted to the Senate in the form of treaties, where ratification was met with opposition. They were still in the finance committee when McKinley died. The president had changed his mind about the tariff, and in a speech the day before his assassination he had promoted reciprocity and spoken of lower rates. Trade advantages obtained as a result of the war were not fair, as they favored some nations over others.

The Dingley tariff angered foreign countries. During the Spanish-American War, European powers except England were pro–Spanish. The Latin American countries were not in favor of the "liberation" of Cuba by the United States. They denounced imperialism by the United States and the military, economic, and cultural encroachments of the "Colossus of the North." A new feeling for England was the war's greatest positive legacy. McKinley and Secretary of State John Hay forged an unwritten alliance between United States and England. All problems and differences between the countries, including Alaskan and Canadian problems, were worked out and they paved the way for the building of the Panama Canal later.

DOMESTIC PROGRAMS

About the time of McKinley's inauguration the depression ended and prosperity returned to stay during his entire presidency. The GOP took credit for it and used as McKinley's re-election slogan "The Full Dinner Pail." Prosperity was based on full production and an excess of exports over imports. McKinley not only changed his ideas about the tariff, but also he changed from a bimetalist to an advocate of the gold standard. The gold standard act of 1900 resulted. McKinley financed the war by raising taxes and selling bonds.

After the war, McKinley undertook a huge program of social and industrial rehabilitation in Cuba. Americans fed the starving and cared for the sick. Sanitary projects were carried out in the cities. Sugar and tobacco plantations were reclaimed, machinery reconstructed, and roads rebuilt. After the war, Puerto Rico was poverty stricken, and the United States sent tons of supplies. Just before McKinley's death, free trade was obtained for Puerto Rico. The president pursued governmental policies providing internal improvements in the newly acquired dependencies. He worked with Hay to pave the way for the building of the Panama Canal. The second Hay-Pauncefote treaty was ratified by the Senate after McKinley's death.

McKinley favored businessmen and industrialists over farmers and laborers. He had always had the support of big business, but he recognized a growing threat from the trusts. At first he favored state legislation, but he soon saw it would not be enough. In 1899 he decided that he would ask Congress for anti-trust legislation in the near future and began gathering material to study the problem. Then he waited until after his re-election. His assassination prevented him from acting against the trusts. For the record though, McKinley allowed monopolistic practices to go unchecked.

The president had a paternalistic attitude toward Filipinos, Puerto Ricans, and Cubans. As a youth McKinley had opposed slavery. He condemned injustices to Negroes in the South after reconstruction. McKinley's secretary of the interior, Ethan Allen Hitchcock, guarded native Americans from exploitation and injustice. McKinley's most important veto was of a bill opening the Navajo reservation to exploitation. As a nation historically devoted to constitutional rights and now becoming a colonial power, the United States was troubled about the status of our new subjects. McKinley believed that the Philippines and Puerto Rico were dependencies to which the Constitution of the United States would not extend. He especially did not want citizenship for Filipinos. In the spring of 1901 the Supreme Court declared the Philippine Islands were dependencies subject to congressional authority, endowing them with a mixture of civil rights and non-citizenship. McKinley's concern about human rights abuses in Cuba was one of the causes of intervention in Cuban affairs that led to the Spanish-American war. After the war, he insisted on humane treatment for people in the dependencies. Under military rule there were some abuses, and McKinley soon replaced military with civilian rule, whereupon the treatment of people improved.

McKinley supported freedom of speech and press and rights of dissent. He supported freedom of religion. Even when confronted by the sensationalism, exaggerations, one-sidedness, and falsehoods of the yellow press, the president did not denounce the press. As a former teacher, McKinley was interested in public education. The president was pleased by the great advances and reforms in education that were made in America in the decade of the 1890s. McKinley helped preserve our historical heritage by establishing a national monument in

Vicksburg in 1899, which later became a national military park. In 1898 he established a national park at Mount Rainier.

ADMINISTRATION AND INTERGOVERNMENTAL RELATIONS

McKinley announced his goals in his first inaugural address. He advocated tariff revision first, then currency legislation. He supported international bimetalism. He was opposed to wars of conquest and wanted no territorial aggression. He favored arbitration, tariff reciprocity, and work toward domestic prosperity. The president engaged in long-term planning, but failed to visualize some of the problems to be overcome, and he changed his mind about some of his objectives. Tariff revision, reciprocity, and prosperity were achieved. Advocacy of international bimetalism changed to promotion of the gold standard, which was then accomplished. He failed to keep the peace.

Early in his administration McKinley made inappropriate choices for cabinet positions, based on political and sectional considerations. Such qualifications as experience, education, and ability were not taken sufficiently into account. Only two members of his original cabinet had a college education, and only three lasted more than two years. Mark Hanna wanted to be a senator, so McKinley appointed Senator John Sherman secretary of state, opening up the senatorial seat to which the Ohio governor appointed Hanna. It was a mistake. Sherman was in poor health. His hearing and memory all but failed and subordinates had to do all the department's business. McKinley and William R. Day, the assistant secretary, made the important decisions. When war came, Sherman was replaced by Day, who in turn was succeeded by John Hay, a much more capable diplomat.

Russell A. Alger, the secretary of war, was involved in a scandal related to conduct of the war and "embalmed beef." McKinley appointed an investigating commission, which found no evidence of poisoned beef, but found many wartime mistakes, and made recommendations which were used to modernize America's army by Alger's successor after 1899.

McKinley put up with Alger and stuck by him too long. When he finally fired him, Elihu Root, a very able person, replaced Alger. McKinley's original cabinet was only average, but the later appointments of Hay and Root strengthened it. Closest to the president among the cabinet members was James Wilson, secretary of agriculture, who was to hold the post under three presidents. McKinley entrusted Wilson with delicate political trips that he gave to no one else. Wilson was the president's prime source of information on trends and events in the West.

McKinley directed the work of the executive branch personnel in a spirit of temperance, conciliation, and affectionate regard. He led by power of esteem, not by fear. He gave his department heads a free hand, except for the State Department. The president's strengths were: ability to delegate, willingness to take advice, and frequent consultations. His weaknesses were procrastination and soft-heartedness that made him refuse to face facts when his appointees failed to meet expectations.

McKinley excelled in spoken communication. He developed an effective two-way communication with executive branch employees, the Congress, and the public. He preferred speeches to writing and preferred talking to someone to writing a note or a letter. He toured the country making speeches to the public, and he loved shaking hands with the people. The Yellow Press, Joseph Pulitzer's New York *World* and William Randolph Hearst's New York *Journal* sabotaged the McKinley peace effort. Pulitzer put all his energy and talent for exaggeration into his newspaper. Richard Harding Davis's account in the Hearst papers of the blowing up of the *Maine* was a major cause of the Spanish-American War. It has been alleged that Davis or Hearst may have even conspired with Americans to blow up the battleship, knowing the disaster would be blamed on Spain.

Throughout his presidency, McKinley had Republican majorities in both houses of Congress. He led Congress by power of friendly persuasion, much as he led his executive branch personnel. McKinley vetoed only fourteen bills. He headed off other bills to which he objected in meetings before they were introduced. Sometimes his foreign policy did not have bipartisan Congressional support. The acquisition of the Philippines was a very controversial issue, opposed not only by Democrats, but by many prominent Republicans, including Speaker of the House, Thomas B. Reed, who resigned his seat in the House rather than go along with his party. Bryan, originally one of the leading opponents, finally supported the treaty, hoping that his proposal to free the Philippines would become a winning issue in the battle for the presidency in 1900. Bryan's change of tactics helped the treaty get the two-thirds majority required for ratification.

During the McKinley administration a satisfactory relationship existed between the president and the courts. As noted above, the Supreme Court in the Insular Cases sustained McKinley's view that Filipinos were not United States citizens. McKinley appointed one Supreme Court justice, Joseph McKenna, who had served in Congress with him, had been a judge, and then was McKinley's first attorney-general.

The president always had the backing of big business and did not want to do anything to offend corporations. This was probably because of McKinley's natural inclinations rather than the result of any particular pressure. McKinley rewarded friends with political appointments, but he wanted to serve the people's best interests, too. He was very aware of public opinion and liked to make decisions accordingly.

LEADERSHIP AND DECISION MAKING

Although not a charismatic leader, McKinley was a kind and gentle man who loved people and wanted everyone to love him. In return, the country showed him a great deal of affection. He could have been a more effective leader had he been more forceful. The president was able to maintain public confidence in the government and to restore confidence after the depression in the previous administration, scandals in the War Department, the war with Spain, and the Philippine insurrection. McKinley was re-elected in 1900 following all of these events. McKinley inspired executive branch personnel by face to face contacts, speaking and listening to them, and by affection for and from him. However, he allowed poor work by personnel to go too far without corrective action. Perhaps he was overly concerned with being well liked. McKinley was very persuasive and usually got his way, even if he did not take the credit himself. McKinley allowed members of his administration to engage in inappropriate behavior, and failed to hold them responsible for performing their duties at a high level of competence and effectiveness. Sherman, Alger, and several generals were incompetent. Others, including Hay, Root, and Leonard Wood achieved at a high level of performance.

McKinley's concept of what the nation and the world should be like changed with his reaction to events and to public opinion. His regrettable public silence on foreign affairs did not indicate a lack of interest. He was aware that the age of isolation was drawing to a close for America and that we would have to assume our place as an international power. He believed in arbitration of differences with foreign powers whenever possible, which led to American participation in the general movement for world cooperation.

McKinley was cautious and careful when making decisions. He weighed alternatives and listened to subordinates and their input. He gathered information needed to make the decision. McKinley possessed a keen intelligence and used it in most problem solving and decision making situations. In emergencies he acted calmly. However, at times he failed to make timely judgments. The president was unwilling to compromise to avoid the war with Spain and the conflict in the Philippine Islands.

PERSONAL QUALITIES

A man of simple and unostentatious tastes, McKinley never forgot his dignity or denied that he relished the powers and prestige of the office. He made people proud to be Americans and made them proud of him as their president. Due to the emergence of the United States as a world power, the stature of the office of president increased. Much of the public thought McKinley was the people's president, that he was on their side. Public opinion counted much with him. He sought input from all segments of the public. He received information from callers and used it. He learned the feelings, hopes, and aspirations of the public on his trips. McKinley used many kinds of formal and informal communication. He was a highly skilled speaker, orator, and conversationalist. However, he was sometimes unwilling to speak out on vital but controversial issues or to take up an unpopular cause. If he had "reached out to the people" and sought their understanding of the extent of the Spanish concessions in Cuba, the Spanish-American war might have been averted. His failure to do so can be regarded not only as a communication failure, but also as an immoral and unprincipled act.

With this one exception, McKinley acted consistently on a firm set of moral values and principles. He was trustworthy and tried to keep his word. McKinley was honest and never used his office to benefit himself personally at the expense of the public. He enhanced the prestige of the office of presidency by the high standard of personal morality he exhibited throughout his life. He was never involved in a personal scandal. He was widely admired for the way he took care of Ida, his invalid wife.

ASSASSINATION AND AFTERMATH

At the Pan-American Exposition in Buffalo, on September 6, 1901, McKinley held a public reception in the exposition's Temple of Music. Among the hundreds of persons in the crowd waiting to shake his hand was Leon F. Czolgosz, an anarchist. As McKinley extended his hand to grasp Czolgosz's outstretched left hand, the anarchist fired two shots into the president's body with a revolver concealed in a handkerchief in his right hand. An ambulance rushed the wounded president to a hospital, where he lingered for eight days. He died on September 14, 1901. After his trial and conviction, Czolgosz was electrocuted at Auburn State Prison in Auburn, New York, on October 29, 1901.

OVERALL ASSESSMENT

McKinley was an intelligent and popular man, but he sometimes did not use his capabilities for guiding the nation in our best interests. His failure to prevent the Spanish-American War was disgraceful. His overall rating was 17 points on a 100-point scale, ranking him in 28th place among the 39 presidents rated.

THEODORE ROOSEVELT
1901–09

	RATING POINTS	RANK
FOREIGN RELATIONS	10	18 tie
DOMESTIC PROGRAMS	12	9
ADMINISTRATION	12	6 tie
LEADERSHIP	17	4 tie
PERSONAL QUALITIES	18	2 tie
OVERALL ASSESSMENT	69	7

BACKGROUND

Theodore Roosevelt was born into a wealthy family in New York City on October 17, 1858. He earned a Phi Beta Kappa key at Harvard University, from which he graduated in 1880. In poor health as a child, he made himself physically fit through living the "strenuous life." He served in the New York legislature from 1882 to 1884, attracting attention as a foe of corruption and an advocate of good government. From 1884 to 1886 he lived as a hunter and rancher in the Badlands of North Dakota. After losing most of his cattle in a blizzard, he returned to New York and concentrated on his writing. A prolific author, he published more than 30 books. He served six years as a member of the Civil Service Commission and two years as president of the New York City Police Commission. In 1897 he became assistant secretary of the navy, but soon resigned to seek action in the Spanish-American War. He became a hero by leading his Rough Riders in a charge up San Juan Hill. In 1898 he became the governor of New York.

NOMINATION AND ELECTION

President McKinley was nominated for a second term in 1900. For his running mate, the convention chose Theodore Roosevelt, partly because of the desire of New York Republican boss Thomas Platt to get the reform-minded governor out of the state. For an account of the election, see the entry on William McKinley. Following McKinley's assassination, Roosevelt became president.

In 1904 the Republicans unanimously nominated him for a term of his own. The Democrats offered Alton B. Parker. The Republican platform called for a protective tariff, increased foreign trade, the gold standard, expansion of the navy and the merchant marine, and praised Roosevelt's foreign and domestic policy. The Democratic platform opposed the protective tariff, favored some progressive legislation, and condemned imperialism and Roosevelt's policies. Roosevelt overwhelmed Parker in the general election by an electoral count of 336 to 140.

Roosevelt declined to run for re-election in

1908, throwing his support to his protégé, William Howard Taft. During Taft's administration, the two men had a falling out and Roosevelt tried for the Republican nomination in 1912. When Taft won the nomination, Roosevelt and his followers formed the Progressive party and engaged in a three-way race against Taft and Woodrow Wilson. On October 14, as Roosevelt was leaving his Milwaukee hotel to address a rally, he was shot in the chest by an anti-third-term fanatic. Fortunately, his eyeglasses case deflected the bullet and he was not seriously injured. With the bullet still in his body, he delivered the speech as scheduled. Afterwards, Taft and Wilson ceased campaigning until Roosevelt recovered. For the outcome of the election, see the entry on Woodrow Wilson.

FOREIGN RELATIONS

Roosevelt used both arbitration and the threat of force to carry out his foreign policies and to prevent wars. He used arbitration to settle a dispute with Great Britain over the Alaska-Canada border. When it appeared that Germany planned to seize Venezuelan territory, Roosevelt gave the Kaiser a week to agree to arbitration or else the U.S. fleet would be sent with orders to shoot. Germany withdrew its warships, and the matter was referred to the Hague Tribunal. When Santo Domingo could not pay its debts to several European nations, Roosevelt announced that the United States would use force if any European powers intervened in the island nation. He ordered American officials to take over the customs system of Santo Domingo, collect taxes, and pay the country's debts. He added the Roosevelt Corollary to the Monroe Doctrine, stating that in flagrant cases of impotence or wrongdoing the United States might exercise an international police power. When an American was kidnapped in Morocco, Roosevelt threatened force and the American was released unharmed. When war loomed in a dispute between Germany and France over the control of Morocco, Roosevelt persuaded the parties to settle the matter at an international conference. He negotiated the Root-Takahira Agreement with Japan in which the two nations agreed not to seek territorial gains in the Pacific. He maintained peace in the Philippines and started the islands on their first steps toward self-government. He served as mediator in the peace talks that ended the Russo-Japanese War. For this effort he received the Nobel prize for peace, the first American to be so honored.

The greatest blemish on Roosevelt's international record occurred in Panama. While Roosevelt was negotiating with Colombia for the purchase of a strip of land across the isthmus, Panamanian rebels set up a revolutionary government. Roosevelt sent troops to prevent Colombia from putting down the revolt, which was instigated by U.S. interests. Roosevelt immediately recognized the Republic of Panama and signed a treaty for the construction of a canal. Roosevelt regarded the Panama Canal as one of his greatest accomplishments, but Latin America was alienated by the way the Colossus of the North treated Colombia.

In order to increase world trade Roosevelt wanted to reduce the high tariff rates enacted in previous administrations, but legislators in his own party kept the rates high.

In keeping peace Roosevelt believed that strength and preparedness were a great help. His motto was: "Speak softly and carry a big stick." He greatly strengthened the navy and sent the Great White Fleet around the world to show U.S. power. World opinion of the United States was enhanced both by Roosevelt's show of strength and by his peacekeeping efforts.

DOMESTIC PROGRAMS

During most of Roosevelt's administration, the country enjoyed prosperity. Bank failures and a stock market slump in 1907 led to a brief depression. Roosevelt dealt effectively with the Panic of 1907. The secretary of the treasury added $25 billion to government funds in the national banks. The president agreed not to take antitrust action against U.S. Steel for purchasing Tennessee Coal and Iron when it was about to fail. Recovery started in the spring of 1908 and was complete by 1909.

Upon Upton Sinclair's expose of unsanitary conditions in the meat packing industry, Roosevelt obtain passage of the Meat Inspection Act and the Pure Food and Drug Act. Congress established the Department of Commerce and Labor.

The president vigorously enforced the Sherman Anti-Trust Act, earning a reputation as a trust buster. During Roosevelt's administration, the government filed suits against 44 corporations. It dissolved J. P. Morgan's Northern Securities Company, ended John D. Rockefeller's oil trust, and James B. Duke's tobacco trust, among others. The Hepburn Act was passed, giving the Interstate Commerce Commission power to fix railroad rates. In a 1905 address Roosevelt challenged the power of business to set its own prices, to keep books and records secret, and to negotiate with labor without governmental intervention. He committed the United States to the view that tyranny of wealth is unacceptable. In a strike of coal miners Roosevelt proposed that the strike be settled by arbitration. When the mineowners refused, Roosevelt threatened to seize the mines. The owners then agreed to accept the findings of a commission that gave the miners most of what they wanted. Roosevelt said he tried to give the miners a square deal. His Square Deal policy changed the pattern of political and social thinking and started the twentieth century domestic reforms continued by Wilson, Franklin Roosevelt, Truman, and Lyndon Johnson.

Far ahead of integration standards of the time, Roosevelt and his family dined with Booker T. Washington at the White House. However, his reputation for racial fairness was tarnished by an affair in Brownsville, Texas, when African-American soldiers were accused of shooting up the community. He ordered the discharge without honor of 160 soldiers, even though they had not been provided with legal representation nor given the presumption of innocence. Roosevelt pressured the San Francisco school board to reverse a decision barring Japanese-American children from the city's public schools, but he made a gentlemen's agreement with Japan severely restricting immigration. Roosevelt opposed Asian laborers working for lower wages and taking white men's jobs. His Native American policy was not so enlightened. The Dawes Severalty Act was amended in 1906, challenging the whole Indian reservation system. The president was authorized to parcel land to individual members in tracts called allotments, making it possible for whites to take over more Indian land by purchasing it from allottees. Many Native Americans sold their land, spent the money, and became impoverished.

Roosevelt supported freedom of speech, press, and religion. He appointed Oscar S. Straus secretary of commerce and labor, the nation's first Jewish cabinet member. Although he did not publicly support women's suffrage until after his presidency, Roosevelt's 1912 Progressive party platform included a plank advocating women's suffrage. Dignity for all was a part of Roosevelt's Square Deal program.

Roosevelt was the Great Conservationist. The Reclamation Act of 1902 provided for the reclamation and irrigation of arid western lands. He started 25 irrigation or reclamation projects, reserved 125 million acres in national forests, 68 million acres of coal lands, and 1,500 water-power sites. He established the first national wildlife refuge at Pelican Island and designated Devils Tower as the first national monument. Although a great conservationist, he was also a big game hunter. In one trip to Africa after his presidency ended, he and his son Kermit killed over 300 animals. At the time no contradiction was seen between killing game and conserving natural resources.

ADMINISTRATION AND INTERGOVERNMENTAL RELATIONS

Roosevelt stated his goals and objectives in his speeches to Congress. He was able to engage in long-term planning and to visualize problems that must be overcome to move the country forward. His long-term peace effort in Europe failed in 1914. His domestic reform program became successful and continued into the future. On day-to-day matters he acted pragmatically, rather than from an organized plan.

At first, Roosevelt kept McKinley's cabinet. Later, he appointed well-qualified people to positions for which they were suited, for example, Gifford Pinchot as chief forester. There were no major scandals involving the president's appointees. He chose the best qualified without regard to sectional or other considerations, but he did not always use personnel efficiently. He did not delegate enough authority and often chose to do the work himself. He sometimes acted alone without consulting his cabinet, communicating afterward to executive branch employees, the Congress, and the public as to his reasons and results. An excellent and prolific writer and a dynamic speaker, he kept people informed after the fact. He established new independent agencies and worked well with them and existing agencies to carry out his reforms.

Except for tariff reform, Roosevelt had overwhelming support from members of his own party in Congress during his first term. Because he started his second term by announcing that he would not run again in 1908, he became a lame duck, losing support and loyalty of his own party, especially in his last two years. He had much support in the opposition party. In fact, Democrats later took over the domestic reform movement started by Roosevelt. He generally had bipartisan support for his foreign policy.

Roosevelt had a good relationship with the courts. The judiciary were especially helpful to him in breaking up trusts and monopolies, the Supreme Court upholding Roosevelt's views in the Northern Securities case. Judge Elbert H. Gray helped him end the Panic of 1907 by not opposing the takeover of Tennessee Coal and Iron by U.S. Steel. Roosevelt appointed three Supreme Court justices, including Oliver Wendell Holmes, perhaps the most highly regarded associate justice in the court's history.

The president had a good working relationship with the press. At first he derisively applied the term muckrakers to journalists uncovering abuses. Later he co-operated with them as he carried out his Square Deal programs. The press delighted in covering the colorful Teddy and his lively children, who made good copy for the journalists.

Roosevelt always acted for what he thought was the public interest. Even when expanding his presidential powers, he acted for the good of the people. He was indeed a president of all the people, including the common man.

LEADERSHIP AND DECISION MAKING

Roosevelt inspired others to follow his lead. Before becoming president he had been a Rough Rider war hero, big game hunter, rancher, mountain climber, conservationist, naturalist, and a participant in strenuous sports, all of which added to his charisma. Through personal example, speeches, and writings, Roosevelt inspired people to accomplish national goals. The president was very persuasive. He was able to get others to follow him by convincing them his was the right course. When that did not work, he used his big stick to get his way.

Following the Panic of 1907, Roosevelt restored public confidence. A strong motivator, he set high standards of performance for himself and others. He unified the nation and created a feeling of togetherness and shared national goals among the people. He warned against the divisiveness of having one camp of prosperous people and another camp of the poor.

Roosevelt was more of a pragmatist than a visionary. Yet, he grasped the moral issues in the U.S. economy. His insight into geopolitics and how the United States fit into the global future was impressive. He had a concept of what the nation and the world should be like and the determination to take it there. He did not conceive much strategy, but acted on each issue as it arose. He acted quickly. He did consider alternatives and made informed judgments about the possible consequences of each action. This also was done quickly.

A student of history, Roosevelt learned much from the past. He made a few mistakes, such as his promotion of simplified spelling. Though pragmatic, he never seemed to learn from his mistakes. He was quite intelligent, with an excellent memory, clarity of conscience, and immunity to indecision, and he used each of these talents to the utmost. He continually evaluated his programs and was skilled at compromise, believing that half a loaf was better than none. Very courageous, Roosevelt made hard decisions and made them promptly. He excelled in handling emergencies.

PERSONAL QUALITIES

Roosevelt conducted himself with appropriate presidential dignity, even when romping with his children, engaging in sports, or hiking. The American people were very proud that he was their president. Many regarded him as an authentic hero. Few presidents have been as popular with the common people as he was. People thought the president was on their side because of his attacks on the trusts and railroads and because of his pro-labor views. Roosevelt received guests from many walks of life, from boxers to ranchers to diplomats. He did not like nightlife and preferred entertaining at noon meals. He sought and received input from each of the varied guests. Roosevelt treated his office as a "bully pulpit" and appealed directly to the people, going over the heads of Congress and other national leaders. The people responded to Roosevelt's flamboyant style and boundless energy. They approved of his policies; they were charmed by his personality; and they regarded him with immense affection and admiration.

Due to the remarkable Teddy Roosevelt, the office of the president received more respect both at home and abroad. By taking bold action, he increased the power of the presidency. He intentionally broadened the use of executive power, believing it was necessary to do so in order to meet challenges at home and abroad. The office was enhanced by his trust-busting, acquiring the Panama Canal, announcing the Roosevelt Corollary to the Monroe Doctrine, ending the Russo-Japanese war, preventing war over Morocco, ending the Panic of 1907, and changing American beliefs about our social and political systems by implementing the Square Deal programs.

Roosevelt acted consistently on a firm set of moral values and principles. He fought immorality in government, in business, and abroad. He kept his promises. He was completely honest. Born rich, he never tried to acquire greater wealth from the public offices he held. A man of high character, Roosevelt was never involved in a scandal in all of his public or private life.

OVERALL ASSESSMENT

Theodore Roosevelt ushered in the twentieth century program of domestic reform. He had been called the first modern president. Completely honest, he fought corruption in government and business. We rated him no better than a tie for eighteenth in Foreign Relations, largely because of his cavalier attitude toward our Latin American neighbors. In every other category he ranks among the top ten American presidents, with his highest ranking being a second place tie in the area of Personal Qualities. Overall, he received 69 points and ranks seventh among all the presidents rated.

WILLIAM HOWARD TAFT

1909–13

	RATING POINTS	RANK
FOREIGN RELATIONS	8	21 tie
DOMESTIC PROGRAMS	11	10 tie
ADMINISTRATION	7	17 tie
LEADERSHIP	0	29 tie
PERSONAL QUALITIES	7	23 tie
OVERALL ASSESSMENT	33	21

BACKGROUND

William Howard Taft was born into a prominent family in Cincinnati on September 15, 1857. He graduated second in his class at Yale University, then attended the Cincinnati Law School. Admitted to the bar in 1880, he became a successful attorney. He served in a variety of public offices: assistant prosecuting attorney for Hamilton County, collector of internal revenue for the Cincinnati district, assistant county solicitor, judge on the Cincinnati Superior Court, solicitor general of the United States, federal judge on the Sixth Circuit Court of Appeals, governor of the Philippines, and secretary of war in the cabinet of Theodore Roosevelt. Taft became an international troubleshooter for Roosevelt and the most popular member of the cabinet.

NOMINATION AND ELECTION

In 1908 Theodore Roosevelt declined to seek another term in the White House. Knowing that Secretary of State Elihu Root was unelectable, Roosevelt chose Taft to become his successor. With the president's help, Taft easily won the Republican nomination on the first ballot. William Jennings Bryan was again the Democratic nominee. Several minor parties entered candidates. With few differences on political principles between the two major parties, the campaign was unexciting. Taft won handily, outpolling Bryan by more than one million votes and taking the electoral college by a count of 321 to 162.

During his term, Taft gradually lost the support of the progressive wing of the Republican party. The chief causes of the split included Taft's defense of the Payne-Aldrich tariff, his removal of Gifford Pinchot as chief forester, and his refusal to support the progressives in their attempt to curb the almost unlimited powers of the Speaker of the House, Uncle Joe Cannon. By 1912 the liberal wing was in open revolt against the president. Theodore Roosevelt decided to try to wrest the Republican nomination from his former protégé. Although the Rough Rider won most of the primaries, the president remained in control of the party machinery. After a battle in the credentials committee, Taft was renominated on the first ballot. Roosevelt's supporters formed a new party, the Progressives, popularly called the Bull Moose party, and nominated Roosevelt for another run at the presidency. With this split in the Republicans, the Democratic candidate won the election. For details, see the entry on Woodrow Wilson.

FOREIGN RELATIONS

There were no wars during the Taft administration. Taft avoided war against Mexico, leaving that to Wilson. In October 1909 he exchanged friendly greetings with President Porfirio Diaz in El Paso and in Ciudad Juarez, becoming the first U.S. president to visit Mexico while in office. He ordered four battalions of troops to the Mexican border, but issued a proclamation warning Americans to observe neutrality laws and abstain from participating in Mexican disturbances. He issued an executive order prohibiting exportation of war materials to Mexico. Taft used the army to protect the Texas border. When Jose Gomez was elected president of Cuba in 1909, Taft ended the U.S. occupation of that land. In 1912 he warned the Cuban government that the United States would intervene if the military continued to interfere in political affairs. In Nicaragua Adolfo Diaz, the provisional president, asked for marines in 1912. Taft sent them, they restored order, and Taft withdrew most of them within months.

Taft was a proponent of peace. An advocate of peaceful settlements of international disputes, he negotiated arbitration treaties with France and England as a first step toward world peace. However, the treaties were killed by amendments in the Senate and dropped. Taft's arbitration proposals and his advocacy of peace enhanced favorable European public opinion. In 1909 he issued an executive order reducing the army by ten percent. As European powers moved toward war, Taft built up our armed forces. In 1911 he sent a special message to Congress asking for funds to begin fortification of the Panama Canal.

The Republican party platform in 1908 pledged tariff revision. Taft called a special session of Congress to fulfill this pledge. He wanted a lowering of tariff rates to promote trade to benefit Americans and people of other countries. He also wanted a provision for a permanent tariff commission. The Payne-Aldrich Act passed Congress and was signed by Taft. This act became very controversial and widened the split within the Republican party. Some sources say it continued the high tariff or raised rates, while others contend it lowered rates. Actually, there were 654 decreases, 220 increases, and 1150 items left unchanged. A tariff board was created to investigate and report each year the facts respecting products whose schedules should be changed. The Payne-Aldrich Act also included provisions for free trade with the Philippines and a corporate income tax.

Taft attempted a reciprocity trade agreement with Canada. It passed the U.S. Congress but was rejected by the Canadian Parliament. Establishment of free trade should have been beneficial to Filipinos. Taft wanted to increase world trade and was successful in doing so. The dollar value of U.S. imports and exports both decreased in Fiscal Year 1909, but increased each year thereafter. The largest increases were trade with Canada and the Pacific area.

DOMESTIC PROGRAMS

Taft took office during a time of prosperity. During 1909–10 he turned a deficit of $50 million into a surplus of $19 million. High prices were blamed on Taft, causing the Republicans to lose the congressional elections of 1910. In 1912 Taft had a deficit of $22 million.

The federal government prosecuted twice as many anti-trust suits under Taft as it had under Theodore Roosevelt. Taft did not deserve his anti-labor reputation. He believed in the right of labor to organize and strike. The secretary of labor was added to the cabinet during his administration. He called for workman's compensation for railway workers and for workers in interstate commerce. He recommended a bill limiting injunctions in strikes. Taft created a separate Children's Bureau in the new Labor Department. An amendment to the

Pure Food and Drug Act in 1911 prohibited the use of misleading labels. He also made certain safety requirements on mines and railroads.

In June 1909 Taft sent a special message to Congress requesting a constitutional amendment to authorize an income tax. The amendment was passed by Congress in July 1909 and ratified by sufficient states to become effective in February 1913. Taft deserves credit for sponsoring it and helping get it adopted. In June 1909 on Taft's recommendation, Congress passed a corporate income tax.

Taft continued Roosevelt's conservation policies. Chief Forester Gifford Pinchot, a popular holdover from the previous administration, was fired for insubordination and for charging Secretary of the Interior Richard A. Ballinger with favoritism to the Guggenheims in their claims to valuable mineral lands in Alaska. A congressional investigation cleared Ballinger. However, Taft's reputation was damaged by Pinchot's charges that Roosevelt's programs were not being continued. Actually under Taft many millions of additional acres were set aside for preservation, including over a million acres of forest reserves in the Appalachian Mountains. In addition he reserved the mineral wealth beneath the surface of public lands offered for sale. He improved the public land laws, established a Bureau of Mines charged among other things with the duty of studying the welfare of miners, a postal savings system, the parcel post system, and the requirement of safety appliances on railroads. He sponsored the Mann-Elkins Act of 1910, which gave the Interstate Commerce Commission jurisdiction over terminals and services of communication by telephone, telegraph, and cable. It placed upon the carriers the burden of proving the justice of contemplated changes. Congress enacted Taft's plan to create a special Commerce Court, composed of experts in commercial law, to which appeals of the ICC might be made.

Taft was a supporter of religious freedom. A Unitarian, he was subjected to religious bigotry by William Jennings Bryan. Nothing in his record is inimical to civil liberties. As governor of the Philippines, he had gone to Rome to discuss with the Vatican matters regarding the landholdings of Catholic friars. He appointed Julia C. Lathrop to head the new Children's Bureau, the first appointment of a woman to a major U.S. government post. He was the first president to address a national convention of woman suffragists. His audience hissed him when he said that he was not altogether in sympathy with their movement. He thought women as a whole were not interested in the vote and that the ballot would be controlled by the less desirable class of women. He may have been freer of racial prejudices than most men of his day. Roosevelt sent him to Tokyo to soothe feelings when California barred Japanese from public schools and forbade them to own land, and to China to persuade the government to lift the boycott against American goods. He vetoed an immigration bill containing a literacy test requirement.

As governor of the Philippines he built roads, harbors, worked toward self-government and led a movement for land reform. He established schools and worked to improve the economic status of people. His record as president was less enlightened. He abolished a Council of Fine Arts established by Roosevelt. He established Glacier National Park and at least five National Monuments. First Lady Helen Herron Taft was largely responsible for the Japanese cherry trees in Washington, D. C.

ADMINISTRATION AND INTERGOVERNMENTAL RELATIONS

In his inaugural address Taft said he planned to submit proposals for constitutional amendments in interstate commerce and trust legislation. He called for a special session of Congress for his first goal of tariff revision. Taft presented to Congress a railroad bill providing for an increase in the powers of the ICC and facilitating the deposition of its orders in the courts, a postal savings bill, a conservation bill, and a number of remedial bills concerning railway safety devices. He recommended a federal incorporation bill to protect investors and insure stability of securities, a bill limiting injunctions, a bill requiring publication of campaign expenditures, and a bill to admit Arizona and New Mexico as states. In his 1912 State of the Union message he called for banking and currency reform and for workman's compensation for railway workers and workers involved in interstate commerce.

Taft created the Children's Bureau and the Bureau of Mines. The Labor Department was split off from Commerce. Taft kept two men from Roosevelt's cabinet. He replaced the others with men of his choice and received a storm of criticism. The president delegated far too much authority. He was too easygoing and trusted his subordinates too much, failing to hold some personnel responsible for results.

His speeches were ponderous and prosaic; his delivery pedestrian. He was colorless in comparison to the flamboyant Roosevelt, who became his opponent after 1910. Taft reported to the public, Congress, and executive branch employees, but Roosevelt outshone the president.

Taft appointed a budget committee of cabinet members to supervise all estimates of federal expenses. In his first month in office he issued an executive order establishing a central agency to purchase all government supplies. He came closer than any previous president to preparing an executive budget. He appointed a Commission on Economy and Efficiency that had recommended the adoption of a budget system, but was unable to induce Congress to accept the innovation.

Prior to Taft's inauguration, the Republican party already had conservative and progressive factions. The combination of progressives and Democrats gave the opposition a majority. However, the Taft administration had an impressive record of legislative accomplishments. Trust-busting and conservation goals were accomplished. Additional power was given to the ICC, postal savings and parcel post were created, civil service was expanded, a secretary of labor cabinet position was created, and the Sixteenth and Seventeenth amendments were passed. Taft's refusal to support the progressives in their successful fight to curb the almost unlimited powers of Speaker Uncle Joe Cannon cost him the support of liberals. The Senate rejected his treaties of arbitration with England and France. Despite his troubles with Congress, he had only one veto overridden — the Webb-Kenyon Bill, prohibiting the interstate shipment of liquor into dry states

Taft wanted to be chief justice more than he wanted to be president. He had excellent relations with the judiciary. He appointed six supreme court justices — more than any previous president. His appointees were able jurists and they came from the Northeast, the South, and the West, and included Catholics and Protestants, Democrats and Republicans. Nevertheless, the appointments were criticized. In 1921 Taft became the only ex–President to serve as Chief Justice of the United States.

Taft was falsely identified with conservative and reactionary groups opposed to reform. Taft tried to act in the best interests of all the people, but the opposition of Roosevelt and the progressives made this difficult.

LEADERSHIP AND DECISION MAKING

Taft was charged with being dull, slow, and lazy. He faced criticism constantly. Lacking charisma, he was dull in the sense of being boring, not in the sense of being dimwitted. He was not energetic and had trouble staying awake in meetings, but he was conscientious. His ponderous style made him unable to inspire people. With the Republican party split, Taft persuaded party regulars to follow him. After the break with Roosevelt, he persuaded conservatives to support his policies.

The president restored public confidence after the Panic of 1907. Prosperity returned and continued. He maintained confidence in government during the Ballinger-Pinchot controversy. His administration was weakened by the split with Roosevelt and the latter's attacks on him prior to the election of 1912.

Taft had a concept of what the nation and the world should be like. He was a proponent of peace and prosperity. However, his administration was marked by divisiveness. The split in his own political party was particularly disruptive. He was unable to communicate his vision in such a way as to get people excited about his goals.

The president was weak at conceiving political strategy. He appeared to be very lacking in political skills. His abilities and attitudes were more appropriate to a judicial position than to a role of political leadership. Often Taft acted against the advice of subordinates. He was a very intelligent man who had devoted his life to public service. He utilized his intelligence in problem solving and decision making, except that he did not always consider all of the ramifications — particularly the political ramifications — of his decisions. His past experience had been in appointive positions rather than elective positions and his decisions were not politically popular. He was inclined to arrive at decisions intuitively rather than by hard work.

Taft might have had more political support if he had been willing to compromise on some issues to appease the progressives. He compromised with the conservatives on the tariff and signed the Payne-Aldrich Act, thus alienating the progressives. His overblown defense of the Payne-Aldrich Act hurt him politically more than if he had just said it was a compromise and he did the best he could. He did not have the political skills to know when to compromise and when not to, and how to defend his decisions. Taft made hard decisions. For example, the firing of the popular Pinchot. He knew this would hurt him politically, but he felt he must do it because Pinchot had broken a government rule.

PRESIDENTIAL QUALITIES

Taft appeared as dignified as his huge size would permit. He always conducted himself with dignity. Americans were so proud of his predecessor that Taft never received enough acclaim to instill pride. The office of the president received more respect in Europe due to Taft's work toward world peace. At home the office received less respect under Taft than it did under Roosevelt. In comparison with the charismatic Teddy, Taft appeared weak and ineffectual.

Taft continued using Roosevelt's powers in trust-busting and conservation. The presidency did not suffer an actual loss of power under the helm of the ponderous Taft. The public wrongly thought Taft had gone over to the reactionaries, representing business interests and not the people. The people did not support his re-election bid. Taft was a genial man who enjoyed being with people. He and his wife did a lot of entertaining. Whether he paid any attention to advice given him during social gatherings is doubtful. Over five thousand guests attended a reception at the White House on New Year's Day, 1910. He and his wife entertained thousands of guests at a White House garden party on their silver wedding anniversary June 19, 1911. Taft spoke to the people often, but he was thought to be dull and boring. He was unable to use the office as a bully pulpit as his charismatic predecessor had done. In 1909 he made a 13,500-mile swing around the country, making more that 250 speeches. He was damaged politically by his statement that the Payne-Aldrich Act was the best bill the Republican party ever passed.

Taft acted consistently on a firm set of morals. He could be trusted. He kept his word. Taft was honest. He never used his office for personal gain. He was criticized for accepting gifts from the public at his silver wedding anniversary party, but there was nothing improper about this. Taft exhibited a high standard of personal morality throughout his life.

OVERALL ASSESSMENT

Although almost devoid of political leadership skills, Taft was an effective president. Overall, he received 33 points and ranks 21st among the 39 presidents rated.

WOODROW WILSON

1913–21

	RATING POINTS	RANK
FOREIGN RELATIONS	13	6 tie
DOMESTIC PROGRAMS	15	6
ADMINISTRATION	16	2 tie
LEADERSHIP	14	9 tie
PERSONAL QUALITIES	18	2 tie
OVERALL ASSESSMENT	76	3 tie

BACKGROUND

Thomas Woodrow Wilson was born December 29, 1856, in Staunton, Virginia. A minister's son, he moved frequently as his father accepted new pastorates. As a child he was called "Tommy," but he dropped his first name soon after graduating from Princeton. He received a law degree from the University of Virginia and opened a law office in Atlanta, but soon entered graduate school at Johns Hopkins University to study history and political science. He received a Ph.D., the only president to earn this distinction. In 1885 Wilson accepted a position as associate professor of history at Bryn Mawr College. In 1888 he became professor of history and political economy at Wesleyan University. In 1890 he became professor of jurisprudence and political economy at Princeton. He became known as a popular lecturer and a distinguished researcher. In 1902 Wilson was named president of Princeton University. Immediately he set about reorganizing the university's undergraduate program. He introduced the preceptorial system and tried to reform the snobbish private eating clubs. Wilson was not successful in getting his reforms implemented, but he earned a national reputation as an educational leader who wanted to make higher education more democratic.

In 1910, James Smith, the Democratic political boss of New Jersey, offered Wilson the party's nomination for the governorship of New Jersey. After receiving assurances from Smith that the machine would not try to control him, Wilson resigned from Princeton to campaign for governor. The power and eloquence of his speeches carried him to a landslide victory. Wilson quickly established his independence from the party machine. He pushed a series of reforms through the legislature, including a corrupt-practices act, a primary-election law, a public utilities act, a workmen's compensation law, and various school reforms. Within two years he had transformed New Jersey from one of the most conservative states in the Union to one of the most progressive.

NOMINATION AND ELECTION

Wilson's New Jersey reforms brought him national attention. By the time the Democratic convention met in 1912, Wilson was one of four leading candidates for the presidential nomination. Progressives were divided between Wilson and Champ Clark. Southern conservatives supported Oscar W. Underwood, while Northern conservatives favored Judson Harmon. Clark led on the early ballots, reaching a majority on the tenth ballot, but still falling short of the two-thirds vote needed for the nomination. Not since 1844 had a candidate received a majority but failed to win the nomination. Wilson prepared to release his delegates, but agreed to stay a little longer. On the fourteenth ballot, William Jennings Bryan, the party's most revered figure, endorsed Wilson. From this point on, Wilson gathered momentum, taking the lead on the 28th ballot, and winning the nomination on the 46th ballot. For vice president, Wilson favored Underwood, who declined. The convention then selected Thomas R. Marshall.

The Republicans nominated President Taft for a second term. Supporters of ex–President Theodore Roosevelt left the Republican party and formed a new Progressive party. The split in Republican ranks almost guaranteed a Democratic victory in the fall. Nevertheless, Wilson campaigned hard, stirring the public with his speeches. He pledged to lower the tariff, end monopolies, restore free competition, and establish the right of labor to bargain collectively. Roosevelt went even further, crusading for the entire Progressive agenda. Overshadowed by his two challengers, the incumbent seemed placid and made few speeches.

The Republican hope was that Wilson and Roosevelt would split the progressive vote, giving the election to Taft, the only conservative in the race. However, the country was clearly in a progressive mood in 1912. In the popular vote Wilson led, Roosevelt was second, while Taft trailed. Eugene Debs, the Socialist candidate, and two minor also-rans totaled more than one million votes. Wilson was thus elected with the smallest percentage (41.56) of the popular vote of any winning candidate since Abraham Lincoln in 1860. The electoral college was another matter. Wilson swept to an easy victory, winning 435 electoral votes to Roosevelt's 88, and Taft's 8 electoral votes.

In 1916 Wilson was renominated by acclamation on the first ballot, with Marshall again selected as his running mate. The Republican candidate was Charles Evans Hughes. Because of the tense international situation, Wilson did not campaign actively, preferring to stay in the White House. His supporters coined the campaign slogan, "He has kept us out of war." Hughes campaigned energetically. He attacked the law creating the eight-hour workday, calling it labor's "gold brick," called for a higher tariff, and criticized Wilson's policies toward Mexico and Germany.

On election night it appeared that Hughes had won the presidency. When most people retired for the night, Hughes had 254 electoral votes, 12 short of a majority, and was leading in California, which had 13 electoral votes. Some newspapers issued extras, prematurely proclaiming a Hughes victory. However, when all the votes were in, Wilson carried California and won the election. The president received 277 electoral votes to 254 for Hughes.

FOREIGN RELATIONS

Wilson kept the United States out of war as long as he could honorably do so. After the sinking of the *Lusitania* in 1915, Wilson negotiated with the Germans and got them to order their submarines not to attack neutral or passenger ships. In less than two years Germany resumed attacking neutral merchant ships. Wilson failed to convince Germany to cease unlimited submarine warfare against all shipping, including American ships. Even when he issued an ultimatum to Germany after the *Sussex* torpedoing, the Germans continued their attacks. Finally, the German submarine attacks forced him to recommend declaration of war. The alternative, of course, was to stop sending supplies to Britain. This was unacceptable to Wilson and probably to the American people as well.

Once the United States entered the fray, Wilson proved himself to be a strong wartime leader. He rallied the people behind the war effort. Not only did he effectively direct the mobilization of America's economic and man-power resources, but he also voiced the moral ideals toward which all the peoples of the world might aspire. He asserted that we were fighting to make the world safe for democracy. In a speech to Congress he set forth in his Fourteen Points his program for peace. The fourteenth point called for the establishment of an association of nations to keep the world peace. The speech inspired Americans, weakened German morale, and gave a basis upon which Germany could appeal for peace.

In an effort to make certain his Fourteen Points would be carried out, Wilson led the U.S. delegation to the peace conference at Paris. He was given a hero's reception in Paris. Everywhere he went in Europe, crowds cheered him as the hope of humanity. But the leaders of France, Britain, and Italy did not share his idealism. He was forced to compromise on several major issues in order to win acceptance of his fourteenth point. His compromises weakened his moral position somewhat, but they did insure the establishment of the League of Nations, for which he was awarded the Nobel Peace Prize in 1920. After compromising in Europe, Wilson refused to accept reservations that Republicans insisted on adding to the Treaty of Versailles. Accordingly, the treaty was rejected by the Senate. Without the membership of the United States, the League was weaker and less effective than it might have been. However, it did have some successes and laid the groundwork for the United Nations that followed.

Relations with Latin American nations suffered a setback during the Wilson administration. Wilson wanted to be their friend and champion upon terms of equality and honor, but his actions did not convince our neighboring nations that he really regarded them as equals. He wanted to convert the Monroe Doctrine from a unilateral policy to a system of mutual security. He failed due to suspicions aroused in Latin America by the record of American military intervention, which increased during the Wilson regime. He twice invaded Mexico and occupied Haiti, Santo Domingo, and Nicaragua to restore order to those troubled lands, but he did accept the offer of the ABC powers (Argentina, Brazil, and Chile) to arbitrate the dispute with Mexico. In

1917 Congress approved the purchase of three of the Virgin Islands from Denmark.

Trouble with Mexico began when Wilson refused to recognize the Huerta government, which came to power in 1913 by means of a bloody *coup d'état*. Wilson permitted Huerta's enemies to obtain arms in the United States to use in a revolt against the dictator. When Huerta's forces arrested a group of American sailors who had gone ashore at Tampico, Wilson refused to accept Huerta's apology and demanded that the dictator salute the American flag. When Huerta refused, Wilson ordered American forces to occupy Veracruz. Eighteen Americans were killed in the action. Wilson then accepted the ABC arbitration and a peaceful settlement. Eventually Huerta resigned and left the country. The government of his successor, Venustiano Carranza, was accorded recognition. Francisco "Pancho" Villa then led a revolt against Carranza. Villa conducted raids on American settlements across the Rio Grande. Many Americans called for war, but Wilson adopted a policy of "watchful waiting." Then, in 1916, he ordered General Pershing to lead an expedition deep into Mexico. Some fighting occurred, but luckily open war was averted. Following the American expedition against Villa, Mexico adopted a new and radical constitution. In 1917 Wilson recognized the Mexican government (with Carranza still at its head) that had been established by the new constitution.

Wilson encouraged the development of democracies in Poland and in the states of the former Austro-Hungarian Empire. The deployment of American troops in Latin America was intended to help provide stable governments there. The troops brought order to lands with no experience with democracy. Wilson denied them self-government, but tried to improve their economies, build roads, improve health conditions, and improve education, perhaps setting the stage for future democracy. The United States supplied food, clothing, and medicine to the war-shattered countries of Europe, providing food to Belgium as early as 1914. These efforts were directed by Herbert Hoover, acting first as a representative of private agencies and later for the Wilson administration.

The Underwood Tariff Act was Wilson's first reform measure. It lowered rates on imports by an average of about 25 percent and removed the tariff completely from many items. The Underwood Tariff, the repeal of the Panama Tolls Act, and Wilson's determination that German submarines should not attack neutral merchant ships are examples of his efforts to enhance world trade. The actions of Wilson at Paris enhanced world opinion of the United States. The perception of this country as strong, peaceful, fair, and a dependable member of the world community has remained in most of the world, even though Wilson's prestige slipped in Europe after the rejection of the League of Nations by the United States Senate.

DOMESTIC PROGRAMS

Wilson proposed legislation reforming the nation's banking and currency laws. Despite the opposition of the banking interests, Congress passed the Federal Reserve Act of 1913, generally regarded as the most effective bank bill in the nation's history. Wilson's reform of the banking and currency laws, the provision of short-term agricultural credit through the federal reserve system, and the Federal Farm Loan Act of 1916 helped maintain the nation's prosperity. Although inflation is almost inevitable in wartime, Wilson kept inflation from becoming excessive.

During his first term, Wilson pushed through Congress the most extensive social reforms of any president up to that time. Under urging from the president, Congress established the Federal Trade Commission in 1914, giving the government the power to investigate and stop unfair trade practices. That same year it passed the Clayton Antitrust Act, strengthening the government's power to stop monopolies and prevent unfair practices of big business. This was followed by the Seaman's Act to provide greater safety for sailors and greater freedom for them in their relations with ship owners. In 1916, the Adamson Act established the eight-hour working day for railroad employees. The Child Labor Act limited children's working hours.

Included in the Clayton Act were provisions that caused it to be called a "Magna Carta" for labor. It exempted labor unions from prosecution under anti-trust laws, limited the use of injunctions in labor disputes, prescribed trial by jury in contempt cases, and legalized strikes, picketing, boycotts, and the collection of strike benefits. Wilson signed the bill creating the Department of Labor. For the nation's first secretary of labor, he appointed William D. Wilson, who had risen through the ranks of the United Mine Workers and whose appointment was urged by the American Federation of Labor. His support did not extend to the radical Industrial Workers of the World, and in 1918 his administration brought the IWW leaders to trial. This is understandable inasmuch as this was wartime and the IWW had openly revolutionary aims. To his credit, Wilson did not use federal force against strikers in the great wave of strikes that hit the country in 1919.

The president promoted the welfare of the people through his regulation of the excesses of big business, his labor policies, his fiscal policies, and his farm bills. Clearly the people benefitted from the economic aspects of his "New Freedom." Wilson's tax policies put the burden of taxation on those most able to pay. The first income tax under the Sixteenth Amendment was enacted during his administration. Wilson began a new series of federal grants in aid of education. The Smith-Lever Act of 1914 provided that the United States should match dollar for dollar the contributions of any states that chose to co-operate in a program of agricultural extension. In 1917 the Smith-Hughes Act appropriated funds, also on a matching basis, for agricultural, commercial, industrial, home economics, and vocational education in public high schools. These acts contributed greatly to the general welfare, as did the Federal Highways Act of 1916, which carried the dollar-matching principle into the area of road building.

Wilson did little to support racial justice. He did, through Bryan, intercede with the California legislature in an unsuccessful attempt to prevent passage of an act prohibiting aliens (Japanese) from holding land in the state. He did nothing to prevent the imposition of segregation in federal departments and agencies. For most of his life Wilson was a strong supporter of freedom of expression. A wave of super-patriotism, foreign-baiting, and suppression of dissent accompanied our entry into the war. An Espionage Act was passed in 1917 and a drastic Sedition Act in 1918. Hundreds of conscientious objectors were sent to jail. Freedom of speech and press were restricted during wartime, with the approval of the Supreme Court. Wilson did not oppose the imprisonment of Eugene Debs for a speech opposing the war in 1918. Wilson supported freedom of religion and refused to use a religious test in his appointments. He appointed Louis Brandeis as the first Jewish member of the Supreme Court.

Wilson twice vetoed restrictive immigration bills. The 1917 bill passed over his veto, provided that adults unable to read would be denied admission. Wilson vetoed it because he thought its real purpose was to discriminate against immigrants from southern and eastern Europe where the literacy rate was much lower than in northern and western Europe. Wilson opposed discrimination based on national origin. The Women's Suffrage Amendment was passed during his watch. He appointed Annette Abbott Adams as assistant attorney general, the first time a woman had been appointed to a government position of that rank. A strong supporter of human rights, both at home and abroad, Wilson treated all persons with respect, regardless of status. He tried to improve the lot of all persons.

ADMINISTRATION AND INTERGOVERNMENTAL RELATIONS

Wilson developed a set of goals and objectives and immediately set out an organized plan for their accomplishment. He laid out his objectives in an eloquent inauguration speech and set the machinery in motion to get his proposals enacted into law. Less than a month after his inauguration Wilson called Congress into a special session. He addressed a joint meeting of the two houses, the first president since John Adams to do so. The president's planning in the area of domestic reform was excellent. His long-term goals for the world were of the highest order.

Wilson organized the executive departments and personnel according to sound administra-

tive principles. He was especially good at delegating to department heads the authority to staff their own departments. The president established communication patterns, used his cabinet effectively, and made excellent use of his advisors and aides to get his programs enacted. Wilson appointed well-qualified men to cabinet positions. As president he hoped to be guided exclusively in appointments by merit, but in practice he found that political considerations had to be taken into account. Legislation initiated by Wilson created two important independent agencies — the Federal Reserve Board and the Federal Trade Commission. To these agencies he made strong, bipartisan appointments.

For the most part Wilson appointed capable cabinet officers. Bryan was not the ideal secretary of state, but the president could not hope to solidify his control over Congress without Bryan's support and the Great Commoner would accept no lesser position. Josephus Daniels, secretary of the navy, had no experience in naval matters but he was an able man, assisted by Franklin D. Roosevelt, who did know about ships. The other cabinet officers were good choices for their respective positions. Wilson insisted that his appointees conduct themselves with honesty and high moral standards. No corruption ever marred his administrations. Wilson delegated authority to department heads and held them responsible for results.

Wilson was an excellent communicator. Open discussion was encouraged in cabinet meetings; he delivered his legislative requests to Congress in person; he was the first president to have regular press conferences; he set aside time each afternoon so that anyone who wished to see him could come in for a brief meeting without an appointment. He was an excellent writer and a superb speaker. He was accessible to the press, and many reporters and editors held him in very high regard.

An outstanding administrator, Wilson controlled expenditures appropriately. Like his predecessors, Wilson had to rely upon his personal relationship with department heads in order to do this. Each governmental agency gave its appropriations requests to the secretary of the treasury, who put them all in a "Book of

Estimates" and sent them to Congress without comment or revision. Wilson proposed giving the president control over budget requests. When Congress passed a bill establishing a bureau of the budget not under the control of the president, Wilson vetoed it.

During his first term Wilson secured overwhelming support from members of his own party and passed a vast array of important, progressive legislation. Toward the end of his second term this support lessened. He secured some support from the opposition party during his first term and on war measures during his second term. After the peace conference, the relationship deteriorated to the point that it damaged his presidency. Opposition from Congress wrecked his foreign policy in the last two years of his administration.

Wilson nominated and secured approval of qualified candidates for judicial positions. The man now usually regarded as the most distinguished of his court appointees, Louis Brandeis, was the one who stirred up the most opposition. Even some reactionaries were said to have been ashamed later of the nature of their opposition to Brandeis. Another of his Supreme Court appointees, James C. McReynolds, who was his first attorney-general, was a noted trust buster and was considered radical in his views, but turned out to be a consistently conservative justice.

Doing what he thought was best for the country was always Wilson's highest priority. Wilson attempted to act always in what he thought was the best interests of all the people, including those sometimes overlooked, such as factory workers, miners, and poor farmers. He fought the "special interests" on their behalf. (He himself may have overlooked blacks and native Americans, but at least he was not hostile to them as many of his predecessors had been.) Although the president was a crusader against the "special interests," he did not so antagonize them that they united to defeat his domestic reforms. Wilson was highly respected by the public. The people respected his ideas and his ideals even more than they supported him as a person. They enthusiastically supported his reforms, which is one reason he was able to overcome the special interests, and they rallied behind him in the war effort to a re-

markable degree. He lost their support with the "failures" of the peace conference.

LEADERSHIP AND DECISION MAKING

Primarily by example, Wilson inspired executive branch personnel to a high level of focused, productive effort. His success in accomplishing significant domestic goals during his first term was surpassed by few, if any, presidents, either before or after him. Wilson did not have the magnetic personality associated with charisma, but he caused people to follow him because of the power of his ideas and the appeal of his ideals. The president was able through his speeches and writings to inspire the people in an all-out effort to accomplish important national goals, such as winning the war. Earlier he used his talents to persuade Congress to pass the most significant reform legislation ever enacted in the nation's history up to that point. Wilson was one of the most persuasive writers and speakers ever to occupy the Oval Office. He was able to win over many opponents by convincing them he was on the right course. The president set incredibly high performance standards for himself and insisted upon high performance by others. He motivated them to achieve.

Although there is a perception that Wilson was cold and aloof, he developed relationships based on mutual respect and trust that enabled him to get his programs implemented. The president was especially skillful at explaining reasons for his actions. He listened, and showed that he was listening, to his subordinates, but seldom changed his mind based on their input. Openness naturally was curtailed during wartime and had deteriorated badly by the end of his second term, especially after his stroke.

The president unified the nation during the war, creating a feeling of togetherness and shared national goals among the people. This unity fell apart during the peace conference. Heads of foreign governments (France, Italy, Britain) respected Wilson's ideals and intellect, although they thought him somewhat naive in not recognizing the immutable demands of realpolitik. They followed his lead on some points because they had to, but they forced him to compromise to achieve anything. Heads of some other governments (especially the new European states) were extremely enthusiastic supporters of Wilson, as were the majority of the European people. He was certainly an international leader, one of the Big Four. He brought America into the arena of international leadership and responsibility more than any previous president.

The president had a very clear vision of what the country and the entire world should be like and tried to get both to conform to his ideal. He was able to conceptualize a strategy for getting the country from where it was to where he wanted it to be. More remarkably, he had a strategy for getting the world to be what he thought it should be. That he was not able to accomplish it was no fault of the conception, but was due to the refusal of others to go along with his plans.

Wilson always weighed various alternatives and made a judgment about the possible consequences of each course of action. He made a mistaken judgment about his failure to agree to the Lodge restrictions on the League of Nations. Perhaps the restrictions would have so weakened the League as to make it useless. But without the participation of the United States, there was no way the League of Nations could play the role that Wilson envisioned for it.

Wilson was a scholar, not only of American but also of European history. His actions as president were guided by a wide knowledge and deep understanding of the past. He was determined to help the world avoid repeating some of its past mistakes. Although Wilson was reluctant to admit his own mistakes, he did learn from them and seldom made the same mistake twice. Wilson did not have any system of reassessment in place, but when events required it, he could change his mind. Although he was strongly against our involvement in the Great War, when the Germans refused to call off their submarines he reluctantly led our country into the war and pursued it with great vigor. Wilson possessed one of the finest intellects of all our presidents. He used his intelligence in analyzing situations and conceptualizing possible solutions.

As president, Wilson quickly learned he had to make some compromises in order to get his programs approved, but he was able to do so without sacrificing any moral principles. He has been criticized for compromising too much with the Allied leaders at the peace conference and has been castigated with equal fervor for not compromising enough with the Senate in order to secure ratification of the peace treaty. Compromise was absolutely necessary in order to secure approval at Versailles. Further compromise was equally essential in order to secure ratification at home, but Wilson would make no concessions to the recalcitrant Republican Senators.

When faced with the necessity to make a decision, the president made the decision firmly and resolutely, regardless of the severity of the consequences. Wilson acted calmly in the international emergency caused by the outbreak of war in Europe. The nation would have eagerly followed him into war earlier, but he waited until the possibilities of staying out were exhausted rather than act precipitously.

PERSONAL QUALITIES

Wilson always acted with the utmost dignity. His comportment reflected well upon the office he held. The people were proud of Wilson, proud that this great man was their president. (This changed after 1918.) The office of the presidency received more respect at home and abroad because of Wilson's stature.

Through his reform legislation and especially through his dollar-matching programs, such as the education and highway construction programs, Wilson enhanced the power of the presidency to promote the public welfare more than perhaps any of his predecessors had. The extraordinary powers conferred upon him in wartime were temporary and had little permanent effect on the power of the presidency, although they did set a precedent that later presidents could call upon when they needed increased powers to meet future crises.

Wilson was very effective at convincing the people that he was the "people's president," that he was on their side against the special interests. Wilson excelled in reaching out to the people through speeches and writings. Many newspapers printed verbatim some of his short speeches. He really had a gift for expressing himself clearly in concise language. He was on a tour of the nation, seeking support for the League of Nations, when he suffered his debilitating stroke. He believed, perhaps mistakenly, that once he explained it to the people they would rally to his side and force the Senate to accept it. Unfortunately for Wilson and for the country, his condition did not permit him to make the case as forcefully as he could have in good health.

Wilson acted consistently on a firm set of moral values and principles. Few presidents were his equal in this regard. He adhered to a strict moral code. Wilson was above reproach as far as his personal honesty was concerned. He never benefitted personally at the expense of the public and was absolutely adamant that others should also meet this standard. Wilson insisted that his appointees conduct themselves with honesty and high moral standards. No corruption ever marred his administrations. Wilson enhanced the prestige of the office of the president through the high standard of personal morality he exhibited throughout his life.

OVERALL ASSESSMENT

In every area on our rating scale, Wilson ranked among the ten best presidents in the history of the United States. His total score was 76 out of a possible 100 points, ranking him in a tie for third place among the 39 presidents rated.

WARREN G. HARDING
1921–23

	RATING POINTS	RANK
FOREIGN RELATIONS	7	26 tie
DOMESTIC PROGRAMS	2	26
ADMINISTRATION	−2	29 tie
LEADERSHIP	−5	35
PERSONAL QUALITIES	−1	35
OVERALL ASSESSMENT	1	33

BACKGROUND

Warren Gamaliel Harding was born on November 2, 1865, on a farm near Corsica (now Blooming Grove), Ohio. He attended a one-room school in Corsica and a public school in Caldonia. He helped with farm chores and learned to set type on the Caldonia *Argus,* a weekly newspaper of which his father was part owner. At the age of fourteen, he entered Ohio Central College. At his graduation in 1882, he delivered the commencement address. Harding taught for one term in a one-room schoolhouse near Marion, Ohio. He also read law and sold insurance before entering the newspaper business. In 1884 he and two friends bought the Marion *Star,* a bankrupt weekly, for $300. He soon acquired full ownership and built the paper into a profitable enterprise. In 1892 he ran for county auditor, but lost. In 1899 he was elected to the Ohio state senate, with the help of Harry Daugherty, who would be his political advisor for more than two decades. During the second of his two terms in the state senate,

Harding served as majority floor leader. In 1903 Harding was elected lieutenant governor of Ohio. In 1910 he was the Republican candidate for governor, but lost in a Democratic landslide. Harding was a delegate to the 1912 Republican national convention, where he placed President Taft's name in nomination. In 1914 Harding was elected United States Senator from Ohio. He introduced no major bills and missed almost half the roll calls during his six year term. He was keynote speaker and chairman of the 1916 Republican national convention. He remained editor and publisher of the *Star* during his political career.

NOMINATION AND ELECTION

When the Republican convention met in 1920, there were three leading candidates for the party's presidential nomination — General Leonard Wood, Governor Frank O. Lowden of Illinois, and Senator Hiram Johnson of California. Harding was considered a darkhorse, but his candidacy was promoted vigorously by his wife and Harry Daugherty. On the first ballot Wood led; Harding was sixth. As balloting continued throughout the day, it became apparent that none of the front-runners would be able to garner a majority. The convention adjourned for the night. Legend has it that a group of party elders met in a smoke-filled room in the Blackstone Hotel at two o'clock in the morning and decided to break the deadlock by supporting the darkhorse Harding, as Daugherty had predicted they would. The next day, on the tenth ballot, Harding won the nomination. Calvin Coolidge was selected as the vice-presidential candidate. The Democratic nominee was Governor James M. Cox of Ohio, with Franklin D. Roosevelt as his running mate. The election was a referendum on the Wilson administration and the League of Nations. Cox endorsed both wholeheartedly. Harding stayed in Marion and conducted a "front-porch campaign" from his home. He made speeches and met visiting dignitaries there. He denounced the League of Nations but promised to work for an association of nations. He avoided specifics on domestic issues by promising a "return to normalcy."

The election resulted in a Republican landslide. Harding won over 60 percent of the popular vote. In the electoral college Harding amassed 404 votes to 127 for Cox.

FOREIGN RELATIONS

Harding had some successes in foreign relations. During his administration peace treaties were signed formally ending the World War, an arms limitation conference was held at Washington with nine nations represented, and a Five Power Treaty was signed with Italy, Japan, Britain, and France. All of these events were intended to be peace making or peace-keeping actions and were successful in the short run. Harding also helped settle disputes between Costa Rica and Panama and between Chile and Peru.

Although Harding opposed the League of Nations, he did favor international cooperation as demonstrated by the disarmament conference and the Five Power Treaty. He greatly improved our relations with Latin America. He spoke in favor of some kind of a voluntary association of nations to replace the League, but did nothing to bring it about. The president maintained a good working relationship with heads of most foreign governments, but was unable to convince Congress to recognize the government of the Soviet Union. Due to intransigence of Congress he did not cooperate with the League of Nations, but played a large role in increasing international cooperation among the nations of the Americas.

Harding withdrew troops from Cuba and Santo Domingo, but kept them in Haiti which he felt was too unstable for withdrawal. He pushed through a treaty with Colombia which included $25 million in reparations for our part in the Panama Revolution of 1903. (It also contained an expression of regret for our actions, but this was removed in order to secure ratification by the Senate.) He also convened a conference which led to the creation of a Central American Tribunal to arbitrate disputes among those nations.

Although the United States itself did not join any alliances, Harding helped in the formation of regional alliances in Latin America. Harding engaged in cooperative endeavors with other nations that helped ease tensions in several places. The Washington Conference was helpful in the short run, but may have been hurtful in the long run because of the failure of Japan to live up to its agreements. Harding's actions enhanced Latin American opinion toward the United States. In other parts of the world opinion was mixed, but on the whole it was positive.

Harding tried to promote democracy in Cuba, Santo Domingo, and the Philippines, among other places. He continued the European relief started during the Wilson administration and extended aid to the Soviet Union. His policies toward Latin America were still exploitive but not so bad as those of the previous four administrations.

With Harding's approval, Congress increased protective tariffs to new highs with the Fordney-McCumber Act of 1922. Although the higher tariff may have been beneficial at first to some segments of the United States economy, its long-run effects were harmful, even to the agricultural community which campaigned vigorously for the high tariffs. The tariff was harmful to world trade.

DOMESTIC PROGRAMS

Inflation had occurred during and immediately after the World War. Deflation came suddenly in the spring of 1920, before Harding's election. Thus, Harding inherited a depression from the previous administration. Recovery was underway when the president died. The extent to which his policies were helpful is debatable. His approach was primarily the trickle-down theory — cut taxes on the wealthy to encourage investment, and thus stimulate the economy. His Farm Loan Act did help ease the recession in agricultural areas, but much more was needed. At the urging of Secretary of Agriculture Henry C. Wallace, and with the support of the president, Congress passed an anti-monopoly act — the Packers and Stockyards Act.

Harding was anti-union. He was strongly against Samuel Gompers. His attorney general got a federal judge to issue an unduly restrictive injunction — the Wilkerson Injunction — against striking railroad workers. However, he helped workers by pressuring the steel industry to end the 12-hour day. He favored improving labor conditions by the voluntary actions of management rather than by collective bargaining, especially if it involved threat of force by labor unions.

Harding thought unemployment could be eased by voluntary means, cooperation among business leaders and state and local governments, rather than by a federal employment program. The idea of a federal welfare program or an anti-poverty program would not have been acceptable to him. Although Harding did not use full governmental powers to promote the health, education, safety, or welfare of the people, he supported the Sheppard Towner bill for the health of women and children.

Harding's fiscal policies may have been partly responsible for the economic recovery that was starting in 1923, but this is by no means certain. His main contribution in the fiscal area was the creation of the Bureau of the Budget. The idea of a federal budget had been first proposed by Wilson. Congress passed a bill that was unacceptable to Wilson, who vetoed it. At Harding's urging, Congress then passed a bill giving the president more control over the budget, and Harding signed it. On the negative side, Harding shifted the burden of taxation from the upper class taxpayers to the middle class.

Harding called for tolerance and an end to discrimination and supported an anti-lynching bill which did not pass. On the other hand, he supported the Per Centum Act, which was designed to discriminate against migrants from southern and southeastern Europe. Harding supported women's suffrage and tried to win support of women voters for the Republican party. He appointed no women or racial minorities to important positions in government, and resisted demands from black leaders that he do so, citing failure to find qualified candidates. In a speech in Birmingham, Harding chided Southerners for not allowing blacks to vote and called for an end to economic, educational, and political discrimination. However, he said there are "eternal and inescapable differences" which make social equality impossible.

A supporter of free speech. Harding did not go along with the extremists during the Red Scare. He released Eugene Debs, who had been jailed under the Sedition Act, and many other political prisoners, including Wobblies. He nearly emptied the nation's jails of wartime political prisoners. Harding was not a deeply religious man. He supported freedom of religion, but did nothing of special importance to advance it.

ADMINISTRATION AND INTERGOVERNMENTAL RELATIONS

At the very beginning of his term Harding announced in a special message to Congress his goals for his administration, but he did not have an organized plan laid out for their accomplishment. He was not much concerned about long-range planning, being more interested in the present than in the future.

Harding organized his departments and personnel according to sound administrative principles. He created the Bureau of the Budget and was the first president to develop an overall budget and submit it to Congress. He suggested a new Department of Public Welfare to coordinate expanding federal activity in education, public health, and sanitation, but never pushed for its creation. He was responsible for creating the Veterans' Bureau, and it became scandal ridden, primarily because of the people he appointed to administer it. In response to pressure group demands that the agricultural sector be represented, Harding changed the composition of the Federal Reserve Board. He tried unsuccessfully to get the Interstate Commerce Commission to reduce rates.

Some of Harding's staffing decisions were excellent. Charles Evans Hughes in the State Department, Herbert Hoover as Secretary of Commerce, and Henry Wallace in Agriculture were all first-rate people and were placed in appropriate positions. These were honest, knowledgeable, dedicated public servants, although Hoover and Wallace engaged in some unseemly turf battles. Some of Harding's other staffing decisions were real disasters and were responsible for the scandals which tarred the administration.

For the most part Harding assigned personnel to appropriate roles and gave them authority to carry out their assignments. He did not insist that they develop clear goals and objectives based on presidential priorities. Sometimes he turned his subordinates loose without giving them sufficient direction or oversight. This may have been the president's greatness weakness. Several members of his administration engaged in inappropriate, dishonest, illegal activity and he did not catch them nor stop them in time to prevent injury to the nation. The public's confidence in its government was shattered after Harding's death by the revelation of scandals that occurred during his administration.

Cabinet members were not always kept well informed. For example, even though he had a cabinet meeting the day of Daugherty's meeting with Judge Wilkerson, Harding said nothing about it and cabinet members did not know about the injunction until they read about it in the newspapers. Policy formulation and decision making were achieved by the president in private conferences with individual cabinet members rather than by the group as a whole. Despite the fact that he moved directly from the Senate to the White House and that many people expected a group of powerful senators to virtually run the government, and despite Harding's reputation for compromise, he did not always consult the Congress before making decisions.

The president reported to the people and to Congress through speeches and written messages. He had more press conferences and more friendly relationships with reporters than any other president between the two Roosevelts. Harding not only had an excellent relationship with the working press, but he also enjoyed editorial support from a majority of the nation's newspapers.

Republicans in Congress supported most of Harding's initiatives, but not the ship subsidy bill to which the President gave the highest priority. There were also some low priority bills they did not support. A small group of isolationists and progressive Republicans opposed the president bitterly. The Democrats opposed most of Harding's proposals, but were unable to defeat many of them. Although the parties were sharply divided on some foreign policy issues, there was enough bipartisan support to pass many of Harding's major foreign policy proposals.

Harding's Supreme Court nominees were all qualified and very conservative. None of his lower court nominees was rejected for confirmation. His nomination of William Howard Taft was widely praised at the time. Justices Sutherland and Butler went on to become two of the Nine Old Men that Franklin Roosevelt tried to purge.

Harding and most of the business interest groups cooperated with each other because they generally shared the same views. Labor unions generally opposed him. He had the support of the Farm Bureau much of the time, but was usually opposed by the other farm organizations. The president was immensely popular with the public at the beginning of his administration. He was liked for his friendly, affable manner and for not putting on airs. His popularity decreased as the recession lengthened, but started to rise as recovery started. As for respect, the public never regarded him as a great man, but they were satisfied with him — until the scandals came. After his death, they lost all respect for him. He is now regarded as one of our least respected presidents, but such was not the case during his lifetime.

LEADERSHIP AND DECISION MAKING

Harding did not provide energetic and creative leadership. Although he worked hard and long hours, he was lax about some things and his easy-going manner and love of recreation did not inspire others to highly focused, productive effort. Lacking charisma, Harding did not inspire people. They followed him mainly because he and they wanted to go in the same direction. Harding was no visionary, but he knew he wanted a nation of peace and prosperity and a world without war. This was a sufficient vision for his countrymen at the time. The president's strategy for peace was through arms reduction and the use of arbitration to settle disputes. His strategy for prosperity was lower taxes, higher tariffs, and reliance on the good sense of businessmen. It worked in the short run, but was disastrous in the long run.

Harding was not an especially persuasive person. Rarely did he marshal a compelling argument to convince others that his was the right course. When he was successful, it was because he and public opinion were in agreement. Harding was not an inspirational leader. He did not call on people to sacrifice for important national goals, except for one memorable speech in which he said: "Ask not what your government can do for you, but what you can do for your government." (Forty years later John F. Kennedy expressed that thought in more elegant language.) The people were tired of sacrifice and all-out effort during the World War. They were ready to get back to "normalcy."

The affable Warren Harding was very considerate of the feelings of others. He had a great need to be liked. Sometimes he waited too long to fire someone not worthy of his trust. Harding explained reasons for his actions and listened to subordinates (but not to all subordinates on all matters). He was able to engage in give and take discussion with those who disagreed with him. The president's great failures were in not setting high performance standards and in not insisting that his subordinates conduct themselves ethically and with a high degree of professionalism.

The nation was unified under Harding because the people were tired of the divisiveness caused by the struggle over the League of Nations. They were tired and ready to settle for normalcy. They wanted what he wanted — peace and prosperity.

Before making a decision the president usually considered one or more alternatives and attempted to foresee at least the immediate consequences of his decision. He was not highly imaginative in coming up with numerous courses of action. The president usually made up his own mind with the help of a few close advisors as to the course of action he wanted to take. If he ran into opposition, he might try to bring others (including the public) into the action in order to try to get his decision implemented or to find a satisfactory compromise.

Harding was not a student of history. He made some of the same mistakes that Grant had made as president. A study of the history of previous presidents might have enabled him to avoid the scandals that tarnished his administration. Harding did not always recognize his own errors in judgment. It should have been obvious to him early on that Daugherty should not have been in charge of the Justice Department, nor one of the president's closest advisors. Yet he either failed to recognize this or out of a misplaced sense of loyalty kept his old friend on too long. Harding was not stupid. He had a good mind. He just did not use it to its fullest. Analysis and contemplation were not his strong points. There is no record of continual or periodic evaluation of Harding's programs to see if they needed to be changed. However, he was only in office two and one-half years.

Harding was usually willing to compromise in order to avoid controversy or to give in on one thing in order to win support for another. Many historians say he was too eager to compromise. On important principles, though, he stuck to his guns, most notably on vetoing the Veterans' Bonus, which he thought the country could not afford.

Although Harding wanted to avoid any

controversy whenever possible, and would frequently postpone action in hope the problem would go away, he had the courage to make hard decisions when necessary and to hold steadfast on things that were important to him as long as he thought he had a chance of winning. His desire to avoid controversy was not due to lack of courage; it was just his style. He wanted everyone to like him and for everyone to get along.

Harding was not good at remaining calm in emergencies. He tended to get flustered if confronted with a crisis or an unresolved conflict. In some such cases he would allow others to make a rash decision, such as allowing Daugherty to get the Wilkerson Injunction against striking rail workers.

PERSONAL QUALITIES

The president usually presented a dignified public appearance, as disreputable as he may have been in private. His failure to exercise sufficient control over dishonest subordinates, however, demeaned the office of the presidency. Until the scandals came out, the country had pride in their president — not as a great, inspirational, visionary leader, but as evidence that a common man could make good. In the early 1920s the country was generally pleased to have him represent their nation to the world. The scandals, of course, destroyed this sentiment.

Harding's political philosophy was that the powers of the presidency should not be expanded. He believed in the constitutional separation of powers as he understood them. The scandals caused the stature of the office to be diminished.

The president allowed the public greater access than had been possible for Wilson during wartime. He also related better to the people than Wilson, who came across as pious and holier-than-thou. As to whether Harding gave thoughtful consideration to input he received from the public, the record is less clear. He did want to remain popular and took public opinion into consideration in a political way. Harding was approachable, friendly, not high-falutin' or strait-laced. The people thought he was one of them, not a member of an elite. The

middle class thought the president was on their side, until they found out some of his underlings had fleeced the country for personal profit.

Harding used many kinds of formal and informal communications to interact with people. The first president to have access to the radio, he took advantage of the new device. He went on a lengthy speaking tour prior to his fatal journey to Alaska. The exhaustion of that trip may have contributed to his death.

Harding did not have an especially firm set of moral values and principles. Religion, moral principles, and philosophy did not play a large role in his life. Harding was trustworthy in that when he gave his word he would keep it. Loyalty was one of his highest values. Unfortunately, he carried it to an extreme and allowed his friends to damage his administration and his reputation.

Getting elected, rewarding friends, and avoiding conflict were high priorities with Harding. He thought he acted for the good of the country, so he would have been chagrined to learn that some scholars thought he failed to put the public interest first. Harding was a typical Midwestern small business man and represented the broad middle class well. He was concerned about the farmer, the laborer, minorities, and even the condition of women and children. The problem was that his proposed solutions were so middle-class oriented that they did not result in beneficial programs for the disadvantaged. He listened to the labor and agriculture interest groups, but thought the business groups had the answers for everybody.

Harding did not exhibit a high standard of morality in his personal life. He had two different mistresses, although this was not widely known at the time. He smoked, chewed tobacco, and openly drank bootleg liquor in the White House, even though he had voted for Prohibition and as president was charged with a duty to see the nation's laws were enforced. He played high-stakes poker and engaged in recreational activities that some people found objectionable in the president of the United States. Yet none of these activities diminished his effectiveness as president. Other chief executives have engaged in many of these same activities and have not been castigated for their behavior.

LAST DAYS

Late in 1922 Harding began to learn of the corruption within his administration. It was disclosed that the Veterans' Bureau had sold war surplus materials at a price far below their value to favored purchasers without competitive bidding, after which new supplies were bought above their normal cost. The head of the Veterans' Bureau, Charles R. Forbes, a poker-playing intimate of the president, resigned. Charles F. Cramer, the attorney for the bureau committed suicide in March 1923. On May 29 another of Harding's close friends, Jesse Smith, shot himself to death in Attorney General Daugherty's apartment.

On June 20, 1923, the badly worried president embarked on a long trip to Canada and Alaska. When his special train reached Kansas City, Harding was visited by Mrs. Albert Fall, whose husband had resigned as Secretary of the Interior a few months earlier. Although their conversation was secret, Harding was visibly shaken by it. (Later Fall was convicted of accepting a bribe in the Teapot Dome scandal and sentenced to prison.) When he reached Alaska in July, Harding received a coded message about other friends who had betrayed him.

On his return trip, Harding was stricken with food poisoning. Further public appearances were canceled and Harding proceeded to San Francisco, where he was felled by pneumonia. He seemed to be recovering. However, on August 2 Harding died. The doctors suspected that a blood clot had been carried to the president's brain and asked for permission to perform an autopsy. Harding's widow refused to allow it. The exact cause of Harding's death is still not known. Gossipers speculated that the president had been poisoned to prevent him from testifying against his friends. In a futile effort to protect her husband's memory, Florence Harding burned all of the president's correspondence that she could find.

OVERALL ASSESSMENT

Harding's scores ranged from a high of seven points in Foreign Relations to a low of negative five in Leadership and Decision Making. Overall, the positives outweighed the negatives by a margin of only one point. He ranks 33rd among the presidents.

CALVIN COOLIDGE
1923–29

	RATING POINTS	RANK
FOREIGN RELATIONS	2	33
DOMESTIC PROGRAMS	–5	33 tie
ADMINISTRATION	–3	31 tie
LEADERSHIP	–2	32 tie
PERSONAL QUALITIES	3	31 tie
OVERALL ASSESSMENT	–4	34 tie

BACKGROUND

John Calvin Coolidge was born on July 4, 1872, at the family home adjoining the Coolidge general store in Plymouth Notch, Vermont. He graduated from Black River Academy at Ludlow, Vermont. After failing the entrance examination for Amherst college, he took college preparatory instruction at St. Johnsbury Academy in Ludlow, qualifying him for automatic admission to Amherst. In college he was an average student his first two years, then improved markedly, graduating cum laude in 1895.

Upon graduation, Coolidge dropped his first name and read law with a firm in Northampton, Massachusetts. Admitted to the bar in 1897, he opened a law office in Northampton and became active in the Republican party. In 1898 he was elected to the city council, and he became city solicitor in 1900. In 1904 he became chairman of the local Republican party. In 1906 he was elected to the Massachusetts state legislature, where he served two one-year terms. In 1909 he was elected mayor of Northampton, serving two terms in this office. From 1912 to 1915 he served four terms in the state senate, with two terms as president of that body. In 1915 he was elected lieutenant governor and was re-elected twice. In 1918 he was elected governor of Massachusetts. He became famous nationally for his handling of the Boston police strike. When bands of hoodlums roamed the streets at night, Coolidge called out the state troops to restore order. He issued the statement: "There is no right to strike against the public safety by anybody, anywhere, anytime." In 1919 Coolidge won re-election by a record vote.

NOMINATION AND ELECTION

When the Republican national convention met in 1920, Coolidge was the favorite son of Massachusetts for the presidential nomination. He was never in serious contention for the top spot on the ticket, however. The party leaders who secured the nomination for Harding agreed upon Senator Irvine Lenroot of Wisconsin as his running mate. After Lenroot's name was placed before the convention, a delegate from Oregon sought recognition from the chair, presumably to second Lenroot's nomination. Instead, he defied the party leadership by proposing Coolidge. The hall was filled with cheers, the stampede was on, and Silent Cal won the nomination on the first ballot. Following the Republican landslide in November, he was vice president of the United States.

Coolidge was the first vice president to attend cabinet meetings regularly, but he took little part in the discussions. He was vacationing at his father's home in Vermont when President Harding died. Because the Coolidge home had no telephone, messengers delivered the news in person. Arriving after midnight, they wakened John Coolidge, who in turn woke his son. The father, who was a justice of the peace, administered the oath of office to his son. The new president then went back to bed and back to sleep.

At the Republican convention in 1924 Coolidge was easily renominated on the first ballot, with only token opposition from the progressive wing of the party. The president wanted Senator William Borah as his running mate, but Borah declined. The convention then nominated Frank Lowden for vice president, but he also refused the office. Finally, the nomination was given to Charles G. Dawes. In 1924 the Democrats held the longest convention ever staged by a major party. The front-runners were Alfred E. Smith and William Gibbs McAdoo. Smith's urban liberalism and his Catholicism were unacceptable to the party's Southern wing. McAdoo's support from the Ku Klux Klan, even though he disavowed it, made him unacceptable to northern liberals and moderates. With the two-thirds rule in effect, neither candidate could win the nomination. At last, on the 103rd ballot, the convention chose John W. Davis and named Charles W. Bryan as his running mate. Unable to support either Coolidge or Davis, liberals formed a new Progressive party and nominated Robert M. La Follette for president and Burton K. Wheeler for vice president.

The Democrats tried to capitalize on the scandals of the Harding administration, but Davis, corporate counsel for Wall Street interests, could not entice the country to rally to him as a reform candidate. On the other hand, La Follette could excite reformers, but third party candidates seldom fare well in presidential elections, and some voters considered him a dangerous radical. Coolidge stayed home and said little, as though it were somehow undignified to campaign. His supporters said, "Keep Cool and Keep Coolidge." The incumbent benefitted from the prosperity which much of the country enjoyed. Coolidge won in a landslide, receiving 382 electoral votes to 136 for Davis and 13 for La Follette.

On August 2, 1927, while vacationing in the Black Hills, Coolidge surprised the nation by handing reporters a terse announcement: "I do not choose to run for President in 1928." He refused to elaborate.

FOREIGN RELATIONS

When a dispute with Mexico became serious, Coolidge recalled the United States ambassador and replaced him by Dwight Morrow, who was able to work out an agreement that was temporarily satisfactory to both sides and any danger of war was averted. Coolidge sent marines to Nicaragua, Honduras, and Panama to restore order. He withdrew marines from Santo Domingo but kept them in Haiti. His supporters said his use of troops was justified as a means of keeping order and protecting our economic interests, but it was denounced as Yankee imperialism by many in Latin America. At the Pan American Conference in Havana in 1927-28 Secretary of State Hughes worked out a multilateral treaty for arbitration. Hughes's successor, Frank B. Kellogg, won the Nobel Peace Prize for negotiating a treaty to outlaw war. The Kellogg-Briand Pact of 1928 was a great symbolic act, even though it had no enforcement teeth.

In his relations with other nations, Coolidge consistently promoted the national interests of the United States as he perceived them. He recognized a constitutional government in Nicaragua, even though it was not recognized by other Central American states or Mexico. He tried to get the United States membership in the World Court, but the Senate attached such reservations to it that the League of Nations refused to accept our conditions of membership. The United States, via Secretary of State Hughes, played a major role in the sixth Pan American Conference.

Although Coolidge contributed to peace in Latin America, his "dollar diplomacy" ruffled feathers. Solid accomplishments were offset by the feeling that his real concern was to protect American economic interests, who were exploiting the population of Latin America. The people of those countries did not regard the United States as a good neighbor. Despite all the actions he took to produce peace and disarmament, Coolidge was never able to convince other nations of the purity of our intentions. Some Latin American nations continued to regard us as a threat. The Dawes plan to help Germany pay its World War reparations should have reduced tensions in Europe, but many Europeans distrusted us. Dawes shared the Nobel Peace Prize in 1925 for his part in developing the plan. The repayment of war debts to us by the Allies and of reparations by the Germans were both nearly impossible given the realities of the economies of Europe.

Coolidge consistently supported high protective tariffs for the benefit of United States manufacturers. His policies had harmful effects on world economy and on the agricultural sector in the United States (and probably long-term harmful effects on the industries they were intended to protect).

DOMESTIC POLICIES

The Coolidge years were a time of prosperity in urban America. The agricultural sector did not share in the general prosperity, and the president strongly opposed the McNary-Haugen Bill, which was intended to help farmers. He also refused to lower tariffs, which hurt farmers. Coolidge used the prestige of the presidency to uphold prices on the stock market when it threatened to collapse due to the price-earnings discrepancy and the overextension of credit. His actions postponed the crash until 1929.

As president, Coolidge was not notably anti-labor. Nothing like the Boston Police strike challenged him during his administration. His policies were definitely anti-agriculture. That he was pro-business is evident. He said the business of America is business, and he seemed to think the function of government is to protect business. The U.S. Chamber of Commerce got its way constantly, not because of its pressure tactics, but because Coolidge agreed with its position on everything. He was not very concerned about enforcing anti-trust laws, even nominating for attorney-general Charles Warren, who had been involved in a scandal when the sugar trust had sought to control the eastern sugar beet industry in 1910. The Senate rejected Warren. William Allen White said the business leaders who advised Coolidge did more harm than the scoundrels who scandalized the Harding administration.

Coolidge placed a high priority on economy in government. He vetoed the veterans' bonus, vetoed a raise for postal employees, vetoed the McNary-Haugen farm relief bill, tried to sell Muscle Shoals to private interests, and showed little interest in protecting the environment or using the powers of government to improve the health, safety, or welfare of the people.

Coolidge lowered taxes on the wealthy, continuing the shifting of the burden from the wealthy to the middle class that had started during the previous administration. Coolidge's fiscal policies reflected his pro-business ideology. He said the government could do more to remedy the economic ills of the people by a reduction in public expenditures than by anything else. He vetoed a bill intended to help farmers cope with the recession that afflicted the agricultural sector during a time of general prosperity.

Coolidge spoke out in favor of better treatment of racial minorities, but took no action to secure such. With misgivings he signed a restrictive immigration bill, which excluded Japanese. To his credit, he pardoned all prisoners convicted under the Espionage Act. As president he engaged in no repressive activities, even though he did little to advance civil liberties. He supported women's suffrage, but generally had a low opinion of women's qualifications for public affairs.

Although Coolidge clearly was impressed by what he perceived as congruence among wealth, wisdom, and character, he did not show disdain or contempt for those of lower social status. Indeed, he retained friendship with people from Plymouth and Northampton who were by no means the social equal of his new associates. He did nothing to try to improve the lot of the less fortunate, believing that hard work would bring the rewards they deserved.

ADMINISTRATION AND INTERGOVERNMENTAL RELATIONS.

Coolidge did not lay out a set of goals and plans for their accomplishment. He wanted to reduce governmental expenditures and keep the peace and prosperity, but he announced no specific plans to bring this about. One of his favorite tactics was delay in hopes any problem would go away. In his first address to Congress after the election of 1924, Coolidge asked for authority for "thorough reorganization of the federal structure with some latitude to the executive." There is no evidence that Congress granted the authorization or that the president pushed for it. No significant reorganization of the executive branch occurred during his presidency. He believed in delegation — hire the best man and leave him alone to do his job. Coolidge probably delegated too much authority to his cabinet members. He did not provide them with much direction or oversight, nor challenge them to develop goals and plans for improving their departments. Executive branch departments and agencies were operated at an acceptable level of effectiveness and accomplished their goals and objectives. The main complaint against them is that their goals were too limited.

Coolidge retained Harding's cabinet members, based on his belief that he had no right to replace them during the portion of Harding's term that he served after the former president's death. At first he defended Daugherty, but he asked for his resignation in March 1924. Denby and Fall both resigned without being asked. The Harding appointees who were untouched by scandal left from time to time for whatever reasons. Wallace's resignation from Agriculture removed some of the contention that had marked the cabinet during the previous administration. Hoover apparently lost influence.

The new appointees were of average caliber, honest but not outstanding in any way, except Kellogg in the State Department and Harlan Fiske Stone as attorney general, who were both excellent choices. Coolidge gave them considerable leeway in running their departments. No new scandals occurred.

Coolidge was a poor communicator. He enjoyed his reputation for being laconic and carried it to extremes. Even so, the communication that he did engage in was one-way, rather than two-way. He did not consult many people, perhaps for fear of seeming under someone's control. He did not consult the progressive members of his own party, with the result that the Republicans in the Senate were divided on his programs.

Coolidge was successful in reducing governmental expenditures, cutting them to less than half what they had been during the war years. He and Harding were the only two presidents of the twentieth century to avoid deficit spending for their entire tenure in office. He did not spend enough money on certain programs to satisfy liberals, but spent enough to satisfy himself and the conservatives who elected him.

Many of the president's proposals were passed by Congress, but by no means all of them. Congress passed a veterans' bonus bill that he opposed, he vetoed it, and Congress passed it over his veto. Congress defeated Coolidge's recommendation to bring the United States into the World Court. It passed a Japanese exclusion bill that Coolidge opposed. It passed a soldier's pension bill, which the president vetoed. It passed a farm aid bill that the president vetoed. Isolationists and progressives within his own party opposed him almost as much as the Democrats did.

Coolidge used federal court appointments as patronage for the Republican party. Chief Justice Taft urged him to make bipartisan appointments, but he refused. Taft thought that many of Coolidge's court appointments were of inferior people. His only appointee to the Supreme Court, Harlan Fiske Stone, was well-qualified and the selection was widely applauded by both parties.

Coolidge was not unduly pressured by the special interests. They got what they wanted largely because he agreed with them, so pressure tactics were really unnecessary. The president thought he was acting in the interests of all of the people because he honestly believed that all of the people would be better off if government was in the hands of the business classes. He gave paramount consideration to business rather than labor or agriculture because he thought that was best for the country.

LEADERSHIP AND DECISION MAKING

Coolidge was not an inspirational leader. He was lacking in charisma and did not inspire executive branch personnel to a high level of effort. But his was not a do-nothing administration, and a malaise did not develop in the country during his incumbency. In trying to persuade others to follow his lead, Coolidge had some successes and some failures. Coolidge restored public confidence in government after the scandals of the Harding Administration. He also kept up confidence in the stock market when things started to look wobbly in 1928. The president set moderate standards of performance for himself and others. He has been criticized as being lazy, but the truth is that Coolidge just did not believe the government should do much. The president was not a visionary. He was a practical, down-to-earth, plain-spoken man of the people, probably more intelligent than is sometimes believed. Conceptualizing long-term strategies for moving the country forward was not his strong suit. He was more interested in maintaining the status quo.

Coolidge was not particularly adept at weighing alternatives and making informed judgments about the possible consequences of each course of action. He was reluctant to seek advice and refused to consult with people who might disagree with him. Although he was something of a student of history, he did not have a really deep understanding of the lessons that can be learned from it. He was a stubborn man, and even when he knew he was wrong he would not admit it, which made it difficult for him to learn from his own mistakes. When Coolidge made a poor decision, it was not so much because of a lack of intelligence as because of a lack of perspective. His unwillingness to consult others caused mistakes. Coolidge was not strong on compromise. He would rather hold firm and suffer defeat than to compromise if a principle was at stake. Sometimes he refused to compromise even though no important principle was involved.

The president had the courage to make a hard decision if it was necessary, but he preferred delaying the decision to see if the need to make it would go away. He remained calm in emergencies. On the death of President Harding he immediately and quietly assumed the presidency and kept the country calm. In some minor emergencies involving Latin American countries he kept his head and never acted rashly.

PERSONAL QUALITIES

Coolidge promoted the "Silent Cal" image of himself as a taciturn, stern, and unsmiling Yankee. After the hail-fellow-well-met Harding and the intellectual Wilson, the public liked this image. Sometimes the president carried it too far, even to the point of rudeness that was embarrassing to all who observed it.

Most Americans were proud of their country during the peace and prosperity period of the Twenties. They tended to be proud of their president who represented their rural origins and the traditional values of America. Coolidge maintained the stature of the office, preventing it from being besmirched by the Harding era scandals. He had a limited view of the powers of the presidency. He did nothing to increase or decrease significantly the power of the office.

Coolidge was definitely the businessman's president. Farmers and laborers were less likely to think the president was on their side. After serving out Harding's term, he was elected to a term of his own by a large majority. The prosperous part of the public generally felt kindly toward him. The protest vote for La Follette, the greatest ever given to a third-party candidate prior to 1968, demonstrated that not all sections of the country shared this feeling.

The president denied the public access to the White House not only physically, but also by shutting himself off from them psychologically. He did not seek input from the public.

Access was limited to a small group of advisors. The president was not interested in reaching out to the people. He was uncomfortable with people, holding himself aloof from them.

Coolidge prided himself on virtues such as integrity and trustworthiness. How solid were his moral values and principles? He was not a particularly religious man, although he gave lip service to religion. His values and principles never seemed to conflict with his respect for business and businessmen.

Despite his respect for money and his frugal spending habits, Coolidge never took advantage of any opportunity to enrich himself at the public trough. He faithfully saved a portion of his salary even when it was pitifully low and lived in cheap hotel rooms whenever the government did not furnish his living quarters.

He even squabbled with the White House chef over how large a ham to serve to guests. In his own financial dealings he was strictly honest. Throughout his life the president always exhibited the highest level of personal morality (except for a tendency to be somewhat cruel in his treatment of others). After the Harding scandals, his example restored the prestige of the presidency.

OVERALL ASSESSMENT

Coolidge received positive ratings only in the areas of Foreign Relations and Personal Qualities. Overall, his score was minus four points, ranking him in a tie for 34th place among the 39 presidents rated.

HERBERT HOOVER

1929–33

	RATING POINTS	*RANK*
FOREIGN RELATIONS	8	21 tie
DOMESTIC PROGRAMS	8	14 tie
ADMINISTRATION	−2	29 tie
LEADERSHIP	−8	37
PERSONAL QUALITIES	1	35
OVERALL ASSESSMENT	7	30

BACKGROUND

Herbert Clark Hoover was born August 10, 1874, in a two-room cottage at West Branch, Iowa. Orphaned at the age of nine, he was raised by relatives on farms in Iowa and Oregon. At the age of 16 he entered Stanford University. In May 1895 he graduated with a degree in geology. He became a mining engineer, working in New Mexico, Colorado, Australia, and China. In 1908 he established his own engineering firm, with headquarters in London. He reorganized mines in many parts of the world. By 1914 he had become a millionaire. During World War I, Hoover organized food relief for Belgium and headed the United States Food Administration. By 1920 he was one of the best known and most respected persons in the world. During the administrations of Warren Harding and Calvin Coolidge, Hoover served as secretary of commerce.

NOMINATION AND ELECTION

As soon as Coolidge announced that he did not choose to run again, Hoover became the strongest contender for the 1928 Republican presidential nomination. He won easily on the first ballot. When the Democrats nominated New York Governor Alfred Smith, a Catholic who favored repeal of Prohibition, the campaign became personal in nature. Hoover stipulated that he and his associates were to wage only a positive campaign, stressing the Republican prosperity, and omitting any mention of religion, Prohibition, or the social bearing of the Irish. Without Hoover's authorization, an anti-Catholic strategy was used by some of his supporters. Hoover won handily, receiving 444 electoral votes to 87 for Smith. He even cracked the Solid South, carrying five states in the region. With one exception, it was the first time that any state from the old Confederacy had voted for a Republican for president since the end of Reconstruction.

In 1932 Hoover again won the Republican

nomination on the first ballot. With millions of people unemployed and the nation's economy in shambles, he had little chance of being re-elected, but his supporters were in firm control of the convention. For details on the election of 1932, see the entry on Franklin D. Roosevelt.

FOREIGN RELATIONS

Hoover brought to the White House a range of international experience greater perhaps than that of any previous president. He determined to make his own foreign policy decisions, but economic problems frequently distracted him from foreign affairs. He used diplomacy to keep the United States from becoming involved in war. There were no threats to the national security of the United States during his administration, but he eschewed many opportunities for military intervention in other countries, especially in Cuba and in Mexico. He did not use the threat of military force against any foreign power.

After the election of 1928, Hoover made a seven-week trip to ten Latin American countries. He promised to withdraw troops from Haiti and Nicaragua. He repudiated the Roosevelt Corollary to the Monroe Doctrine. Hoover had long advocated freedom for the Philippines, but when Congress passed a bill providing for Philippine independence in ten years, he vetoed it, citing our responsibility for the islands. Congress overrode his veto.

An advocate of disarmament, Hoover wanted the London Naval Disarmament Conference of 1930 to be a success. At the time the treaty was hailed as a great victory, but it had no great endurance and only limited, immediate effect. At the World Disarmament Conference in Geneva in 1932 he asked for a 30 percent reduction in armed forces. Little progress was made.

He announced that he would recognize governments if they promised to hold elections in due course and to honor international agreements. His 1930 meeting with Ramsey Mac-Donald was regarded as a diplomatic triumph. In a meeting with Pierre Laval in 1931 he secured a promise that France would remain on the gold standard. Hoover was highly respected by foreign governments because of his relief work during and after World War I. His meetings with MacDonald and Laval enhanced this prestige. Hoover built up the foreign service and increased the budget of the State Department.

When Japan occupied a strategic rail line in Manchuria in 1931, the League of Nations and the United States requested Japan to withdraw. When Japan refused, the Stimson Doctrine was announced, stating that the United States would refuse to recognize any agreement contrary to the Kellogg-Briand Peace Pact, the Open Door Policy, or American rights in China. Despite the Stimson Doctrine, Japan threatened Shanghai with firebombing. Hoover assured Japan that the United States would not intervene. When Stimson proposed economic sanctions against Japan, Hoover overruled him, feeling that sanctions would lead to war.

Hoover wanted a strengthened tariff commission which with executive approval could raise or lower rates by up to 50 percent. He was unable to secure congressional approval for the commission. Although he signed the Smoot-Hawley tariff in the spring of 1930, he was angered by its high rates, which were hurtful to the economies of the United States and Europe.

During his presidency, Hoover's greatest contribution to economic well being abroad came from the moratorium. Before the depression, he had thought that war debts should be paid. The world-wide depression altered his views. On June 20, 1931, he proposed a one-year moratorium on all intergovernmental payments, war debts, and reparations. It averted panic and financial disaster in Europe.

World opinion of the United States was enhanced by the election of Hoover, who was much more highly regarded throughout the world than his immediate predecessors. This opinion was enhanced by his policy in Latin America, his meetings with foreign leaders, his efforts toward peace and disarmament, and the moratorium on war debts.

DOMESTIC PROGRAMS

Like some other presidents, Hoover was blamed for a depression that he did not cause. Before he became president, he had frequently warned against speculation in stocks. He had repeatedly asked President Coolidge to seek additional control over private banking and financial practices. Two days after he took office, President Hoover conferred with Federal Reserve officials about restraining stock speculation. The crash came on October 23, 1929. Hoover responded quickly. He began meeting with business leaders, asking for voluntary arrangements to keep workers employed at decent wages. He asked Congress to help workers keep their jobs and wages. He requested greater public works appropriations. The government focused on reviving finance rather than dealing directly with unemployment, unprofitably low prices, and agricultural unemployment. Although Hoover initiated a few new government programs, some of which foreshadowed the New Deal, he relied mainly on publicity and voluntary response. The depression worsened throughout his term

The public perception of Hoover as a man who favored capital over labor is not entirely justified. Although he had earned an anti-union reputation during his engineering days, his actions as president were not anti-labor. As a presidential candidate in 1928, he called for a shorter work day and an augmentation of the laborer's purchasing power. As president he signed the Norris-LaGuardia Act in 1932, outlawing yellow dog contracts and limiting injunctions except when danger or injury was threatened. He refused to exempt oil companies from compliance with the anti-trust laws. More indictments for violating anti-trust laws came under Hoover than during any previous presidential term.

Hoover had a genuine concern for child welfare and public health. He urged passage of a Rural Health Bill, which was defeated by a Senate filibuster. He proposed creation of a federal Department of Health, Education, and Welfare. Congress ignored his recommendation, but did create the National Institutes of Health. Hoover appointed a fact-finding committee on housing and zoning. The Reconstruction Finance Corporation (RFC) lent funds for the eradication of slums. He prodded Congress into passing the Agricultural Marketing Act of 1929, a community-oriented and politically progressive act, promoting private cooperation with government help. He was the first conservationist

president since Theodore Roosevelt. Hoover prevented a private power company from building a dam above scenic Cumberland Falls in Kentucky. He supported the building of Boulder Dam on the Colorado River and planned to build Grand Coulee Dam on the Columbia. He vetoed a bill providing for government operation of Muscle Shoals.

All of these progressive measures were outweighed in the mind of the public by two negatives — his rhetoric against the "dole" and his treatment of the veterans. He gave substantial personal contributions to private relief and instituted several government programs to help the poor, but he said that making the government responsible for alleviating poverty would destroy private initiative. He hoped that more fortunate Americans would freely rescue their neighbors. Even when evidence showed private philanthropy was not up to the job, he continued to talk about volunteerism. He vetoed a bill for federally subsidized state employment agencies. When he finally decided that federal relief was needed, he used the RFC, but it was ineffective as a relief agency. He signed the Wagner-Graham Stabilization Act, but delayed for months in appointing a director.

His treatment of the veterans' "Bonus Army" dealt a serious blow to his reputation. Some 20,000 unemployed veterans, who came to Washington to seek early payment of the soldier's bonus, settled in abandoned government buildings and established a tent city in Anacostia. Hoover had the district police provide food and supplies to the veterans. The House passed the Bonus Bill; the Senate defeated it. Hoover initiated federal loans for transportation home to any veteran who applied. Ten thousand stayed. When some veterans camped out on the Capitol lawn and occupied the building's steps, Hoover agreed to the selective arrest of militant leaders. The army, under General MacArthur, evicted the veterans from the downtown area. MacArthur used cavalrymen with drawn sabers and infantry with tear gas to disperse the crowds. Ignoring orders from the president, MacArthur and his troops crossed the bridge to Anacostia and set the tents on fire. Privately, Hoover reprimanded MacArthur for his insubordination, but supported him in public.

Hoover wanted to lower federal income taxes on "earned" income as against "unearned" income. He ordered all government tax rebates to be made public. Until September 1931 he had opposed the raising of taxes, preferring that the budget be balanced by borrowing and moderately reducing spending. Then he supported a manufacturer's sales tax, insisting that it apply neither to food nor to inexpensive clothing. The tax was defeated in the House. Hoover favored an increase on excise taxes on luxuries and non-essentials. He wanted to raise the income tax on the upper brackets and raise estate taxes. He signed the Revenue Act of 1932, the most progressive tax law of the decade.

In his earlier days Hoover had made numerous racist comments, but his record improved. He and his wife refused to sign a restrictive covenant against Negroes and Jews at their Washington residence. They entertained many blacks at the White House. In the presidential campaign of 1928, Hoover favored an anti-lynching law. He appointed more blacks to middle-level government jobs than Coolidge and Harding combined. He proposed helping blacks secure ownership of land on which they worked as tenants and sharecroppers. He purged the Republican party in the South of some corrupt Negro leaders. He ordered an end to discrimination in the pay of white and black workers on government projects, but few changes actually occurred. His Indian policy was to help Native Americans become independent and to preserve Indian culture. He favored collective tribal ownership of Indian lands. He wanted integration, but not assimilation of Indians into the nation. He thought the reservation system should be ended. He doubled appropriations for Native Americans

Hoover defended civil liberties. He asked for the release of Communists who had peacefully picketed in front of the White House, secured the resignation of an assistant attorney general who had used espionage agents in a domestic investigation, and opposed wiretapping and illegal searches and seizures.

Hoover said he would like to appoint a woman to a distinguished position, but was unable to find a distinguished woman to appoint. The Inter-American Commission of

Women in 1930 approved a treaty providing there shall be no distinction based on sex in laws relating to nationality. At the ensuing Hague Conference the United States refused to sign a convention codifying international law because it lacked this provision. The Economy Act of 1932 required reductions in the number of employees at the expense of those whose spouses worked for the government. Hoover protested this provision, but he signed the act. Late in 1932 he issued an order against sex discrimination in hiring for new jobs. He agreed to sharp restrictions on immigration. He felt that the national origins quota system had great flaws, but agreed to a law setting quotas based on the 1890 population.

Hoover favored prison reform, but accomplished nothing in this regard. He was a humane individual and favored humane treatment of all. Hoover wanted to improve the lot of the homeless, to alleviate poverty, and to insure justice for any unfavored group or individual. His policies and programs, however, did not achieve these ends.

ADMINISTRATION AND INTERGOVERNMENTAL RELATIONS

The depression made it impossible for Hoover to adhere to a long-range plan for the accomplishment of his goals and objectives. He was unable to visualize the problems that had to be overcome in order for him to move the nation forward.

For the most part, Hoover organized the executive departments and personnel according to sound administrative principles. In some cases he may have delegated too much authority to subordinates. Hoover retained only Andrew W. Mellon and James J. Davis from the Coolidge cabinet. Three of his appointees were first rate — Henry L. Stimson in State, Charles Francis Adams as secretary of the navy, and William D. Mitchell as attorney general. Others were not so strong. Among his cabinet appointees, all were white males. None were Catholics, Jews, or Southerners. Most were millionaires. To his credit, he put many postmasters under Civil Service. His appointees conducted themselves well, preventing scandal or corruption from marring his administration.

He assigned personnel to appropriate roles and gave them authority to carry out their duties. He did not work closely with them in developing their goals and objectives, nor did he closely supervise their activities. He was frequently brusque with employees. and seldom discussed their concerns with them. Most executive branch departments and agencies were well-administered. They had many accomplishments, but were unable to pull the country out of the economic depression.

Communication was a serious problem for Hoover. He had intended to have frequent press conferences, and said he sometimes would allow reporters to quote him, but he did not keep his promise. He felt the press invaded his privacy. His secretary asked the press to consult with his office before sending out potentially damaging economic news. Hoover was concerned about leaks; the press was concerned about censorship. Hoover had a flat, metallic speaking voice, and his public speeches were stilted. His inability to deal intimately and openly with people hurt him in his relations with the press, with Congress, and with the general public.

Hoover exercised strict control over government expenditures, permitting no excessive or wasteful spending. He failed to secure ample funds from Congress to combat the depression effectively. He tried to balance the budget at a time when deficit spending was needed.

Hoover was uncomfortable in working with Congress. He did not like to wheel and deal, to cajole, or to compromise. He had almost as much difficulty working with members of his own party as with the Democrats. He suffered only two major defeats by Congress — rejection of a Supreme Court nominee and the overriding of his veteran's bonus veto. But there were many "minor" defeats that were not inconsequential.

Hoover's appointments to the federal judiciary were made strictly on merit. He appointed fewer members of his own party than any president since Cleveland (except Taft). To the Supreme Court, he named Charles Evans Hughes, Owen Roberts, and Benjamin Cardozo. The one mistake Hoover made was his nomination of John J. Parker, who early in his career had upheld an injunction enforcing a yellow-dog labor contract and who had said in 1920 that the Negro was not yet ready to participate in politics. The Senate refused to confirm this nomination.

Hoover is sometimes mistakenly viewed as a tool of the special interests. Actually, he tried to put the public interest ahead of everything else. His inability to overcome the depression caused the public to lose its respect for him, but he still tried to do what was best for the people. His strategy was at fault, not his intent. Hoover simply did not have the vision to be an effective chief executive of a nation suffering through the worst depression in its history.

LEADERSHIP AND DECISION MAKING

Hoover was not an inspiring leader. His inability to capture the public mind made his efforts to fight the depression seem even less effective than they really were. Hoover had limited success in persuading others to follow him. He relied too much on dry facts, on logic, rather than using emotional tactics. He was unable to reassure people that things would get better. The president was unable to communicate a vision that would unite the people behind his efforts to fight the depression. Hoover's strategy for bringing the country out of the depression proved to be inadequate. He relied too much on voluntary efforts and did not get the full force of the government into the fight, but the failure was less in conception than in leadership.

As an engineer, Hoover knew very well how to make a scientific decision. As a political leader, however, one must enter human beings into the equation. Hoover never learned how to do this. His assumptions were always that if people behaved rationally, certain results would follow. He could not predict the consequences of what he regarded as irrational behavior. He had a lot of facts at his command, but the facts alone do not always provide the answer, and he failed to enter into discussions with those who had a different perspective. Therefore, his attempts to weigh the consequences of each course of action were flawed. Hoover was too unwilling to compromise in order to win wider support for a proposal. He was unwilling to engage in the give and take of political compromise, feeling that such shenanigans were improper.

Hoover was capable of making hard decisions and dealing with emergencies, as he had demonstrated many times in his career. As president, facing the emergency of the depression, he remained calm and did not act rashly. Perhaps he waited too long before taking forceful action. If so, his delay was not from fear, but was based on his sincere beliefs.

PERSONAL QUALITIES

Hoover usually conducted himself with dignity. As president, he seldom engaged in behavior that could be characterized as petty or mean-spirited. Hoover had such a reputation as a great humanitarian that people were at first proud that a man such as he was their president. As the depression worsened, more and more people blamed Hoover for it. During the depression they felt less pride in themselves and their country. The office of the president received more respect abroad under Hoover than under Coolidge or Harding. At home, this was not true, especially as the depression continued. Hoover did not increase the power of the presidency because he did not push his powers to the limit in dealing with the depression.

Many people came to feel that the president sided with business against them. They perceived that he thought banks were more important than people, that he lacked sympathy for them. This is a misperception, but it was widely held. Hoover decreased public access to the White House. More importantly, his heart and mind were not accessible to the public. He was such a private person that the people felt cut off from him. They thought he did not care about them. One of Hoover's great weaknesses was his inability to reach out to the people. During World War I he had been very successful in arousing a favorable response in people and involving them in food conservation and other measures. Somehow he was not able to make the same appeal as president.

Hoover acted consistently on his values and principles. His political philosophy was ill-formed and incomplete, but he adhered to his moral principles. As president, Hoover acted on the belief that a public office is a public trust and never used his office to benefit himself personally. Hoover's personal life was above reproach.

OVERALL ASSESSMENT

Hoover received a total of seven points and ranks in 30th place among the 39 presidents rated.

FRANKLIN D. ROOSEVELT

1933–45

	RATING POINTS	RANK
FOREIGN RELATIONS	17	1
DOMESTIC PROGRAMS	18	1
ADMINISTRATION	9	14 tie
LEADERSHIP	16	7
PERSONAL QUALITIES	16	8 tie
OVERALL ASSESSMENT	76	3 tie

BACKGROUND

Franklin Delano Roosevelt was born into a prominent and wealthy family on January 30, 1882, in Hyde Park, New York. Educated by tutors and in private schools, Roosevelt graduated from Harvard and the Columbia University Law School. He married his fifth cousin, Eleanor Roosevelt, niece of Theodore Roosevelt. Eleanor became the most active First Lady in American history. In 1910 Franklin was elected to the New York State Senate. In 1913 he was appointed assistant secretary of the navy by President Wilson. After losing a 1914 bid for the U.S. Senate, he remained with the Navy Department throughout World War I. In 1920 he was the vice-presidential candidate on the ticket headed by James C. Cox that lost to Harding and Coolidge. After the election he bcame a partner in a law firm in New York City and took charge of the New York office of a surety bond firm. In 1921 he was stricken with polio. Although he could never again walk unaided or without braces, he concealed the ex-

tent of his disability from the public. In 1928 he was elected governor of New York. He was re-elected by a record margin in 1930.

NOMINATION AND ELECTION

When the Democratic national convention met in 1932, Roosevelt was the front-runner for the presidential nomination. He received a majority of the votes on the first ballot, but it took considerable maneuvering before he received the requisite two-thirds majority on the fourth ballot. Plans for recovery from the depression and the repeal of prohibition were the main issues in the campaign. Roosevelt won the election handily, winning 472 electoral votes to 59 for the incumbent President Hoover. In 1936 Roosevelt was nominated for a second term by acclamation. The election was a referendum on the New Deal. Roosevelt buried the hapless Alfred M. Landon in a landslide, carrying 46 of the 48 states for the most lopsided electoral college victory (523–8) since James Monroe ran unopposed in 1820. In 1940

Roosevelt was again nominated on the first ballot. The president and the Republican candidate, Wendell Willkie, were not far apart on the issues, so the election hinged largely on the question of whether the country should depart from the two-term tradition. Roosevelt won with 449 electoral votes to 82 for Willkie. In 1944 Roosevelt was again nominated overwhelmingly on the first ballot, but a fight raged over the vice-presidential nominee. Roosevelt had forced Henry Wallace upon a reluctant convention in 1940, but was unable to do so again. Harry Truman was selected as a compromise candidate. The Republicans nominated Thomas E. Dewey. Again there was no great division between the two candidates on political principles. Dewey attacked Roosevelt's advisors and questioned the president's health. Roosevelt won with 432 electoral votes to Dewey's 99. Less than three months after his fourth inauguration, Roosevelt died from a cerebral hemorrhage.

FOREIGN RELATIONS

In the area of Foreign Relations, Roosevelt was our most outstanding president. For details, see the Criteria and Ratings section of this book.

DOMESTIC PROGRAMS

Roosevelt ranks first among all the presidents in the area of Domestic Programs. See the Criteria and Ratings section for an account of his contributions in this area.

ADMINISTRATION AND INTERGOVERNMENTAL RELATIONS

At the beginning of his administration Roosevelt had one main goal — bring the country out of the depression. Later his major goals were keeping out of the war, then preparedness, then winning the war, and finally shaping the postwar world. He did not have an organized plan for the accomplishment of each of these goals. His was more of a pragmatic, experimental administration. Despite help from his brain trust, he was not able to develop a long-range plan for dealing with the nation's economic problems. On the other hand, his long-range plans for winning the war were sound.

Roosevelt did not organize the executive departments according to orthodox administrative principles. Duties of different departments were not clearly differentiated. The executive branch was not disorganized nor run in a haphazard manner, but many administrative principles were violated. Although the president was remiss in not following accepted best practices in organizational structure, he was very creative in inventing new structures that worked.

Some departments were overstaffed. Roosevelt's cabinet was quite mixed in competency, ranging from superb to mediocre. Department heads did not always cooperate with one another. The president relied more upon personal advisors than upon his cabinet. Although not all of his appointees were scrupulously honest, no major scandals or corruption occurred during Roosevelt's watch.

Roosevelt was not particularly good at defining work roles, delegating authority, and holding subordinates responsible. As a manager, he was adequate but not exceptional. He developed and usually maintained an effective system of two-way communication with executive branch personnel, the Congress, and the people. Sometimes he failed to engage in adequate discussions before embarking on a course of action, resulting in congressional opposition that perhaps could have been avoided or lessened. One of the president's strong points was in reporting to the public. His fireside chats were especially effective. Although Roosevelt was opposed, often bitterly, by the majority of publishers, he established a good working relationship with reporters. He manipulated his press conferences by allowing friendly reports to ask the key questions, but did it in such a way as not to antagonize many of the others.

Roosevelt submitted and secured congressional approval of appropriate budgets. He was accused of wasteful or excessive spending, but such charges were unfounded. He generally exercised adequate control over departmental expenditures. The Truman Committee, however, found a great deal of inefficiency in defense spending, over-charging by defense contractors, and excess profiteering. Although the culprits were mainly businessmen, Roosevelt had failed to set up a system for careful monitoring.

Even though executive branch departments and independent agencies were not administered according to accepted principles or best practices, they did accomplish important goals and objectives. They were effective.

During his first term Roosevelt had such overwhelming support that almost anything he proposed could have passed. This support gradually waned and he did not receive backing from his own party on packing the Supreme Court and on one tax bill. When he tried to purge conservative Democrats, his attempt backfired. His overall record though was highly positive. The Republican membership of Congress was so small as to be inconsequential during his first term. As Congress became more evenly divided, the opposition strengthened.

Roosevelt was unable to get cooperation from isolationists in Congress prior to Pearl Harbor. After that he had near unanimous support for his foreign policy and leadership in the war effort.

His court packing scheme hurt him politically and was a real slap at independence of the judiciary. The justices who had declared much of the New Deal unconstitutional retired soon after that anyway, so his attempt was unnecessary as well as unwise. Eventually, Roosevelt appointed nine Supreme Court justices, more than any other president. Included were some outstanding jurists, such as Hugo L. Black, Felix Frankfurter, and William O. Douglas. Some others were less distinguished, but all were competent.

Roosevelt mobilized powerful interest groups in support of many of his programs. Even after he had a falling out with John L. Lewis, he was still able to get support from the rank and file union membership.

Although winning elections was very important to Roosevelt, there is no evidence that he ever failed to put the public interest, as he perceived it, first. Would he rather be right than president? He thought he was both. Looking at his administration, it is very clear that he acted in the public interest. He tried to be president of all the people, from the forgotten man at the bottom of the economic pyramid to his social equals among the wealthy elite. When men of wealth rejected him, he continued to do' what he thought was best for all the people. Despite accusations by some right-wingers, he was never a tool of the labor unions or any other special interests. This is demonstrated by looking at his record in office. When he thought they were wrong, he opposed the unions as vehemently as he opposed any economic royalist.

Bitterly hated by a minority, Roosevelt was highly popular with most of the public, with their feelings toward him at times bordering on adulation. Although his popularity gradually diminished over time, he still used it to help further his goals for the nation.

LEADERSHIP AND DECISION MAKING

Among the most charismatic of all presidents, Roosevelt was an inspirational leader, both in the early days of the New Deal and in leading the war effort. His exuberant spirits gave the people hope in the dark days of the depression, when he assured them that "We have nothing to fear, but fear itself." He restored confidence of the people in the government, in the nation, and in their own futures. Charming and gregarious, he seemed genuinely interested in people and their problems. He was very adept at persuading others to follow his lead.

Roosevelt set high standards of performance for himself and others. He motivated people to achieve at a high level. Some of his cabinet officials and other high-ranking appointees did not perform up to expectations and he was loath to fire them. More likely he would bypass them by assigning their duties to someone else. This caused some friction among departments and some confusion and inefficiency in government.

During the depths of the depression, Roosevelt unified the nation, only to see the unity disappear in controversies over court-packing, the third term issue, and isolationism versus aid to the allies. Then the unity was restored by the Japanese attack on Pearl Harbor. Perhaps never before in all of our history and never since has the nation been so united as it was under Roosevelt's leadership during World War II. In financial crises and in wartime the people rallied behind their president.

Roosevelt had a vision of a prosperous nation with all people sharing in the fruits of the prosperity and of a peaceful world, with all peoples governed by a government of their own choosing and a world organization to enforce peace. Implementing the New Deal, winning the war, and creating the United Nations were his strategies for bringing this dream to fruition.

Before making a decision the president usually, but not always, weighed the alternatives and made an informed judgment about the possible consequences of each course of action. His skill in this regard seemed to improve during the war, despite his deteriorating health. Although he was not a scholar, Roosevelt was a student of history and learned from it, particularly from studying the mistakes and accomplishments of previous presidents. He was quick to discover when he was headed the wrong way and showed no hesitation in changing directions. (There are a few exceptions to this generalization, such as the Supreme Court packing attempt, but it was true to a greater extent of Roosevelt than of most presidents.) His intelligence was probably underrated by his critics and even by some neutral observers. He not only utilized his own keen mind, but surrounded himself with the brightest advisors he could find.

Roosevelt was usually willing to compromise on details in order to accomplish an objective, but on a few occasions he was unwilling to do so and it hurt him. Perhaps he compromised too much with Churchill in delaying the invasion of France until after invasions of North Africa and Italy.

Roosevelt seldom shied away from making a hard decision, no matter how awesome the consequences. He was at his best in emergencies.

PERSONAL QUALITIES

Roosevelt conducted himself in such a way as to reflect honor upon the country he represented before the world. The way he overcame his physical handicap was particularly admired. In public the president conducted himself with the dignity that his office required. He reinforced the feeling of pride in America that most citizens had. Many of them (but by no means all) were intensely proud of their president. The office of the president received much more respect both at home and abroad because of Roosevelt's stature.

His bold actions increased tremendously the power of the presidency to act for the good of the nation. Some people opposed his assumption of power as a step toward dictatorship. Others felt it was necessary in order to prevent the arrival of "a man on horseback" or a radical revolution during the depths of the depression. During wartime he assumed emergency powers, similar to Wilson's in World War I, but less than Lincoln's during the Civil War (when the threat to national security was greater).

Roosevelt made most people think that the president was on their side. They identified with the "forgotten man" whom Roosevelt wanted to help. The president received (without necessarily seeking it) input from all segments of the public. He acknowledged much of this unsolicited input, but whether he was influenced by it is not certain. Serious discussions of important issues were restricted to a small number of advisors. He used more means of effectively reaching out to the people than did most of his predecessors. His fireside chats over the radio were particularly effective, as were his press conferences. He made people think that he cared about them.

Not noted for acting consistently on a firm set of moral values and principles, Roosevelt was more interested in finding out what worked. He was trustworthy and seldom went back on his word. Personally honest, he never used his office for personal financial advantage. He was embarrassed and enraged when some of his sons used their relationship in order to feather their own nests. He did not exhibit the highest standards of morality in his private life, but since this was not known to the public at the time, it did not diminish the office of the president nor hurt his effectiveness as president.

OVERALL ASSESSMENT

Among all our presidents, Roosevelt scored highest in Foreign Relations and in Domestic Programs. He served his nation well in times of depression and war. Overall, he received 74 out of a possible 100 rating points and ranks in a tie for third place among all the presidents rated.

HARRY TRUMAN

1945–53

	RATING POINTS	RANK
FOREIGN RELATIONS	14	3 tie
DOMESTIC PROGRAMS	16	4
ADMINISTRATION	13	4 tie
LEADERSHIP	12	13 tie
PERSONAL QUALITIES	15	10
OVERALL ASSESSMENT	70	5 tie

BACKGROUND

Harry Truman was born on May 8, 1884, at Lamar, Missouri. Family financial reverses prevented him from attending college. He worked at various clerical positions, managed the family farm, served as election clerk, road overseer, and postmaster, and joined the Missouri National Guard. During World War I he was in command of a field artillery battery in France. Discharged with the rank of major, he opened a men's haberdashery, but it failed during the farm depression that began in 1921. With the support of the corrupt Pendergast machine, Truman won election as county judge in 1922. From 1923 to 1925 he attended the Kansas City School of Law. In 1924 he was defeated for re-election as county judge, but he was re-elected in 1926 and served until 1934 when he was elected to the U.S. Senate. Re-elected to the Senate in 1940, he chaired a committee to investigate the national defense program. The Truman Committee uncovered waste and inefficiency, saving the government about $1 billion and greatly speeding war production. A poll of Washington newspaper correspondents named Truman as second only to President Roosevelt in contribution to the U.S. war effort.

NOMINATION AND ELECTION

In 1944 President Roosevelt refused to name publicly a preference for the vice-presidential nomination. After considerable backstage maneuvering, the party leaders decided to support Truman. Henry Wallace led on the first ballot, but Truman won the nomination on the second ballot. Less than three months after Roosevelt was inaugurated for his fourth term, the president died and Truman succeeded him.

In 1948 the Democratic party was badly divided. The progressive wing favored the president's civil rights program, but wanted someone even more liberal as the candidate. The conservative Southerners were anti-labor, anti–New Deal, and violently against civil rights. Others had no particular agenda, but were opposed to renominating the president because they thought he would lose in November. An effort to unite the dissidents behind Dwight D. Eisenhower failed when the general said he would not accept the nomination. After a serious fight over the civil rights plank in the platform, some Southern delegates walked out. Truman won the nomination on the first ballot.

The Southerners formed a new States' Rights (Dixiecrat) party and nominated J. Strom Thurmond for president. The Progressives nominated Henry Wallace. With a three-way split in the Democratic party, the Republican candidate, Thomas E. Dewey, appeared a shoo-in. Truman, however, came out fighting. He called Congress into a special session and laid before them an agenda of the country's needs. When Congress refused to act, the president embarked on an extended campaign tour, blasting the "Do-nothing Eightieth Congress." Confident of victory, Dewey ignored the president's challenges. So certain were they of a Republican triumph, the pollsters stopped polling. The president was greeted by large and enthusiastic crowds, but the pundits still failed to recognize Truman's popular support. Thurmond won 38 electoral votes in the South; Wallace siphoned away enough votes to cause the Democrats to lose New York and Michigan; but Truman carried almost all the West to garner 303 electoral votes to Dewey's 189.

FOREIGN RELATIONS

Less than one month after Truman took office, Germany surrendered, ending the war in Europe. Three months later the president ordered the use of the atomic bomb in Japan, bringing World War II to a conclusion and saving the lives of American troops who were preparing to invade Japan. At the end of the war the Soviet Union installed communist governments in the countries of Eastern Europe that had been liberated from Nazi occupation. Determined to prevent the further spread of communism, the president announced the Truman Doctrine, guaranteeing aid to any nation resisting communist aggression. As the first implementation of this doctrine, he secured appropriations from Congress for aid to Greece and Turkey.

Truman gave full and vigorous support to the fledgling United Nations at a time when U.S. support was vital to any hope of viability for the new organization. In 1949 Truman led in the creation of the North Atlantic Treaty Organization (NATO), in which member nations agreed that an attack on one would be considered an attack on all. Under Truman the United States sought not to liberate countries from communism, but to prevent its spread, a policy known as containment. When the Soviets blockaded Berlin, Truman ordered an airlift that flew supplies to the city until the blockade was ended. Truman's support of the United Nations was a peacekeeping effort of great magnitude. Support of NATO, aid to Greece and Turkey, and the Berlin airlift all demonstrated his determination to deter aggression through strength.

The policy of containment and Truman's actions in Europe should have been enough to convince anyone of his resolve. However, it was not clear to North Korea that the protection of South Korea was included in his view of our national interest. When North Korea invaded, Truman acted swiftly and decisively, securing United Nations approval after he had committed the first U.S. troops. He achieved his goal of preventing the Communists from gaining control of the entire peninsula. Whether the Korean War was in the long-term interests of the United States is controversial. At the time it seemed clear that Communist aggression must be stopped somewhere. If the line were not drawn in Korea, it was believed other lands would fall like dominoes. Truman insisted that the Korean War be kept within bounds, that it not become a nuclear nightmare, and he showed tremendous courage in removing the widely popular General MacArthur from command when that became necessary.

Truman improved our relations with Latin America, especially Mexico. He continued Roosevelt's Good Neighbor policy. Although he continued support of some oppressive governments in the region, doing so contributed to security and stability in the hemisphere. He was the first U.S. president to visit Mexico while in office. While there he laid a wreath at the monument to Los Niños Héroes, six teenage cadets who had lost their lives during the war with Mexico. This act helped end a 100-year-old wound and made Truman immensely popular in Mexico.

Secretary of State Marshall's European Recovery Program helped rebuild Europe from the ravages of World War II. The Marshall Plan was one of the greatest examples in all of world history of the use of economic aid to encourage the development of stable democracies. The rebuilding of Germany and Japan were superb efforts to increase the standard of living in countries devastated by the war. Truman set up a Point Four program to provide aid for countries threatened by communism in Southeast Asia. Although it was very controversial, Truman's quick granting of recognition to the new state of Israel was in our national interest, as was his recognition of the German Federated Republic.

Truman's strong stand against communist expansion led to the Cold War and increased tension between the United States and the Soviet Union. The United States was determined to prevent the communists from expanding their empire. Given the determination on both sides, it is doubtful that the Cold War could have been avoided without the United States making unacceptable concessions.

DOMESTIC PROGRAMS

Truman took strong action to maintain prosperity through intervening in labor-management disputes and using the powers of government to help in the transition from a wartime to a peacetime economy. When he left office, unemployment had all but disappeared. Farm income, corporate income, and dividends were all at an all-time high. Real living standards were considerably higher than when he took office. The postwar economic collapse that was widely predicted in 1947 did not occur. Whether Truman's economic policies were responsible for staving off disaster is not provable, but his policies worked, and the anticipated depression was averted. As long as he could, Truman kept price controls and fought vigorously against attempts by labor to raise wages and by management to raise prices. Although prices did go up somewhat, there was no runaway inflation during the Truman years.

In 1948 Truman proposed a "poor man's" tax cut, whereby each taxpayer could deduct from his final tax bill forty dollars for himself and each dependant. When Congress passed instead what Truman called a "rich man's" tax bill, he vetoed it.

In 1947 Truman called for strengthening anti-trust laws, but Congress took no significant action in this regard. Truman vigorously opposed strikes by coal miners, railroad workers, and steel workers when he regarded such strikes to be against the national interest. He even went so far as to propose that striking railroad workers be drafted into the army. On the other hand, he courageously vetoed the popular Taft-Hartley Act, which he regarded as anti-union. He proposed increased support for farmers, including crop insurance. Truman favored hydroelectric projects, irrigation, and conservation of natural resources. He established the Everglades National Park. He created the Atomic Energy Commission and placed it under civilian control.

Truman proposed increased unemployment compensation, an immediate increase in the minimum wage, federal aid to housing, and many other steps aimed at helping the status of low income persons. Part of his proposals were enacted into law, and he reaffirmed his support of the program, popularly known as the Fair Deal, in speeches and messages to Congress. He vetoed a Republican bill to remove persons from Social Security. During his administration Social Security benefits doubled, the minimum wage was increased, and eight million persons attended college through the GI Bill, forever changing the nature of higher education in America. Progress was made in slum clearance, and millions of new homes were built through government financing, including many made available to veterans through low interest loans. Truman battled hard for federal aid to education and for medical insurance programs. Although he could not get his health plan through Congress, his proposal was an indication of his vision and his concern for people.

In a courageous and controversial action, Truman desegregated the armed forces. He also ordered desegregation of the federal civil service, another forward-looking step. He did more than any president since Lincoln to awaken the American conscience to the issue of civil rights. He created the U.S. Commission on Civil Rights. He called for a federal anti-lynching law, protection for the right to vote, a law against poll taxes, the establishment of a Fair Employment Practices Commission with the authority to stop discrimination by employers and unions alike, and an end to discrimination in interstate travel. He asked Congress to act on claims made by Americans of Japanese ancestry who had been placed in detention camps during World War II.

Although Truman was generally supportive of freedom of expression, he established a Federal Employees Loyalty and Security Program. While this program was not nearly so bad as some of the congressional inquisitions, it infringed upon First Amendment rights, as Truman himself later admitted. He campaigned for a change in the Displaced Persons Act that discriminated against Catholics and Jews, favoring a more liberal immigration policy. He appointed highly qualified persons to office, regardless of religion. Although he appointed very few blacks or women to high office, he was outspoken in his opposition to discrimination in employment against Catholics and Jews and acted on his convictions in this regard. Women and blacks benefitted, of course, from the Fair Employment Practices Commission and the civil rights legislation.

Truman's immigration policy, his civil rights proposals, his actions to end discrimination, and his help to the economically needy both at home and abroad demonstrated his commitment to human rights. The cause of dignity for all was advanced by Truman's economic programs and his civil rights and anti-discrimination measures.

ADMINISTRATION AND INTERGOVERNMENTAL RELATIONS

The death of Roosevelt thrust Truman into the White House unprepared because Roosevelt had not taken his vice president into his confidence on many important matters. After the initial period of adjustment, Truman developed a set of goals and objectives for his ad-ministration and tried to plan for their achievement. Intervening occurrences kept getting in his way: a recalcitrant Congress, a new threat from abroad, and unexpected events everywhere in the world impinged upon his presidency, but the president never lost sight of his goals.

Truman improved the organization of the executive branch, both through his own efforts and by implementing recommendations of the commission headed by former president Herbert Hoover, whom Truman had restored to public life. One of his great accomplishments was the unification of the armed services under the Defense Department.

To his cabinet Truman appointed men of the first rank — George Marshall, Dean Acheson, James Byrnes, Tom Clark, James Forrestal, Averill Harriman, and Robert Lovett, for example. Other appointments were equally brilliant — David Lilienthal to the Atomic Energy Commission, despite bitter opposition, and General Ridgway to replace MacArthur in Korea. There were some mistakes, but on the whole Truman's appointees match those of any president in this century. His cabinet members tended to be strong-minded individuals, not hesitant to voice their opinions, even when those opinions differed from those of the chief executive. He made some outstanding appointments to independent agencies and maintained an appropriate relationship with them. Although he held appointees to a high standard of conduct, a few of them violated their trust and brought the aroma of scandal to his administration. The most notorious was Harry Vaughan, who did nothing illegal, but exercised poor judgment and a lack of propriety in dealing with people who sought to benefit from his influence with the president.

Truman knew how to delegate authority while retaining responsibility. "The buck stops here" was no empty slogan to him. While he gave his cabinet members ample authority, he did not relinquish the president's prerogative to make the final decision. Despite coming into office during wartime with the utmost need for secrecy in military matters, Truman never practiced undue secrecy in his administration. In domestic matters he shared information with subordinates, the press, and the public.

Reporting to the people was one of the president's strengths.

The president secured ample funding to operate all existing government programs, plus such new programs as he could get Congress to approve. Congressional refusal of programs such as national health insurance was based on political or philosophical grounds rather than on costs. Truman was a very frugal administrator, keeping an eye open for waste and unnecessary expenditures of public funds. He ran a very tight ship. He had first gained a national reputation for exposing waste and fraud in the defense industry while in the Senate, and he was determined to prevent any abuses while he was president.

For the most part, departments and programs under the jurisdiction of the executive branch operated very effectively. When an officeholder tried to put his personal agenda ahead of the administration's priorities, that individual was removed from office, whether he was a secretary of state or a general of the army. The achievements of the Truman administration were quite impressive. Truman's Supreme Court nominees were well-qualified and compare favorably with those nominated by other presidents.

Truman seldom enjoyed support from interest groups. The powerful business interests generally opposed him, as did some labor unions. Truman invariably acted in the public interest, as he saw it. With great courage he fought for civil rights at great expense to himself politically. With equally great courage he removed General MacArthur from command at a time when the general's popularity greatly exceeded his own. He had to do it, in his view, because the national interest required it. Truman was president of all the people. He was a loyal Democrat, and he enjoyed taking on the Republicans in a political battle. But he was an American first, and a Democrat second. He courageously fought for measures that he thought were in the best interests of all the people, even when it divided the party and alienated its Southern wing or its extreme left wing.

Truman was not always respected by the American public. People who controlled the mass media tended to underestimate Truman and their biases influenced public opinion.

Polls varied widely, sometimes showing strong approval and sometimes showing disapproval of him by the public. When the chips were down in the 1948 election, Truman went directly to the people in his famous whistle stop campaign and won them over. Despite the defection of the Dixiecrats and the Progressives, he won re-election because he appealed to the public and the people believed he told them the truth.

LEADERSHIP AND DECISION MAKING

Not a charismatic leader, Truman was unable to charm people into following him. However, he was able to inspire devotion in those who knew him best. Truman was usually able to persuade people to follow him by convincing them that he was on the right course. As he attempted to break new ground, he was not always successful, as with his national health program. On the other hand, Truman persuaded Congress to pass forward-looking civil rights legislation, and the president used executive orders to end segregation in the armed forces and federal civil service. Although there was much opposition to these steps, Truman prevailed by convincing enough people that they were the right thing to do.

For the most part Truman maintained public confidence in government, but at times that confidence waned. The charges of Communist influences in government, levied by Senator McCarthy and others, the petty scandals involving some of Truman's aides, and even the failure of the Chinese Nationalists to control mainland China were some of the factors that sometimes undermined public confidence.

The president set very high standards for himself and others. While he was loyal to his subordinates, he removed them from office when they failed to meet his standards. He was quite effective in motivating others to achieve at a high level.

Truman had a concept of what the nation and the world should be like. He wanted a nation where all people are free to live and work where they please, where the constitutional guarantees of individual liberties and of equal protection of the laws are honored, where the "common man" has access to education, a job at a fair wage, medical care, and a decent standard of living. He aspired to a world governed by the rule of law, free from tyranny and the threat of war. He identified the nation's needs and developed plans and strategies for moving the nation forward.

Before making an important decision, Truman carefully considered the alternatives and tried to estimate the consequences of various courses of action. Once the best alternative was identified, he made the decision and did not agonize over it. When the decision had been made and a course of action set upon, Truman found it difficult to change his mind. He did not like to admit publicly to being wrong, and he seldom was convinced that he had made a mistake. However, if it became clear to him that a mistake had been made, he acted with dispatch to correct it.

Although Truman was not regarded as a scholar, he was a student of history and far more knowledgeable than most people realized. Military history and biographies of military leaders were his favorite reading materials. He knew a lot of American and European history and applied what he had learned. Truman was quite intelligent, much more so than was recognized by his critics. The fact that he was not a college graduate led many people to underestimate the keenness of his intellect and the depth of his knowledge. He used his intelligence and his knowledge in making decisions about the critical issues he faced as president.

Above all, Truman was a man of principle. He found it difficult to compromise for political expediency when he felt a principle was at stake. If a compromise did not violate his sense of right and wrong, he could go along in order to prevent a stalemate or to avoid losing the whole thing. One area in which no one could fault Harry Truman was in his ability to make a hard decision. No matter how tough the choice or how severe the consequences, this president made decisions when they had to be made. He kept his cool in emergencies, utilizing as careful a decision-making process as time permitted, but making a timely decision. He was more apt to act rashly if a member of his family was criticized than he was when faced with a momentous decision of war or peace.

PERSONAL QUALITIES

Although Truman's behavior was exemplary in a moral sense, he did not always conduct himself with the dignity that some people think the president should exemplify. Sometimes he lost his temper in public; he engaged in nasty name-calling with a syndicated columnist; and he intemperately threatened to do bodily harm to a music critic who wrote a scathing review of his daughter's singing. There were times when his petulant outbursts were viewed as demeaning the presidency. The people were not pleased that the president came from the background of the Pendergast political machine. But most Americans were proud of this feisty little man of enormous courage and integrity. Moreover, they were proud of themselves for confounding the "experts" and re-electing him in 1948. The "man-on-the-street" regarded the outcome of that election as much a vindication of Americans as a victory for Truman.

Although President Truman commanded a great deal of respect, both at home and abroad, he did not increase the stature of the office. He acted nobly in great things and pettily in little things, and the pettiness tended to cancel out the nobility. His immediate predecessor had increased the power of the presidency far beyond what it had been when he took office in 1933. Truman increased the power still further by his use of executive orders in desegregation and his use of the power of commander-in-chief to commit troops to combat in Korea.

Truman was the people's president. He induced the people to think that the president was on their side in the battle against privilege and special interests. He sought input from all segments of the public. He had more press conferences, talked to more people on his morning walks, and engaged in more repartee with ordinary citizens than his predecessors. His accessibility to the public was a worry to the secret service agents assigned to protect him. Truman used many means of formal and informal communications to interact with the people. The most outstanding example of reaching out to the people was his campaign tour in 1948 when he appealed to the people to support him and defeat the special interests that he said were running the Republican party.

All his life Truman acted consistently on a firm set of moral values and principles. His integrity matches that of any other individual to hold the office of president. Among the moral values to which Truman was committed, trustworthiness ranked high. To Truman a promise made was a moral contract to be fulfilled. Truman was scrupulously honest in both his private life and his public life. The virtues of truth, honesty, loyalty, courage, devotion to duty, hard work, and modesty were instilled in him as a child, and he never turned away from them. He was taught that "right is right, and wrong is wrong." He believed it, and he acted on his belief.

OVERALL ASSESSMENT

Truman scored well across the board. With 70 points, he ranks in a tie for fifth place among all the presidents.

DWIGHT D. EISENHOWER
1953–61

	RATING POINTS	RANK
FOREIGN RELATIONS	1	34 tie
DOMESTIC PROGRAMS	−3	30 tie
ADMINISTRATION	11	11 tie
LEADERSHIP	10	17 tie
PERSONAL QUALITIES	11	15 tie
OVERALL ASSESSMENT	30	24

BACKGROUND

David Dwight Eisenhower was born in Denison, Texas, on October 14, 1890, but grew up in Abilene, Kansas. He soon reversed the order of his given names. In grade school he acquired the nickname Ike. After graduating from high school, Ike worked in a creamery while trying to save enough money to attend college. He applied for an appointment to the Naval Academy, but he finished second in the competitive examinations his sponsor required candidates to take and settled for an appointment to West Point, from which he graduated 65th in a class of 170.

Upon graduation from West Point, Eisenhower was assigned to the infantry at Fort Sam Houston. His request to join the expedition against Pancho Villa was turned down, as was his request to serve in Europe during World War I. Instead, he remained stateside, training troops and coaching football. In 1919 he accompanied an army truck convoy across the country from Maryland to California, which dramatized the nation's need for better roads and bridges. Ike was promoted to major in 1920, and he remained in that rank for 16 years. He served three years in Panama, graduated first in his class at the Command and General Staff School, served as an aide to General Pershing, attended the Army War College, and was assigned to the War Department in Washington. He served as an aide to General MacArthur from 1932 to 1939. In 1936 he was promoted to lieutenant colonel; he was made a full colonel in 1941. After that, promotions came quickly, until he reached the highest rank, general of the army, in 1944. Five days after the Japanese attack on Pearl Harbor, General Marshall brought him to Washington to the army's War Plans Division. He became head of the Operations Division of the War Department. Then he was named commanding general of American forces in the European Theater of Operations. By 1944 he was in London directing the Supreme Headquarters of all the allied forces. He did not lead troops in battle, but planned and coordinated military operations, including the Normandy invasion in 1944 and the final assault on Nazi Germany. To Americans and to many of the allies he became the most prominent military hero of the war. In 1945 he replaced General Marshall as army chief of staff. In 1948 he retired from active duty, became president of Columbia University, and wrote the book, *Crusade in Europe.* In 1950 he returned to active duty as supreme commander of NATO forces in Europe.

NOMINATION AND ELECTION

Both the Democrats and the Republicans had made overtures to Ike about the presidential nomination in 1948. He turned them down. When Robert A. Taft, the likely 1952 Republican nominee, refused to commit to the principle of collective security for the defense of Europe, Eisenhower entered the fray. He returned from Europe and resigned from the army. Taft was the favorite of many party leaders. Eisenhower's popularity with the people, however, enabled him to make a superior showing in the states that had presidential primaries. Going into the convention, Taft was the front-runner, with Ike a close second. The Eisenhower forces mounted a credentials challenge against Taft's southern delegates, winning a bitter and hotly contested fight, assuring his nomination on the first ballot. Adlai E. Stevenson, the Democratic candidate, had little chance against the popular war hero, who promised to clean up "the mess in Washington" and pledged to go to Korea to end the unpopular war. The Republican slogan was "I like Ike." The voters proved at the polls that they shared this sentiment. Ike received 442 electoral votes to Stevenson's 89.

In 1956 Eisenhower was again nominated, this time without serious opposition. The general election was a re-run of 1952, and the results were similar. Eisenhower received 457 electoral votes to 73 for Stevenson.

FOREIGN RELATIONS

As president, Eisenhower believed that his primary responsibility was to promote and maintain American national security. He intended to be first and foremost a foreign policy president. To him the Communist threat was real and was directed from Moscow. Third world countries were dominoes in the big-power games. A stable, supportive Western Europe was the chief anchor of American global security.

Eisenhower fulfilled his promise to bring the Korean War to a speedy conclusion. His policies kept the cold war against the Soviet Union and China alive, but did not lead to a shooting war. His peacekeeping efforts in Viet Nam and the Mideast were temporarily successful, but had serious deleterious effects later. The Eisenhower Doctrine, a commitment of economic aid, military assistance, and direct American troop intervention on behalf of friendly Arab states, did not prevent a successful coup by radical officers in Syria in 1957 or the assassination of Iraq's King Faisal in 1958. In 1953 Eisenhower ordered the CIA to organize and carry out a coup in Iran because Iran had nationalized the oil wells. Prime Minister Mossadeq was overthrown, and the Shah was returned to power. The resentment of religious and nationalist groups in Iran festered until the Ayatollah Khomeni came to power a quarter of a century later.

Eisenhower refused to authorize air strikes against the Viet Minh unless the Western Allies cooperated and Congress agreed. The Allies refused, so the United States funneled aid to Ngo Dinh Diem to build up a separated South Viet Nam. Ike refused to support Britain and France in their effort to retake the Suez Canal and topple Nasser. At the request of the president of Lebanon, Eisenhower sent Marines onto the shores of Beirut to counter an anticipated revolution. The revolution did not materialize.

The threat of military force was a key component of the brinkmanship policy of John Foster Dulles and the president. The massive retaliation policy did nothing to prevent the Soviets from consolidating their hold on the satellite nations of Eastern Europe. American threats of massive response did not lead to action when Soviet tanks crushed resistance which broke out in East Berlin and in Hungary. Threats of air strikes against China, including the possible use of nuclear bombs, led to the signing of the Korean armistice on

July 26, 1953. Threats of atomic reprisal against mainland China if the Communists continued bombing Quemoy and Matsu led to a warning from Khrushchev that an attack on the Chinese People's Republic would be viewed as an attack on the Soviet Union. Both sides then backed down somewhat and war was averted.

Eisenhower helped form the Southeast Asia Treaty Organization (SEATO), which proved to be ineffective, and eventually was disbanded. The United States assumed the role formerly held by the French in Indo-China. In an address to the United Nations, Ike proposed the "Atoms for Peace" program that led to the International Atomic Energy Agency. In 1955 the leaders of France, Britain, the Soviet Union, and the United States met in Geneva for a summit conference. Ike proposed that the United States and Russia allow air inspection of each other's military bases. The Soviets rejected this "Open Skies" proposal. Ike and Khrushchev met again at Camp David in 1959 and planned a new conference to be held in Paris. Before the meeting could take place, a U.S. U-2 spy plane was shot down over Russia. Ike claimed it was a weather research craft that had lost its bearings. But the Russians captured the pilot and the aircraft wreckage intact, exposing the U.S. lie. The conference was scuttled. Ike expanded covert action by the CIA in the Third World. He favored the status quo against an increasingly militant anti–Western and anti-colonial nationalism. The coup in Iran proved to be harmful to our long term interests, as the restored Shah was overthrown by more radical Iranian nationalists.

Ike was not a good neighbor to the countries of Latin America. In Guatemala President Jacobo Arbenz had initiated a badly needed land reform program and expropriated some uncultivated land owned by the United Fruit Company. The CIA trained Guatemalan insurgents and bombed Guatemala City. A military junta took over and restored United Fruit's lands and removed taxes on foreign investors' dividends. This caused intense hatred of the United States. In 1959 Ike authorized secret training and equipping of Cuban exiles in Guatemala, hoping they could overthrow Castro. Strained relations between the United States and Cuba have continued to this day.

Ike made some attempts to relieve international tension, such as his proposal that the nations of the world share atomic information and materials for peaceful purposes. But these were more than offset by his brinkmanship policy, by talk of massive retaliation, talk about liberation of Eastern Europe, and CIA incursions in Third World countries. Most of the CIA actions were secret, and the American people were unaware of them at the time. CIA operatives conducted illegal sabotage in North Vietnam, airlifted supplies to Indonesia in an attempt to overthrow President Sukarno, established a secret training base for Tibetan guerrillas in Colorado and organized a covert action to rescue the Dalai Lama. A CIA-led revolt in the Republic of Congo led to the seizure of power by Joseph Mobutu and the assassination of Premier Patrice Lumumba. Ike set up a structure for the CIA to continue counterrevolutionary activities abroad without presidential approval, so he could honestly deny knowledge of specific incidents.

Ike's brinkmanship and his hostility to nationalist movements in Third World countries alienated public opinion toward the United States. The bombing of Guatemala City was particularly hurtful in Latin America. Eastern Europeans felt betrayed when after all the talk about liberating Eastern Europe, no aid was given to the Hungarians when they tried to throw off the Soviet yoke and were crushed by Soviet tanks.

Eisenhower preferred to leave all assistance to underdeveloped nations to private investors. Until 1957 he refused to use U.S. trade and government aid packages to the Third World as a means of contributing to more stable economic and political relations and to a reduced need for covert action. He had supported the Marshall Plan for aid to Western Europe, for he believed that a stable, supportive Western Europe was the chief anchor of American global security. While Eisenhower was successful in keeping the peace and maintaining American national security during his administration, his policies were hurtful to the long-term national interests of the United States.

DOMESTIC PROGRAMS

Eisenhower wanted to restore the United States as a self-disciplined, cooperative society marked by enlightened corporate leadership. He disdained the government paternalism that he saw in the New Deal and the Fair Deal. He disliked the factional clamor of the special interests. (He regarded farm groups, labor unions, and minority advocates as special interests, but did not consider businessmen as pleaders for special interests.) He did not vigorously enforce anti-trust laws. Farmers were upset at Ike's efforts to reduce government price supports. The anti-union provisions of the Landrum-Griffin Act of 1957 pleased corporate lobbyists, while the administration's reluctance to invoke injunctions against strikes pacified labor. Ike counted among his best friends and most influential advisors the chief executive officers of some of the nation's largest corporations. He much preferred their company to that of farmers or labor leaders. He appointed business representatives in huge numbers to government regulatory boards and commissions and expanded the number and role of industrial advisory committees.

Among the economic problems facing Eisenhower were inflation, unemployment, and budget deficits. He had some success with each, most notably with inflation. Although the national debt increased by 27 billion dollars during the Eisenhower years, a surplus was achieved in three of the eight years. Ike feared inflation far more than he feared unemployment. During the 1954 recession he privately urged bankers to lower interest rates and loosen credit. He encouraged the private sector to assume greater responsibility for business revival. He believed that voluntary action by business leaders was preferable to government controls. Another business recession occurred in 1957 and 1958. Again Eisenhower opposed a broad government spending program, believing such a program would lead to inflation. Business picked up by the summer of 1958. Eisenhower lowered taxes on industry and capital. The Tax Code of 1954 was a major overhaul of the nation's tax system.

Ike opposed governmental programs to alleviate poverty, provide health care, or to regulate business in the interests of the public. Although he disapproved of Social Security, he knew it was too popular to be attacked; he broadened it. He removed price and wage controls, but increased the minimum wage. He created a national advisory committee to address the housing shortage. The panel consisted almost exclusively of realtors, builders, bankers, and politicians opposed to federal public housing. The resultant Housing Act of 1959 did little to alleviate housing shortage for low-income people.

Ike endorsed the creation of the St. Lawrence Seaway Development Corporation in 1956 to build a deep-water navigation channel. He promoted the Interstate Highway Act. This was a major improvement for automobile travel, but it led to erosion of the urban tax base through suburban sprawl, disincentives to mass transit and energy conservation, and to an increase in air pollution. He turned the tideland underseas oil reserves over to the states and private industry. He pushed for the deregulation of natural gas. He withdrew official obstacles to private hydroelectric power projects in Idaho and California and placed obstacles in the path of any expansion of TVA. Under Ike the federal government enacted legislation that ended the public monopoly of nuclear energy development in the United States. The St. Lawrence Seaway and the Interstate Highway System are usually regarded as Ike's greatest domestic achievements as president.

During his first term, Eisenhower implemented armed forces desegregation (started by Truman) and integrated public facilities in Washington, D.C. He ordered the drafting of a noncommittal Justice Department brief in the school segregation cases. He repeatedly refused to take a public stand on the merits of public school desegregation, although privately he was quite skeptical about it. Nevertheless, when segregationists attacked black students attempting to enter Little Rock Central High School, he nationalized the Arkansas National Guard and dispatched army paratroopers to help the guardsmen protect the students and escort them to school. He hesitantly supported the Civil Rights Act of 1957. Prodded by the U.S. Commission on Civil Rights, he sought and obtained additional voting rights legislation in 1960.

He supported legislation to remove the citizenship of those convicted of conspiring the violent overthrow of the government, to force witnesses to give up Fifth Amendment protections and to testify in national security investigations, and to broaden espionage and sabotage laws. He created a new federal internal security review program, which broadened employee requirements beyond loyalty to suitability, making it possible to dismiss federal workers for drinking, homosexuality, and other characteristics unrelated to political beliefs. He continued to prosecute Communist party leaders under the Smith Act and supported the FBI's programs to infiltrate and disrupt party activities. He approved plans for the FBI to round up suspected subversives without charges in the event of a national emergency. He endorsed the decision to remove J. Robert Oppenheimer's security clearance, even though he admitted privately that there was little evidence to justify such an action. Eisenhower did not challenge Senator Joseph McCarthy until the winter of 1953-54 and then only when McCarthy's attacks had shifted from Truman holdovers and career diplomats to Ike's own appointees. Even then he refrained from a personal public denunciation of the senator.

Eisenhower believed in the humane treatment of all individuals, but he supported military dictators abroad who violated human rights. Anti-communism took precedence over human rights with him. He urged private business to improve the lot of the working classes, feeling it was not government's responsibility to do so. His own circle of friends and advisors were exclusively wealthy, white business executives.

He opposed federal aid to education and the college student aid program. He reluctantly signed the National Defense Education Act in 1958. As an outcome of the recommendations of the Hoover Commission on the Reorganization of Government, Congress created the Department of Health, Education, and Welfare in 1953. Eisenhower appointed Oveta Culp Hobby as secretary of HEW. She became the second woman cabinet member in United States history, joining a cabinet of white males, all but one of whom were millionaires. Eisenhower did not support government aid to the arts and humanities. He was not a noted proponent of national parks; the only park established during his administration was located in the Virgin Islands.

ADMINISTRATION AND INTERGOVERNMENTAL RELATIONS

Eisenhower organized the executive branch appropriately. He made each cabinet officer responsible for his area, and made Sherman Adams chief of staff, thus freeing the president of many routine jobs. For advice on foreign relations, Ike relied on the National Security Council, not the cabinet. Eisenhower's cabinet included a number of men who had achieved outstanding success in private business, law, or politics. They were strong, capable people who represented well the president's programs, but they tended not to have fresh ideas about improving the condition of the American people. Foster Dulles in the State Department was a foremost advocate of brinkmanship and would have gone even further in foreign adventures had not Ike restrained him. Ezra Taft Benson in Agriculture was unpopular with family farmers who felt he represented the interests of corporations more than those of small farmers. A conflict of interest appeared when an advisor who wrote an administration report urging private development of power needs in the Tennessee Valley turned out to be also a consultant to the firm underwriting the Dixon-Yates effort to build a power plant to supply power to Memphis and the Atomic Energy Commission. More serious was the scandal involving Sherman Adams who was accused of influence peddling on behalf of a textile manufacturer in return for personal gifts. Adams resigned under congressional pressure.

Ike carried military practices over to the White House. He delegated authority to his department heads and did not engage in micromanagement of their activities. He left coordination of their work to Sherman Adams. His staff prepared one-page summaries freeing the president from the necessity of reading long memoranda, but leading to the charge that he was uninterested in the details of governing. For the most part the executive departments were administered well and important goals were accomplished.

Ike was skilled at public relations. He created a standing White House Committee on public relations, marketed his programs through television, presenting campaign ads and formal presidential addresses. He allowed televising on a selective basis of excerpts from news conferences. Although he did not take reporters into his confidence, he had good relationships with editors and publishers. His communications were much more about public relations than they were about sharing information. In addition to members of the National Security Council and the corporate executives with whom he golfed and played bridge, only a few cabinet members and White House aides had real access to the president. He had a concealed taping system secretly installed in the Oval Office.

Eisenhower attempted to control government expenditures. Nevertheless, the federal budget increased almost continuously during his administration and the federal debt grew. Despite the end of the Korean War, the deficit increased more during his administration than during Truman's.

The Democrats won control of both the House and the Senate in the off-year elections of 1954 and retained control of both during Ike's second term. He tried to charm the Republican Old Guard and sought compromise with the Democrats in order to build a domestic consensus. Often he had more support from Democrats than from conservative Republicans in Congress. He learned how to use his veto power effectively

In public Ike supported the independence of the judiciary and used his powers as commander in chief to enforce court decisions that he may have privately disagreed with. He appointed Earl Warren, who became one of our most effective chief justices. Other Eisenhower appointees to the High Court included John Marshall Harlan, William J. Brennan, Jr., Charles E. Whittaker, and Potter Stewart. Three of these men had long and distinguished careers on the court. All of his Supreme Court appointees were much more liberal than the man who appointed them.

People who did not know his political views

liked Eisenhower and trusted him. His public relations efforts successfully preserved the image of Ike as the patriotic leader, above partisan politics, for the people, against the evil special interests. The special interests that Ike castigated may have actually been better friends of the people than were the corporate leaders with whom Ike hobnobbed, but the people did not see it that way. The majority of the people continued to think that Ike acted in their best interests.

LEADERSHIP AND DECISION MAKING

Eisenhower had been an inspirational wartime leader. His infectious grin, his friendly attitude, and his carefully orchestrated public relations campaign kept him a hero to the American people. He was viewed as an ideal person by much of the public. Ike could be very persuasive. Even working with a Congress controlled by the opposition party, he was able to get many of his programs enacted.

Ike was no visionary. He wanted to restore the United States as a self-disciplined, cooperative society marked by enlightened corporate leadership. He foresaw a government-business partnership, with government as the junior partner. In the international arena he was so blinded by the perceived threat of communism that he failed to envision a Third World not dominated by either the United States or the Communists. He talked about liberating the captive countries of Eastern Europe, but did nothing in that direction. The president did not conceptualize a grand strategy for bringing about the kind of society he envisioned for the United States nor one that was effective in freeing Eastern Europe from Soviet domination

The president was able to maintain public confidence in the government. Even during the recessions, the Dixon-Yates mess, and the scandals involving Sherman Adams the people did not lose confidence in Ike or in their government. Many of them did lose confidence in some government personnel during the McCarthy era. Ike should have defended more quickly and more vigorously those charged by McCarthy with disloyalty.

Ike usually set high standards of performance

for himself and others in his administration. His apparent hands-off attitude toward work of the various departments and his delegation of many duties to Sherman Adams left him much time for golf and relaxation. During his first term he did not appear to be a hard-working president. After his health problems, he seemed to buckle down and work harder.

Eisenhower carefully considered alternatives before making a decision. He tried to predict the possible consequences of each course of action. He listened to advice from only a few trusted subordinates or friends. He kept his decision-making strategies and tactics secret, except when there was a public relations advantage to making them public. Ike possessed a keen intelligence and utilized it in problem solving and decision making situations. He made few major blunders. Eisenhower was able to compromise when necessary in order to get his programs through. Early in his presidency he tried to appease McCarthy, but he finally stood up to him and refused to turn over notes of private strategy sessions. He compromised with the Democratic controlled Congress. In none of his compromises did he violate his principles.

Eisenhower had proven in wartime that he could make hard decisions and remain calm in emergencies. As president, he still had this ability. When an important decision had to be made, he made it and took full responsibility for it. He did not believe in shared decision-making; it was the responsibility of the president alone to make crucial decisions. On decisions that he did not regard as crucial he was willing to delegate authority to subordinates or to delay the decision in hopes that the need for it would pass.

PERSONAL QUALITIES

Eisenhower comported himself with the dignity that the office requires. He had much respect for the presidency and wanted his conduct and appearance to reflect favorably upon the position. He paid particular attention to his public style and to tactics of presidential leadership. He constantly emphasized his formal duties as chief of state instead of his role as a partisan leader. He did not wish to engage in any unseemly controversies.

The people were proud of Ike — proud that he was their president, and proud to be Americans. Many of them saw him as a father figure or as a genial grandfather. Others still viewed him as the military hero who had led us to victory over Hitler and who was standing up to the Communists. Ike convinced the majority of the people that he was their friend, that he would do what was right for them and their country. They liked Ike and trusted him.

The office of the president received respect at home because of the caliber of the person who occupied it. Overseas, the same was true except among those who thought they had been betrayed by the president's false promises or his failure to embrace their causes. The power of the presidency declined a bit early in Eisenhower's watch. The two-term limit weakened the presidency somewhat. Congress strove to achieve dominance, thinking Ike would go along. He fought them and won when the Bricker Amendment to require Senate approval of executive agreements with foreign powers was defeated. Ike's use of the veto reasserted presidential power.

Access to the president was strictly and skillfully controlled. His mangled syntax at press conferences was induced by his desire to maintain secrecy over administration's policy deliberations without appearing unwilling to respond to questions. He did not seek input from broad segments of the public, nor give serious consideration to much of the input he received. Ike was able to reach out to the people and garner their support, even though he denied them access and ignored their input. He was an expert at winning approval from the people.

Eisenhower had a reputation for integrity and trustworthiness. He misled friends and foes alike in international affairs, but this is accepted behavior in that arena. His reputation did not suffer because of it. He is still viewed as a man of high moral standards and principles. Eisenhower never used his office to benefit himself personally at the expense of the public. He allowed his desire to get re-elected and his desire to see the Republican party victorious to influence his actions or failures to act in certain instances, but he never consciously in any major way went against the good of the country in order to promote himself or his party.

Eisenhower enhanced the prestige of the office of the president by the high standard of morality that he was perceived as exemplifying.

OVERALL ASSESSMENT

Eisenhower accumulated 30 points on the rating scale, and ranks 24th among the 39 presidents rated.

JOHN F. KENNEDY
1961–63

	RATING POINTS	RANK
FOREIGN RELATIONS	12	12 tie
DOMESTIC PROGRAMS	14	7 tie
ADMINISTRATION	13	4 tie
LEADERSHIP	13	11 tie
PERSONAL QUALITIES	13	12
OVERALL ASSESSMENT	65	8

BACKGROUND

John Fitzgerald Kennedy was born May 29, 1917, in Brookline, Massachusetts. His father was a self-made millionaire. His maternal grandfather had been a Congressman and mayor of Boston. The family had a summer vacation home at Hyannis Port on Cape Cod and a winter vacation home at Palm Beach, Florida. Jack attended Choate Preparatory School. In the summer of 1936 Jack studied at the London School of Economics, where he contracted jaundice. That fall he entered Princeton University, but a recurrence of jaundice forced his withdrawal. When he recovered, he entered Harvard University, from which he graduated cum laude in 1940. He attended the Stanford University Graduate School of Business briefly. He volunteered for the army but was rejected for health reasons. Soon thereafter he enlisted in the Navy and was stationed in Washington, D.C. Following the attack on Pearl Harbor, he applied for sea duty. On August 2, 1943, the PT boat he commanded was cut in half by a Japan-ese destroyer. For his heroism in rescuing members of his crew, he was awarded the Navy and Marine Corps Medal. He injured his bad back, for which he received the Purple Heart. His back gave him great pain the rest of his life. Kennedy worked briefly as a newspaper reporter. In 1946 he was elected to Congress and was twice re-elected. In 1952 he was elected to the U.S. Senate. At the Democratic convention in 1956 Kennedy made the nominating speech for Adlai Stevenson. When Stevenson opened the vice-presidential choice to the floor, Kennedy worked furiously for that nomination, but lost to Estes Kefauver. He immediately began working for the 1960 presidential nomination. In 1958 he was re-elected to the Senate, but his eye was on the big prize of 1960.

NOMINATION AND ELECTION

Because no Catholic had ever been elected president, Kennedy thought his only chance was by proving his vote-getting ability in the primaries. He entered eight primaries; his chief rival, Hubert Humphrey, entered five. The other leading contenders — Stuart Symington and Lyndon Johnson — stayed out of the primaries, pinning their hopes on political maneuvering during the convention. The first primary was in Wisconsin. Kennedy won, carrying the Catholic districts but losing in Protestant areas. The crucial test came in West Virginia, which was 95 percent Protestant. Kennedy won easily. Humphrey withdrew from the race, and Kennedy swept the remaining primaries, virtually guaranteeing him the nomination. He was nominated on the first ballot. In order to shore up his southern support, Kennedy chose Johnson as his running mate. The Republicans nominated Richard Nixon for president and Henry Cabot Lodge, Jr., for vice president. A number of minor parties fielded candidates, but none posed a serious threat.

Kennedy had three themes in his campaign: the missile gap, a stagnant economy, and a failure to meet the needs of a growing population. He charged that the United States was falling behind the Soviet Union in military power and was lagging behind both the Soviets and the nations of western Europe in the rate of economic growth. He said the United States was failing to modernize itself. Needs in public services, health, transportation, and urban renewal were not being met. The race appeared to be very close. The pollsters gave Kennedy an early lead, but after the campaign got underway Gallup polls showed Nixon ahead. Four televised debates decided the contest. Kennedy not only made a better appearance, but he clearly outclassed Nixon in the style and substance of his arguments. Kennedy won by a narrow margin, receiving a plurality but not a majority of the popular vote, the first president to be so elected since 1916. Kennedy received 303 electoral votes to 219 for Nixon.

FOREIGN RELATIONS

Kennedy replaced "massive retaliation" with "flexible response." He used a show of strength and skillful diplomacy to keep us out of war in Cuba, Berlin, and Laos. Just three months after his inauguration, JFK permitted the Bay of Pigs invasion, planned in the Eisenhower administration, to go ahead, even though he had learned about it soon enough that he could have stopped it. This was a major mistake. The fiasco dealt U.S. prestige a blow from which we did not recover until the successful resolution of the Cuban missile crisis a year and one-half later, when Kennedy's naval blockade led to the dismantling of Soviet missiles in Cuba. In return, Kennedy pledged that the United States would not invade Cuba. He used a combination of a military buildup and hard-nosed diplomacy to prevent the Soviets from giving East Germany control over the West's air and land supply routes to Berlin. In a 1961 meeting with Khrushchev in Vienna, the two leaders had agreed to support a neutral and independent Laos. A coalition government was created in that Asian country a year later. The United States and 13 other nations agreed to guarantee Laotian independence.

Kennedy ordered U.S. troops and equipment to Vietnam and Thailand. Eisenhower had had sent two thousand advisors to Southeast Asia. Kennedy sent may thousands more. He officially refused to commit U.S. combat troops to the region, but some of our "advisors" were involved in battles; some were killed. What his policy would have been in 1964 and beyond is not known. His last draft on Vietnam said that both military and economic aid would be higher in 1964, but that the United States planned to withdraw some troops before the end of 1963. The draft authorized secret military operations up to thirty miles inside Laos. It contained a statement that Cambodia was now of first importance to the United States. It also suggested covert action against North Vietnam with "plausible deniability."

Kennedy promoted international cooperation. In 1961 the United States established the Alliance for Progress, a program to aid Latin American countries that agreed to begin democratic reforms. The Canadian Air Defense System was armed with nuclear warheads under U.S. control. In 1962 Congress appropriated $100 million in bonds to help finance the United Nations. Even though JFK was unable to convince De Gaulle to commit France to a NATO nuclear force, NATO remained strong, When the USSR broke an unofficial atomic weapons test ban, the United States stopped wheat sales to the Soviets. The hot line linking

Washington and Moscow was established on June 2, 1963. After five years of negotiations, an agreement to halt nuclear tests in the atmosphere, in outer space, and under water was signed in Moscow on August 5, 1963, and ratified by the U.S. Senate in September. The Nuclear Test Ban Treaty was a major accomplishment of JFK's administration.

Kennedy convinced the USSR by our actions during the Cuban missile crisis and the Berlin crisis that we were determined to protect our national interests against Soviet threats. The political and psychological impact of U.S. advances in the space race enhanced world opinion of the United States, as did Kennedy's actions in Cuba, Berlin, and Southeast Asia. The establishment of the Peace Corps was also a significant plus.

Congress passed the President's Trade Expansion Act, giving the president the power to cut tariffs so the United States could trade freely with the European Common Market. Kennedy had called for reciprocal tariff reductions on January 25, 1961. These positives were partially offset by the embargo on trade with Cuba, which had a negative effect on the economy of that island nation.

A major innovation of the Kennedy administration was the Peace Corps, launched by executive order on March 1, 1961, and later authorized by Congress. The Peace Corps, the Alliance for Progress, and the Agency for International Development were all aimed at improving the standard of living for people in other countries. Kennedy suggested foreign aid should be called mutual assistance in order to make it more acceptable to the public.

DOMESTIC PROGRAMS

Kennedy inherited a sluggish economy. The recession of 1960-61 ended soon after he took office. Inflation was low, and he resolved to keep it low. To combat inflation he established voluntary wage-price guidelines. In 1962 the steelworkers agreed to a contract with no wage increase, but several companies raised prices anyway. Kennedy went on television and denounced the steel executives. Under administration pressure, the companies rolled back the price increases. In 1963 he proposed a tax cut to stimulate the economy. The cut had not been acted upon at the time of his assassination.

Kennedy adopted a generally pro-labor stance. Attorney General Robert Kennedy vigorously prosecuted both labor racketeering and anti-trust violations. John Kennedy's farm program was not passed by Congress. In April 1961 Congress appropriated aid to economically depressed areas. He aided business by increasing tax benefits for companies investing in new equipment. His proposed 1963 tax cut included reduced corporate taxes.

By Executive Order No. 1 on his first day in office Kennedy doubled the food rations of four million needy Americans. His proposals to create a Department of Urban Affairs and medical care for the aged were both rejected by Congress. He increased aid to dependent children. He increased social security benefits. He proposed an increase in the minimum wage from $1 to $1.25. His aid to depressed areas bill passed. Kennedy promoted conservation and environmental protection. He introduced measures against air and water pollution. He also proposed aid for mass transit.

Kennedy asked the Civil Rights Commission to slow down and tried to get the freedom riders to call off their rides, but when they went ahead anyway and were violently attacked, JFK sent U.S. marshals south to protect them. He ordered federal troops to Mississippi after James Meredith tried to enter the University of Mississippi. He federalized the Alabama National Guard to insure the desegregation of the University of Alabama and the public schools. He urged Congress to pass legislation requiring hotels, motels, and restaurants to serve all. By the end of 1961 "White" and "Colored" waiting rooms had been ended in all interstate terminals. Although he delayed in coming to the support of civil rights, he eventually responded with executive action, a legislative program, and moral leadership. His legislative program was enacted later under President Johnson.

John F. Kennedy strongly supported separation of church and state. He opposed religious bigotry very effectively. Through executive action, Kennedy ordered an end to racial discrimination in housing owned, operated, or financed by the federal government. He established the President's Committee on Equal

Employment Opportunity. He appointed blacks to prominent federal positions. He opposed legislation requiring equal pay for women. He asked the Justice Department to dig up dirt on rival candidates, and did not try to stop J. Edgar Hoover from abusing the FBI's investigative powers.

He believed in the dignity and equality of all human beings and spoke eloquently to this point in his address following Governor George Wallace's defiance at the University of Alabama, challenging Americans to live up to the promise of American ideals and abide by the Golden Rule.

Kennedy supported federal aid to public but not to parochial schools. He established the President's Advisory Council on the Arts. Many artists, writers, musicians, and Nobel Prize winners were invited to the White House. The atmosphere of Camelot supported culture; disdain and contempt for intellectuals ended. The White House had a cultural coordinator for the first time. John Kennedy proposed manpower development and training.

ADMINISTRATION AND INTERGOVERNMENTAL RELATIONS

Kennedy's goals were to improve the economy, strengthen our position vis-à-vis the Soviet Union, and improve the lives of Americans at home. He planned to move quickly into action. Although he accomplished some of his goals, he was unable to remain focused on his long range plans because he had to respond to unexpected events, such as the civil rights revolution, and emergencies in Cuba, Berlin, and Southeast Asia.

Kennedy ran very much of a hands-on operation. He did not delegate nearly as much as Eisenhower did and tried to get the very best talent available. He had a strong cabinet, including Dean Rusk, Douglas Dillon, Robert McNamara, and Arthur Goldberg. His appointment of Robert Kennedy as Attorney General led to charges of nepotism. He appointed Robert C. Weaver, an African-American, to head the Housing and Home Finance Agency and made it a cabinet post. He recruited distinguished scholars to the Kennedy team. Several Republicans were appointed to high positions in his administration. Most of his appointees were assigned to appropriate roles. Kennedy held his subordinates responsible for results. Most departments and agencies were well-administered and accomplished goals. Some officials in the military, the FBI, and the CIA may have at times put their agencies' agendas ahead of those of the president.

John Kennedy was outstanding as a communicator. In his first two months he made 12 speeches, held 7 press conferences, and had 28 communications with foreign leaders. More reporters covered his press conferences than those of any previous president. His were the first press conferences to be televised live.

Of the bills introduced by the administration, most of those making it to the floor passed. Others were held up in committee, frequently by conservative Southern Democratic chairmen. In the off-year elections of 1962 the Democrats gained four seats in the Senate and lost only two in the House. This was only the third time in the 1900s that the party in power had increased its representation in Congress in the mid-term elections. Although the president was unable to get all of his domestic agenda enacted because of a coalition among southern Democrats and Republicans, he worked well with Congress and received bipartisan support on some domestic programs as well as foreign policies. Kennedy exercised appropriate control over the nation's expenditures. He was sometimes unable to get full funding from Congress for some of his proposals.

The president's appointments to the Supreme Court were Byron White and Arthur Goldberg, both very competent individuals. To the lower federal courts, however, he made some bad appointments. Senator Eastland chaired the Senate Judiciary Committee and had the power to hold up appointments of pro–civil rights judges. Kennedy made a deal with him. He appointed the racist William Howard Cox as the price for Eastland accepting the appointment of Thurgood Marshall to a federal Court of Appeals. The president did not review carefully the records of some of the people he appointed to the district courts.

The president was not the tool of any special interests. He wanted always to the do what was best for the country. He placed the power of government behind efforts for social justice, for example. However, he was not unaware of pressure groups and used them when possible to secure enactment of his programs, and sometimes moved more quickly on an issue if he knew there was powerful support for it than if there was strong opposition. He placed a very high priority on getting re-elected and was reluctant to take any action that appeared to diminish his chances. On occasion, though, he did what was morally right even though he felt it would hurt him politically.

LEADERSHIP AND DECISION MAKING

John Kennedy was an inspirational, charismatic leader. He inspired his subordinates to all-out effort. Many had an intense loyalty to him, and he could often persuade others to follow him by convincing them that his was the right course. He was an excellent speaker and had talented speechwriters to help him persuade the public. In private he could make a forceful presentation of his point of view. Public confidence in government was seldom higher than in the Camelot years of the Kennedy presidency. The president set high standards for himself and others. He worked hard at his job and motivated others to perform at a high level. Slipshod performance was not tolerated.

When Kennedy had a vision of the future, such as putting a man on the moon or revitalizing the spirit of America, he communicated it so well that he seemed to be a man of great vision. He unified the nation on foreign policy and on the space race, but was unable to heal racial divisions.

Kennedy was good at analyzing situations and conceiving strategies to improve the nation's lot or to extricate it from a dangerous situation. He found that the job of the president was reactive, not proactive. He had to respond to events unpredictable and forces unseen. Before making a decision the president weighed the alternatives carefully, and then, with cool objectivity, tried to forecast the possible consequences of each course of action. He engaged in as much information gathering as time would permit. He listened to subordinates, from some of whom he received bad advice, particularly those in the Defense Department who were carryovers from previous administrations. He learned from his mistakes and soon learned to discount advice from certain sources. Kennedy utilized a keen intelligence in decision making and problem solving situations. He could engage in dispassionate analysis. Once a decision was reached he would not be swayed by sentiment, subjective, or moral arguments.

John Kennedy understood the art of compromise. In order to win wider support for a proposal he frequently gave up part of what he wanted. His compromise in the Cuban missile crisis (removing our missiles from Turkey) was a masterstroke, as he gained far more than he lost, yet enabled Khrushchev to save face. His compromises with Senator Eastland were less admirable.

Kennedy made tough decisions time after time during his brief presidency. He held firm, remained calm, and steadfastly upheld what was best for the nation during dangerous times — the Cuban missile crisis and the Berlin crisis, for example.

PERSONAL QUALITIES

In public Kennedy conducted himself with a style that the public admired. Even his touch football games with the clan presented an image of healthy, youthful vitality and energy. His White House invitations to leaders in the worlds of art and culture enhanced the office of the president. This president made people proud to be Americans. The country was moving again, it was standing up to the Soviets in Cuba and Berlin, and was catching up and surpassing them in the space race. The people were proud of their handsome president and his beautiful, stylish wife.

Because of public perceptions of Kennedy, the office of the president received more respect both at home and abroad. It was believed that he brought strength, courage, and determination to bear upon our foreign relations and hope and pride to the American people. By appearing to be a vigorous, take charge president JFK restored presidential powers that had apparently diminished during the less energetic Eisenhower years.

Although elected by a minority of the voters in 1960, JFK soon won overwhelming support from the public, who readily adopted him as their hero. He received only 49 percent of the popular vote in 1960. Three years later 59 percent of those polled said they had voted for him. This means that many people overcame their initial doubts and came to feel that JFK was "their" president.

John Kennedy received input from many segments of society. Although he put his greatest trust in those closest to him, he included in his administration many Republicans, such as McNamara, Bundy, Gilpatric, Clay, McCloy, and Lodge. Kennedy used many kinds of formal and informal communications to interact with the people. He was the first president to master television. Through his style and pizzazz he excelled in nonverbal communication as well.

In his official duties, JFK acted with integrity and trustworthiness. Although he was aware of and gave high priority to the political implications of his actions, he never betrayed his duty to his country. He never used his office to enrich himself at public expense, nor did he allow his appointees to do so. No financial wrongdoings by himself or his associates tainted his administration.

Although during his lifetime JFK enhanced the prestige of the presidency by the public image he presented, the image was maintained only through the complicity of a friendly corps of reporters. In his private life, JFK was careless about standards of morality. Some of his associations, such as that with Judith Campbell Exner, who was also a lover of reputed Mafia boss Sam Giancana, were not only ill-advised but could have compromised national security. J. Edgar Hoover's knowledge of Kennedy's affairs prevented the president from exercising control over the FBI chief.

ASSASSINATION AND AFTERMATH

On November 22, 1963, Kennedy was riding in an open car in a motorcade through the streets of Dallas, when shots were fired and he slumped in his seat, fatally wounded. He was pronounced dead at Parkland Memorial Hospital. Lee Harvey Oswald was arrested as a suspect in the assassination. On November 24 while being transferred under custody to the county jail, Oswald was shot to death by Jack Ruby in full view of millions watching on live television. Because Oswald did not live to stand trial, President Johnson appointed a commission, headed by Chief Justice Earl Warren, to investigate the assassination. The Warren Commission reported that Oswald was guilty and had acted alone. Despite this finding, many persons have accepted one or another of various conspiracy theories.

OVERALL ASSESSMENT

Kennedy received 65 points on our 100-point rating scale and ranks eighth among the 39 presidents rated.

LYNDON B. JOHNSON
1963–69

	RATING POINTS	RANK
FOREIGN RELATIONS	1	34 tie
DOMESTIC PROGRAMS	16	4 tie
ADMINISTRATION	12	6 tie
LEADERSHIP	15	8 tie
PERSONAL QUALITIES	2	33
OVERALL ASSESSMENT	46	15

BACKGROUND

Lyndon Baines Johnson was born in a farm house near Stonewall, Texas, on August 27, 1906. His father was a farmer and schoolteacher who served five terms in the Texas legislature. When Lyndon was five, the family moved to Johnson City, Texas, a town founded by his grandfather. At the age of 15 Lyndon graduated from Johnson City High School. He and five friends went to California in a used Model T Ford, camping along the way. Lyndon hitch-hiked up and down the coast, working as a waiter, dishwasher, and farm laborer. For a time he clerked in the law office of a relative. After he hitchhiked back to Johnson City, he worked on a road-building gang. In 1927 he entered Southwest Texas State Teachers College at San Marcos where he paid his expenses by working first as a janitor then as a secretary to the college president. For a year he taught elementary school in Cotulla, Texas, earning enough money to return to college. In 1930 he graduated with a B.S. degree in history and a

teacher's certificate and became a public school teacher. In 1931 Richard Kleberg was elected to Congress and appointed Johnson as his private secretary. In 1935 Johnson became the Texas state director of the National Youth Administration. He was elected to Congress in 1937 and was re-elected six times. In 1941 he was narrowly defeated in a Senate race by W. Lee O'Daniel. He enlisted in the Navy the day after Pearl Harbor, serving as lieutenant commander and winning a Silver Star when his plane was attacked by the Japanese over New Guinea. He resigned his commission in 1942 when President Roosevelt ordered all Congressmen in the service to return to their legislative duties.

In the 1948 Senate Democratic primary Johnson defeated Coke Stevenson by just 97 votes in an election marked by alleged ballot box fraud and other irregularities. He was re-elected by a huge majority in 1954. In 1951 he was elected Democratic whip and in 1953 minority leader. When the Democrats took control of the Senate in 1955, Johnson became majority leader. He was a dynamic, skilled parliamentarian with an instinct for finding workable compromises. He was obsessed with politics and acquired an extraordinary mastery of political skills.

As a young Congressman, Johnson had been an ardent New Dealer and an all-out supporter of Franklin Roosevelt. He was less supportive of President Truman, however, and his record in the House and in the Senate became more conservative as the years went by. While he was majority leader, his party was deeply divided between Southern conservatives and Northern liberals and had a majority of only two in the Senate. A Republican was in the White House. A coalition of Republicans and conservative southern Democrats constituted a working majority. Yet Johnson became one of the most effective and powerful leaders in the history of the U.S. Senate, a truly remarkable achievement. His two major accomplishments as majority leader were passage of the act creating the National Aeronautics and Space Agency and the Civil Rights Act of 1957.

In 1960 Johnson was one of the leading contenders for the Democratic presidential nomination, but sat out the primaries in which John Kennedy sewed up the nomination. To the surprise and disappointment of the party's liberals, Kennedy selected Johnson to be his running mate in the hope that the Texan could help him carry the Lone Star State and some other Southern states. Johnson came through and helped Kennedy win in November. As vice president, he chaired the President's Committee on Equal Employment Opportunity and the National Aeronautics and Space Council. He made eleven separate foreign trips to 33 countries. He was in office, but out of power. He detested every minute of his vice-presidency.

NOMINATION AND ELECTION

Johnson was unopposed at the Democratic convention in 1964. He and his choice for running mate, Hubert H. Humphrey, were both nominated by acclamation on the first ballot. The Republicans nominated Barry Goldwater as their presidential candidate. Goldwater's "extremism" became the main campaign issue. Goldwater called for a firmer stand against Communism, for use of greater military force to win the war in Vietnam, for cutting back on federal government programs, for returning power to the states, and he deplored the moral decay in society, which by implication he blamed on the Democrats, especially on the wheeler-dealer in the White House. Johnson campaigned on the theme of peace and prosperity — no widening of the war in Vietnam, no finger on the nuclear button, and for building a Great Society at home. It was no contest. Johnson won in a landslide, with a plurality of almost 16 million votes. The electoral count was 486 to 52 in favor of the Johnson-Humphrey ticket.

FOREIGN RELATIONS

United States troops were already in Vietnam when LBJ took office. His advisors told him that the Communist North Vietnamese had invaded the non–Communist nation of South Vietnam and that if South Vietnam fell other countries in Southeast Asia would also fall like dominoes. In February 1965 U.S. planes bombed North Vietnam. In March. U.S. marines were sent to South Vietnam — the first admittedly combat troops. In April LBJ announced his willingness to begin peace negotiations. In December a holiday truce was declared. U.S. emissaries were sent to various capitals to explore negotiation possibilities. In July 1966 U.S. planes attacked Communist bases in the demilitarized zone. In August LBJ agreed to proposals for an all–Asia Vietnamese Peace Conference. In March 1967 proposals for peace talks were rejected by Ho Chi Minh. Johnson's advisors unanimously recommended escalation of the war. Escalation continued along with calls for negotiations and occasional bombing halts from 1965 to 1968. Until the Tet offensive in the spring of 1968, none of his advisors recommended withdrawal from Vietnam. In March 1968 Johnson announced a partial halt to bombing North Vietnam and again called upon Ho Chi Minh to enter into peace talks. Peace talks started in Paris in May, but little progress was made. In October 1968 LBJ announced a complete halt to bombing in Vietnam. Unable to get Ho Chi Minh to negotiate peace, LBJ had to continue the war or abandon South Vietnam. He, along with all of his top advisors and (at first) the majority of the American people, regarded the struggle in Vietnam not as a civil war or a revolution but as an invasion of one independent country (South Vietnam) by another (North Vietnam, aided by other Communist powers). In line with the domino theory he did what he thought was right. In hindsight, it now appears that he was wrong. Johnson used military force in a way he thought promoted our national interests. His use of military force was endorsed and authorized by Congress in the Gulf of Tonkin resolution of August 4, 1964. The Vietnam war turned out to be a disaster for the United States.

In 1968 the United States and the USSR signed a two-year cultural agreement. From 1963 to 1967 LBJ conferred with the heads of state or governmental leaders of more than twenty nations. In 1966 he denounced the white supremacist regimes in Africa and pledged assistance to developing African nations. A nuclear planning group was created by NATO (except France) in 1966. In the same year the United Nations general assembly unanimously accepted a draft treaty prohibiting nuclear weapons in space. Johnson concluded a Columbia River power and flood control agreement with Canada. Relations with Panama were restored in 1964. In April 1965 U.S. marines landed in the Dominican Republic, but they were soon replaced by OAS patrols. He declared that the United States sought conciliation, not conquest in Asia. Our actions in Vietnam probably increased rather than decreased international tensions. Johnson planned a summit conference with Kosygin to lay the groundwork for a new détente with the USSR, but it was canceled when Soviet tanks invaded Czechoslovakia. World opinion of the United States probably suffered as a result of our actions in Vietnam. This was partially offset by good deeds elsewhere.

The president proposed a Southeast Asia development program, a TVA-like program for Vietnam. Of course, it was never implemented because the Vietnamese did not really want it. In 1966 he authorized grain shipments to India and proposed a food for freedom program. His foreign aid program stressed self-help and population control.

DOMESTIC PROGRAMS

During LBJ's administration profits soared and poverty declined. The goal of reducing unemployment to four percent was finally reached. The minimum wage was increased to $1.60 per hour and coverage was expanded. Prices started going up in 1965. In 1966 LBJ urged suspension of the business tax credit as an anti-inflation measure. He refused to raise taxes or impose mandatory wage-price controls, preferring voluntary adherence to guidelines. He asked for cutbacks in spending to offset sharp increase in prices. Price increases in aluminum, copper, and steel were rescinded or modified under LBJ pressure. However, his anti-inflation actions were not entirely successful.

On January 4, 1965, LBJ proposed his Great Society program, featuring Medicare for the elderly, educational assistance for the young, food for the hungry, housing for the homeless, poverty grants for the poor, legal protection for blacks, rehabilitation for the disabled, higher benefits for the unemployed, fair labeling for consumers, civil rights and a safer environment for all. Congress enacted much of his program within a matter of months. An Appalachian aid bill was passed in March, aid to elementary and secondary education in April, Medicare in July, a voting rights bill in August, a housing bill with rent subsidies in August, a bill appropriating $300 million to combat heart disease, cancer and strokes in October. Also in October he signed a $1.785 billion anti-poverty bill, doubling the amount appropriated in 1964. In 1966 he recommended but did not secure enactment of a subsidized minimum income. He signed legislation establishing automobile safety standards, a water pollution control bill, and a clean air restoration act.

At the beginning of Johnson's administration, tax rebates were given to business. In June 1965 excise taxes were cut. By 1966 the country was quite prosperous and inflation was becoming a problem. At first LBJ refused to raise taxes. In January 1967 he asked for a six percent surcharge on income taxes to support the war and his domestic programs, but Congress did not pass it until 1968.

Johnson's televised talk after Selma was a

speech that shaped human events. He showed moral leadership and a greatness of spirit as well as a mastery of techniques. He had become a true believer in civil rights. He took the most advanced position on civil rights of any president in history. He called up the Alabama National Guard to protect the Selma to Montgomery march. On July 2, 1964, he signed the Civil Rights Act of 1964, followed by a voting rights bill in 1965, and a White House Conference on Civil Rights in 1966. The Civil Rights Act of 1968 barred discrimination in the sale and rental of housing and stiffened criminal penalties for civil rights violations. An age discrimination in employment act was passed in 1967.

Johnson was a promoter of religious freedom. He accepted a compromise in the Elementary and Secondary Education Act of 1965 allowing parochial school students to benefit from most provisions of the act. He accepted the right of peaceful protest among opponents of the war, but objected when the protests became violent and when urban riots broke out among the African-American population. His record in regard to freedom of the press was not pristine. He tried to manipulate reporters, used rewards and punishment against them, and berated editors who published unfavorable stories. He installed a taping system in the White House.

Johnson signed an immigration bill eliminating national origin quotas. He appointed Thurgood Marshall to the Supreme Court, the first black so named and appointed Robert Weaver, another black, as the first Secretary of Housing and Urban Development. He believed all persons were deserving of respect, regardless of status. He tried to improve the lot of the homeless, to alleviate poverty, and to insure justice for any unfavored group.

Johnson secured passage of the Elementary and Secondary Education Act of 1965, the most massive and comprehensive federal aid ever given to the public schools of this nation. He proposed improved schooling for Indians, vocational training for the unskilled, and federal participation in the JFK Center for the Performing Arts. In November 1965 he signed the Higher Education Act, including federal aid to colleges and the creation of a National Teacher Corps.

ADMINISTRATION AND INTERGOVERNMENTAL RELATIONS

When LBJ assumed the reins of government after the assassination of Kennedy, he retained the former president's staff and goals. When elected to serve his own term, LBJ created seventeen task forces to identify major issues in each area, analyze the most significant problems, and recommend specific programs. In 1965 he transmitted 63 separate documents requesting legislative action. He established two new cabinet level executive departments — Transportation and Housing and Urban Affairs. He appointed the Heiman Commission to study governmental reorganization.

He convinced all of JFK's cabinet and White House staff to stay on while he served out the slain leader's unexpired term. He kept them informed, constantly requested their advice and asked for their help. When he was elected on his own, he began replacing them with his own selections. He developed a loyal staff of intelligent and energetic men. He had no chief of staff, but communicated directly with his top aides. He demanded a great deal from them, but he never drove an assistant harder than he drove himself.

The president's staff grew in influence at the expense of the cabinet. He assumed personal control over decisions on budget and personnel, further weakening the power of department. heads. This concentrated more power and responsibility in the hands of the president and was administratively sound. Johnson assigned personnel to appropriate roles, gave them limited authority, and held them responsible for producing desired results

Lyndon Johnson regarded the press as an interest group. His motto was: "Keep their daily bread (information) in your own hands so you can give it out when and to whom you want." He used access to the president as a means of reward and punishment. He held press conferences when he wanted rather than on a regular schedule. If leaks occurred and the press published something he did not want published, he would sometimes change his plans in order to embarrass the reporter and the person responsible for the leak. All presidents feel a need for secrecy in wartime. Perhaps LBJ carried this penchant for secrecy further than he should have. The full extent of the U.S. commitment in Vietnam was kept secret as long as possible.

Johnson sponsored Program Planning and Budgeting Systems designed to evaluate programs according to definite objectives and to expand the president's control over the budget-making process. He did not give department heads control over their own budgets, believing the president should be in charge of the entire government. He tried to finance the Great Society and the War in Vietnam simultaneously without raising taxes enough to cover the entire costs, which increased the national debt and contributed to inflation. He assigned very high priority to both areas and felt the increased expenditures were not only desirable but necessary.

The executive branch departments and agencies were well-administered. In the domestic arena more was accomplished in Johnson's administration than in almost any other administration in history. His goals in Vietnam were not accomplished because he and his top advisors miscalculated the nature of the conflict there.

Johnson tried to crack the wall of separation between the executive and legislative branches. enough to give Congress a feeling of participation in his bills without exposing his plans to advance congressional opposition. He sought congressional advice on strategy, but not on goals. He involved selected Representatives and Senators on his task forces. He required cabinet members to consult with key legislators on drafts of bills. He held White House briefings, at which he would display a chart showing where each of his bills was at the moment and discuss strategies for moving the bill forward. The major item of every cabinet meeting through 1965 (before Vietnam became the top priority) was pending legislation. He gave a detailed breakdown on head counts on bills, with the status of each member's position. If a bill was in trouble, what compromises should be made? He would hold the line unless a compromise was absolutely necessary to secure passage. His personal calls to members of Congress were legendary, but were used only as a last resort. He was much more sophisticated in congressional relations than the press reported. He secured overwhelming support for his domestic programs. In foreign affairs he maintained a bipartisan approach. Even after the war became unpopular he received more support from Republicans than from Democrats for his Vietnam policy.

He appointed two members to the Supreme Court — Abe Fortas, his personal attorney and a very capable man, who resigned after allegations of minor improprieties in 1969 and Thurgood Marshall, the Court's first African-American member, who became one of the great liberal justices of the century. Johnson's appointments to lower federal courts were not all distinguished. He was criticized for discussing politics with Fortas after the latter joined the court, but such interaction between presidents and justices have been very common.

Johnson was able to create an unusual unity of national mood in the first months of his presidency. He met with leaders of labor, business, civil rights, and other groups. He immediately focused public attention of the skillfully ordered legislation that was to mark the first years of his presidency. He made poverty an issue of public concern, making visits to poverty-stricken regions and calling for an unconditional war on poverty. He handled it with remarkable deftness. Using his consensual skills he was able to enlist support or at least mute potential opposition from interest groups leaders. He met with groups ranging from the DAR to the Socialist Party, from the Business Council to the AFL-CIO. The powerful interest groups at first supported his Vietnam policy. When they turned against him on the war, he decided not to run for re-election in 1968.

LEADERSHIP AND DECISION MAKING

In the first four months after Kennedy's assassination LBJ displayed brilliant leadership and political skill. He positioned himself as a "faithful agent of Kennedy's intentions and as the healing leader of a stunned and baffled nation." [59] Although not everyone responded positively to LBJ's Texas-style charisma, he was an extremely successful leader. He inspired others by his personal example of hard work.

When the war in Vietnam went badly, he was unable to preserve a sense of unity in the nation, but that would probably have been an impossible task for anyone.

In private conversations LBJ was one of the most persuasive men ever to occupy the White House. He learned as much as he could about the person he was trying to persuade and adapted his means to fit the situation. He was also extraordinarily effective in small groups, less so with large audiences. Johnson did an outstanding job in reassuring the country, calming its fears, and restoring confidence after the assassination. Later, he lost the confidence of many people due to his handling of the war in Vietnam.

The president set high standards of performance for himself and others. He insisted on hard work and motivated others by all means at his disposal.

At first LBJ devoted himself to accomplishing Kennedy's goals. When he won the election of 1964, the presidency was legitimately his; he was no longer bound by the JFK legacy. He proposed a Great Society, which was his vision for America. His ideal was a land in which every person shared in the progress and responsibilities of his country. He conceptualized a strategy to bring his vision into reality. His strategy was amazingly successful, until he and the nation were sidetracked by Vietnam.

The president carefully weighed alternatives and made an informed judgment about the possible consequences of each decision. If he made mistakes in Vietnam, it was not due to his failure to consider alternatives. He made incorrect judgments about the possible consequences of his actions, but these judgments were unanimously shared by the small group of state department and military advisors with whom he conferred. Perhaps he should have operated with less secrecy and engaged in fair and honest deliberations with a wider circle of people.

Johnson was much more intelligent than the eastern press credited him with being. He used his intellectual abilities in decision making and problem solving situations, but also relied somewhat on his gut instinct and his sense of what was right and wrong.

Lyndon Johnson was a master of compromise, extremely skillful at giving no more than he had to in order to achieve his goals. His willingness to compromise in order to achieve results was confined within the limits imposed by the requirements of the presidency and his knowledge of just how far a particular man or group might be pushed. One of his problems with Ho Chi Minh was that the latter was unwilling to compromise, making negotiations fruitless. Johnson preferred negotiations or compromise over hard-nosed decision-making, but if a tough decision had to be made, he made it. He did not pass the buck, or allow himself to be paralyzed into non-action.

PERSONAL QUALITIES

When LBJ succeeded to the presidency upon the death of Kennedy, he checked his arrogance and conveyed a deep humility, but expressed confident determination that JFK's goals would be pursued and reached. In his first major address he said the ideas and ideals which JFK so nobly represented must be translated into effective action. He said no memorial could more eloquently honor JFK's memory than the passage of a civil rights bill. The American people were never particularly proud of LBJ. The contrast to the Camelot image of the Kennedys was too great. He never completely lived down his wheeler-dealer past and the reputation he got from the irregularities in his election to the Senate. Despite his outstanding leadership and vision, LBJ did not enhance the stature of the office of the president. He did not exemplify some of the characteristics that people want in their ideal president. In contrast to the urbane and sophisticated Kennedy, Johnson seemed loud, boisterous, and uncultured. At times he could be crude and vulgar, but he generally was cognizant of the decorum expected of a president.

Certainly LBJ increased the power of the presidency. He assumed personal control over decisions on budgets and personnel. He controlled legislation through his intense preparation and careful monitoring. The Tonkin Gulf resolution greatly increased the power of the president to send and use troops without specific authorization from Congress.

Lyndon Johnson tried very hard to be a

"people's president." Except for the war in Vietnam, he would have been successful at it. Opposition to the war led many people to believe that the president was not on their side. His popularity plummeted as the war dragged on. Early in his presidency LBJ appointed many task forces and met with leaders of many interest groups. As the years went by he began to restrict access. Although the press covered the Vietnam war much more intimately than any previous war, reporters complained about the secrecy with which Johnson made decisions relating to the war.

Johnson was not entirely successful in reaching out to the people. Although he could be masterful in dealing with individuals or small groups, he did not relate well to large audiences. A common man, he related well to common people, and did more for them than almost any other president in history, yet the people did not totally accept him.

Johnson's integrity is frequently questioned, mainly because of charges of improper activities in some of his early political campaigns. Yet he had a set of moral principles and values on which he operated. He did not swerve from these. He was more honest than his reputation implies. There was no graft in his record. His wife's ability to catapult a small radio station into a multimillion dollar communications empire may have been enhanced by the offices her husband held, but there is no evidence of any wrongdoing. He appointed some friends to office, but no more than most presidents. He was a manipulator and a conniver, who may have been involved in election frauds when he was first elected to the Senate. Johnson did not always meet high standards of morality. He diminished somewhat the prestige of the office, but he was not a dishonest or corrupt president.

OVERALL ASSESSMENT

Johnson was a very complex man, who could have been a great president. We rate him in the top ten presidents for Domestic Programs, for Administration and Intergovernmental Relations, and for Leadership and Decision Making. We rate him among the lower-ranking presidents in Foreign Relations and Personal Qualities. Overall, he received 46 points on the rating scale, and ranks in fifteenth place among the 39 presidents rated.

During the Johnson administration, the country made its greatest advances in civil rights since the end of Reconstruction. The civil rights movement not only helped African-Americans, but it also laid the groundwork for progress by other minorities, women, and persons with handicaps or disabilities. Johnson's Great Society program carried the nation a step beyond the New Deal and was well on the way toward improving the lot of the underprivileged when it was sidetracked by the war. His administration was also marked by civil unrest, a wave of political assassinations, urban riots, and a revolution in moral standards among the youth of the land.

RICHARD M. NIXON

1969-74

	RATING POINTS	RANK
FOREIGN RELATIONS	12	12 tie
DOMESTIC PROGRAMS	−5	33 tie
ADMINISTRATION	−10	38
LEADERSHIP	4	24 tie
PERSONAL QUALITIES	−9	38 tie
OVERALL ASSESSMENT	−6	36

BACKGROUND

Richard Milhous Nixon was born on January 9, 1913, in Yorba Linda, California. When he was nine years old the family moved to Whittier, California. At an early age the boy worked at many different jobs to supplement the family income. He graduated from Whittier High School, Whittier College, and Duke University Law School, where he ranked third in the 1937 graduating class. During World War II he served as an officer with a naval air transport unit in the Pacific. In 1946 he was elected to Congress, where he gained fame for his probing of Alger Hiss. After a second term in Congress, he was elected to the Senate in 1950. He charged his opponents in both the congressional and the senatorial races with being soft on communism. In 1952 he was elected vice president. President Eisenhower sent him abroad on good will visits to more than fifty countries.

In 1960 Nixon was the Republican candidate for president. For an account of this election, see the entry on John F. Kennedy. After the 1960 election, Nixon returned to California where he ran for governor in 1962, but lost. In 1963 he moved to New York where he became a partner in a Wall Street law firm. In 1966 he campaigned vigorously for Republican candidates in congressional elections, earning him the party's gratitude.

NOMINATION AND ELECTION

In 1968 Nixon overcame his loser image by winning presidential primaries by large margins in several states. At the convention he was nominated on the first ballot. He selected Spiro Agnew as his running mate. The Democrats, badly split over the Vietnam war, nominated Hubert H. Humphrey. George Wallace ran as a candidate of the American Independent Party. Nixon and Humphrey both promised to seek peace in Vietnam. Nixon proposed that other nations take more of the responsibility for preserving world peace and helping underdeveloped countries. He also promised to strengthen law enforcement in the United

States. Humphrey pledged more federal aid for the needy and proposed to rebuild slum areas in the cities. Wallace ran a populist, anti-intellectual, anti-government campaign, capitalizing on his stand against racial desegregation. There were no presidential debates. Early in the race Nixon was heavily favored, but Humphrey cut into his lead in the final days of the campaign. The popular vote was extremely close, with Nixon winning a plurality. His margin over Humphrey was less than one percent. In the electoral count Nixon received 301 votes to 191 for Humphrey and 46 for Wallace.

In 1972 Nixon was nominated by acclamation for a second term. The Democrats chose George S. McGovern as their presidential candidate. Fresh from diplomatic triumphs with China and the Soviet Union and faced by an opponent widely regarded as too liberal to be elected, Nixon was an overwhelming favorite for re-election. Nevertheless, he set up the Committee to Re-elect the President (CREEP), which collected a record-breaking $60 million campaign fund. Much of this money was collected illegally and used for illegal purposes. The Committee was also responsible for the break-in and illegal wiretapping of Democratic headquarters in the Watergate building. Nixon won a landslide victory in November, receiving over 60 percent of the popular vote and swamping McGovern in the electoral college by 520 to 17.

FOREIGN RELATIONS

Nixon's use of military force in the Vietnam war was appropriate under the circumstances. He gradually withdrew American troops while trying to turn the defense of South Vietnam over to the Vietnamese. The bombing of Cambodia was controversial, but was probably justified as a part of the strategy to end the war. His implied threat of military force elsewhere deterred further Soviet expansion. Nixon showed the Soviet Union and China that the United States had the strength, courage, and will to defend its national interests against any threats from them. His ending the war, his maintaining U.S. strength, while making diplomatic overtures to the Soviet Union and China were appropriate peacekeeping efforts.

A supporter of NATO and the United Nations, Nixon maintained existing American alliances. The Nixon Doctrine attempted to shift more of the responsibility for resisting leftist subversion to the nations affected rather than having the United States bear the brunt of the burden. Early in his presidency he visited Europe and improved our relations with France and Great Britain.

Nixon supported the military junta that overthrew the elected president of Chile, Salvador Allende. Nixon's actions were widely supported in the U.S. and by the governments of most Latin American nations, but were regarded as gross interference by the common people of Chile and other Latin America countries. Nixon emulated other recent U.S. presidents in supporting friendly or anti–Communist governments, regardless of their legitimacy in the eyes of their own people.

The long-drawn out process leading to the end of the war in Vietnam eased international tensions. So did the overtures to the Soviets and Nixon's visit to China. He started the Strategic Arms Limitations Treaty (SALT) process with the Soviets. The breakthrough toward normalizing relations with China was in our national interest. Ironically, this is viewed as one of Nixon's greatest triumphs, although he was one of the major forces making it impossible for any of his predecessors to have done so (by his soft on communism charges). Opening up China to American markets was a positive step.

As far as his conduct of foreign policy is concerned, Nixon enhanced public opinion toward the United States in much of the world. During his administration the United States appeared to be a strong and dependable member of the world community.

DOMESTIC PROGRAMS

Nixon attempted to maintain prosperity by reducing inflation without creating unemployment, but was unable to do so during the first two years of his administration. Instead inflation increased, unemployment increased, and the gross national product declined during the president's first two years in office. This was the worst possible combination — rising inflation coupled with rising unemployment. The president then instituted wage-price controls and urged the Federal Reserve to adopt an expansionary monetary policy. These steps had a favorable short-term effect on the economy, helping pull the country out of a recession that was looming in 1970. The imposition of wage-price controls brought inflation down temporarily in 1971, but after the removal of the controls, inflation soared after the 1972 election.

Although Nixon did not propose pro-labor legislation, he courted labor leaders, especially George Meany, and secured support from much of the rank-and-file for his social issues. On the whole, Nixon's was not a pro-labor administration. His administration did not put much emphasis on regulation of trusts and monopolies.

Nixon's record on fighting poverty was mixed. He advocated a welfare reform plan, the Family Assistance Plan (FAP) that offered virtually a guaranteed annual income to former welfare recipients who found work, but he eventually dropped this plan, which was never enacted by Congress. Nixon fought hard to abolish the Office of Economic Opportunity. Congress refused to eliminate legal services, economic development, and community action programs. Nixon impounded the funds Congress had appropriated for these programs. Nixon continued the Social Security program, with an index to increase payments to keep up with inflation. He opposed mandatory national health insurance. He supported the food stamps program. He was a strong "law and order" advocate, but his protection against crime was mainly rhetoric.

Bored by economists, Nixon had no consistent fiscal policy. At one point he favored tax reform that included repealing the investment credit, reducing the corporate tax rate by two percent, and cutting the personal tax rate. Eventually, he signed a Democratic bill that he had threatened to veto. Nixon campaigned for a balanced budget, but was unable to achieve it. The effects of inflation, recession, and demands for lower taxes were too much to overcome. Only in 1969 did government receipts exceed outlays. The 1971 and 1972 deficits were higher than those of any year since the end of

World War II, except 1968. In an attempt to lower expenditures, he cut the budget for welfare programs despite great needs in that area.

By executive order Nixon established an Office of Minority Business Enterprise within the Commerce Department. He attempted to crack the long-standing color barriers in the construction trades by supporting the so-called Philadelphia plan to require contractors doing business with the government to hire a segment of minority workers. These controversial initiatives were offset by his attempts to slow down school desegregation. Nixon thought he had an exemplary civil rights record and could not understand the opposition to him by most blacks. His record was one of opposing school desegregation, of opposing affirmative action (except in the Philadelphia Plan) and generally opposing anti-discrimination programs. He opposed extending the Voting Rights Act of 1965.

Nixon was incensed by anti-war protesters, especially when their protests involved violence. He attempted to stop publication of the Pentagon Papers, convinced by Henry Kissinger that their publication would undermine peace negotiations. These actions by the president could be justified by the fact we were actually at war in Vietnam. His civil liberties record is marred by his support of wiretapping, of "no-knock" entry by police, by opposition to the Miranda ruling, and for his secret taping of visitors to the White House. Nixon has been accused of anti–Semitism, and some of his remarks certainly support those charges. Yet he appointed several Jews to high positions in his cabinet and in the White House advisory councils.

Nixon made no important changes in our immigration policy. He made a determined effort to win the votes of so-called ethnics for the Republican party and for his own candidacy. Nixon took no strong position on women's rights, pro or con. Although he had pledged support for the Equal Rights Amendment as a candidate, he refused to reaffirm support for it as president. He appointed no women to high posts in his administration. The Equal Employment Opportunity Act of 1972 was passed by Congress during Nixon's administration, strengthening the powers of the

Equal Employment Commission. The president opposed giving the commission cease-and-desist power, and the chairman resigned because of a lack of administration support. His entire cabinet and top White House staff as well as all of his Supreme Court appointees were white males.

In private as well as in public, Nixon strongly preferred the company of self-made millionaires. He was uncomfortable with "aristocrats" who had inherited wealth. He also identified with small businessmen. In public he praised working class Americans. He derided college students who protested the war. His private conversations included anti–Semitic talk. He did little to try to improve the lot of the homeless, to alleviate poverty, or to insure justice for unfavored groups. The White House tapes reveal a man who had little respect for human dignity.

ADMINISTRATION AND INTERGOVERNMENTAL RELATIONS

Nixon had a set of goals and objectives for his foreign relations and a plan for their accomplishment. In the domestic arena he was much less focused. He was not good at long-range planning. His administration was marked by considerable inconsistency.

Originally, Nixon was a strong proponent of cabinet government, but in common with most recent presidents soon found himself relying far more heavily on the White House staff than on the cabinet. He was not particularly adept at establishing organizational patterns and communication channels. His most significant organizational change was the creation of the Office of Management and Budget (OBM).

With a few notable exceptions, the executive branch departments were headed by capable, but not distinguished appointees. National security advisor Henry Kissinger was the dominant cabinet member. He shared the Nobel Peace Prize in 1973 for his role in negotiating the end of the war in Vietnam. There was considerable bickering among cabinet members and in-fighting among agency heads within some departments. Attorney General John Mitchell was very corrupt, and his actions tar-

nished the Nixon administration. The president's personal staff were more loyal to him than to the country, as evidenced by their complicity in the Watergate cover-up. Among presidential advisors were some first-rate people, such as Pat Moynihan. The president wanted to reduce the size of the bureaucracy, but did not do so to any significant degree. The failure to assign subordinates to appropriate roles and to hold them responsible for results was one of the causes of the Watergate scandal.

Nixon attempted to utilize two-way communication, but was not particularly effective at it. The Watergate cover-up was one example of withholding information, not only from the public, but from Congress and investigating committees. Nixon had long maintained an antagonistic relationship with the press, reaching its nadir after his defeat for the California governorship in 1962. As president, the relationship did not much improve. He had the support of most publishers and editors, but the working press was against him. The attempt to suppress the Pentagon Papers and the Watergate cover-up destroyed the relationship utterly.

Nixon reported to the people and Congress through speeches, writings, and press conferences on his perception of national needs and problems. He was not forthcoming on plans and withheld information related to Watergate.

Working with an opposition Congress, Nixon was unable to secure approval of budgets that reflected his perceptions of national needs and priorities. He had to compromise. Nixon exerted presidential control over executive branch and agency expenditures to the extent possible, even going so far as to impound Congressional appropriations. Despite his efforts to cut domestic programs, government spending increased every year during his administration.

Even before Watergate, Nixon was not entirely successful in dealing with Congress. After his cover-up became apparent, he lost whatever control he did have. Early in his presidency Nixon compromised with the Democratic majority in Congress to get part of what he wanted in return for giving them part of what they wanted, but on the whole the relationship was adversarial. Nevertheless, Nixon secured bipartisan support for some of his foreign policy initiatives. (The Democrats supported him on overtures toward China and the Soviet Union for which he would have crucified them had their roles been reversed.)

Two Supreme Court nominations — Clement Haynsworth, Jr., and George Carswell — were turned down by the Senate. The nomination of Carswell was especially bad. His other Supreme Court appointees were quite competent — Harry Blackmun, Lewis Powell, William Rehnquist, and Chief Justice Warren E. Burger. His appointments to the lower federal courts were decried by many liberals and advocates of civil rights.

Perhaps because he lacked a coherent agenda, the president was unable to mobilize powerful interest groups in support of his domestic programs. He was trying to build a new coalition of disparate interests who did not have much in common except their opposition to "too-liberal" Democrats. The Democratic control of Congress further inhibited his efforts to gain solid support from the interests who had to cover their flanks. He was much more successful in getting their support for his election than he was in getting support for his programs. Getting re-elected was the most important thing for Nixon. He did the honorable thing in obeying the court order to surrender the White House tapes, instead of destroying them as some of his friends urged. Resigning rather than undergoing an impeachment trial was probably in the public interest also. Nixon tried to be president of all the people, but some of the people did not like him, his policies, or his methods.

LEADERSHIP AND DECISION MAKING

Although Nixon had leadership ability, his lack of focus and inconsistency on domestic issues reduced his effectiveness as an administrative leader. Nixon was not a charismatic person, but he was frequently able to persuade others to follow him by convincing them that his was the right course. Nixon did not inspire the people to an all-out effort to accomplish important national goals.

The president had difficulty developing warm, friendly relationships with some subordinates, but he inspired a great deal of loyalty from others. Nixon listened to subordinates, usually engaged in discussions with those who agreed or disagreed with him within his administration. Sometimes he failed to accomplish his goals because he neglected to consult congressional leaders of both his own and the opposition party. He developed his plans with only a small group of advisors.

Nixon had overwhelming support from the public during his first term. He was re-elected by one of the largest margins in history. He lost this support because of Watergate. His actions in the cover-up and other revelations of misconduct caused the people to lose respect for him. Watergate destroyed public confidence in government, not only at the time but for years to come. Its effects are still being felt. The office of the independent counsel, which caused President Clinton so much grief, was created in response to the Watergate cover-up. Although Nixon was an extremely hard worker, he did not set high standards for himself or others in his administration. He wanted to bring the country together again after the divisiveness of the Sixties. Watergate destroyed any hopes of success in this regard.

Nixon had a view of what the nation and the world should be like. He wanted a world at peace, led by a strong United Nations. At home he wanted an end to domestic discord and a healthy economy. Nixon had a strategy for accomplishing his international goals, but no workable strategy for achieving his domestic objectives. The president was not good at long range planning, especially in the domestic arena.

In most cases Nixon carefully weighed alternatives before making a decision and tried to make an informed judgment about possible consequences. In other cases he just jumped right in without considering the consequences. However, he was willing to reassess his position when circumstances changed, as on wage-price controls, for example. In attempting to work with an opposition Congress, the president found it necessary to compromise, sometimes on principles as well as on details.

Nixon was a student of history and learned (but not enough) from it. In some cases Nixon recognized and admitted his own errors in judgment and changed his programs as a result. He did not seem to be able to recognize that his fears, insecurities, and ambition led him to the kind of personal missteps that culminated in the Watergate cover-up. Nixon was a very intelligent, clever man. He applied his keen intelligence to foreign relations and earned a reputation as an outstanding foreign relations president; he applied his cleverness to political affairs and earned a reputation as "Tricky Dick" and became our only president to be driven from office in mid-term.

Nixon had ample courage to make tough decisions. Sometimes he acted rashly in what he perceived as emergencies. In some cases he overreacted with unfortunate consequences.

PERSONAL QUALITIES

Nixon demeaned the office of president by petty, small-minded, mean-spirited, and crude conduct. After the revelations of Watergate, Americans could take no pride in their president. Nixon's actions brought the office of the president into disrepute. Although Watergate diminished the stature of the presidency, it did not seriously weaken the power of the presidency in the long run.

Nixon led the "new Republican majority" to think the president was on their side, but this did not carry over to the thinking of the minority. The public did not have much direct access to the president. They communicated with him through telegrams of support or demonstrations in protest. He was buoyed by the support and angered by the opposition. It is doubtful that he gave much thoughtful consideration to their input. On occasion he tried to reach out to the people through emotional speeches. Because of his disdain for the protesters and for the media, he did not interact much with the people.

Long before Watergate, Nixon had a reputation for being untrustworthy. He abandoned all moral principles in the Watergate cover-up. Nixon was personally honest as far as handling public funds was concerned. He enriched himself in office through legal means, not through bribes or mishandling funds. However, he was accused of improprieties in handling his income taxes and paid nearly one-half million dollars in back taxes in April 1974. Two of Nixon's top men, Attorney General Mitchell and Vice President Agnew, were very corrupt. The whole atmosphere of Watergate added to governmental scandal.

Nixon exhibited appropriate standards of morality in his personal life. It was his public life that was lacking in morality.

RESIGNATION

On February 3, 1973, the Senate voted unanimously to conduct an investigation of the Watergate incident and the 1972 presidential election campaign. The investigating committee began televised hearings on May 17, 1973. The Watergate grand jury revealed on June 6, 1974, that Nixon had been named an unindicted co-conspirator in the Watergate cover-up. The House Judiciary Committee began public debate on articles of impeachment on July 24, 1974. The committee voted in favor of impeachment. Before the full house voted, the president resigned on August 9, 1974. One year later, President Ford granted Nixon a full pardon for all offenses committed during his administration. Nixon's two top aides, ex–Attorney General Mitchell, and several functionaries were sent to prison. Ex–Attorney General Kleindienst received a suspended sentence.

OVERALL ASSESSMENT

Nixon's scores ranged from a high of 12 points in Foreign Relations to a low of negative 10 in Administration and Intergovernmental Relations. Overall, he had a score of negative six and ranks 36th among the presidents rated.

GERALD R. FORD

1973–77

	RATING POINTS	RANK
FOREIGN RELATIONS	11	15 tie
DOMESTIC PROGRAMS	–4	32
ADMINISTRATION	–7	35
LEADERSHIP	–2	32 tie
PERSONAL QUALITIES	4	29 tie
OVERALL ASSESSMENT	2	32

BACKGROUND

On July 14, 1913, in Omaha, Nebraska, a son was born to Dorothy Gardner and Leslie King, a western wool dealer. They named their only child Leslie Lynch King, Jr. In 1915 the Kings were divorced. Dorothy and her two-year-old son moved to her parents' home in Grand Rapids, Michigan. A year later she married Gerald R. Ford. Formal adoption papers were taken out for her son, who was renamed Gerald R. Ford, Jr. When Jerry graduated from South High School in Grand Rapids in 1931, he received a scholarship to play football at the University of Michigan, where he graduated in 1935 with a B average and a liberal arts degree. Ford became an assistant football coach at Yale University. In 1939 he was admitted to Yale Law School. He finished in the top third of his class, earning his degree in 1941 and returning to Grand Rapids, where he opened a law office. In 1942 he joined the Navy. Commissioned as an ensign, he was assigned to a physical training unit with the V-5 program at the Univer-

sity of North Carolina. He requested sea duty, received gunnery training, and was assigned to the light aircraft carrier *Monterey* as director of physical training and assistant navigation officer. The ship participated in many major naval engagements in the South Pacific. Ford served nearly four years, earning ten battle stars, and rising to the rank of lieutenant commander.

After his discharge, he returned to Grand Rapids where he joined a law firm. In 1948 he was elected to Congress, to which he was re-elected 12 times. In 1951 he secured an appointment to the Appropriations Committee, which he thought would help him toward his goal of becoming Speaker of the House. In 1963 he became chairman of the House Republican Conference. After Kennedy's assassination, President Johnson appointed Ford to the Warren Commission. In 1964 he became minority leader in the House. He opposed Johnson's conduct of the war in Vietnam, believing the president was requiring our troops to fight a limited war instead of making decisive sea and air moves that might produce victory. He also opposed Johnson's open housing bill forbidding discrimination in the sale or rental of housing, but voted for the bill when his Republican colleagues revolted against his leadership. After Nixon's election, Ford supported him down the line. He supported Nixon's Indochina policy, his opposition to civil rights, and his stance on other social issues. Ford lost much credibility when he sought the impeachment of the distinguished Justice William O. Douglas.

When Vice President Agnew resigned in disgrace, Nixon chose Ford as his successor. In a bizarre televised ceremony in the East Room of the White House, the president, already himself threatened with impeachment for his involvement in the Watergate cover-up, announced his selection to an assembly of dignitaries. Ford's appointment had to win confirmation from a Congress controlled by Democrats. His perceived integrity outweighed ideological differences, and the Michigander was confirmed by an overwhelming margin in both houses. On December 6, 1973, he was sworn in as the first non-elected vice president in the nation's history.

The vice president steadfastly protested his belief in Nixon's innocence of major wrongdoing in the Watergate affair, but urged the president to release evidence and be more frank in his dealings with the courts and Congress. After Nixon's resignation, Ford took the oath of office as president of the United States on August 9, 1974.

NOMINATION AND ELECTION

Ford is the only president in the history of the United States to ascend to the Oval Office without having been elected to either the vice presidency or the presidency.

The beginning of the end of Ford's presidency came a month after he took the oath of office. He pardoned Richard M. Nixon. Ford's popularity rating declined 21 points. To compound his woes, the country's economic condition deteriorated and the news from Southeast Asia was unpalatable to many Americans. Unemployment and inflation were both on the rise. By 1975 Communists had taken over Cambodia and marched into Saigon. The war

in Vietnam ended with a complete Communist victory.

Despite all this, Ford announced that he would be a candidate for his party's nomination in 1976. In 1975 two women in separate incidents tried to kill Ford. Lynette Fromme tried to shoot the president, but the gun failed to fire. Sara Jane Moore fired at Ford, but the shot missed. Both women were convicted and sentenced to life in prison. Ronald Reagan entered the contest for the Republican nomination. Ford and Reagan ran neck and neck in the primaries. At the convention, Ford won a first ballot nomination with 1187 votes to Reagan's 1070. As his running mate, he picked Senator Robert Dole.

Ford ran an inept campaign. Early in the race he was hurt by the country's economic condition, by his disregard for the plight of the cities, his seeming callousness toward the poor and needy, and his pardon of Nixon. Democrat Jimmy Carter got off to a head start in the race, but he ran a poor campaign, and the lead narrowed. The economy improved with inflation and unemployment both falling. The deficit was increasing rapidly, but few people paid much attention. Ford nearly closed the gap. However, he made a major gaffe in the televised debates when he insisted that Eastern Europe was not under Soviet domination. Ford received only 240 electoral votes to 297 for Carter.

FOREIGN RELATIONS

The war in Vietnam ended on April 30, 1975 with the unconditional surrender of the South Vietnam government. Three days before Saigon fell, President Ford ordered the evacuation by helicopter of the remaining Americans. The United States became involved in no new wars during the Ford administration.

When the American merchant ship *Mayaguez* was seized by a Cambodian naval vessel, Ford ordered it retaken by U.S. forces. Several Americans were killed or wounded. Whether the ship could have been retrieved by diplomatic means with no loss of life will never be known. Many Americans would have supported an even greater use of military force than Ford employed. Ford's action in the

Mayaguez incident showed our determination and ability to protect our national interests.

Through diplomacy Ford tried to ease international tensions. The establishment of diplomatic relations with East Germany was a positive step. Secretary of State Kissinger tried, but failed to bring about accommodation between Egypt and Israel. President Ford and Soviet leader Leonid Brezhnev conferred in Vladivostok on limiting the number of offensive nuclear weapons. They agreed to negotiate a new ten-year agreement on strategic arms limitations. The United States and the Soviet Union signed a treaty to limit the size of underground nuclear explosions; on-site inspection was allowed. Ford became the first U.S. president to visit Japan, but no notable achievements were made there. He also visited South Korea, but again nothing significant happened. He conferred with the leaders of West Germany, Israel, France, and other countries, and visited at least five European capitals.

After the Soviet and Cuban success in Angola, Ford came out for majority rule in the countries of Africa having a black majority, provided there was a guarantee of white minority rights, but said the United States would not provide the guarantee. He continued the negotiations begun by Lyndon Johnson for the gradual transfer of operation of the Panama Canal to Panama.

World opinion of the United States was enhanced by Ford's diplomatic efforts. This was partially offset by the final collapse of American hopes and the ruin of our friends in Indochina and by our inability to prevent the Organization of Oil Exporting Countries (OPEC) from raising the price of oil to an amount that was harmful to our national economy. There were no significant changes in our tariff policies during the Ford administration. The sale of U.S. grain to the Soviet Union was helpful to that nation.

DOMESTIC PROGRAMS

Ford inherited an economy that was not in good shape, and things got worse before they got better. Inflation in 1974 was the worst since 1947. Unemployment peaked 1975, the highest since 1941. Three days after taking the oath of office, the president addressed Congress, calling for measures to fight inflation, which he called "public enemy number one." He announced a Whip Inflation Now (WIN) program and called on industry to exercise restraint. As a result of his speech, two major steel companies and the Ford Motor Company reduced their planned price increases. In further attempts to avoid price increases, Ford vetoed environmental controls on strip mining, recommended that Congress repeal the requirement that the auto industry strengthen emission standards, and vetoed a bill that would have required the transport of twenty percent of imported oil in high-cost U.S. tankers, employing union labor. Although much of the public ridiculed Ford's WIN buttons, he was successful in reducing the rate of inflation by 1976 to one-half the 1974 rate.

Ford's main anti-recession proposal was a combination of tax rebates and investment tax credits. Congress passed a tax reduction bill that was greater than the president had requested; as a result deficits skyrocketed. The 1976 budget deficit was the greatest ever in the nation's history up to that time. Efforts to get the economy moving were thwarted by the rising price of petroleum, due to price increases announced by OPEC and by U.S. oil companies. A shortage of fuel oil became so severe that many factories, office, and schools were closed throughout January 1977 because of lack of heat. In order to combat the fuel shortage, Ford proposed to reduce consumption of petroleum by increasing the price rather than by setting quotas and allotments. To combat the inflationary aspect of price increases, he proposed to return to the public and industry billions of dollars in tax rebates, tax reductions, and direct grants.

Clearly, Ford favored capital over labor and industry over agriculture. He vetoed one bill that would have enlarged the power of construction unions to shut down projects, breaking his promise to sign it. His secretary of labor resigned in protest. Ford's tax reductions applied both to individuals and to corporations, but industry was the main beneficiary.

Ford did not cut poverty programs in absolute dollar amounts, but held the level of increase below the rate of inflation, thus in effect reducing the benefits. Thinking it should be solved by individual initiative rather than by government action, Ford did little to try to alleviate poverty. Like Nixon, he tried to destroy the community action program and the legal services program. He did not favor using the power of the presidency to promote the welfare of the people.

As president, Ford took little or no action to support education, culture, and national parks and recreation areas. He did not use governmental power to promote internal improvements. He did not favor legislation to promote conservation, and he vetoed environmental legislation.

Although he spoke in favor of human rights, Ford took no action to help secure human rights abroad. He did not use the power of government to enhance racial justice in the United States. As president he took no action for or against affirmative action or voting rights legislation. In Congress he had opposed open housing legislation and gone along with Nixon's anti-rights programs. Ford showed little interest in employment opportunities for minorities. He appointed one woman and one black man to cabinet positions. Ford supported civil liberties. He established a commission to investigate charges of illegal domestic surveillance by the CIA and made public the report of the Rockefeller Commission confirming domestic espionage by the CIA. He appointed George Bush as new Director of the CIA and gave him control of the entire intelligence community.

ADMINISTRATION AND INTERGOVERNMENTAL RELATIONS

Succeeding unexpectedly to the office, Ford had not established a set of goals and objectives for his presidency. He immediately announced that combating inflation would be a top priority of his administration. He was able to develop plans that, while ridiculed by much of the press and the public, helped bring about a significant reduction in inflation. He also laid out plans to improve the economy. In other areas of domestic policy he seemed to have no long range plans for improving the nation.

Ford was not adept at establishing clear organizational patterns and communications channels. At times the executive branch appeared to be run in a disorganized, haphazard manner. Ford reduced the size of the White House staff. He inherited Nixon's staff and cabinet, of course. Some of these were able people; others should have been replaced sooner than they were. During less than a full term as President, Ford had three different chiefs of staff. Although all three were people of some competence, none was particularly successful in the role. He appointed Nelson Rockefeller as vice president and intended for him to be an active participant in the administration. Although Rockefeller did have one or two important assignments, his appointment did not work out as intended. One of the Nixon holdovers, Secretary of Agriculture Earl Butz, was an embarrassment to the president and the country until he resigned.

At first, Ford delegated appropriately to his department heads and intended to hold them responsible for results. His plans were to have each department head report directly to him, rather than going through a chief of staff. Frictions, animosities, and disillusionments developed among cabinet members. Ford fired Secretary of Defense James R. Schlesinger, who clashed with Secretary of State Henry A. Kissinger. Other department heads had major difficulties with the various chiefs of staff and with Bo Callaway, Chairman of the President Ford Committee. The president failed to provide sufficient direction to prevent disarray. His administration was marked by in-fighting and back-stabbing among the White House staff. Ford is a gentle and forbearing man who abhors dissension, but the jealousies, rivalries, and hatred among his people required a firm hand at the controls. The frictions among department heads and staff became public knowledge. It was a time of confusion for the public.

Ford had communication problems. He was not a good public speaker and his words were not always well chosen. Although he had a reputation for being open, frank, and candid, his actions as president did not bear this out. His decision to pardon Nixon, for example, was made secretly. When he announced it, his press secretary resigned in protest. Sometimes he engaged in informal brainstorming with his staff. Other times he did not discuss, but simply listened without comment to the ideas of others, and then made his decision alone later. Without clearly delineated areas of authority and channels of communication, cabinet members and top staffers contradicted each other and it was not clear what the official position of the government was.

Ford exercised control over governmental expenditures. Whether he correctly identified national priorities is doubtful. He inherited a recession when he took office, and chose to fight it by reducing taxes to stimulate business. The deficit increased more during his presidency than during that of any previous president.

As a long-time member of the House, Ford thought he would be able to get along with Congress. He tried "communication, conciliation, compromise, and co-operation," but without success. The Democratic-controlled Congress checked military spending and further potential involvement in Southeast Asia and in Angola against the wishes of Ford and Kissinger. Congress ignored his petroleum supply and conservation proposals and passed a greater tax cut than he recommended. Ford vetoed sixty-six bills and was overridden twelve times.

Ford made one appointment to the Supreme Court — John Paul Stevens, a moderate who became a highly respected jurist. Ford's vendetta against Justice Douglas was not forgotten, however, so it cannot be said there was mutual respect between the president and the courts.

The president's view of the public interest was somewhat limited. He was perhaps more concerned about business and industry than other parts of the economy. The public regarded him as a decent and honorable man, but as somewhat of a bumbler. He was unable to mobilize public opinion in support of his programs.

LEADERSHIP AND DECISION MAKING

Lacking in charisma, Ford was not an inspiring speaker. He was unable to stimulate ex-

ecutive branch personnel to a high level of focused, productive effort. He was only moderately successful in convincing others to adopt his proposals or carry out his programs. Although Ford was able to restore the public's confidence in the integrity of government, after the Watergate scandals, his pardon of Nixon hurt. His administration was marked as a period of confusion and despondency for the American public. Ford did not set particularly high standards of performance for himself or for others. In contrast to some other presidents, he seemed lazy or unmotivated. He did not have a forward-looking vision of what the country should be like. He was a poor communicator and did not do a good job of unifying the country. Ford was not particularly good at conceptualizing strategies to improve the lot of the country.

Before making a decision, Ford listened to the advice of subordinates. Sometimes he engaged in fair and honest discussions of alternatives. Other times he made the decision in private. He was not well informed by a wide knowledge and deep understanding of history. Ford was more intelligent than some critics give him credit. His problem solving and decision making techniques were no better than average.

Ford was usually willing to compromise on almost anything in order to achieve his objectives. With one exception (the pardon of Nixon) Ford did not rush to make decisions until it was necessary they be made. He did not panic in emergencies, but remained calm. He was not afraid to make tough decisions when it was necessary to do so.

PERSONAL QUALITIES

The president did not demean the office by crude or inappropriate behavior. Although he gave the appearance of bungling, he generally was in control of himself. His contrast to Nixon reflected favorably on the office. Only in contrast to Nixon was Ford able to make people proud that a man such as he was their president, but he did restore some of the pride that we had lost. Ford also restored to the office of the president some of the respect that it had lost both at home and abroad because of the actions of his predecessor. Ford did not increase the power of the presidency. Indeed, Congress probably increased its power at the expense of the presidency during Ford's administration.

People did not regard the president as their enemy or think he was not on their side, but some people, especially those in the lower income brackets, thought the president was less concerned about their problems than he might have been. Ford did not seem especially interested in seeking input from all segments of the public. Access was limited mainly to government officials and people of wealth and influence. Because of his poor communication skills and lack of charisma, Ford was unsuccessful in reaching out to people. He was amiable, but he just could not "connect" with people and make them think he was empathetic to their needs.

Ford had a reputation for integrity and trustworthiness. On occasions he could break a promise if circumstances changed. Ford was personally honest. Although he liked to hobnob with wealthy people and naturally sided with business against labor, his vote was not for sale. If he received favors from wealthy business and supported their positions, it was not a matter of being bribed to support them but a genuine mutuality of political philosophy. Ford's personal morality stood in such a marked contrast to that of certain other recent presidents that it enhanced the prestige of the office of president.

OVERALL ASSESSMENT

With a score of two points, Ford ranks in 32nd place among the 39 presidents rated.

JIMMY CARTER
1977–81

	RATING POINTS	RANK
FOREIGN RELATIONS	11	15 tie
DOMESTIC PROGRAMS	11	10 tie
ADMINISTRATION	6	21
LEADERSHIP	6	21
PERSONAL QUALITIES	8	21 tie
OVERALL ASSESSMENT	42	16 tie

BACKGROUND

James Earl Carter, Jr., was born in Plains, Georgia, on October 1, 1924. Jimmy grew up in a wooden clapboard house alongside a dirt road on a farm in the community of Archer, three miles southwest of Plains. Jimmy attended public schools, graduating from Plains High School in 1941. At the age of 17 he entered Georgia Southwestern College. After one year he transferred to the Georgia Institute of Technology as a Naval ROTC student. In 1943 he realized his boyhood dream — an appointment to the United States Naval Academy at Annapolis. He graduated in 1946, ranking 59th in a class of 820. In the Navy Carter served on battleships and submarines for seven years, attaining the rank of lieutenant commander. While in the Navy he took graduate courses in nuclear physics at Union College for one semester. After he left the Navy he returned to Plains to run the peanut business he had inherited from his father. By the early 1970s Carter Warehouses had become one of Georgia's largest peanut wholesalers.

Carter entered into civic affairs, becoming a deacon in the Plains Baptist Church, president of the state Certified Seed Organization, district governor of the Lions Club, chairman of the local planning commission, and a member of the local library board, hospital authority, and county school board. In 1962 he was elected to the state senate. He was re-elected in 1964. In 1966 he ran for governor, but lost. He was elected governor in 1970. In his inaugural speech the governor declared that the time for racial discrimination was over. The speech gave him national attention as a liberal voice of the "New South." His chief accomplishment as governor was the reorganization of state government, in which 278 agencies and departments were abolished. Ineligible to succeed himself when his term as governor expired in 1974, Carter became chairman of the Democratic National Committee.

NOMINATION AND ELECTION

When Carter announced his candidacy for president, few national observers took his candidacy seriously. However, after he surprisingly won pluralities in the Iowa caucuses and the New Hampshire primary, he was recognized as a legitimate contender. Carter won some and lost a few other primaries, but his run-everywhere strategy paid off. At the Democratic national convention Carter received the nomination on the first ballot. He selected Walter Mondale as his running mate. In a very close contest with Ronald Reagan, President Ford captured the Republican nomination. Robert Dole was Ford's choice for vice president.

Carter campaigned as an outsider who would inject a sense of ethics, morality, and justice into government. He spoke of the need for a national health system, proposed cuts in the defense budget, and suggested policies needed to help the poor and to boost employment. Ford was hurt by his inability to deal with unemployment and inflation. He was also damaged by his pardon of Nixon and his seeming indifference to the plight of the poor. The campaign started in earnest on Labor Day, with early polls showing the challenger with a 15-point lead. In a dull and uninspiring campaign, the Georgian frittered away his lead. In the final polls before election day the two contenders were almost even. The election was as close as the final polls predicted. Carter received 40,828,929 votes (50.4 percent) to 39,148,940 for the incumbent. He won the electoral vote by a count of 297 to 240, with one Republican elector from the state of Washington casting his vote for Reagan.

In 1980 an economic depression, along with high inflation and the holding of American hostages in Teheran, made President Carter extremely vulnerable. Ted Kennedy and Jerry Brown challenged Carter for the Democratic nomination. However, Carter won a majority of the primaries and won the nomination convincingly on the first ballot. The Republicans nominated Ronald Reagan, with George Bush as his running mate. Congressman John Anderson of Illinois ran as an independent. A gasoline shortage, inflation, and the Iranian hostage crisis hurt the president immensely.

Walter Cronkite, the respected CBS newsman, closed his nightly telecasts with a reminder of the number of days American had been held hostage in Iran. The televised debates allowed the Republican candidate — a handsome former movie actor and broadcaster — to shine. Reagan won by a landslide.

FOREIGN RELATIONS

When militants stormed the U.S. embassy in Teheran, took 66 hostages and demanded the return of the Shah, who was undergoing medical treatment in the United States, Carter resisted warmongers and used diplomatic measures in an attempt to free the hostages. This was an exceedingly unpopular course, which probably cost him re-election to the presidency, but it was the right thing to do. A helicopter mission to rescue the hostages in Teheran was called off because of equipment failure.

As president and in his post-presidential career, Carter was quite active in promoting peace throughout the world. He met with Israeli Prime Minister Menachem Begin and Egyptian President Anwar Sadat at Camp David, leading to the signing of the Camp David accords, ending strife between Egypt and Israel. Six months later Israel and Egypt signed a formal peace treaty in Washington. Sadat and Begin received the Nobel Peace Prize as a result. In 1979 Carter recognized the People's Republic of China and established full diplomatic relations with China.

Relations with our neighbors in the Americas improved during the Carter administration. The United States and Canada agreed on a joint project to build a 2,700 miles long natural gas pipeline from Alaska to the lower 48 states. Negotiations on transfer of the control of the Panama Canal to Panama had been going on since 1964. In 1977 negotiators announced an agreement on treaties, which were signed by President Carter and Panamanian President Omar Torrigos Herara. After long, bitter debate and intense lobbying by both sides, the Senate approved the treaties in 1978.

Following the Soviet invasion of Afghanistan, Carter announced an embargo on sales of technology and a drastic reduction in grain sales to the USSR. He secured a United Nations resolution calling for the withdrawal of Soviet troops from Afghanistan. In response to presidential urging, the U.S. Olympic Committee voted to boycott the 1980 Olympic Games in Moscow. These measures did not secure the desired result, but were indicative of the U.S. resolve to use means short of war to stop Soviet aggression.

Carter's moderation in his response to the taking of hostages in Iran and in his reaction to the Soviet invasion of Afghanistan, as well as his according full diplomatic recognition to China, all served to ease international tensions somewhat. The Panama Canal treaties and Carter's role in the Israel-Egypt peace accords greatly enhanced world opinion of the United States. This was offset somewhat by Carter's failure to take stronger action against Iran after the taking of the hostages. Some viewed this as a sign of weakness.

Carter imposed an oil-import fee for the purpose of reducing the U.S. consumption of oil from OPEC countries. Congress passed a resolution denying Carter authority to impose such a fee. Carter vetoed the resolutions, but Congress overrode his veto. Carter's attempts to lessen U.S. dependence on foreign oil did not hurt the standard of living in the OPEC countries, where the profits went to the wealthy and were not shared with the poor. His foreign policy was based on a concern for morality, justice, and human rights.

DOMESTIC PROGRAMS

Carter inherited an economy that was not in good shape. The Ford administration had been marked by inflation, rising unemployment, and huge deficits. Conditions had started to improve in 1976, but deteriorated again because of rising oil prices. The trade deficit for 1977 was the greatest in history up to that point. Under Carter the budget deficit stayed under its 1976 peak, and unemployment was lower each year than it had been in any of the Ford years, but inflation increased during each year of Carter's administration. Congress stalled on passing Carter's energy program, which was intended to check inflation. In order to prevent further unemployment in the auto industry, Congress granted $1.5 billion in federal aid to the financially imperiled Chrysler Corporation. In 1980 the President announced that a recession had begun.

Carter did not interfere in the 110-day coal miner's strike, the longest in U.S. history. He signed legislation deregulating the airlines, and proposed deregulating the trucking industry and natural gas prices. The administration offered to buy grain off the market to keep the domestic price up so farmers would not be hurt by the wheat embargo on the USSR.

As a committed Christian, Carter was determined to improve conditions for the poor and the deprived and to reduce unemployment. He planned to reduce government spending, but redirect it by targeting scarce resources toward the most needy. He wanted to reform the income tax and the welfare system in the interests of lower income groups. He also wanted to create a national health program, but all of his plans were foiled by a recalcitrant Congress and troublesome economic conditions.

Carter called for higher taxes on petroleum to force Americans to cut back on energy consumption. Congress passed a bill taxing windfall profits in the oil industry, although it was somewhat weaker than Carter had proposed. In 1980 Carter successfully resisted pressure from Congress to enact a massive tax cut.

Carter was concerned about the environment, especially about energy conservation. His first fireside chat focused on energy conservation. Energy became his number one domestic priority. He wanted to encourage domestic production, promote energy conservation, and develop alternative sources, such as solar heating. The Department of Energy was created in 1977. Carter introduced an energy package, with five bills finally passed by Congress in 1978. By 1980 there had been an 11 percent drop in oil consumption and an 8 percent drop in imports. Carter signed a ban on dumping raw sewage in the ocean. He introduced legislation to protect the environmental quality of the land and seas. New laws were passed in 1977 regulating strip mining and in 1978 controlling the leasing of offshore drilling areas. Late in 1980 a lame duck Congress passed additional energy legislation and bills to clean up toxic waste and to protect 150 million acres of Alaskan wilderness.

As one of the world's leading advocates of human rights, Carter naturally supported civil liberties. He gave more attention to racial and religious discrimination and to the mistreatment of dissidents than to other areas of the civil liberties spectrum. Carter believed in racial justice. He was not directly involved in the civil rights struggle, but did gain the respect of the country's civil rights leaders. Carter's immigration policy was non-discriminatory. He opposed discrimination based on national origin or citizenship status. He was concerned about these issues both at home and abroad. He supported equal employment opportunities. He appointed three women to cabinet positions and the first African-American ambassador to the United Nations. He appointed more women, blacks, and Hispanics to federal judgeships than any previous president. Carter made human rights a cornerstone of his foreign relations policy. He tried to improve the lot of the homeless, to alleviate poverty, and to insure justice for all both at home and abroad.

Carter was one of the greatest friends of public education ever to sit in the oval office. He strengthened compensatory education, extended and improved the Elementary and Secondary Education Act in 1977 and 1978, doubled the percentage of the discretionary portion on the nondefense budget going to education, and overcame opposition to secure creation of the Department of Education. During his administration federal support for education was increased by 25 percent in constant dollars and college student loan programs were tripled.

ADMINISTRATION AND INTERGOVERNMENTAL RELATIONS

Carter developed a laudable set of goals and objectives for his administration and planned for their accomplishment. He was unable to overcome the problems that prevented some of his goals from being realized. He created two new executive departments — Energy and Education — to give greater emphasis to two areas of national concern. Organizational patterns and communication channels were appropriate.

Carter's staffing of executive departments was not distinguished. Except for Cyrus Vance and Ed Muskie in the State Department, most of his appointees were not national figures, and too many were outsiders who did not know how to operate well in the Washington political scene. Bert Lance, Director of the Office of Management and Budget, resigned when allegations were made of improprieties in his career as a banker before joining the government. No evidence of wrongdoing while in office was ever proved. The mass resignations of five cabinet members in June 1979 gave an impression of presidential ineptitude.

Except for a tendency to micromanage, Carter did an adequate but not outstanding job of directing the work of the executive branch personnel. He reformed civil service to enable him to base promotions on job performance, not simply length of service. Executive branch departments were administered moderately well and accomplished some important goals and objectives, but were prevented by forces beyond their control from accomplishing all of the president's goals for his administration.

Carter was not an effective communicator. His hesitant speech and Georgia drawl were not conducive to rapport with sophisticated audiences. Although Carter had many press conferences, the relations between the White House and the press corps were not good. Many reporters thought some of Carter's advisers were immature and naive.

Carter tried to direct government spending toward priority areas, frequently against the opposition of Congress. Despite inflation, he was able to reduce the budget deficit to below the levels of the Ford administration while increasing spending on education and the environment.

Although Carter was successful in getting many of his proposals enacted into law, he is generally regarded as being ineffective in working with Congress. He was not skilled at working with or leading legislators of his own party. A fair look at the legislative record leads to the conclusion that his performance was not as bad as his reputation.

Carter had no opportunity to appoint any Supreme Court justices. His appointments to lower courts brought a greater diversity to the federal judiciary than those of any previous president. His appointments were not only diverse (women, blacks, Hispanics), but they were of high quality. He established a merit system for selecting appeals court judges. He also had a system to recruit women and minorities to the federal bench. The American Bar Association rated a higher proportion of his nominees as well-qualified or exceptionally well qualified than those of any of his five immediate predecessors.

Carter put the public interest first. He was not the captive of any special interests, nor was he able to garner the support of the interests on behalf of his programs. Because of inflation and other economic problems and the inability of his administration to free the hostages from Teheran, the president gradually lost respect of a large segment of the public, so he was unable to mobilize public opinion as a force in behalf of his programs. There is no doubt, however, that Carter acted in the best interests of the people. Two decades after the end of his presidency, many people have regained their respect for him.

LEADERSHIP AND DECISION MAKING

Carter was not a charismatic leader. His personal example inspired some people to view him as an ideal person and to follow his lead, but he did not appeal to all people. Many times Carter was able to persuade others to follow him by convincing them that his was the right course, but in some instances he was unable to do so. He helped heal the wounds caused by the Vietnam war and Watergate. (He granted amnesty to Vietnam war draft dodgers.) However, he was not able to instill confidence in the people. The state of the economy and the intransigence of Iran led to a crisis in the American spirit, which the press dubbed a national malaise, and attributed to Carter.

Carter had a vision of an America and of a world of justice, equality, and human dignity. He was unable to communicate this convincingly enough to unify the nation and create a feeling of togetherness and shared national goals. The president's strategy for moving the country forward, however well conceived it

may have been, was unable to overcome the road blocks in his way (the economy, the hostages). Carter set exceptionally high standards of performance for himself. He was unable to motivate all others to achieve at the same high level.

A trained engineer, Carter knew the importance of gathering facts, weighing alternatives, and predicting possible consequences of various courses of action. His consideration of alternatives was limited by his lack of experience in the national and international arena and by shortcomings in some of his advisors. Among presidents he was probably about average in his ability to weigh alternatives. Carter possessed a keen intelligence and utilized it in problem solving and decision making situations. He did not go off half-cocked. He sometimes made mistakes, but that was not the fault of his intellect.

Occasionally, but perhaps not often enough, Carter would compromise on details in order to win wider support for a proposal, but he would never compromise on principle. In refusing to compromise he sometimes failed to calculate the political consequence of his action to the detriment of his chances of accomplishing his goal. He made tough decisions when necessary. He made difficult, unpopular, and politically damaging decisions when he thought it was the right thing to do.

PERSONAL QUALITIES

The president usually conducted himself with the dignity the office requires. He was not stuffy. He carried his own suitcases into the White House and he preferred to be known as Jimmy rather than as James, but these common touches were applauded by most people. His unfortunate *Playboy* interview during the 1976 presidential campaign was, however, undignified. The people were not proud that Carter was their president. Toward the end of his term some people were viewing him with contempt. Anyone who has followed his post-presidential career must be proud of his good work in recent years, but that does not count in rating him as a president.

At first Carter probably increased the stature of the presidency through his honesty and openness. However, his stature and the stature of the office declined as the hostage crisis dragged on and the country suffered its economic woes. The power of the presidency remained unchanged by the Carter administration.

Early in his presidency Carter was successful in making the people think he was on their side. His unpretentiousness, informality, and common touch were viewed positively. As his term ended he had lost much of the early good feelings, largely because of the failure to rescue the hostages. Carter welcomed input from all segments of society and gave some consideration to the input he received. Access to all recent presidents has been limited in contrast to that of most of the earlier presidents. Carter attempted to reach out to the people. He was successful in the early part of his term, less so during the latter part.

Carter acted consistently on a set of high moral principles. His integrity was quite exceptional. Carter believed that public office is a public trust and never benefitted financially from his office at the expense of the public. He put his peanut business in a trust, which lost a large sum of money during his presidency. Throughout his life Carter exhibited a high standard of personal morality. He is a devoutly religious man, who tries far harder than most to live up to the ideals of his religion.

OVERALL ASSESSMENT

Carter received 42 out of a possible 100 points on the rating scale. He ranks in a tie for sixteenth place among the 39 presidents rated.

RONALD REAGAN

1981–89

	RATING POINTS	RANK
FOREIGN RELATIONS	3	31 tie
DOMESTIC PROGRAMS	–8	39
ADMINISTRATION	–8	36
LEADERSHIP	2	27
PERSONAL QUALITIES	7	23 tie
OVERALL ASSESSMENT	–4	34 tie

BACKGROUND

Ronald Wilson Reagan was born February 6, 1911, in a five-room apartment above a bakery in Tampico, Illinois. As a child he lived in various Illinois communities. After graduating from Dixon High School, he attended Eureka College on a partial football scholarship, earning the remainder of his expenses by washing dishes and serving as a lifeguard. He made average grades. Reagan graduated from Eureka College in 1932. He worked as a lifeguard and at odd jobs until he secured a position as a radio announcer in Davenport, Iowa. After he transferred to WHO in Des Moines, he became one of the best known sports announcers in the Midwest. In 1937 he secured an acting contract with Warner Bros. During the next 20 years Reagan appeared in dozens of films. Often he was the leading man. If not quite a star, he was constantly on the verge of stardom. A member of the cavalry reserves, Reagan was called to active duty in 1942 and assigned to a motion picture unit of the Army Air Corps to make training films.

In 1947 Reagan was elected president of the Screen Actors Guild, a position he held for five consecutive terms. In 1949 he was selected chairman of the Motion Picture Industry Council. In the mid–1950s he became host and program supervisor of the *General Electric Theatre,* a popular television show. While under contract to GE, he gave hundreds of speeches to corporate leaders and to civic or service clubs. The GE tours were an excellent training ground for the political career that would follow. From 1962 to 1965 Reagan was host and a performer on *Death Valley Days,* another television series.

In 1966 Reagan was elected governor of California; in 1970 he was re-elected. As governor, he signed a liberalized abortion bill, cut the state budget, won numerous battles with the University of California system, and raised the state sales tax, the personal income tax, and taxes on banks and corporations. In his second term, Reagan achieved welfare reform, improved school financing, and secured property tax relief. When his second term as governor ended in 1975, Reagan wrote a syndicated newspaper column, made radio commentaries, and made speeches on the conservative banquet circuit. He tried for the 1976 Republican presidential nomination. His battle with President Ford was bruising and lasted for several months. He campaigned on a radical tax-cutting, free-market, staunchly anti–Communist platform and projected himself as an outsider fighting the corrupt Washington insiders. He won ten primaries and narrowly lost at the Republican national convention.

NOMINATION AND ELECTION

Immediately after the 1976 convention, Reagan began planning for the 1980 election. During the next three years he continued his newspaper column and radio programs and made hundreds of speeches across the country. The Reagan campaign got off to a bad start in 1980 when he lost the Iowa caucuses to George Bush, but he rebounded with a victory in the New Hampshire primary. By early spring Reagan had the nomination virtually wrapped up. On May 26 Bush dropped out of the race. In a party unity move, Reagan picked Bush to be his running mate. Without serious opposition, Reagan was nominated on the first ballot.

Many voters were attracted by Reagan's message of economic rebirth through a return to the free enterprise system and his tough, patriotic foreign policy stance. He campaigned for a reduction in taxes, curbs on public spending, decentralization of many governmental programs, deregulation of industry, easing of environmental protection regulations, and for large scale military rearmament. Impressive to the voters was his speaking style, which enabled him to come across as a sincere, caring person. His use of apocryphal anecdotes was legendary and effective. He projected a jaunty, optimistic demeanor. Calling attention to the country's economic problems under President Carter, he adopted a question as his campaign slogan: "Are you better off now than in 1976?" Carter's inability to secure the release of the American hostages in Iran doomed the incumbent. Reagan won a slight majority of the popular vote. In the electoral college Reagan amassed 489 votes, while Carter garnered only 44 votes.

In 1984 Reagan was unopposed for the Republican nomination. He ran an image-based campaign of confidence, strength, success, and optimism. Release of the hostages from Teheran, the reduction in the inflation rate, and the economic expansion that started in 1982 enabled Reagan to espouse a new campaign slogan: "It's morning again in America." The voters bought wholeheartedly into this scenario. Most of them were totally unconcerned about the balance of trade and the skyrocketing budget deficits. Reagan was re-elected in a landslide. He carried 49 states with 525 electoral votes. Vice President Mondale, the Democratic candidate, received only 13 electoral votes.

FOREIGN RELATIONS

The United States was involved in no wars during Reagan's administration, although it did participate in several military actions. When terrorists drove trucks packed with explosives into the U.S. Marine headquarters at the Beirut airport, killing 241 servicemen, Reagan responded by withdrawing the marines to ships offshore. Terrorist attacks continued, and more Americans were killed. Reagan charged that Muammar Qaddafi of Libya was the world's principal terrorist. Twice U.S. planes shot down Libyan fighter planes engaged in maneuvers off the Libyan coast. In April 1986 U.S. planes bombed the Tripoli area, striking Qaddafi's home and killing his infant daughter. Many countries condemned the bombing as an act of terrorism by the United States.

In 1983 Reagan ordered a force of U.S. troops to invade Grenada, after the government of that island nation had been overthrown by extremist members of the prime minister's own party. The pretext was to prevent a takeover by Cuba and to protect the lives of American students attending a medical school on the island. The U.N. Security Council voted to condemn the invasion. In Nicaragua the Reagan administration provided funds, arms, and training to the Contras, rebels who were dedicated to overthrowing the government of that nation. CIA complicity in the mining of Nicaraguan harbors was proven. Congress eventually cut off military aid to the Contras.

In 1987 the United States intervened in the war between Iran and Iraq. Iran tried to stop the transportation of oil by seeding the Persian Gulf with mines. Eleven Kuwaiti oil tankers were re-registered as American vessels and escorted through the Gulf by U.S. Navy warships. Missile attacks were exchanged. In the most significant U.S. naval surface battle since World War II, 20 percent of the Iranian navy was destroyed. An American warship shot down an Iranian jetliner that it mistook for hostile aircraft, killing all 290 passengers. Two weeks later Iran accepted a UN plan that called for a cease-fire in its war with Iraq. Reagan's policies had succeeded in protecting the free flow of oil, but at a great cost in human lives.

After Mikhail Gorbachev became General Secretary of the Communist Party in the Soviet Union and began espousing *glasnost* and *perestroika,* Reagan agreed to four summit meetings. The November 1985 meeting between the president and Gorbachev in Geneva was the first between U.S. and Soviet heads of state since 1979. Following lengthy negotiations the two heads signed the Intermediate-Range Nuclear Force Treaty eliminating medium range missiles, the most sweeping arms limitation agreement of the Cold War era. It led to the destruction of 2,600 warheads and permitted on-site inspection of missile facilities in both the Soviet Union and the United States.

Reagan's invasion of Grenada and his support of the Contras against the government of Nicaragua were unneighborly, to say the least. His siding with Britain against Argentina in the Falkland Islands dispute, while defensible, was also regarded by some of our neighbors as inappropriate. Reagan continued supporting repressive military dictatorships in some Central American countries, most notably El Salvador.

Since the Truman administration, the U.S. policy had been to contain communism, but Reagan attempted to go further and roll back communism in countries where unpopular regimes were propped up by the Soviets. He used the CIA to give covert aid to anti–Communist insurgencies in the Third World. This policy became known as the Reagan Doctrine. It had some success in Afghanistan and Angola. During his first term, when Reagan denounced

the Soviet Union as an evil empire, he built up American military strength. In 1983 he deployed U.S. ground-based cruise missile in England in response to an ongoing buildup in Warsaw Pact countries. Later, as the Cold War began to thaw under Gorbachev, the United States and the Soviets mutually reduced their missiles. In contrast to these successes, Reagan's attempts to deal with international terrorism were disastrous. Among the pledges that had helped him win the presidency in 1980 were his promise of swift retribution against terrorism and his vow never to negotiate with terrorists. His retributions failed to secure the desired results and his secret negotiations led to an embarrassing scandal and criminal activity on the part of some of his aides.

International tensions increased notably during Reagan's first term, at least partly because of Reagan's harsh rhetoric. He condemned the Soviet system as the "focus of evil in the modern world." Relations between the two countries reached a nadir in 1983 when the Soviets shot down a South Korean airliner that had strayed into Soviet airspace, killing all the passengers, including a U.S. Congressman. The Soviets increased the number of medium-range missiles aimed at Western Europe, and the United States, with the approval of other NATO members, began deploying missiles in Europe. These tensions began to relax with the advent to power of Gorbachev in the Soviet Union. Events in Libya and in the Persian Gulf and the spread of international terrorism contributed to international tension. By the end of Reagan's second term, relations with the Soviets had improved and the world was probably less tense than when he took office.

Reagan's conduct of foreign policy had different effects on world opinion in different parts of the world. In some places, notably England, it probably had a positive effect. On the other hand, in Latin America it probably had a negative impact. The Iran-Contra affair was decried by most people. However, improved relations with the Soviets during Reagan's second term were well received by world opinion.

Reagan and Canadian Prime Minister Brian Mulroney pushed through their respective legislatures approval of a trade pact that promised to establish virtually free trade between the two countries, gradually abolishing tariffs on goods and services with the goal of completely free trade by 1999. Reagan was always a low tariff advocate.

The Reagan administration opposed sanctions against the white minority government of South Africa on the grounds that such action would hurt the black workers. Nevertheless, Congress overrode a presidential veto and enacted sanctions, barring certain imports and new investments in South Africa and suspending commercial air traffic between the two countries. Reagan's efforts to keep the oil flowing through the Persian Gulf were beneficial to world trade. The actions against Nicaragua and the continuing boycott of Cuba were harmful both to world trade and to the standard of living of people in those two nations.

DOMESTIC PROGRAMS

Reagan's plan for dealing with the economy was a version of supply-side economics that became known as "Reaganomics." The theory was that cutting taxes on corporations and high income individuals would lead to greater investment and enable businesses to expand and to modernize equipment, thus increasing production, strengthening the economy, generating more jobs, and creating more revenue, which in combination with spending cuts would balance the budget and curb inflation. When Reagan took office the inflation rate was over 11 percent and interest rates had risen to 20 percent. The Federal Reserve Bank instituted a tight-money policy, which drove the rate of inflation down. The president's proposal for a three-stage tax cut, the largest in history, was approved by Congress. Deep cuts were instituted in federal spending for social programs, including funding for health, food, housing, and education. A severe recession resulted, the worst since the great depression of the 1930s, and by November 1982 the unemployment rate reached a 42-year high, with nearly 12 million people out of work. In 1983 the nation's poverty rate reached its highest points since President Johnson instituted his War on Poverty in 1965.

However, the tight-money policy helped the economy. During 1984 the inflation rate fell and unemployment returned to the same rate that existed when Reagan took office. The stock market reached record heights, and the state of the economy helped Reagan win re-election. Not all segments of the economy were in good health, though. The economy continued improving throughout the remainder of Reagan's administration.

The belief that tax cuts would initially cause a revenue shortfall, but that economic growth would eventually bring revenue into line with expenditures, was misplaced. The average annual deficit in the fiscal years 1982 through 1987 was more than $180 billion, producing total deficits of $1.1 trillion. The United States had to borrow hundreds of billions of dollars from foreign countries and was transformed from the world's largest creditor nation to one of the largest debtor nations. The national debt grew more during Reagan's tenure than in the administrations of all previous presidents combined. The yearly cost of debt service more than doubled during the Reagan years. Reagan blamed Congress for the deficit, saying it engaged in wanton social spending. He urged a balanced budget amendment to the Constitution. However, of the six budgets that produced a $1.1 trillion deficit about 93 percent of the total was proposed to Congress by the Reagan administration. Spending added by Congress accounted for only one-fourteenth of the deficit.

Reagan clearly favored the interests of capital over those of labor and agriculture. In 1981 he ordered the firing of 13,000 striking air traffic controllers because federal employees are not allowed to strike. They were replaced by less-qualified personnel, which was a blow to the union movement and posed serious threats to airline safety. With a farm credit crisis posing the greatest threat to U.S. agriculture since the depression, the administration in 1985 eased rules governing a $650 million loan-guarantee program, but refused additional funding.

In 1983 Reagan signed into law a measure designed to ensure the solvency of Social Security beyond the year 2050. Included among its provisions were accelerated increases in the Social Security tax rate, taxing for the first time the Social Security benefits of higher income retirees, a formula restricting cost-of-living increases, incentives for postponing retirement past age 65, mandatory enrollment for federal employees, and a gradual increase in retirement age to 67 by the year 2027. In 1988 the Reagan administration prohibited federally funded family planning centers from providing any assistance to women seeking abortions. Reagan cut federal allocations for health care, decreased food for the poor, and opposed environmental standards.

Reagan's 1981 tax cut was the biggest in U.S. history. In 1986 he signed into law the most thorough revision of the tax code in more than forty years. The 1986 reforms restricted the use of tax shelters, shifted more of the burden from individuals to corporations, and dropped millions of low-income people from the tax rolls, but it also made the income tax less progressive by reductions in the higher brackets and provided the greatest windfall for the wealthiest Americans. The shifting of many social programs from the federal to the state level made it necessary for states to raise their taxes. Other federal taxes and certain user fees went up sharply. The overall tax burden on the average taxpayer changed little or perhaps even worsened during the Reagan years. Reagan's refusal to raise taxes during his second term contributed to the exploding deficit. When he left office, he cited as his major regret his failure to fulfill his 1980 campaign pledge to balance the budget. He blamed the failure, however, not on his administration, but on Congress, the special interests, and the media!

Reagan's anti-regulations stance meant he opposed governmental efforts toward conservation of natural resources and protection of the environment. To him "environmentalist" was a pejorative term. He appointed as secretary of the interior James Watt, who wanted to open up wilderness areas to energy exploration, to greatly expand the amount of offshore leasing for oil exploration, to dismantle the Office of Surface Mining, and to declare a moratorium on national park acquisition. Watt was one of the leaders of the so-called "Sagebrush Rebellion" and Reagan proudly called himself a "Sagebrush Rebel." As president he sought to weaken air pollution controls and was unresponsive to those who warned of the dangers of acid rain. He opposed use of federal funds for mass transit or for rebuilding the nation's infrastructure. Reagan opposed federal aid to education. He showed no interest in improving our national parks and recreation areas. He did not use the government to support arts and humanities, nor did he advance the educational use of television and other media.

Although he had opposed the 1964 Civil Rights Act, Reagan was not a bigot. He repudiated support offered him by the Ku Klux Klan. He saw nothing wrong with affirmative action, as long as it did not involve rigid racial quotas. He was unfamiliar with Supreme Court decisions on the subject, and allowed the Justice Department to set administration policy. He proposed no new programs concerned with racial justice. Reagan supported civil liberties, including freedom of religion. Reagan supported minority rights. He was the first president to appoint a woman to the Supreme Court.

Reagan took no action to help secure human rights abroad. He treated all persons with respect, regardless of status. He called a halt to the war on poverty, not because he was contemptuous of the poor, but because he believed they would be helped more by trickle-down economics than by government programs.

ADMINISTRATION AND INTERGOVERNMENTAL RELATIONS

Among Reagan's major goals were improving the economy and increasing our military superiority over the Soviets. His chief plans for accomplishing these goals were his version of supply-side economics and increasing our missile delivering capability and the Strategic Defense Initiative, better known as Star Wars. Other major goals included reducing international terrorism and easing governmental regulations on business. He had no long range plans for accomplishing these goals.

Reagan failed to establish a structure or procedure to maintain high standards of performance or to keep himself informed about the actions of his top subordinates. Reagan made numerous poor judgments in filling top staff positions. Attorney General Edwin Meese, Secretary of the Interior James Watt, some members of the White House staff, National Security Advisor Robert McFarlane and his successor John Poindexter and their aide Oliver North, were among those who either betrayed their trust or were unsuited for their positions. Meese resigned under fire for alleged influence peddling and bribery. North and Poindexter were indicted for conspiracy, fraud, and theft of government funds. McFarlane pleaded guilty to misleading Congress. Reagan delegated far too much authority to executive branch personnel. He failed to keep himself informed about their activities and did not exercise the administrative oversight expected from a chief executive. He was criticized by the Tower Commission for failing to oversee the implementation and consequences of his own policies.

Ironically, Reagan was known as the "Great Communicator" because of his ability to sell himself and his programs to television audiences. He was a gifted raconteur with a storehouse of anecdotes and a winning delivery style. However, as president he did not provide sufficient two-way communication between himself and his subordinates, or for sufficient horizontal communication among executive departments. He held few press conferences and provided little information in those he did hold. The Reagan administration undertook a campaign of disinformation, planting false stories in the newspapers regarding our intentions in Libya; State Department press spokesman Bernard Kalb resigned in protest. In the Iran-Contra affair White House officials destroyed documents and drafted a false chronology of events in order to cover up the arms sales and diversion of funds. National Security Advisor John Poindexter admitted that he had approved the plan to divert profits to the Contras, but did not inform the president in order to provide him with "plausible deniability." He also admitted he had destroyed documents. Oliver North admitted that he had lied and destroyed documents.

In a time of peace and prosperity Reagan drastically increased the national debt. The budget deficits caused the cost of debt service to rise so much he was unable to keep government expenditures in check. The annual interest payments on the national debt exceeded all the savings in federal spending obtained through cuts in domestic programs.

With some exceptions, the executive branch departments and agencies were not well administered and failed to achieve goals or accomplished inappropriate objectives. Under Reagan the Department of Housing and Urban Development was deeply involved in fraud, theft, patronage, and favoritism, which cost taxpayers hundreds of millions of dollars. The savings and loan industry collapsed due to inadequate supervision during the Reagan years. Taxpayers had to contribute half a billion dollars to bail out what had been, before Reagan, a viable industry.

Reagan generally secured support for his programs from Republicans in Congress. Congress went along with his disastrous deficit spending. He secured bipartisan support for some, but not all, of his foreign policy initiatives. Congress did override his veto of sanctions against South Africa and brought a virtual halt to military aid to the Contras.

Reagan appointed Sandra Day O'Connor as the first woman justice to serve on the Supreme Court. He promoted William Rehnquist to the chief justiceship and appointed Antonin Scalia to the court. He nominated Robert Bork, who was rejected by the Senate as too radically conservative. Finally, he appointed Anthony Kennedy. Reagan's appointees to the district and appeals courts were overwhelmingly conservative. Advances in civil liberties and racial justice were imperiled by these appointments.

Reagan was not the tool of special interests. He put the public interest, as he interpreted it, first. If he favored business, it was because of his political beliefs, not that he was giving in to pressure. The president had the respect of most of the public, including that of many who were hurt by his policies.

LEADERSHIP AND DECISION MAKING

Reagan had charisma. Through his superb speaking ability he was able to charm and inspire others. However, he did not use his abilities to lead executive branch personnel to accomplish important national goals. Instead, his hands-off administrative style allowed them to engage in inappropriate behavior. Reagan had the ability to be a great leader, but failed to utilize it fully. Very persuasive, he was usually able to get others to follow him and carry out his programs.

Reagan was able to restore public confidence in the government and in America after the malaise of the Carter years. His calm reassurance and inspirational speeches maintained this confidence even in the face of the recession of 1981-82, the mounting deficit, the scandals of Iran-Contra, the savings and loan debacle, and other evidence of inept administration. Nothing rubbed off on Reagan to destroy public confidence in him; thus his was the "Teflon Presidency."

The president had a lax management style and failed to exercise control over the execution of his policies. The most notable example of this was the Iran-Contra affair, but it was endemic throughout his administration. He worked short hours, frequently was inattentive in staff meetings, and was astonishingly uninformed about important national and world affairs.

Reagan had a vision of America and was able to communicate this vision well. It was one of the sources of his great popularity. But it was not a forward looking vision; it was a vision of our glorious past. It was a pleasant vision, but perhaps not an appropriate one for the leader of a great nation in the troubled times of the 1980s. He did not dream of a great society to be attained, but of a return to the simpler times of yesteryear.

Analyzing and conceptualizing were not the president's strong points. Reagan was not much interested in engaging subordinates in discussions about alternatives and possible consequences of decisions. He did not have a particularly wide knowledge or deep understanding of history. He seemed to believe that he could make decisions intuitively. Reagan was intelligent enough, but did not apply disciplined intelligence to problem solving and decision-making strategies.

Reagan was usually willing to compromise in order to win wider support for a proposal or in order to avoid controversy. He was prag-matic, but in the few instances where he felt an important principle was at stake, he held firm. The president kept calm in emergencies. He was never afraid to make a decision. He did not always engage in a careful and prudent decision-making process, but he did make timely decisions when he felt they were necessary.

PERSONAL QUALITIES

Reagan almost always conducted himself with appropriate dignity. He appeared to be calm, confident, and genial. Even when he told anecdotes that were mean-spirited, such as those about welfare mothers, he did so with such style that he did not sound cruel to most listeners.

Reagan made people proud to be Americans and made most of them proud that a man such as he was their president. Even the scandals of his administration failed to dim the luster of the "Teflon President." The office of the president probably received more respect because of the perceived stature of the man who occupied it. Reagan did not utilize fully the powers of the presidency. He delegated too much to underlings and failed to exercise sufficient oversight.

The Great Communicator convinced the vast majority of the public that he was on their side. His poll ratings were among the highest of all presidents. He did not seek input from the public, nor give much consideration to the input that he received, except to add to his store of anecdotes. Reagan was a master of public relations. He used television effectively to sell himself to the public.

Reagan was viewed as a man of integrity. He was deemed trustworthy and as one who kept his promises when possible. Serious doubt about his integrity was raised during the trial of John Poindexter. Over one hundred times the president answered "I don't know," or " I don't remember" when he should have known and remembered. The Teflon President must be downgraded because of his role in the Iran-Contra cover-up. Reagan never enriched himself in public office. He made millions by investing his movie and television earnings in California real estate.

Reagan was not a moral exemplar, but he

did not diminish the prestige of the office nor his own effectiveness as president by any shortcomings in his personal morality.

OVERALL ASSESSMENT

Reagan had a score of negative four on our rating scale. He ranks in a tie for 34th among the 39 presidents rated.

GEORGE BUSH

1989–93

	RATING POINTS	RANK
FOREIGN RELATIONS	8	21 tie
DOMESTIC PROGRAMS	−7	37 tie
ADMINISTRATION	3	25 tie
LEADERSHIP	5	22 tie
PERSONAL QUALITIES	5	27 tie
OVERALL ASSESSMENT	14	28 tie

BACKGROUND

George Herbert Walker Bush was born in Milton, Massachusetts, on June 12, 1924. While he was very young the family moved to Greenwich, Connecticut. He attended Greenwich Country Day School and Phillips Academy. Upon graduation, Bush enlisted in the Navy. Commissioned as an ensign, he was assigned to a torpedo bomber squadron aboard a light aircraft carrier. Twice his plane was shot down. He flew 58 missions and was awarded the Distinguished Flying Cross. After discharge, Bush entered Yale University where he majored in economics and earned a Phi Beta Kappa key. Upon graduation in 1948 he went to Texas to learn the oil business. Within a few years he was president of Zapata Offshore with headquarters in Houston.

In 1962 Bush was elected chairman of the Harris County Republican Party. In 1964 he ran for the United States Senate, but lost to the Democratic incumbent. In 1966 and again in 1968, he was elected to Congress. In 1970 he again ran unsuccessfully for the Senate. President Nixon appointed him ambassador to the United Nations. Later Bush became chairman of the Republican national committee. When Gerald Ford became president, he appointed Bush chief of the U.S. Liaison Office in Peking, then named him director of the Central Intelligence Agency. In 1977 Bush left the CIA and went back to Houston where he joined several corporations as director or well-paid consultant.

In 1980 he scored an upset victory in the Iowa caucuses. However, Ronald Reagan won most of the primaries to clinch the nomination. Reagan selected Bush as his running mate. The Reagan-Bush ticket easily defeated Carter and Mondale in 1980 and repeated that triumph with a victory over Mondale and Geraldine Ferraro in 1984. For details on these elections, see the entry on Reagan.

NOMINATION AND ELECTION

Bush was the early front-runner for the 1988 Republican presidential nomination. The Iran-

Contra affair was his biggest political liability, contributing to his defeat in the Iowa caucuses, where he came in third behind Robert Dole and Pat Robertson. After months of leading in the polls, his defeat in Iowa appeared devastating. But Dole lost the New Hampshire primary, partly because of his surly and mean-spirited attacks on Bush. Bush swept the Super Tuesday primaries in the South and locked up the nomination. Bush was nominated by acclamation on the first ballot. He named Dan Quayle as his running mate. At first Bush campaigned on the Reagan record, which he characterized as one of peace and prosperity. Bush spoke of his hopes for a kinder, gentler America where dependence on government aid would be replaced by volunteerism emanating from a thousand points of light. He promised to cut the capital gains tax and to impose no new taxes, pledging: "Read my lips; no new taxes." Meanwhile, the Democrats had nominated Michael Dukakis, who surged to an early lead in the polls. For a while Dukakis presented a positive campaign, offering a detailed health insurance plan, federal tuition loans, financial incentives for teachers, federal child-care facilities, and the appointment of a drug czar. Then the campaign turned vicious. Bush implied Dukakis was unpatriotic for vetoing a bill that required all public school teachers to lead their classes in a daily Pledge of Allegiance. He pounded Dukakis for the pollution of Boston Harbor and for financial problems in Massachusetts. He denounced Dukakis as soft on crime and for his membership in the American Civil Liberties Union. The new, tougher Bush called for the execution of major drug traffickers. He blasted Dukakis for opposing the death penalty. He charged the governor's opposition to certain land-based missiles and to the proposed Star Wars space-based system would threaten national security and undermine the U.S. leverage in negotiating with the Soviet Union. One televised ad featured Willie Horton, a black convict who had attacked some white women while on furlough from prison. The ad emphasized Horton's color, thus appealing to the worst instincts of voters who might harbor racist feelings. The negative campaign was effective and Bush pulled ahead in the polls. Under attack, Dukakis also turned

negative. He made some mistakes and responded inappropriately to some questions from reporters. Nevertheless, in the final three days of the campaign he put on a spurt. Still he fell short. Bush won with 426 electoral votes to 111 for Dukakis.

In 1992 Bush was renominated by acclamation. He was opposed by Bill Clinton, Democrat; Ross Perot, Independent; and a host of minor candidates. For details on the campaign and election, see the section on President Clinton.

FOREIGN RELATIONS

In August 1990 Iraqi troops invaded Kuwait, seizing control of the country and its rich oil fields. The UN Security Council, under urging from President Bush, passed resolutions requiring Iraq's withdrawal, backed up a demand for sanctions, and authorized the use of force if Iraq did not comply by January 15, 1991. Bush put together a coalition of troops from many nations. U.S. forces were sent to Saudi Arabia and naval vessels to the Persian Gulf to prepare for military action. On January 12, 1991, the Senate and House passed a joint resolution authorizing the use of military force if Iraq did not meet the deadline. When that date passed without withdrawal by Iraq, coalition air strikes began, followed by an invasion by multi-national ground forces under the control of American generals. Within four days the Iraqi forces had been expelled from Kuwait and military action ceased. Allied governments made a greater financial contribution to the war than did the United States.

In a flagrant violation of international law U.S. forces invaded Panama in 1989 to capture General Manuel Noriega, the de facto leader of that independent nation, who was wanted in Florida on drug trafficking charges. Twenty-three Americans and about 500 Panamanians, including many civilians, were killed. Property damage exceeded $1 billion. Many Panamanian homes destroyed by U.S. forces were not rebuilt or replaced. Nevertheless, the invasion was popular among Americans and a CBS poll claimed a majority of Panamanians believed the invasion was justified.

During the civil war in Yugoslavia, the

United States acknowledged national dissolution and recognized the independence of Bosnia and Herzegovina. The United States participated in the UN Security Council vote to impose sanctions against the Serbian government in an unsuccessful effort to stop attacks on Bosnia and Herzegovina.

At a summit meeting in Washington in 1990, Bush and Gorbachev agreed to a reduction in strategic arms and chemical stockpiles and to cooperate on atomic energy research. Bush and the leaders of the NATO and Warsaw Pact nations signed a mutual non-aggression pledge. The Warsaw Pact disbanded in 1991. The United States withdrew the last of the cruise nuclear missiles that the Reagan administration had installed in Britain. In 1992 Bush and Gorbachev signed the Strategic Arms Reduction Treaty, which promised deep cuts in nuclear arsenals over seven years. In 1993 Bush flew to Moscow to sign START II Treaty with President Boris Yeltsin, greatly reducing the permissible number of nuclear arms. These actions virtually ended the Cold War.

Humanitarian aid to the contras in Nicaragua was extended until elections were held in that country. With the election of Violeta Chamorro, Bush lifted the economic sanctions against Nicaragua, promised more direct aid, and encouraged the contras to disband. This positive step was more than offset by our invasion of Panama, which the Organization of American States condemned by a vote of twenty to one.

The Persian Gulf war and the invasion of Panama demonstrated that the United States was determined to protect our national interests against threats from weaker nations. No challenges from major powers were made during the Bush years. Our actions toward the Soviet Union eased international tensions. Our withdrawal from military action against Iraq as soon as the Iraqi army had been evacuated from Kuwait showed we had no designs for conquest in that area. World opinion was highly supportive of the ending of the cold war against the Soviet Union. Much of the opinion also supported our actions in the Persian Gulf. The invasion of Panama was roundly criticized in most of the world.

On December 17, 1992, Bush signed the North American Free Trade Agreement (NAFTA) with Canada and Mexico. Bush supported low tariffs, NAFTA, and the General Agreement on Trade and Tariff (GATT) as being beneficial to world trade and helping raise the standard of living in other countries. He dispatched troops to Somalia to help feed starving people during a civil war there. He called on the United Nations for aid in protecting relief supplies sent to Bosnia and Herzegovina. Bush supported a plan to induce international banks to forgive part of the debt owed by developing countries.

DOMESTIC PROGRAMS

Bush inherited an economy in disarray. Deteriorating productivity, growing deficits, increasing unemployment, a rapidly growing national debt, and declining living standards for the poor and middle class were the result of Reaganomics. Bush failed to take decisive action to confront the problem. The budget soared to the highest in history. Federal spending under Bush rose to 25 percent of the GNP in 1992, the highest since World War II. During the Bush administration, inflation continued to fall, reaching a low of three percent annually. Other economic indicators worsened. Unemployment rose. Fewer jobs were created and more businesses failed than during any other administration since the depression. The number of American qualified for food stamps jumped to a record ten percent of the population. The gap between rich and poor continued widening. The annual budget deficit doubled to $350 billion. Bush signed a bill bailing out hundreds of savings and loan institutions that had failed due to mismanagement, corruption, or inability to meet the competition after deregulation. The estimated cost would be $300 billion, spread over a 30-year period.

Following the collapse of the savings and loan industry, Bush signed a bill imposing tough new restrictions on the accounting and lending practices of banks and thrifts and providing funds to prosecute in the case of fraud. His support of NAFTA and GATT were helpful to business, including the large agribusiness combines, but were opposed by labor unions and small farmers. Bush favored capital over labor and agriculture.

Bush failed to respond adequately to the cries for help from veterans suffering from the Gulf War syndrome. He approved legislation requiring places of business, public transportation, and public accommodations to make their facilities accessible to persons with physical disabilities. The Americans with Disabilities Act was the most far-reaching anti-discrimination legislation since the Civil Rights Act of 1964. He vetoed a $27 billion tax bill to create enterprise zones designed to aid residents of inner cities. He failed to support calls from his own secretary of housing and urban development for a renewed war on poverty, a national housing policy, and enterprise zones. Bush signed a Child Care Bill in 1990 after he induced Congress to include parental choice and federal aid for church-related child care. He favored tax credits to help lower-income people buy insurance, reform of insurance by pooling smaller businesses into larger groups, the reform of medical malpractice laws, and the encouragement of managed care programs to contain costs. He did not send a detailed bill to Congress.

Breaking his no new taxes pledge, Bush agreed to a series of tax hikes aimed at the middle class and the wealthy. These included sharp increases in federal taxes on gasoline, cigarette, alcoholic beverages, and luxury items, and an increase in the top income tax rate. The bill also included tax credits for the working poor. Nevertheless, Democrats claimed the taxes were regressive in that the cigarette, gasoline, and beer taxes would take a disproportionately larger portion of the incomes of the poor. Bush also raised Medicare premiums. Although breaking the pledge cost him dearly in the 1992 election, it was the right thing to do.

Bush proclaimed himself the environmentalist president. He called for elevating the Environmental Protection Agency to a cabinet-level Department of Environment. However, he sided with the Council on Competitiveness against the EPA and attacked environmental rules vigorously. By executive action he canceled the public's right to contest Interior Department decisions to grant grazing permits, mining leases and oil exploration licenses. He proposed eliminating restriction on development in one-half of the nation's wetlands. By executive action he allowed industry to raise emission standards without public notice. On the other hand, Bush signed the Clean Air Act of 1990, which strengthened anti-pollution standards. He dispatched federal troops to Alaska to help clean up an oil spill. At the Earth Summit in Rio de Janeiro, Bush defended his opposition to major environmental initiatives, saying that he was protecting U.S. businesses and jobs from environmental extremists. But he increased foreign aid for conservation of Third World forests and changed rules in the United States to discourage clear-cutting. Citing safety reasons, Bush's secretary of energy, James Watkins, postponed the restarting of the Savannah River nuclear reactors. Watkins encouraged opening up part of the Arctic National Wildlife Refuge in Alaska to oil drilling.

In 1990 Bush vetoed the Civil Rights Act intended to restore job discrimination protections cut by recent Supreme Court decisions. In 1991 he signed a new Civil Rights bill very similar to the one he had vetoed a year earlier. Bush's Solicitor General, Kenneth Starr, sought to convince the High Court to reject affirmative action considerations in the awarding of broadcast licenses. He supported several school systems in their successful efforts to end federal court supervision of their desegregation status, even when shifting residential patterns were causing resegregation.

Bush supported the proposed constitutional amendment to exclude flag-burning from First Amendment protection. When the amendment was defeated he unsuccessfully urged the Supreme Court to uphold a statute passed by Congress that intended to accomplish the same aim. He was a member of various clubs that discriminated on the basis of race or religion. Starr sought to get the court to uphold graduation prayers in public schools. He urged an expansion of the police search and seizure authority and a narrow interpretation of the entrapment doctrine. Bush opposed affirmative action hiring practices. He appointed Clarence Thomas, an opponent of affirmative action, to succeed Thurgood Marshall on the Supreme Court. He appointed no women to the High Court. His original cabinet included one woman, one black, and one Hispanic.

Bush had a sense of *noblesse oblige*. He did

not favor the use of government to alleviate poverty or improve justice for unfavored groups or individuals, preferring to rely upon voluntary actions and philanthropy. He lifted the sanctions against South Africa.

Insensitive to the differences between public and private schools, Bush supported a voucher system that would subsidize private schools. His education initiatives included ensuring literacy for all adult Americans, but failed to provide the funds to accomplish it. He did not support federal aid to the arts and humanities. He met with the nation's governors to set national goals for education. This meeting resulted in an America 2000 proposal, setting six goals for educational improvement. Bush also favored a proposal for a New American School Development Corporation by which businesses would raise money to create an innovative school in a congressional district. It would have allowed funding of parental choice for private and religious as well as public schools. Bush's education initiatives had little actual effect on education.

ADMINISTRATION AND INTERGOVERNMENTAL RELATIONS

Bush did not have a comprehensive set of goals and objectives and a well-thought-out plan for their accomplishment, other than continuing the peace and prosperity of the Reagan administration and to do it without raising taxes. The Iraqi invasion of Kuwait, the economic recession, and the growing federal deficit prevented him from achieving his goals.

Bush favored a centralized organization structure in order to enhance the communications flowing through his office. As soon as he took office, he appointed a chief of staff. At times he appointed councils and task forces to deal with problems, but few of them produced recommendations that were implemented. Bush appointed the first head of the new Department of Veterans Affairs. As a result of the savings and loan fiasco, the Federal Home Loan Bank Board and the Federal Savings and Loan Insurance Corporation were scrapped. Two new agencies were established — the Office of Thrift Supervision and the Resolution Trust

Corporation. Bush was much more of a take-charge president than his predecessor had been.

Bush's cabinet was comprised for the most part of competent, but undistinguished white men. There were no superstars, although Dick Cheney in Defense became something of a hero through the Gulf War. Jack Kemp in Housing and Urban Development and Lamar Alexander in Education later became contenders for the Republican presidential nomination. Bush did not support Kemp's proposals to help the inner cities and the poor. Alexander had ties with a for-profit corporation that bid to operate public schools and that gave public schools television sets if they would broadcast certain commercial programs. John Sununu as chief of staff and Richard Darman as director of the Bureau of Management and the Budget were probably more influential than the department heads.

Although Bush was much better than Reagan at directing the work of executive branch personnel, he was not an outstanding administrator. In foreign policy Bush made it clear that he was in charge. On most domestic matters he expected the cabinet secretaries and other senior advisors to work out disagreements among themselves. If consensus was not reached, inaction was likely.

Bush was an adequate but not unusually effective communicator. He did not engage in excessive secrecy or misinformation, and the public was better informed about the Gulf War than any previous war. He spoke to the press more than other modern presidents, but without great positive effects. His informal speaking style was uneven and irregular. He seemed to have difficulty in focusing on a linear thought pattern from beginning to end of a response. He was generally conciliatory and willing to bring people into full consultation. During crises, however, he had an insular management style that did not extend far beyond the executive suite. In the Gulf crisis he did not consult with experts on the region prior to making his decisions.

Due to circumstances beyond his control, expenditures increased during the Bush administration. Bush was unfairly blamed for these increases and for breaking his no new taxes pledge. Expenditures had to increase and taxes had to be raised because of perceived national emergencies.

Executive branch agencies were for the most part adequately administered. The Defense Department was credited with an outstanding performance in the Gulf War. The most significant development of the Bush years — the end of the Cold War — was due more to the efforts of Gorbachev and Yeltsin and to the downfall of Soviet communism than to U.S. efforts, but Bush took full advantage of opportunities to bring about rapprochement and arms reduction, taking the lead himself rather than leaving it to the State Department.

Bush faced a Congress controlled by the Democrats. At first he called for amicable relations and bipartisanship. He tried hard to break down the barriers between the Hill and the White House. However, his congressional support turned out to be lower than that of most other recent presidents. Still, Bush had some success in his relations with Congress. He usually had the support of moderates in both parties, with his opposition coming from liberal Democrats and ultra-conservative Republicans. Only one of his 46 vetoes was overridden. He used the threat of a veto to exact compromises from Congress. He secured bipartisan support for many of his foreign policy initiatives. By the end of his term, relations with Congress had soured, gridlock had developed, and Bush campaigned against Congress in the 1992 elections.

Bush's nomination of Clarence Thomas for a position on the Supreme Court was the low point in his relationship with the judiciary. This was partially, but not totally, offset by his appointment of a well-qualified moderate, David Souter. Bush appointed to the lower federal courts judges believed to share his political views, utilizing the President's Committee on Federal Judicial Selection for ideological screening. He did, however, resume the practice of submitting names of nominees to the American Bar Association for their review. Only one of his nominees failed confirmation by the Senate. He expressed an interest in securing women and minorities for judgeships. However, he appointed mainly middle-aged, well-to-do, white, male Republicans.

Bush put the public interest, as he saw it, ahead of self-interest. He did not mobilize powerful interest groups to exert pressure in behalf of his programs, nor did he give in to pressure groups. On the other hand, his pardon of six persons convicted or charged in the Iran-Contra scandal may have been motivated as much by self interest as by humanitarian concerns. The pardons deprived the country an opportunity for public hearings on whether Bush's contentions of non-involvement were truthful.

LEADERSHIP AND DECISION MAKING

In small group situations Bush usually emerged as the leader. However, his charisma did not come through when speaking to large groups. He lacked Reagan's appeal to the television viewer. He had more leadership ability than he used, probably because he did not have programs that he was determined to push. He failed to provide leadership on key issues confronting the nation. When Bush had a specific cause to promote, he was usually able to persuade others that they should follow him because he was on the right course. Too often, however, he lacked conviction that a certain course was the right one. Bush set high standards of performance for himself and others. He was an adequate but not an outstanding motivator. His major weakness was that he failed to set a direction for addressing substantive problems.

On maintaining public confidence in the government, Bush's record was mixed. His foreign policy triumphs led to great feelings of pride and confidence among many Americans. On the other hand, many people did not believe his contention that he shared no responsibility for the Iran-contra scandals. Confidence in our economic stability was shaken by the growing budget deficit, the loss of jobs to overseas competitors, and the savings and loan debacle.

Bush was unable to communicate a vision to the American people. He recognized this shortcoming, but he lacked the imagination or the communication skills to overcome this weakness. He was not committed to a definite and clear political program. He has been described as a president without a cause. He talked about a New World Order but did not present a vision of what it should be or what the U.S. role in it should be.

Analyzing situations and planning how to move the country forward were not Bush's strengths. He relied heavily on his senior advisors and almost always followed their consensus. If a consensus was not reached, he postponed action if possible. He required advocates of contending views to debate issues in his presence. When making domestic policy decisions, a range of options were presented, refined, criticized, and assessed around the table. More important issues were dealt with by senior advisors. John Sununu was Bush's top legislative strategist, political advisor, and domestic policy maker. After being charged with excessive use of government perks and abuse of travel privileges, Sununu was replaced by Samuel Skinner. Sununu was brilliant, acerbic, arrogant, quick-tempered, and impatient. He was not liked by the press or by the public. Skinner kept a much lower profile.

Not a rash or reckless person who rushed into decisions without considering the possible consequences, Bush preferred to postpone a decision rather than risk making the wrong one. He had a broad experiential background for decision making. He had won a prize for economics at Yale, and correctly diagnosed Reaganomics as "voodoo economics." Yet he made his foolish pledge of no new taxes. Bush was intelligent, but he sometimes failed to utilize fully his intelligence in decision-making situations.

When necessary, Bush was willing to compromise. Working with a Congress controlled by the opposition, Bush had to compromise constantly in order to get anything accomplished. He effectively used the threat of a veto as leverage in making compromises with Congress. As a man of few convictions, Bush did not have to betray his principles in order to compromise. Bush did not like to make tough decisions, preferring to wait and see if the situation would resolve itself. When necessary, though, he could make the tough ones — such as invading Panama and his Operation Desert Storm. In emergencies he remained calm and behaved in a rational manner.

PERSONAL QUALITIES

With few exceptions, Bush conducted himself with the dignity appropriate to the President of the United States. Only during political campaigns did he engage in petty, mean-spirited behavior. Some of Bush's actions, especially the victory in the Gulf War, increased the pride that Americans had in their country and in their president. However, something about Bush, perhaps his aloofness, prevented the people from ever acclaiming him as their hero. Instead, that role went to Colin Powell, and to a lesser degree to General Schwartzkopf. Even Dick Cheney got more credit than Bush. Yet when doubts began to arise as to whether we had accomplished enough, with Saddam Hussein still in power, Bush was the one whose leadership was questioned.

Bush neither increased nor decreased the stature of the office of president. Perhaps he weakened the presidency a bit when he agreed to cut off aid to the Contras unless he received letters of approval from four Democratic-controlled committees in Congress. He secured congressional approval before sending U.S. troops to the Persian Gulf, but not prior to invading Panama. His leadership in working with Gorbachev, Yeltsin, and leaders of ex–Soviet satellites in eastern Europe counterbalanced any weakening from the other events cited.

Bush was not particularly adept in appealing to public opinion. His aloofness and "preppy" style prevented the people from feeling close to their president. He really was out of touch with the people. He was so far removed from ordinary life that he did not even understand the question when asked during the 1992 presidential debates how the state of the economy affected him. Bush was not noted for seeking input from large segments of the public, or for giving thoughtful consideration to the advice he received from those not in his inner circle. He paid attention to public opinion polls, but paying attention to numbers is not the same as paying attention to individual people. He did not hold town meetings or public forums that would bring him into contact with average people. He did not visit with citizens to keep his finger on the public pulse.

Bush's aristocratic aloofness made it difficult

for him to reach out to the people. He attempted to use the office as a "bully pulpit," but he failed to inspire public support because he did not come to grips with specifics. He said he was for better schools and against illegal drugs, but failed to propose specific programs.

Bush generally acted on a set of moral values and principles. He believed in family, order, and hierarchy. His integrity was seldom doubted. He broke his most famous promise: "Read my lips; no new taxes." But breaking this inappropriate promise was the right thing to do. Bush was personally honest. Having been born into a wealthy family, he never benefitted financially from his public offices. He never

used his office to benefit his friends financially, either. Although he appointed many of them to office, public service was as often a financial sacrifice as a benefit.

Throughout his life Bush exhibited a high standard of personal morality, deviating from the high road only during his presidential campaigns of 1988 and 1992.

OVERALL ASSESSMENT

Bush obtained 14 out of a possible 100 points on the rating scale and ranks in a tie for 28th place among the 39 presidents rated.

WILLIAM JEFFERSON CLINTON

1993–

	RATING POINTS	RANK
FOREIGN RELATIONS	13	6 tie
DOMESTIC PROGRAMS	14	7 tie
ADMINISTRATION	7	17 tie
LEADERSHIP	10	17 tie
PERSONAL QUALITIES	–3	36
OVERALL ASSESSMENT	41	18 tie

BACKGROUND

William Jefferson Blythe IV was born in Hope, Arkansas, on August 19, 1946. His father drowned when his car skidded off the road into a ditch before the future president was born. When he was 16, Bill legally changed his surname to Clinton in honor of his stepfather. He graduated from Hot Springs High School and from Georgetown University, where he majored in international relations and won a Rhodes Scholarship, our only president to earn this distinction. In 1970 he accepted a scholarship to Yale University Law School where he met Hillary Rodham. She became the first presidential spouse to maintain her own career. Hillary headed the President's Task Force on National Health Care and became the first First Lady to have an office in the West Wing of the White House.

Upon graduation from Yale Law School in 1973, Clinton accepted a position at the University of Arkansas Law School. In 1974 he ran for Congress, winning the Democratic nomination, but losing in the general election. In 1976 he was elected attorney general of Arkansas. In 1978 he was elected governor. Clinton raised the state gasoline tax and automobile registration fee to pay for road improvements and increased spending on education. He was defeated for re-election in 1980. During 1981 and 1982 Clinton practiced law in Little Rock. In 1982 he was again elected governor and was re-elected three more times. Clinton made numerous reforms in public education. The improvements were paid for by increases in the state sales tax and local property taxes. Clinton used Arkansas's low wage base and tax incentives to entice new businesses into the state. He expanded health insurance coverage and improved health care for pregnant women and babies. Clinton created the Minority Business Advisory Council to oversee efforts to increase purchases from minority-owned enterprises. He appointed more blacks and women to high state offices than any previous Arkansas governor.

While he was governor, Clinton became prominent nationally. He chaired the Democratic Leadership Council (1990-91), the Southern Growth Policy Board (1985-86), the Education Commission of the States (1986-87), the National Governor's Association (1986-87), and the National Governor's Association Task Force on Child Care (1990-91). In a poll of governors conducted by Newsweek in 1991, Clinton was named the most effective governor in the nation.

NOMINATION AND ELECTION

In 1991 Clinton announced his candidacy for the Democratic presidential nomination. Tom Harkin won the Iowa caucuses, and Paul Tsongas took the New Hampshire primary. Clinton's candidacy appeared to be in trouble as charges were made of marital infidelity and improper manipulation to avoid the draft during the war in Vietnam. However, Clinton won the majority of the remaining caucuses and primaries. Before convention time Clinton had the nomination locked up, and won on the first ballot. For his running mate, Clinton chose Senator Al Gore. His platform emphasized economic growth, welfare reform, a strong defense, abortion rights, universal access to health care, expanded child care, unpaid work leave for family emergencies, new public works, and environmental protection.

President Bush won the Republican nomination on the first ballot. Ross Perot entered the contest as an independent. Early polls showed he would run well against Bush and Clinton. Voter dissatisfaction with the declining economy and concerns about Clinton's character contributed to this phenomenon. However, divisions developed within the Perot campaign and for a time the Texan dropped out of the race. When he entered it again, he was unable to win back the affection of many who felt he had deserted them.

Clinton took a large lead in the polls, and Bush reverted to the negative campaign tactics that had worked four years earlier. He attacked Clinton as a tax-and-spend liberal. He blasted

him for avoiding the draft during the War in Vietnam and for participating in anti-war demonstrations while a student at Oxford. He sought to portray Clinton as untried, untrustworthy, and unpatriotic. Bush called for a cut in the capital gains tax as a stimulus to the sluggish economy, for tax credits to offset the cost of health insurance, and for a constitutional amendment to restrict abortions. Perot made deficit reduction a top priority, proposing to raise taxes on gasoline, cigarettes, and Social Security benefits. Clinton proposed raising taxes on the richest two percent of Americans and modest tax cuts for the middle class. He would rely on economic growth to gradually reduce the deficit. He also called for public works projects to provide high speed rail service, to develop a national computer network, and to repair the nation's infrastructure. He proposed working toward a national health insurance program, financial aid for all qualified college students, and welfare reform. All three candidates agreed that the defense budget should be cut and that education should be improved. Three presidential debates were held. Bush's strategy to hammer away at Clinton's character was stymied by the questioners' insistence that the candidates stick to the issues.

Clinton received a plurality, but not a majority of the popular vote. In the electoral college he received 370 electoral votes to 168 for Bush. While Perot made a respectable showing in the popular vote, he received no electoral votes.

In 1996 Clinton was unopposed at the Democratic convention in Chicago as he and Gore were nominated for second terms. After a hard-fought campaign, Senator Bob Dole won the Republican nomination. Ross Perot secured the nomination of his own Reform party. Clinton campaigned on his record. Reversing a stand of years, Dole embraced supply-side economics. He pledged a 15 percent tax cut, costing $548 billion, and overhaul of the education system, giving vouchers for attendance at private and church-related schools, and balancing the federal budget within five years. Although tax cuts pledges are usually popular with voters, few believed that Dole could deliver on his promise. Perot attacked the two-party system. Two debates were arranged between Clinton and Dole, with Perot excluded. Dole intensified his attacks on Clinton's character, while Clinton ignored the charges and emphasized his accomplishments. The lackluster campaign produced a small voter turnout. Clinton rolled to a decisive victory, receiving 379 electoral votes to 159 electoral votes for Dole and none for Perot.

FOREIGN RELATIONS

With varying success, Clinton used negotiations and or the threat of military force in efforts to bring peace and stability to many parts of the world. When a military coup ousted Haitian President Jean-Bertrand Aristide, the UN Security Council authorized a U.S. force to invade Haiti, oust the coup leaders, and restore the elected president. A team headed by former President Carter negotiated a peaceful settlement. The coup leaders surrendered power to President Aristide and left the country. U.S. forces stayed to help keep order. U.S. forces were also involved in actions in Somalia and Bosnia in cooperation with the United Nations in humanitarian ventures. U.S. peacekeepers reduced the level of clan violence in Somalia and checked the specter of famine, but were unable to get a stable government in place. Clinton participated in the UN arms embargo against Bosnia. In 1998 Clinton negotiated a truce, which led to a temporary halt to the violence in Northern Ireland. He sent troops to Kosovo as part of a NATO peacekeeping force.

Troubles with Iraq continue. Clinton has been unable to convince other governments that Hussein's possession of chemical and biological weapons poses an immediate threat to its Arab neighbors or to Europe. Nevertheless, when U.S. weapons inspectors were expelled from Iraq, diplomatic means were used to get Iraq to allow them back in. Restrictions placed on the inspections made them of such limited value that the inspectors withdrew. In 1998 Clinton ordered U.S. airstrikes on suspected sites for manufacturing or storing proscribed weapons. In 1999 several incidents occurred as the United States attempted to enforce no-fly zone restrictions in Iraq.

Representatives of Israel and the Palestine Liberation Organization met at the White House in 1993 and signed a declaration of principles for interim Palestine self rule. It was hoped the accord would lead to a lasting and comprehensive peace settlement. Under urging from Clinton, Prime Minister Yitzhak Rabin and Yasser Arafat shook hands. The hopes were dashed with the assassination of Rabin. In 1998 Clinton hosted a meeting at the Wye conference center in Maryland between Benjamin Netanyahu and Arafat, which led to renewed hopes of a peace settlement.

Following a meeting of the presidents of Ukraine, Russia, and the United States, Ukraine agreed to give up its nuclear arsenal. The United States and Russia agreed that none of their strategic weapons would be aimed after May 30, 1994, at the territory of any country. Clinton was unable to persuade the Senate to ratify the Comprehensive Nuclear Test Ban Treaty, but he pledged that the United States would abide by terms of the treaty.

Clinton proposed sanctions against North Korea. As a result, North Korea agreed to freeze its nuclear program and allow inspectors access to its facilities. Clinton proposed a one hundred percent increase in tariff on Japanese cars. In response, Japan agreed to import more parts from the United States and to increase production of Japanese cars in this country. In 1996 the United States agreed to give up an air base in Okinawa and scale back our military presence there. The United States and Vietnam agreed to exchange diplomats. Vietnam agreed to pay $208.5 million to settle claims on U.S. property confiscated at the end of the Vietnam war. The United States unfroze $130 million in Vietnamese assets in this country.

Clinton's tariff policies were helpful to world trade. The United States and Mexico ratified NAFTA in November 1993. Canada gave final approval a month later. Clinton signed it into U.S. law effective January 1, 1994. Clinton extended Mexico an $18 billion dollar line of credit to avert a financial collapse and used his emergency authority to provide a $20 billion loan. Clinton attended a meeting on Asia-Pacific Economic Cooperation, at which summit leaders endorsed reduction or elimination of tariffs on a wide range of goods. Congress approved the tariff-cutting provisions of the so-called Uruguay round of GATT in December 1994.

Peacekeeping and humanitarian efforts by Clinton enhanced world opinion of the United States, although his 1998 bombings in Afghanistan and the Sudan in response to the bombings of U.S. embassies was considered an overreaction.

DOMESTIC PROGRAMS

The unemployment rate was over seven percent when Clinton took office. The deficit in 1993 was $327.3 billion and shortfalls for 1994–98 were foreseen as nearly as large. The one bright spot was the low rate of inflation. In 1993 Congress passed an economic stimulus package that fell far short of what Clinton wanted. Nevertheless, the economy improved. By 1997 the unemployment rate was the lowest it had been in two decades. In his 1999 State of the Union address the president reported the lowest peacetime unemployment since 1957. The president further claimed that nearly eighteen million new jobs had been created during his administration, that wages were rising at twice the rate of inflation, and that the nation had the highest home ownership in history, and the lowest welfare rolls in 30 years. Layoffs at Kodak and shutdowns by Levi Strauss and Fruit of the Loom cost a few thousand jobs; these were highly publicized and blamed on NAFTA. Overall gains from the explosion in foreign trade have been tremendous, but some individuals have been hurt. Under Clinton the economy has improved and the deficit has been eliminated. In 1998 the United States had its first budget surplus since 1969.

Labor unions and representatives of small farmers have criticized NAFTA and GATT as being harmful to their interests. Whether the trade agreements have accelerated the loss of jobs is debatable, as the total number of jobs is up greatly. Clinton signed side agreements to NAFTA firming up labor and environmental standards and guarding against the negative impact of a sudden flood of imports. The agreements have been favored by agri-business and corporate farms, not by family farmers. Farmers have not shared in the general prosperity of the country during the Clinton administration. Clinton reluctantly signed the Freedom to Farm Act, which hurt small farmers.

Within the first month of his administration Clinton issued an executive order overturning restrictions on abortion imposed by Reagan and Bush, ordered the armed forces to no longer ask recruits about their sexual orientation, ordered that openly gay personnel would be placed on standby reserve rather than being discharged, and signed a Family and Medical Leave Act, similar to bills that Bush had twice vetoed. In his most ambitious move Clinton appointed a Task Force on National Health Care Reform. His health care package was announced in September 1993. The AMA declared its opposition. As the bill ran into trouble in Congress, Clinton said that he would settle for a health bill guaranteeing coverage to 95 percent of the population. The Senate leadership gave up on universal health insurance coverage as a result of opposition from the business, insurance, and medical industries. In 1995 Clinton endorsed proposed Food and Drug regulations aimed at curbing the use of tobacco by young people. A bill controlling tobacco usage was defeated by the Senate in 1998. In 1996 a health care bill was blocked by disagreements between Republicans and Democrats over Medical Savings Accounts.

In 1993 Congress approved a motor-voter bill so people in any state could register to vote when applying for a driver's license. By executive order Clinton required stricter licensing of gun dealers and banned imports of semi-automatic assault style weapons. He signed a Handgun Violence Prevention Act. In 1994 Congress approved a crime bill, supported by Clinton, that provided funds for additional police officers, expanded state prison construction, expanded federal death penalties, banned nineteen kinds of semi-automatic weapons, and contained a "three strikes and out" provision. It included some money for community social programs in high-crime areas, but these were greatly reduced in a compromise to secure passage. A 1997 National Crime Victimization Survey showed the lowest crime rate since the government began keeping records in 1973. The FBI reported the lowest homicide rate since 1969. In 1996 Clinton signed a defense bill which contained a provision requiring that troops with AIDS be discharged, but he promised not to enforce that provision. In the same year he vetoed a ban on late-term abortions, vetoed a limit on punitive damages for faulty products, signed a bill raising the minimum wage, and approved a new law allowing workers to retain health insurance coverage when they change jobs and assuring coverage of pre-existing conditions. Regulations requiring more scientific tests for bacteria in meat inspection were issued.

Clinton signed a welfare reform bill in 1996, which will require welfare recipients to go to work within five years or lose their benefits. It does not guarantee they will be able to find jobs. Although it provides some funds for job training and child care, these provisions are not adequate. The bill ends federal guarantees of cash assistance for the poorest children. It gives lump sums to states to run their own programs. The Clinton administration increased the suffering of poor disabled children by adopting standards more stringent than Congress intended. Disability benefits have been cut for 142,000 persons and two-thirds of new claims have been denied since Clinton signed the bill.

Soon after taking office, Clinton proposed to raise the personal income tax on high-income families, raise the corporate income tax, and reduce business deductions for meals and entertainment. He wanted to raise the tax on gasoline and fuel oil, reduce government spending, and impose new limits on Medicare payments. After a long and acrimonious debate, a compromise deficit reduction and tax increase bill was passed. All Republicans in both houses voted against the bill.

After a Republican filibuster killed a stronger plan, Clinton proposed to limit logging on federal old-growth forests in the Northwest and to protect endangered species. This plan did not have to be authorized by Congress, but required court approval. By administrative regulations Clinton doubled fees the government charged ranchers to graze their animals on public lands. The regulations also include stricter environmental protection on grazing lands. Clinton made a commitment to no net loss of wetlands. In 1994 the Senate broke a Republican filibuster and set aside 6.6 million acres of California desert wilderness. The Environmental Protection Agency proposed to move against as many as 36 pesticides within two years. In the 1998 budget compromise Clinton secured an additional $1.7 billion to treat polluted runoff, research greenhouse gases, and protect endangered species. In 1996 Clinton signed a bill to promote rivalry among local telephone companies, long distance carriers, and cable operators. In the same year he signed a Clean Water Act to help states upgrade their municipal water systems and to require that the public be given information about contaminants. By executive order Clinton created the Grand Staircase–Escalante National Monument in Utah.

Clinton tried to defend affirmative action plans against attacks in Congress, the courts, and the states. His appointment of a Chinese-American as top civil rights administrator in the Justice Department was blocked in the Senate because of his support of affirmative action. He appointed two Jews to the Supreme Court. The court had been without a Jewish member for several years and had never before had two at the same time. Clinton made diversity an important criterion in his appointments. He wanted a cabinet that "looked like America." His first cabinet included at least two blacks, two Hispanics, and three women. He was the first president to appoint a woman as secretary of state and the first to appoint a woman as attorney general. In order to reduce the flow of refugees from Cuba and Haiti he attempted to find safe havens for them elsewhere. Clinton sought to prevent Congress from taking benefits away from aliens, legal and illegal, and successfully restored some benefits to legal immigrants.

Clinton sent U.S. troops to Somalia, Bosnia, and Haiti to try to secure more humane treatment of individuals in those countries. He met with Jiang Zemin in 1993 and said we might not renew China's most favored nation status unless they improved their record on human rights, but he renewed that status despite Chinese inaction. However, in 1997 after Clinton publicly challenged Jiang's human rights record in a face-to-face exchange, Jiang released Wei Jinsheng, one of China's leading dissidents.

With some success, Clinton has proposed a number of educational reforms. He constantly struggled with Congress over educational funding — Clinton wanting to give federal aid to public schools only and Republicans in Congress wanting to give some aid to private and parochial schools. Clinton's first veto was of a bill that would have cut education spending. Congress then passed a bill restoring funds that Clinton wanted for education, training, and environmental programs. In 1993 Congress approved Clinton's National Service bill. In the 1998 budget agreement Congress gave Clinton an extra $1.1 billion for the hiring of additional public school teachers. Clinton has also secured additional funds for college scholarships and for tax credits for parents of college students.

ADMINISTRATION AND INTERGOVERNMENTAL RELATIONS

Clinton had a set of goals and objectives for his administration. He developed organized plans for their accomplishment. For example, he created a task force on health care reform which held months of hearings, heard testimony, and presented a detailed plan. But Clinton was unable to get it through Congress. The fault was not in the planning but in the execution.

Early in the Clinton administration the White House staff was not well organized. There were too many meetings, too much discussion, an inability to get decisions made quickly. Clinton tried to do too many things at the same time. Political consultants played too large a role in the administration. The staff gave Clinton indecisive and ineffective support. Clear organization patterns and communication channels did not exist. After Leon Panatta became chief of staff, the consultants were reined in. Things tightened up. Panatta reviewed all papers before they went to the president. Walk-in privileges to the Oval Office decreased. After Panatta resigned, some of his reforms remained in place.

On the positive side, Clinton announced a plan to "reinvent government." Eight hundred recommendations were put together under Vice President Gore's leadership to make government leaner, more efficient, and more responsive. Budgets and appropriations were to go on a two-year cycle. (Congress did not ac-

cept this.) The plan would make it easier to dismiss employees, reduce the number of reports, and give more decision-making authority to mid-level managers. The federal work force would be cut by 252,000. Many regional offices would close, saving $108 billion over five years. Many of these recommendations required congressional approval, and were not implemented due to lack of legislative action. Nevertheless, Clinton streamlined government, eliminating more than one hundred thousand federal jobs.

Clinton appointed the most diverse cabinet ever, including some strong people, but few of exceptional stature. He nominated several persons who ran into political opposition during or prior to the confirmation process and backed off, giving an impression of indecisiveness, weakness, or poor preparation. Clinton was not particularly adept at directing the work of executive branch personnel. After some initial fumbling, he assigned them to appropriate roles, gave them sufficient authority, and held them responsible for results. His weaknesses were in failure to give clear assignments and in helping subordinates develop clear objectives.

Clinton's communications improved during his time in office. His task force on health reform was accused of keeping some of its plans and data secret too long, but his problem has generally not been secrecy, but rather giving too much information so that people do not focus on important matters. This has been compounded by the tendency of the media to give more attention to trivialities or to investigations and rumors of scandals than to important policy matters. Clinton hired ex-Reagan aide David Gergen to help keep public attention on major policy initiatives, but with limited success. Clinton has done a better job communicating with the public than the media recognize. He reports through weekly radio addresses, televised press conferences, and televised speeches on his plans, priorities, and hopes for the nation.

Except for cutting welfare payments to poor people, Clinton has not done great harm to social programs while reducing government expenditures. He has had remarkable success in balancing the budget and producing a surplus. He has accomplished some important goals and objectives. Given the fact that he has faced a hostile Congress, some of his accomplishments are very noteworthy.

Clinton took office with a Democratic majority in both the House and the Senate. He was able to get quite a bit of legislation through early. On the NAFTA agreements he received more support from Republicans than from Democrats. However, as time went by, the Republicans became more and more obstructionist. The congressional session ended in gridlock. Republican senators had used filibusters and other delaying tactics to prevent adoption of bills that appeared to have majority approval, among them bills on lobbying reform, restrictions on spending in congressional campaigns, special interest contributions to campaigns, and several environmental bills. The Republicans swept to victory in the 1994 midterm elections, gaining control of both the House and the Senate. The House Republicans had remarkable success in their first one hundred days, passing a large part of their Contract with America, but few of these bills made it through the Senate. By its August recess the 104th Congress had enacted only twenty public bills. In 1995 Congress refused to pass a budget or continuing resolutions to keep the government functioning. The government shut down in December. In January 1996 Clinton signed a bill to resume many government operations. The public blamed Congress more than Clinton for the stalemate. However, in November they re-elected both the president and a Republican Congress. There have been no more government shutdowns, but the Republicans have continued to block action by refusing to hold hearings on Clinton appointees. Sometimes the Democrats are recalcitrant. Democratic votes denied Clinton fast-track authority to make trade agreements even though a majority of Republicans voted with the president. A government shutdown was avoided in 1998 when the Republicans agreed to a last minute compromise with the president.

Since the Republicans gained control of Congress in 1994, Clinton has had some implacable foes in the House and Senate. Some members of the so-called religious right bear the president intense animosity. Efforts to control the marketing of tobacco products and to provide a patients' "bill of rights" have been casualties of congressional opposition. Senate filibusters have prevented a vote on campaign finance reform. By a highly partisan vote the House of Representatives impeached the president despite evidence that the public overwhelmingly opposed impeachment and that the Senate almost certainly would not convict. Indeed, conviction failed to receive even a simple majority in the Senate, much less the two-thirds majority required to remove the president from office.

Clinton nominated and secured approval of two well-qualified Supreme Court Justices — Ruth Bader Ginsburg and Stephen Breyer. Republican senators have blocked hearings for many appointments to lower courts by refusing to hold confirmation hearings.

Although getting re-elected was a high priority for Clinton during his first term, he put the public interest first. He was not afraid to anger powerful constituents, such as labor unions over NAFTA and Jesse Jackson over his criticism of Sister Souljah.

LEADERSHIP AND DECISION MAKING

Clinton is not an inspirational leader. He is immensely likable and has some charisma, but his style of trying to do too many things at the same time makes it difficult for him to inspire executive branch personnel to a high level of focused, productive effort. Clinton can be very persuasive, but he is not always able to convince others that his is the right course. Although he has had considerable success in getting his programs adopted, he has lost on some important issues.

Despite rumors, investigations, and charges, Clinton maintained public confidence in government until the release of the Starr report in September 1998. Most people saw the charges as politically motivated. The revelations about Clinton's affair with Monica Lewinsky and the cover-up attempts destroyed some of this confidence. Many people are disgusted with the president's behavior, with Starr's vindictiveness, and with the partisanship of Republicans in Congress.

Clinton's vision for America is of a nation in which the American Dream is a reality for all who are willing to work for it, where the diverse American community is growing stronger together, and where our leadership for peace, freedom, and prosperity continues to shape the world. His strategy to pursue this vision involves creating opportunity for all Americans, demanding responsibility from all, and forging a stronger American community. He has not been able to communicate this vision well enough to create a sense of shared national goals among all the people, but neither are we drifting aimlessly. The president has conceptualized programs that would move the country in the right direction, but he has difficulty in getting them approved by Congress.

In considering alternatives Clinton listens to subordinates, consultants, and friends. He seeks out various points of view. He enjoys philosophical and political discussions. A voracious reader, he has considerable knowledge and understanding of history. Clinton is very bright. He is not mentally lazy. He uses his intelligence in problem solving and decision making situations. Clinton is perhaps too quick to compromise. He believes that half a loaf is better than nothing, but the quickness with which he compromises gives the impression of being "soft" or of "waffling." His efforts to keep conflicting constituencies in his corner sometimes mute his message.

Clinton remains calm in emergencies. He is prudent and does not rush into an emergency decision if it can be avoided, but if necessary he can make the tough decision. He hardly ever appears flustered or rattled. He is able to shake off distractions and stick to the main point. Many people were surprised that he was able to keep his focus on foreign relations and domestic programs during the impeachment trial.

PERSONAL QUALITIES

In public the president usually conducts himself with dignity. Perhaps he appeared on too many talk shows and answered too many personal questions. The contents of his grand jury testimony were very damaging to his dignity and demeaned the office he holds.

Until his grand jury testimony was made public, Clinton had little effect on the pride that people have in being Americans. Most were moderately but not overly proud that he was their president. Some were ashamed of him because of the allegations against him. Public revelation of Clinton's unseemly private conduct diminished the stature of the presidency.

Congress gave Clinton the line-item veto, increasing the power of the presidency temporarily, until the courts declared it unconstitutional. During Clinton's administration, the power of the presidency was temporarily weakened by the authority given to the independent prosecutor and by court rulings requiring the president to testify in a civil suit and denying executive privilege to secret service agents and White House lawyers. On the other hand, Clinton's refusal to give in to demands for his resignation strengthened the presidency. The abuse of power by the special prosecutor will almost certainly lead to the abolition of that office or stricter controls on its operations. The office of the presidency has great resiliency and will suffer no permanent effects from Clinton's wrongdoings.

The majority of the people still see Clinton as having their best interests at heart. They think he is on their side, interested in them, and working for them. Although big campaign contributors enjoy special access, Clinton seeks input from all segments of the public. Early in his presidency he gave dinners for 40 people twice a week at the White House. Clinton circulated among the guests and talked with all of them. He enjoys talking with people and will plunge into a crowd, engaging strangers in conversation when the secret service lets him. Although Clinton reaches out to the people through his speeches and his travels, he has not gone over the heads of Congress with direct appeals to the people as much as he might.

The president is not seen as a man of great integrity because of attacks upon his character and because of his willingness to compromise. His failure to support some of his prospective cabinet members when they were attacked by his political enemies contributed to this perspective. His legalistic defenses in his grand jury testimony confirmed the view.

Charges that Clinton used his position as governor of Arkansas to benefit himself financially were not proven. There is no evidence that he used the presidency to benefit himself personally at the expense of the public.

Clinton's failure to adhere to high standards of morality in his personal life diminished the prestige of the office of president somewhat. Charges about Whitewater, Paula Jones, and improper fundraising also hurt, but to this point there is no evidence of illegal behavior on his part in those matters. However, most people believe his relationship with Monica Lewinsky involved immoral conduct. Furthermore, most people believe the president gave misleading testimony to the grand jury and lied to his family, his staff, and the public. Overwhelmingly, however, they think these offenses do not warrant his removal from office.

OVERALL ASSESSMENT

Although his second term is not over yet, we can give Clinton a preliminary rating of 41

points and rank him in a tie for eighteenth among the 39 presidents rated. Much can still happen that would affect his ratings. Additional terrorist attacks, the outbreak of a major war, the advent of a world-wide economic depression are all within the realm of possibility, with potentially devastating effects on the president's ratings. Continued prosperity, additional successful peacekeeping acts, and congressional approval of Clinton's proposals for health care reform, campaign finance reform, or other progressive measures could conceivably raise his ranking. Past experience indicates that most presidents have less success in the later parts of their terms than in the earlier, so we do not expect Clinton's ratings to climb.

ENDNOTES

1. Clinton Rossiter, *The American Presidency*. New York: New American Library, 1960, p. 137.

2. Barry D. Riccio, "The U.S. Presidency and the Ratings Game," *The Historian*, 52 (August 1990): 583.

3. Robert K. Murray, and Tim H. Blessing, "The Presidential Performance Study: A Progress Report," *The Journal of American History*, 70 (December 1983): 535.

4. Arthur M. Schlesinger, Sr., "Historians Rate U.S. Presidents," *Life* (Nov. 1, 1948): pp. 65–66, 68, 73–74.

5. Quoted by Thomas A. Bailey, *Presidential Greatness: The Image and the Man from George Washington to the Present*. New York: Appleton-Century, 1962, p. 24. The instructions do not appear in the *Life* article.

6. Arthur M. Schlesinger, Sr., "Our Presidents: A Rating by 75 Historians," *New York Times Magazine* (July 29, 1962): pp. 12–13, 40–41, 43.

7. *Ibid.*, p 12.

8. Gary M. Maranell, "The Evaluation of Presidents: An Extension of the Schlesinger Polls," *Journal of American History* 57 (June 1970): 104–131.

9. *Ibid.*, p. 107.

10. David Porter, "American Historians Rate Our Presidents" in William Pederson and Ann M. McLaurin (ed.) *The Rating Game in American Politics*. New York: Irvington Publishers, 1987, p. 33.

11. Steve Neal, "Our Best and Worst Presidents," *Chicago Tribune Magazine*, (January 10, 1982): pp. 8–13, 15, 18.

12. Murray and Blessing (1983), pp. 535–55.

13. Robert K. Murray, and Tim H. Blessing. *Greatness in the White House: Rating the Presidents Washington through Carter*. University Park: Pennsylvania State University Press, 1988.

14. William J. Ridings, Jr., and Stuart B. McIver. *Rating the Presidents*. Secaucus, NJ: Citadel Press, 1997.

15. Arthur M. Schlesinger, Jr., "The Ultimate Approval Rating," *New York Times Magazine* (December 15, 1996), pp. 46–51.

16. Bailey, p. 21.

17. *Ibid.*

18. Rossiter (1960).

19. *Ibid.*, p. 96.

20. *Ibid.*

21. Morton Bolden (ed.), *America's Ten Greatest Presidents*. Chicago: Rand McNally, 1961.

22. Herman Finer, *The Presidency: Crises and Regeneration*. Chicago: University of Chicago Press, 1960.

23. *Ibid.*, pp. 120–147.

24. Eric Sokolsky, *Our Seven Greatest Presidents*. New York: Exposition Press, 1964.

25. Bailey (1962).

26. *Ibid.* pp. 262–266.

27. *Ibid.*, p. 267.

28. *Ibid.*, p. 293.

29. *Ibid.*, pp. 308, 312.

30. *Ibid.*, p. 322.

31. *Ibid.*, p. 328.

32. *Ibid.*, pp. 334–35.

33. Frank R. King, *America's Nine Greatest Presidents*. Jefferson, NC: McFarland, 1997.

34. James David Barber, "Analyzing Presidents: From Passive-Positive Taft to Active-Negative Nixon," *The Washington Monthly*, 1 (October 1969): 33–54.

35. Pederson and McLaurin (1987).

36. Ann M. McLaurin, and William D. Pederson, "Dimensions of the Rating Game," in Pederson and McLaurin (1987), p. 6.

37. Barber, reprinted in Pederson and McLaurin (1987), pp. 39–40.

38. *Ibid.*, p. 54.

39. *Ibid.*, p. 68.

40. *Ibid.*, pp. 56, 62.

41. William D. Pederson, "Amnesty and Presidential Behavior: A 'Barberian' Test," in Pederson and McLaurin (1987), p. 73.

42. *Ibid.*, p. 73.

43. *Ibid.*, p. 72.

44. *Ibid.*, p. 73.

45. *Ibid.*, p. 76.

46. *Ibid.*, p. 77.

47. *Ibid.*, p. 76.

48. *Ibid.*, p. 80.

49. *Ibid.*, p. 79.

50. *Ibid.*

51. Thomas E. Cronin, *The State of the Presidency*. Boston: Little, Brown, 1973, p. 251.

52. Murray and Blessing (1988), p. 46.

53. Bailey (1962), pp. 262–66.

54. Charles A. McCoy, *Polk and the Presidency*. Austin: University of Texas Press, 1960, p. 3.

55. Bailey (1962), p. 268.

56. John E. Ferling. *The First of Men: A Life of George Washington*. Knoxville: University of Tennessee Press, 1988, p. 416.

57. Irving Brandt. *The Fourth President: A Life of James Madison.* Indianapolis: The Bobbs Merrill Company, 1930, pp. 644–45.

58. Robert J. Rayback. *Millard Fillmore.* Buffalo: Buffalo Historical Society, 1959, p. 253.

59. Doris Kearns. *Lyndon Johnson and the American Dream.* New York: Harper and Row, 1976, p. 173.

BIBLIOGRAPHY

Alden, John R. *George Washington: A Biography.* Avenal, NJ: Random House Value, 1995.

Ammon, Harry. *James Monroe: The Quest for Identity.* New York: McGraw-Hill, 1971.

Ariail, Dan, and Cheryl Heckler-Fritz. *The Carpenter's Apprentice.* Grand Rapids: Zondervan, 1996.

Bailey, Thomas A. *Presidential Greatness.* New York: Appleton-Century, 1966.

Barber, James David. "Analyzing Presidents: From Passive-Positive Taft to Active-Negative Nixon." *Washington Monthly* (1966).

Barber, James D. *Presidential Character: Predicting Performance in the White House.* 4th ed. Paramus, NJ: Prentice-Hall, 1992.

Barilleaux, Ryan J. *The Post-Modern Presidency: The Office After Ronald Reagan.* Westport, CT: Greenwood, 1988.

Bishop, Joseph Bucklin. *Theodore Roosevelt and His Time, Shown in His Own Letters.* 2 vols. New York, 1920.

Blakesley, Lance. *Presidential Leadership from Eisenhower to Clinton.* Chicago: Nelson-Hall, 1995.

Bolden, Morton, ed. *America's Ten Greatest Presidents.* Chicago: Rand McNally, 1961.

Bourne, Peter G. *Jimmy Carter: A Comprehensive Biography from Plains to Postpresidency.* New York: Lisa Drew Books/Scribner, 1997.

Brandt, Irving. *The Fourth President: A Life of James Madison.* Indianapolis: Bobbs Merrill Co., 1930.

Brody, Richard A. *Assessing the President: The Media, Elite Opinion, and Public Support.* Stanford, CA: Stanford University Press, 1991.

Burk, Robert F. *Dwight D. Eisenhower, Hero and Politician.* Boston: Twayne Publishers, 1986.

Burner, David. *Herbert Hoover: A Public Life.* New York: Alfred A. Knopf, 1979.

Burns, James McGregor. *Roosevelt: The Lion and the Fox.* New York: Harcourt, Brace, Jovanovich, 1956.

Busch, Noel F. *T R. The Story of Theodore Roosevelt and His Influence on Our Times.* New York: Morrow, 1963.

Cannon, Lou. *Reagan.* New York: G.P. Putnam's Sons, 1982.

Carroll, John Alexander, and Mary Wells Ashworth. Completing the biography by Douglas Southall Freeman,. *George Washington.* vol. 7. *First in Peace.* New York: Charles Scribner Sons, 1957.

Carter, Jimmy. *Keeping Faith: Memoirs of a President.* New York: Bantam Books, 1982.

Chitwood, Oliver Perry. *John Tyler: Champion of the Old South.* Newtown, CT: American Political Biography Press, 1990. (Originally published by the American Historical Association, 1939.)

Clinton, Bill. *Between Hope and History.* New York: Random House, 1996.

Collier, Peter with David Horowitz. *The Roosevelts: An American Saga.* New York: Simon & Schuster, 1994.

Coolidge, Calvin. *The Autobiography of Calvin Coolidge.* New York: Cosmopolitan Book Corporation, 1929.

Cormier, Frank. *LBJ: The Way He Was.* Garden City, NY: Doubleday, 1977.

Corwin, Edward S. *The President: Office and Powers.* 5th rev. ed. New York: New York University Press, 1984.

Cronin, Thomas E. *The State of the Presidency.* Boston: Little, Brown, 1973.

Cunningham, Noble E., Jr. *The Pursuit of Reason: The Life of Thomas Jefferson.* Baton Rouge: Louisiana State University Press, 1987.

Davis, Burke. *Old Hickory: A Life of Andrew Jackson.* New York: Dial Press, 1977.

Davis, James W. *The American Presidency.* 2nd ed. Westport, CT: Greenwood, 1995.

DeGregorio, William A. *The Complete Book of Presidents.* Avenal, NJ: Random House Value, 1997.

Derbyshire, Ian. *The United States from Carter to Bush.* Edinburgh: W. & R. Chambers, 1990.

Di Clerico, Robert E. *The American President.* 4th ed. Paramus, NJ: Prentice-Hall, 1994.

Donald, David Herbert. *Lincoln.* New York: Simon and Schuster, 1995.

Drew, Elizabeth. *On the Edge: The Clinton Presidency.* New York: Simon & Schuster, 1994.

Duffy, Herbert S. *William Howard Taft.* New York: Minton, Balch, 1930.

Duffy, Michael, and Dan Goodgame. *Marching in Place: The Status Quo Presidency of George Bush.* New York: Simon & Schuster, 1992.

Eckenrode, H. J. *Rutherford B. Hayes, Statesman of Reunion.* New York: Dodd, Mead, 1930.

Edwards, David V. *The American Political Experience.* 2nd ed. Englewood Cliffs, NJ: Prentice Hall, 1982.

Ellis, Joseph J. *Passionate Sage: The Character and Legacy of John Adams.* New York: Norton, 1993.

Evans, Rowland, Jr., and Robert D. Novak. *Nixon in the White House: The Frustration of Power.* New York: Random House, 1971.

Ewald, William Bragg. *Eisenhower the President.* Englewood Cliffs, NJ: Prentice-Hall, Inc. 1981.

Fehrenbacher, Don. E. *The Leadership of Abraham Lincoln.* Problems in American History Series. New York: Wiley , 1970.

_____. *Prelude to Greatness.* Stanford, CA: Stanford University Press, 1962.

_____. *The Changing Image of Lincoln in American Historiography.* Oxford: Clarendon Press, 1968.

Ferling, John E. *The First of Men: A Life of George Washington.* Knoxville: University of Tennessee Press, 1988.

Finer, Herman. *The Presidency: Crisis and Regeneration.* Chicago: University of Chicago Press, 1960.

Freeman, Douglas Southall. *George Washington.* Vol. 6. *Patriot and President.* New York: Charles Scribner Sons, 1954.

Friedman, Leon, and William F. Levantrosser. *Richard M. Nixon, Politician, President, Administrator.* New York: Greenwood, 1991.

Fuess, Claude M. *Calvin Coolidge: The Man from Vermont.* Westport, CT: Greenwood, 1965.

Gara, Larry. *The Presidency of Franklin Pierce.* American Presidency Series. Lawrence: The University Press of Kansas, 1963.

Grant, Ulysses S. *Personal Memoirs of U. S. Grant.* 2 vols. New York: Charles L. Webster, 1885, 1886.

Green, Fitzhugh. *George Bush: An Intimate Portrait.* New York: Hippocrene Books, 1989.

Hamilton, Holman. *The Three Kentucky Presidents.* Lexington: The University Press of Kentucky, 1978.

_____. *Zachary Taylor,* (2 vols.) Indianapolis: Bobbs-Merrill, 1941, 1951.

Haynes, Sam W. *James K. Polk and the Expansionist Impulse.* New York: Longman, 1997.

Hecht, Marie. *John Quincy Adams: A Personal History of an Independent Man.* New York: Macmillan, 1972.

Heckler-Feltz, Cheryl, and Daniel G. Ariail. *The Carpenter's Apprentice.* Grand Rapids: Zondervan, 1996.

Hesseltine, William B. *Ulysses S. Grant, Politician.* New York: Dodd, Mead, 1935.

Hill, Dilys M., and Phil Williams, eds. *The Bush Presidency: Triumphs and Adversities.* New York: St. Martin's, 1994.

Hoyt, Edwin D. *James Buchanan.* Chicago: Reilly & Lee, 1966.

Jewett, Robert ed. *The Captain America Complex.* Santa Fe, NM: Bear, 1984.

Kane, Joseph Nathan. *Facts about the Presidents.* 6th ed. New York: H. W. Wilson, 1993.

Kearns, Doris. *Lyndon Johnson and the American Dream.* New York: Harper and Row, 1976.

Kellerman, Barbara. *The Political Presidency: Practice of Leadership from Kennedy Through Reagan.* New York: Oxford University Press, 1986.

King, Frank R. *America's Nine Greatest Presidents.* Jefferson, NC: McFarland, 1997.

Klein, Phillip S. *President James Buchanan.* Signature Series on American Politics. University Park: Pennsylvania State University Press, 1962.

Krog, Carl E., and William R. Turner, eds. *Herbert Hoover and the Republican Era.* Lanham, MD: University Press of America, 1984.

Lasky, Victor. *Jimmy Carter: The Man and the Myth.* New York: Richard Marek, 1979.

Leech, Margaret. *In the Days of McKinley.* New York: Harper, 1959.

Lerner, Max. *Thomas Jefferson: America's Philosopher-King.* New Brunswick, NJ: Transaction, 1996.

Light, Paul C. *The President's Agenda: Domestic Policy Choices from Kennedy to Reagan.* 2nd rev. ed. Baltimore: Johns Hopkins Press, 1991.

Link, Arthur S. (ed.) *Woodrow Wilson: A Profile.* New York: Hill & Wang, 1968.

Lorant, Stefan. *The Glorious Burden.* Lenox, MA: Authors Edition, 1976.

_____. *The Presidency.* New York: Macmillan, 1951.

_____. *The Life and Times of Theodore Roosevelt.* Garden City, NY: Doubleday, 1959.

Loth, David. *Woodrow Wilson: The Fifteenth Point.* New York, J. B. Lippincott, 1941.

Lyons, Eugene. *Herbert Hoover: A Biography.* Garden City, NY: Doubleday, 1964.

McCormac, E. L. *James K. Polk: A Political Biography.* Newtown, CT: American Political Biography Press, 1922.

McCoy, Charles A. *Polk and the Presidency.* Austin: University of Texas Press, 1960.

McCullough, David. *Truman.* New York: Simon & Schuster, 1992.

McElroy, Robert. *Grover Cleveland, the Man and the Statesman: An Authorized Biography.* 2 vols. New York: Harper & Brothers, 1923.

Mapp, Alf J., Jr. *Thomas Jefferson: Passionate Pilgrim.* Lanham, MD: Madison Books, 1981.

Maranell, Gary M. "The Evaluation of Presidents: An Extension of the Schlesinger Polls." *Journal of American History* 57 (June 1970): 104–131.

Marble, Harriet Clement. *James Monroe: Patriot and President.* New York: G. P. Putnam's Sons, 1970.

Mariniss, David. *First in His Class: The Biography of Bill Clinton.* New York: Simon & Schuster, 1995.

Mason, Alpheus Thomas. *William Howard Taft: Chief Justice.* London: Oldbourne, 1965.

Michaels, Judith E. *The President's Call: Executive Leadership from FDR to George Bush.* Pittsburgh: University of Pittsburgh Press, 1997.

Morgan, H. Wayne. *William McKinley and His America.* Syracuse: Syracuse University Press, 1963.

Morgan, Ted. *FDR: A Biography.* New York: Simon & Schuster, 1985.

Morrill, Martha McBride. *Young Hickory: Life and Times of President James K. Polk.* New York: E.P. Dutton, 1949.

Murray, Robert K. *The Harding Era: Warren G. Harding and His Administration.* Minneapolis: University of Minnesota Press, 1969.

Murray, Robert K., and Tim H. Blessing. *Greatness in the White House.* University Park: Pennsylvania State University Press, 1988.

Murray, Robert K., and Tim H. Blessing. "The Presidential Performance Study: A Progress Report."

Journal of American History 70 (December 1983): 535–555.

Myers, Elisabeth P. *Benjamin Harrison.* Chicago: Reilly & Lee, 1969.

Nagel, Paul C. *John Quincy Adams: A Public Life.* New York: Alfred A. Knopf, 1997.

Neal, Steve. "Our Best and Worst Presidents." *Chicago Tribune Magazine* (January 10, 1982): 8–13, 15, 18.

Nelson, Michael. *Presidency: A History of the Office of the President of the United States from 1789.* New York: Smithson, 1996.

Neustadt, Richard E. *Presidential Power and the Modern Presidents: The Politics of Leadership from Roosevelt to Reagan.* New York: Free Press, 1989.

Nichols, Roy Franklin. *Franklin Pierce: Young Hickory of the Granite Hills.* Philadelphia: University of Pennsylvania Press, 1931.

Niven, John. *Martin Van Buren: The Romantic Age in American Politics.* New York: Oxford University Press, 1983.

Osborne, John. *White House Watch: The Ford Years.* Washington: New Republic Books, 1977.

Parmet, Herbert S. *Richard Nixon and His America.* Boston: Little, Brown, 1990.

Peckham, Howard. *William Henry Harrison: Young Tippecanoe.* Indianapolis: Bobbs-Merrill, 1962.

Pederson, William D. *The Barberian Presidency: Theoretical and Empirical Readings.* American University Studies: Political Science, Ser. X, vol 14. New York: Peter Lang, 1989.

Rayback, Robert J. *Millard Fillmore,* Buffalo: Buffalo Historical Society, 1959.

Reeves, Richard. *President Kennedy: Profile of Power.* New York, 1993.

Reeves, Thomas C. *Gentleman Boss: The Life of Chester A. Arthur.* New York: Alfred A. Knopf, 1975.

Riccards, Michael P. *Ferocious Engine of Democracy: A History of the American Presidency.* 2 vols. New York: Madison, 1995.

Riccio, Barry D. "The U.S. Presidency and the 'Ratings Game.'" *Historian* 52 (August 1990: 566–583.

Ridings, William J., Jr., and Stuart B. McIver. *Rating the Presidents,* Secaucus, NJ: Citadel Press, 1997.

Rossiter, Clinton. *The American Presidency.* New York: New American Library, 1962.

Russell, Francis. *The Shadow of Blooming Grove: Warren G. Harding in His Times.* New York: McGraw-Hill, 1968.

Schlesinger, Arthur M., Jr. *The Age of Roosevelt.* vol. 2. *The Coming of the New Deal.* Boston: Houghton Mifflin, 1959.

———. *The Age of Roosevelt.* vol. 3. *The Politics of Upheaval.* Boston: Houghton Mifflin, 1960.

———. "The Ultimate Approval Rating." *New York Times Magazine* (December 15, 1996):

Schlesinger, Arthur M., Sr. "Historians Rate U.S. Presidents." *Life* (November 1, 1948): 65–66, 68, 73–74.

———. "Our Presidents: A Rating by 75 Historians." *New York Times Magazine* (July 29, 1962): 12–13, 40–41, 43.

Seager, Robert II. *And Tyler Too: A Biography of John and Julia Gardiner Tyler.* New York, McGraw-Hill, 1963.

Sidey, Hugh. *A Very Personal Presidency: Lyndon Johnson in the White House.* New York, 1968.

Sievers, Harry J. *Benjamin Harrison, Hoosier President.* 3 vols. Chicago: H. Regnery, 1952–1969.

Sinclair, Andrew. *The Available Man: Warren Gamaliel Harding.* New York: Macmillan, 1965.

Smith, Elbert B. *The Presidencies of Zachary Taylor and Millard Fillmore.* American Presidency Series. Lawrence: The University Press of Kansas, 1988.

Smith, Page. *John Adams.* 2 vols. Garden City, NY: Doubleday, 1962.

Smith, Richard Norton. *An Uncommon Man: The Triumph of Herbert Hoover.* New York: Simon & Schuster, 1984.

Sokolsky, Eric. *Our Seven Greatest Presidents.* New York: Exposition Press, 1964.

Taylor, Tim. *The Book of Presidents.* New York: Arno Press, 1972.

Ter Horst, Jerald F. *Gerald Ford and the Future of the Presidency.* New York: Joseph Okpaku, 1974.

Thelen, David, ed. *The Constitution and American Life.* Ithaca, NY: Cornell University Press, 1987.

Thomas, Benjamin P. *Abraham Lincoln.* New York: Alfred A. Knopf, 1952.

Thomas, Lately. *The First President Johnson: The Three Lives of Andrew Johnson the Seventeenth President of the United States of America.* New York: Morrow, 1968.

Tugwell, Rexford Guy. *Grover Cleveland.* New York: Macmillan, 1968.

Welch, Richard E., Jr. *The Presidencies of Grover Cleveland.* American Presidency Series. Lawrence: The University Press of Kansas, 1988.

White, William Allen. *A Puritan in Babylon: The Story of Calvin Coolidge.* New York: Capricorn Books, 1938.

Whitney, David C., and Robin Vaughn Whitney. *The American Presidents.* Pleasantville, NY: Readers' Digest Association, 1996.

Wills, Garry. *Reagan's America: Innocents at Home.* Garden City, NY: Doubleday, 1987.

Wright, Anna Marie Rose. *The Dramatic Life of Abraham Lincoln.* New York: Grosset & Dunlap, 1925.

INDEX